ALL YE LANDS

World Cultures and Geography

Make a joyful noise unto the Lord, all ye lands!
Serve the Lord with gladness!
Come before his presence with singing!
Know ye that the Lord he is God;
It is he that hath made us and not we ourselves;
We are his people, and the sheep of his pasture.
Enter into his gates with thanksgiving,
And into his courts with praise.
Be thankful unto him, and bless his name.
For the Lord is good;
His mercy is everlasting;
And his truth endureth to all generations!
—Psalm 100

Volume 6

ALL YE LANDS

World Cultures and Geography

Contributors to Volume 6

Ellen Rossini

Carl Rossini

Rollin Lasseter

Anne Carroll

Christopher Zehnder

Mary O. Daly

General Editor

Rollin A. Lasseter

Produced and developed by:
Catholic Schools Textbook Project

In cooperation with:
Ave Maria University

Ignatius Press   San Francisco

Project Manager: Douglas Alexander
Editing: Patricia Bozell and Bridget Neumayr
Design and Production: Hespenheide Design, Lindsey Altenbernt, Stephanie Davila, Gary Hespenheide, Randy Miyake, Leslie Weller, Patti Zeman, and the DLF group
Acknowledgments: to all of our spiritual, intellectual, and material benefactors, especially Dr. Dominic Aquila, Mr. and Mrs. William Burleigh, Mark Brumley, Sr. John Dominic Rasmussen, O.P., Fr. Joseph Fessio, S.J., Dan Guernsey, Dr. James Hitchcock, Dr. Ken Kaiser, Helen Lasseter, Ruth Lasseter, Ron Lawson, Carolyn Lemon, Mother Assumpta Long, Luke Macik, Esq., Jan Matulka, Dr. John Nieto, Rose Nieto, Fr. Marvin O'Connell, Dr. Andrew Seeley, Luke Seeley, Mary Ann Shapiro, Mr. and Mrs. Charles Van Hecke, Jessie Van Hecke, and Karen Walker (StudioRaphael). In memoriam, Jacqleen Ferrell and Hal Wales, Esq.

Also, gratitude is due the following organizations for their contributions: Ave Maria University, Dominican Sisters of Nashville, Sisters of Mary Mother of the Church, Sisters of Mary Mother of the Eucharist, Joseph and Laurel Moran, and St. Augustine Academy.

Cover Image: All images supplied by Corbis (clockwise from top) Elio Ciol; Gian Berto Vanni; Araldo de Luca; Eric Curry; The Corcoran Gallery of Art

Photo Credits: All images supplied by Corbis **p. 1** Eric Curry; **p. 11** Galen Rowell; **p. 13** Roger Ressmayer; **p. 19** Bettmann; **p. 20** Archivo Iconografico, S.A.; **p. 21** Archivo Iconografico, S.A.; **p. 23** Gianni Dagli Orti; **p. 25** Yann Arthus Bertrand; **p. 28** David Lees; **p. 29** Bettmann; **p. 30** Gianni Dagli Orti; **p. 31** Gianni Dagli Orti; **p. 33** Paul Almasy; **p. 34** Carmen Redondo; **p. 35** Archivo Iconografico, S.A.; **p. 36** Charles Lenars; **p. 37** Roger Ressmeyer; **p. 38** below left, Archivo Iconografico, S.A., below right, Araldo de Luca; **p. 39** below left, Gian Berto Vanni, below right, Gianni Dagli Orti; **p. 40** left, Bettmann, middle, Roger Wood; Archivo Iconografico, S.A.; **p. 41** Sandro Vannini; **p. 43** Philip de Bay; **p. 45** Philip de Bay; **p. 46** above, David Lees, below, Oriol Alamany; **p. 47** Bettmann; **p. 49** upper left, Dave G. Houser, upper right, Carmen Redondo, below, Christine Osborne; **p. 50** Bettmann; **p. 51** Arte & Immagini srl; **p. 53** Archivo Iconografico, S.A.; **p. 54** Gianni Dagli Orti; **p. 55** right, Nik Wheeler, left, Bettmann; **p. 56** Philip de Bay, Historical Picture Archive; **p. 57** above, Elio Ciol, below, Bettmann; **p. 58**, National Gallery Collection; by kind permission of the Trustees of the National Gallery, London; **p. 60** Richard T. Nowitz; **p. 64** Bettmann; **p. 65** Rugero Vanni; **p. 67** Wolfgang Kaehler; **p. 68** Bettmann; **p. 71** Bettmann; **p. 72** Wolfgang Kaehler; **p. 73** Bettmann; **p. 74** above, unknown, below, Dallas & John Heaton; **p. 75** row 1, row 4, Philip de Bay/Historical Picture Archive, row 2 left, Philip de Bay, row 2 right, row 3 right, Bettmann, row 3 left, Archivo Iconografico, S.A.; **p. 76** Bettmann; **p. 77** both, Gianni Dagli Orti; **p. 78** Leonard de Selva; **p. 79** left, Francis G. Meyer, right, Gianni Dagli Orti; **p. 80** Ted Spiegel; **p. 81** right, Archivo Iconografico, S.A, left, Araldo de Luca; **p. 82** Araldo de Luca; **p. 85** Richard A. Nowitz; **p. 87** Araldo de Luca; **p. 88** John Turner; **p. 89** Werner Forman; **p. 90** Charles Lenars; **p. 91** Araldo de Luca; **p. 93** Bettmann; **p. 94** both, Bettmann; **p. 95** Bettmann; **p. 97** Araldo de Luca; **p. 98** above, Bettmann, below, National Gallery Collection; by kind permission of the Trustees of the National Gallery, London; **p. 103** Gianni Dagli Orti; **p. 104** Bruce E. Zuckerman; **p. 105** Archivo Iconografico, S.A.; **p. 106** Archivo Iconografico, S.A.; **p. 107** above, Arte & Immagini srl, below, National Gallery Collection; by kind permission of the Trustees of the National Gallery, London; **p. 109** Archivo Iconografico, S.A.; **p. 110** Elio Ciol; **p. 112** Elio Ciol;

Credits continue on page 345

Table of Contents

Our Lady of Grace

Preface

Dear . . . .

Many years ago, when embarking upon a career as an educator, I was confronted with only two options in teaching history: beautifully designed secular texts with a definite anti-Catholic bias, or photocopied versions of old Catholic texts, which were outdated and, in many respects, overly parochial. I realized that Catholic schools were forced by default to use one option or the other. This was not serving our students. I was not satisfied with this limitation, and I found others, teachers and parents, who were not satisfied either. The Church has always been a blend of heaven and earth, the material and the spiritual; and we dreamed of a textbook that combined the beauty of secular texts with the expansive and hopeful vision of history that is truly Catholic.

For more than a decade we have been working to make this dream a reality, to answer the prayers of countless teachers and parents. Now educators and families can have both beautiful illustrations and accurate text that is true to the Catholic vision of history as set forth in the Second Vatican Council's guiding document: *Lumen Gentium.*

The Catholic Schools Textbook Project fills the void in the historical education of youth who know little of the accomplishments and contributions of their parents and grandparents, and even less about the men and women who have given us our civilization, our country and, most importantly, our Catholic Faith. This vacuum of historical knowledge is not our true heritage. Ours is a culture of life and of hope, of faith, vast and deep, and rich achievements for the common good.

The Catholic Schools Textbook Project restores what has been lost in the secular texts and offers beautiful illustrations to accompany the story. We extend to teachers and students the first distinctively Catholic history textbooks since the 1960s.

As a teacher and administrator, I cannot fully express my satisfaction at finally having an option for Catholic schools, an option to educate with the tool of a textbook which is balanced and supportive of our Faith. The Catholic Schools Textbook Project restores what has been forgotten—for the good of the Church, for the good of society and for the good of our children.

—Michael J. Van Hecke, M.Ed.
President
The Catholic Schools Textbook Project

Introduction

Since the Second Vatican Council, Catholics have been aware of the deficiencies in religious education which afflict the Church at all levels, from kindergarten to graduate school, and some efforts have been made to correct these.

But the faith is more than theology. Because the Second Person of the Trinity became man, entered human history, that history must have deep religious significance for believers. The Judaeo-Christian tradition sees historical events as governed by Divine Providence, while at the same time warning believers against thinking that they are able to read the meaning of that Providence.

It is not insignificant that the Gospels were written not as theological treatises but as historical narratives, nor is it coincidental that the most radical attacks on Christianity have been on its historicity.

Just as Catholics have been deprived of much of their authentic theology over the past forty years, so also they have been deprived of their history, a deprivation which has been much less noticed. This has several damaging effects. Catholics now have little sense of their tradition, little understanding of how the faith can and should permeate a culture and serve as a leaven in that culture. They have little sense of what the lived faith was like through the centuries. Indeed they are extraordinarily present-minded, with little understanding of the faith as anything beyond their own immediate communities. They have little sense of the Communion of Saints—that they are intimately linked with all those who have gone before them with the sign of faith. They have little sense that history itself has a religious meaning.

The Catholic Schools Textbook Project is one of the most promising enterprises of the post-conciliar era, with its determination to once more make available to Catholics an understanding of "secular" subjects which helps illumine the richness of the faith.

The curricula of the Catholic schools prior to Vatican II has often been criticized for its alleged parochialism, the assumption that there was such a thing as "Catholic mathematics," for example, or the tendency to look at the past exclusively through apologetic eyes. These mistakes, to the extent that they were real, will not be made by the Catholic School Textbook Project. As this volume shows, it will be a series which on the one hand honors the Catholic faith and on the other is not afraid to be honest and comprehensive in its treatment of the past. It is a project which deserves the support of every serious Catholic.

—James Hitchcock
St. Louis University

Chapter 1 Introduction to Geography

God's Creation, God's Gift

The stories of the world have not occurred in a vacuum. They have taken place on this remarkable planet called Earth, created by God to be our first home on our pilgrimage to heaven. The planet Earth is ours to enjoy and share—its different environments range from the fertile farmlands of central Europe to the volcanic islands of Japan. We have been given it as stewards of creation; we are to care for it, enjoy it, improve it, and pass it along to the next generations.

The Written World

The study of the Earth—including its land and landforms, rivers and seas, and the people that have carved out homes in its various regions—is called geography. This word comes from the Greek: *geo* for "Earth," and *graph* for "writing." By learning about this "written world," you will make better sense of the stories in this book and other books. People and events will fill your imagination. When you read, you will travel; and when you travel, you will read, seeing the past in a landscape that does not change much over time.

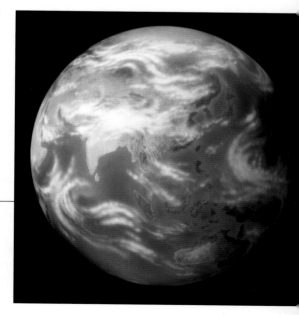

An enhanced photo of Earth taken from space in 1972 by the Apollo 17 astronauts during their mission to the Moon.

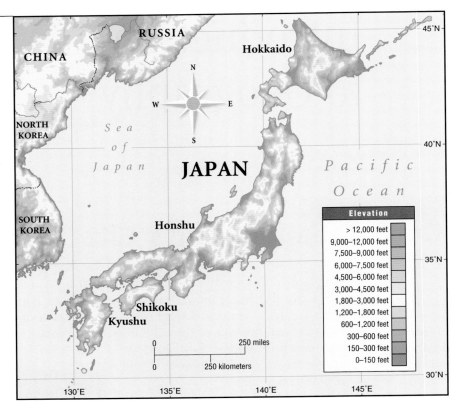

Map of the islands of Japan, showing latitude and longitude lines, and a color-keyed elevation scale.

Reading Maps

Maps are flat drawings of the world or certain places on it. Maps, in some form, have existed since the earliest civilizations. People want to know where they are (physical geography) and what territory is theirs (political geography). A book of maps is called an atlas, a name that comes from ancient Greek mythology. Atlas was a giant who held up the sky. Early mapmakers liked to draw him underneath a map of the world, which he appeared to carry on his shoulder.

Map Directions   Most maps are usually positioned with North at the top, but some maps place another direction at the top. Look on the map for a compass rose, a small circular symbol pointing to North, East, South, and West. This is like a compass of the map.

Legend or Key   Because a map is a small picture of a large area, it can include symbols to represent places or features. A blackened triangle may stand for a mountain and a crooked line for a river or a boundary. A dot is usually a city; the larger the dot, the larger the city. A broken line or lines with arrows can show someone's travels or an army's invasion.

Scale   This helps show distances and is a horizontal bar on a map. The bar will compare a small length with a larger one; for example, a line like this — may stand for 200 miles. With a scale, you can measure the distances between cities or compare the sizes of regions.

Sometimes a map's scale can appear distorted, especially when you put the entire three-dimensional globe onto a two-dimensional map. Greenland may appear larger than Africa, but it isn't. This is the problem with transferring the rounded surface of the globe to a flat surface. Areas at the top and bottom must be enlarged. This kind of map is called a Mercator Projection, after its inventor, Gerardus Mercator (1589). Today some maps try to correct that distortion by drawing the North and South in rounded shape. This kind of map is called a Robinson Projection. (All maps are distorted in some way.)

Latitude and Longitude

Latitude and longitude are the imaginary lines used by mapmakers to show places on a map, or by sailors and other travelers to learn where they are on the Earth. These imaginary lines crisscross the globe, running East-West (latitude) and North-South (longitude). These are the chief ways of showing a location on the map.

Mercator Projection—A map showing the meridians parallel to each other and the lines of latitude spaced farther apart as their distance from the Equator increases. This kind of map is especially useful for sea navigation.

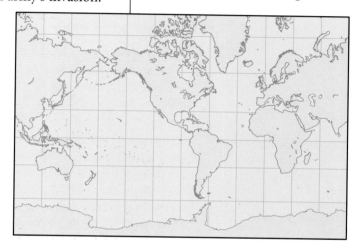

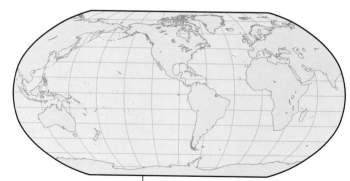

Robinson Projection—A map showing shapes and areas more accurately than other maps. The poles are shown as lines, not points. Lines of latitude are straight, and meridians are curved and get closer as they approach the poles.

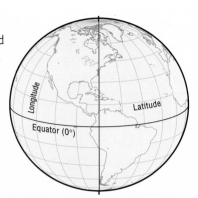

Since the Earth is a sphere—a three-dimensional circle—it can be divided like a circle into 360 degrees. Lines of latitude and longitude are described as degrees and subdivided into "minutes" (60 minutes = 1 degree) and "seconds" (60 seconds = 1 minute).

- a degree symbol looks like this: °
- a minute symbol like this: ′
- a second looks like this: ″

Equator: an imaginary circle, equally distant from the two poles, around the middle of the earth.

The central line of latitude is the **equator**, which circles the center of the globe, halfway between the north and south Poles. All latitude lines run parallel to the equator. For example, the North Pole, shown as a dot, not a line, is 90 degrees north latitude, because the distance between the Equator and the Pole is one-fourth of the whole way around the Earth (one-fourth of 360 is 90). The South Pole is 90 degrees south latitude. Beijing, in China, and Philadelphia, in the United States, are both at about 40 degrees latitude, even though they are on opposite sides of the Earth. If regions are in the same latitude, their climates might be the same.

Prime Meridian: The only great circle of the earth that passes through both poles of the earth and the Royal Observatory in Greenwich, England. All other meridians are numbered from this meridian which is the 0° (degree) meridian.

Longitude is also measured in degrees, with the imaginary center of 0 degrees, called the **prime meridian**, being the line passing through Greenwich, England. Since there is no natural way to show where east and west start or end on a globe, mapmakers simply had to decide. In 1884, 25 nations agreed on the Greenwich Meridian. Our maps still go along with that starting point to number longitude. What is on the western border of the map depends on the continent the map uses as the central point. Some world maps show the Americas in the middle, cutting Asia in two between the western and eastern sides of the map.

The Geographical Directions

The Earth is a sphere, spinning as it moves around the sun. That is not what our immediate senses tell us, of course, but what our scientists have discovered over the last several centuries. The Greeks, and possibly the

Egyptians, knew the Earth was a sphere, but they thought it stood still and the heavenly bodies moved around it, not it around the sun.

The imaginary line through the Earth that the sphere spins around is called the Earth's **axis**. The ends of the axis are called poles—North Pole and South Pole. The spin creates a magnetic field, so that magnets are drawn toward the poles. But the magnetic field is not quite in line with the actual spin of the sphere, so that Magnetic North, the pole of the magnetic field, is slightly off from true North. Still, a magnetic compass is close enough for most purposes.

Axis: the line around which a body rotates.

The Earth spins so that the sun's light (day) moves over half the Earth as the sphere spins. The senses feel that the sun "rises" in the morning, and "sets" in the evening. The fact is that our point on the Earth has moved into the sun's light, or out of it when the Earth spins.

Directions are given in terms of the "rising" (east) and the "setting" (west) of the sun, and of the poles of the Earth's axis, north and south. It has become the custom to draw our maps with north at the top and east on the right.

The Continental Plates

About a hundred years ago, scientists of the Earth's history learned something that changed the way everyone thinks about geography. It is called the theory of "continental drift," or "plate **tectonics**." It seems that all the lands of the Earth were once one large mass. Rock cliffs in South America exactly match and fit cliffs like them in Africa. Far back in the beginnings of the planet, there seems to have been one huge landmass above water. Historians of natural history call this landmass Pangaea. Around 120 million years ago, this landmass began to split into two parts—a northern section called Laurasia and a southern one called Gondwanaland. The waters of the ocean that was to become the Atlantic Ocean poured in to separate the Americas from Africa and Europe. India moved north to collide with Asia and Antarctica moved south.

The top surface of the Earth's crust broke into plates. Some of these plates were already beneath the waters of the oceans, others tipped,

Globe showing the difference between magnetic north and polar north.

Tectonics: Geological structural features; geology dealing especially with the faulting and folding of a planet or moon's surface.

throwing up part of the plate and lowering the other end into the waves. These pieces, or plates, became the continents. The continents are the land above water of a continental plate.

The ice-bound continent of Antarctica, for instance, was once covered with jungles and was the home of dinosaurs. Now nothing can live there. Fossils and soil samples dug from beneath the ice show that the climate was once hot, not cold, and that the continent was connected to Africa and Asia.

The continental plates have moved apart and driven up against each other. When this happens, great mountain ranges are raised up. Where they move apart, the waters of the ocean move in to make new bodies of water. In the short history of humankind on Earth, the continents have been just about the same as they are now. They are moving, but so slowly that we

Beneath the oceans are continental plates which come together to form the surface of the earth. This map shows the boundaries of the plates.

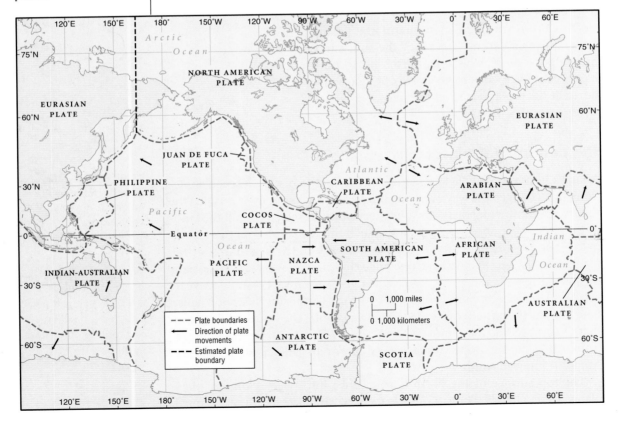

cannot tell it. Only measurements at one or two known plate edges can show that the theory of continental drift is true. Human history has been very short compared to the Earth's history.

The Seven Continents   There are seven continents: North America, South America, Asia, Europe, Africa, Australia, and Antarctica.

Asia and Africa are the largest continents. Australia and Antarctica are the smallest. On a map it looks as if Europe and Asia form one continent, but there is a European continental plate and an Asian one. The Ural (YOO•rahl) Mountains, the Caucasus Mountains, the Black Sea, and the Caspian Sea separate these two continents. The eastern end of Europe is flat and was once covered with dense forests and wide grasslands. The western end of Asia is also flat and cold or desertlike. These physical

Map of the world showing the continents, the oceans, and the equator.

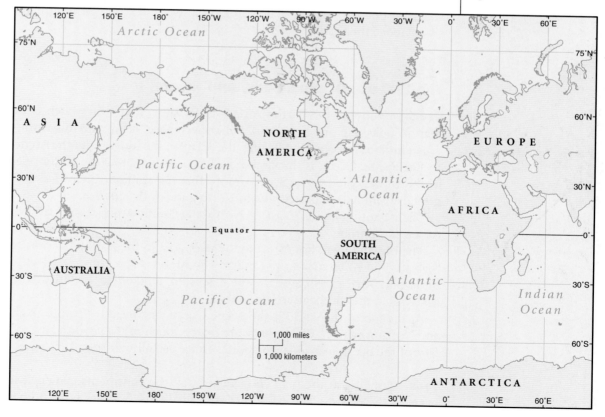

boundaries prevented travel and reenforced the different civilizations that developed on the two continents.

The two Americas are connected by the bridge of Central America, between the southern tip of Mexico and the Isthmus (a narrow strip of land) of Panama. Mexico and Central America are part of North America, but are semitropical like most of South America.

Peninsulas   A body of land surrounded on three sides by water is called a peninsula (from Latin *paene* meaning almost, and *insula* meaning island—an "almost-island"). Greece and Italy are on large peninsulas jutting in the Mediterranean. Spain and Portugal are on the Iberian Peninsula.

Islands   A body of land surrounded on all sides by water is called an island. Greenland, the largest island, is a continental island, one of a class of islands separated from their continents by water but connected underwater on one continental plate. Some islands are the tops of mountains rising above the waters.

The Waters: Oceans, Seas, and Rivers

Oceans   Most of the Earth's surface is actually covered by water. On a map it looks like one big ocean. For convenience, we divide this world-ocean into four oceans: the **Pacific**, the Atlantic, the Indian, and the Arctic.

Pacific: Calm, peaceful.

The Pacific Ocean is the largest ocean, so large that all the landmasses in the world could fit in it. It is more than 64 million square miles. It extends from Asia and Australia to North and South America.

The Atlantic Ocean is east of North and South America and west of Africa and Europe.

The Indian Ocean has Africa to the west, Asia to the north, Australia to the east, and Antarctica to the south. The Arab traders sailed across it·to India and Africa and brought their Muslim religion to the islands of Malaysia at the southeastern tip of Asia.

At the top of the world is the Arctic Ocean, encircled by Europe, Asia, and North America. All its waters are frozen much of the year, and a good part of the ocean lies under the northern ice cap all year round.

Seas   Looking at the map you can see that the continents can enclose parts of the oceans. These pockets are called seas. Seas are large bodies

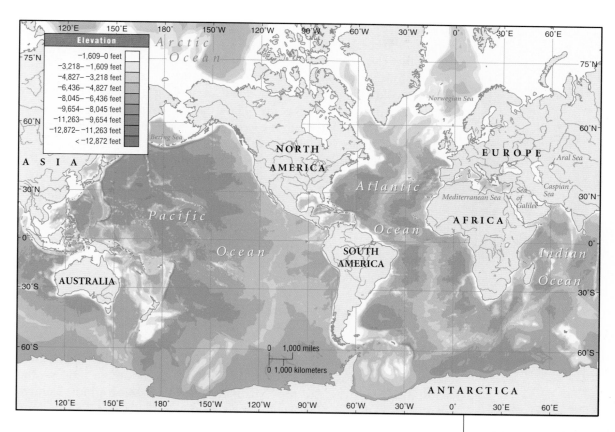

World map showing seas, oceans, lakes, and rivers, with an elevation scale keyed to the colors of the map.

of salt water. Some are connected to the larger oceans, and are surrounded by land on three sides. Some are really saltwater lakes, such as the Sea of Galilee in Israel, or the Aral Sea and Caspian Sea in Asia. Relatively small compared to the oceans, these seas have been important in history.

A student of history should be able to find the Mediterranean Sea on a map. Our civilization began in lands along its shores. The Mediterranean—Latin for "in the middle of land"—is surrounded by the three continents of Europe, Asia, and Africa. This sea was traveled by the ancient people of Phoenicia (foe•KNEE•shah) and Greece and early on brought Europeans to the north coasts of Africa. The Mediterranean Sea drawn on a map has been said to look like a winged sea horse.

Rivers   One body of water found on every continent except Antarctica is a river. A river is a large stream that carries fresh water into an ocean, lake, or another river. Rivers are essential to life because their water is drinkable. It is fresh water, unlike the salt water of oceans.

The world's longest river is the Nile River in Africa; it gave life to the civilization of the ancient Egyptians. The Amazon River in South America is the second longest, although it carries more water than the Nile. At some places the Amazon is so wide you cannot see across it. The Yangtze River in China is the longest river in Asia; the Mekong of Southeast Asia is the second longest. The Mississippi River is the longest in the United States, and combined with the Missouri River that flows into it, one of the longest in the world. The Danube River and the Rhine River are the longest in Europe; they form the center of much of the continent's history. The great river valleys of the world have been the most hospitable to human life. The first human civilizations began in valleys, because they were beside the life-giving waters of great rivers.

Ice   Much of the world's water is frozen. The two poles of the planet are covered with thick layers, or caps, of ice. These ice caps are called the Arctic (North) and the Antarctic (South) Ice. The southern continent of Antarctica carries a mile-thick ice cap. The Arctic ice cap is just as thick but smaller in area. Rivers of ice form in certain high mountain ranges—the Alps, the Himalayas, and the Canadian Rockies—that are almost as huge and thick as the ice caps. These ice rivers are called glaciers. During long periods of prehistory, called the Ice Ages, the northern ice cap grew or shrank in size, and glaciers descended from it over the continents of Asia, Europe, and North America, keeping animal life in the middle part of the planet.

The Ice Age glaciers carved out clefts and hollows in the land that filled with water and became northern lakes. The glaciers pushed Earth and rocks ahead of them which left glacial hills. Rainfall that might have returned to the oceans was locked up in these glaciers, lowering the level of the oceans, so that land bridges could be seen between continents; shores were also opened but they have since returned to the sea.

Mountains   Mountains are often made by plates shoving up against each other, cracking, and reconnecting. The surface of the Earth is constantly shifting. Mountain ranges have risen and fallen over the millions of years of Earth history. (A humbling sight when visiting mountains is to see the exposed layers of rock—rock that was once a flat surface under the sea, but has been thrust up, sometimes vertically, layer beside layer. These layers represent so much time and age that our mere human history is nothing by comparison.)

Look at a physical map of the world and find the great mountain ranges. Find the Alps in Europe, the Himalayas in Asia, the Rockies in North America, and the Andes in South America.

The world's tallest mountain is Mt. Everest, soaring 29,000 feet high—that's more than five miles—at the border of Nepal and Tibet (which happens to be the world's largest and highest plateau). Mt. Everest is part of the Himalayas, the largest mountain system, with eight of the world's ten highest mountains. The higher mountain ranges are the youngest in Earth's history, though still unimaginably old by human history. As a mountain range ages, it is worn down by wind and rain, and so becomes smaller.

Volcanoes   Some mountains are formed by molten rock and ash erupting out of the hot magma layer beneath the Earth's crust. Breaks in the plates allow the molten rock to pour up. Then the molten rock cools and

Mount Everest, 29,035 feet high, located in Nepal, is named after the English surveyor, Sir George Everest.

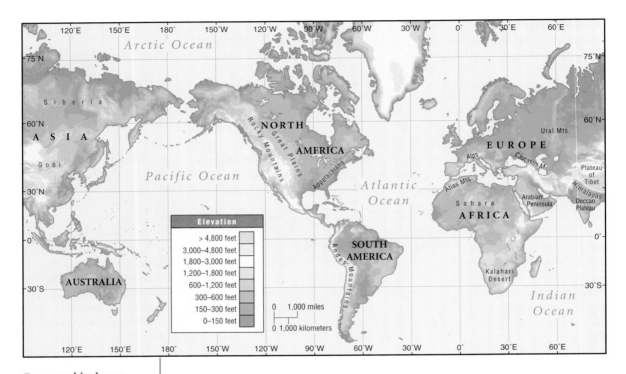

Topographical map showing mountain ranges of the world with color-keyed elevation scale.

Obsidian: Dark, natural glass formed by the cooling of molten lava.

hardens, and forms cone-shaped mountains. Volcanoes surround the Mediterranean Sea and the North Pacific Ocean.

The soil that their ash leaves behind is rich and fertile and has given some of the best farming. Human beings have chosen to live under volcanoes for the rich farmland. The natural volcanic glass, **obsidian**, gave human toolmakers the first really sharp knives and cutting tools and was treasured by prehistoric man.

The most famous volcanoes in history are Mt. Vesuvius in southern Italy, and Mt. Aetna on the island of Sicily. Vesuvius buried the Roman town of Pompeii in ash. It left a perfectly preserved ancient town for our archeologists to uncover. Mt. Fujiyama in Japan has been revered by the Japanese for its majestic size and beauty. The eruption of Krakatoa in Indonesia during the 1890s sent a cloud into the atmosphere that left ash all over the world.

Plains   The large, flat areas of the world are called plains. Plains are not truly flat; they have a rolling surface, but have no mountain ranges. Plains

Mount Vesuvius, a volcano in Italy near Naples, erupted in A.D. 79, destroying the ancient cities of Pompeii and Herculaneum.

have been historically the home of **nomadic** people, people who follow the herds of game or riding animals. The plains of eastern Europe and western Asia, huge expanses of thousands of miles of grassland, are called **steppes**. The Great Plains of the North American continent were covered in grasses that grew as tall as a man. Such grasslands are called prairies. The plains areas nearer the tropics are too hot to grow tall grasses, but they support small stands of trees and low grasses that are called **savannahs**. Plateaus are plains high above sea level, usually part of a mountain, where the air is cooler and the winds from the mountains are strong. Central Mexico is a plateau, as are Tibet, north of the Himalayas, and the central portion of India called the Deccan Plateau.

Nomad: A member of a people who move from place to place with no fixed residence.
Steppe: Dry, level grasslands with few to no trees.
Savannah: Grasslands containing scattered trees.
Plateau: Large area of high land.

Deserts A desert is land with very little or no water. Human life is difficult in deserts, and they are unfriendly to human travel and development.

Africa contains the largest desert—the Sahara, which stretches the whole width of the continent. The other major deserts that have affected history are the Arabian Desert, in the center of the Arabian peninsula, and the Gobi Desert, cutting off China from the West. In North America, the Southwestern Desert may also have affected history by forming a natural barrier to invasion of Mexico from the north, which protected the development of Meso-American civilization. Between the sea and the Andes Mountains on the west of South America are high, windswept coastal deserts. The civilizations of Peru were also protected from invasion by the difficulty of crossing those miles of barren waste.

Climates

The climate is all weather conditions, including rainfall, cloud cover, and temperature. Latitudes affect climates because a region is cooler farther from the Equator, but so do other factors such as altitude, the amount of water in the area, and the wind patterns. Water currents can make a difference too. The Gulf Stream carries warm water from the Gulf of Mexico making England's climate moderate. At the same latitude is Labrador, a frozen wasteland most of the year because of the icy Labrador Current coming down from the Arctic.

Water holds a more stable temperature than air. Because of a lack of water, the world's deserts are interesting because of their extreme temperature variations. This is especially so in central Asia. Temperatures may rise to 130 degrees in the day, and then drop to below freezing at night.

The climatic regions of the Earth are called zones, the Greek word for belt, because they run around the globe. At the center of the globe are the Tropics, zones north and south of the Equator to the latitude lines 23 degrees 27 minutes. These latitudes are the Tropic of Cancer (north of the Equator) and the Tropic of Capricorn (south) that roughly show the path of the sun as it appears to move north or south during the year. The polar regions are frozen year-round, and inhospitable to life. But the Temperate Zones, the latitudes between the frozen Polar Zones and the Tropics, have been the site of most of human history.

The climatic regions of the Earth have remained somewhat the same through all of human history. The cold regions of the polar north and south and the heights of mountain chains have grown or shortened through the ages, but have essentially stayed the same. Europe has enjoyed

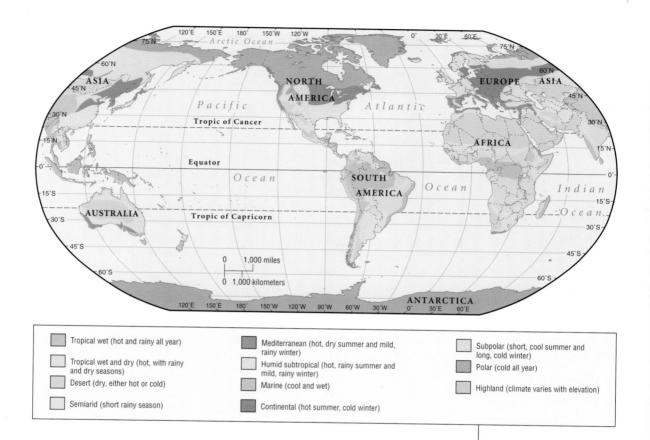

▦ Tropical wet (hot and rainy all year)	▦ Mediterranean (hot, dry summer and mild, rainy winter)	▦ Subpolar (short, cool summer and long, cold winter)
▦ Tropical wet and dry (hot, with rainy and dry seasons)	▦ Humid subtropical (hot, rainy summer and mild, rainy winter)	▦ Polar (cold all year)
▦ Desert (dry, either hot or cold)	▦ Marine (cool and wet)	▦ Highland (climate varies with elevation)
▦ Semiarid (short rainy season)	▦ Continental (hot summer, cold winter)	

A climate map of the world.

a temperate and moist climate through recent centuries, as have China and Japan. The Middle East, North Africa, and India have remained warm and semitropical. The Americas have been much as they are today throughout human history.

The chief climate event in human history has been the coming and going of several Ice Ages, when the northern glaciers spread down over parts of Europe, Asia, and North America. No Ice Age has occurred since human beings have been able to write and record their history. Only warming and cooling periods have been noted in recorded history. In the northern half of Africa, the plains of the Sahara were a fertile grassland when the last glaciers withdrew and the world's climate changed. Rainfall shifted away from northern Africa, the rich pastureland dried, and the **oases** disappeared. Dry sand and rock desert are there now.

Oasis (oases): A fertile, green area in an arid, or dry, region.

Chapter 1 Review

Let's Remember   Write your answer in a single complete sentence.
1. What determines the directions? East? West? North? South?
2. Name the seven continents. Which continents touch another continent? Which continents stand alone?
3. What is the difference between an island and a peninsula?
4. How many oceans are there? What are they named?
5. The longest river on Earth is called _____. What is the second longest? What is the longest river in the U.S.A.?
6. How can scientists tell which mountain range is the older?
7. What is a desert? Where are the largest deserts of the world?
8. Where are the Tropics? What makes the Temperate Zones temperate?

Let's Consider   For silent thinking and a short essay, or for thinking in a group with classroom discussion:
1. Why does a lack of water cause deserts to vary in temperature from night to day?
2. What is the possible effect of mountain ranges on the spread of civilization? Why could so many ancient civilizations have developed on one continent, Asia, so differently?
3. Why do civilizations begin in major river valleys?
4. Consider what the Mediterranean Sea must have offered to human development in earliest times.

Things to Do
1. Find all the continents on a globe. Make a map on a flat surface of the continents you have seen on the globe. Consider why it is difficult to draw a flat map of a round surface.
2. Trace the course of the following rivers on your globe with your finger. What countries do they run through? The Nile in Africa. The Yangtze in Asia. The Rhine in Europe. The Danube in Europe. The Mississippi in North America. With a piece of string, measure these rivers on the globe as well as you can. Find the legend or key. About how many miles does your string show the river runs?
3. Using your measuring string, find out how far your state is from the Equator, and then from the North Pole. Use the legend or key on your map. Consider what other weather-makers determine the climate of your state. (mountains—open plains—winds—seacoast)

Chapter 2 Prehistory: Beginning Man's Story

The Infancy of Man

The prehistory of our world is a bit like your own childhood. You could not write when you were a baby, nor can you tell any stories from your babyhood. Try as you might, you cannot remember farther back than the ages of three or four. Of course, you have your parents' memories, but you have none of your own. Yet, you know you existed as an infant because you see that other people don't come into being at the age of four. They are first formed in the darkness of their mother's womb, emerge at birth, and live as infants, then toddlers. And so, you conclude, the same was true for you.

There are other clues to your earliest years—photographs, baby spoons at the back of the drawer, a baptismal candle, a box of baby toys in the attic, a birth certificate and medical records. Written records are as valuable to history as your memories are to your sense of your life. But even without these memories, you can discover something from your past.

Like your infancy and growth, the history of mankind began with the first written records, even though life had gone on for some time before the written records. Written records appeared 3,500 years before the coming of Christ.

Other life on our planet is much older than human life. For instance, the dinosaurs lived for 40 million years! They had disappeared millions of years before the first people were created, for which we can be very thankful! Before them, trilobites lived in the seas for 250 million years, and before that there were algae, including the archeons that still live in unbelievable pressure and temperature in the deep places of the Earth.

The time before Christ's coming is called by historians, B.C., before Christ. The years after the coming of Christ are called A.D., *Anno Domini*, which means in Latin "In the Year of the Lord." We live in the 21st century after the coming of Christ. The years before the coming of Christ are counted backwards; the larger the number in B.C., the farther from the birth of Christ, as well as from our own time. For instance, 2000 B.C. is older than 200 B.C.

Human-like beings have existed only for approximately 1 million years, and they may have been only animals. Our faith tells us that humankind had two ancestors, a first father and first mother, Adam and Eve. Where those parents lived or when they lived is a mystery. But how our first parents came to be is no mystery. God has told us that he made them, and that—like Adam and Eve—we have his love and special concern. Yet, all of recorded history—that is, the whole life of mankind since anyone was able to write down what was happening—has existed only a little more than six thousand years.

Yet what about all the thousands of years of mankind before there was writing? This time, which we call "prehistory," is not a dark and silent age about which nothing can be known, any more than an individual life in its infancy is dark and unknown. Of course, our earliest ancestors did not know how to write. They left no written story about themselves and their lives. What they did leave was shards and scraps, skulls, bones, and stone tools. We know they were human, like us, because they did what humans—not animals—have always done. They left objects that show they were concerned for the soul. They left carefully prepared graves to honor their loved ones who died. They tried to make themselves beautiful with body ornaments. They constructed enormous stone structures all over the world. They made beautiful paintings deep inside caves. They built homes in cliffs and, later, they cultivated the soil and built cities and discovered the arts of writing and music. All these things are the work of thinking, personal creatures—animals do not paint their surroundings nor carefully bury their dead. Yet, our earliest ancestors also were not innocent; they knew about warfare and, so, probably, about sin and death.

The evidence shows that these creatures also knew how to kill their own kind. Our faith explains this tendency to evil as coming from the Fall. That is, revelation tells us that the first parents, Adam and Eve, placed in this beautiful world to guard and improve it, did not know disease or death until they disobeyed the one command of God. When they came to know good and evil, not just good, they fell from grace and began the sad history of death and disease, domination, conquest, murder, treachery, and deceit.

Based on the artifacts and tools they uncovered, the first paleontologists—those who describe history—organized the prehistory of ancient man into three ages: the Stone Age, the Bronze Age, and the Iron Age. The tools and technology of the earliest human societies were made of stone, and thus gave the name Stone Age to man's beginnings. The first metal to be mastered was bronze, and tools and weapons of bronze gave their name to the Bronze Age. But the mastery of iron gave an advantage in weaponry, and the Iron Age has lasted from the time of the Greeks to the modern world. These names have remained ever since as a useful though not very precise description of the years of human existence on our planet.

Old and New Stone Age

The Stone Age has been divided into two parts: Old and New Stone Age. In the Old Stone Age (Paleolithic), mankind lived only by hunting; in the New Stone Age (Neolithic), farming and city-building began to transform human life.

The people who discover and tell the story of prehistoric man are paleontologists, archaeologists, and anthropologists.

1. Paleontologists study the traces left by mankind during those long years before writing. The word paleontologist is from the Greek words *palaea*, meaning the past, and *ontologia*, meaning the study of what is.
2. Archeologists find and dig up the lost cities and campsites of mankind; they study the bones and buildings and rubbish left there for signs of man's life. Archeologist comes from the Greek *arche*, beginnings, and *logia*, study.
3. Anthropologists study different human cultures and behaviors among ancient peoples. The word comes from the Greek *anthropos*, meaning mankind, and *logia*, study.

These scientists are not actual historians; they don't write history. But by finding human tools and foods, by using the insights of physics to date these findings, and by comparing these findings with the activities of modern people living under similar circumstances, these scientists can guess a lot about prehistoric mankind. As more discoveries are made, parts of the ancient tale either come into better focus or must be completely reworked.

The paleontologists of the 20th century developed a method called radiocarbon dating, which shows the age of organic material, and by implication, the age of people who

These prehistoric blades are chipped laboriously from flint, chert, or obsidian (volcanic glass). Flint or obsidian blades are still used in modern surgery because the edge is hundreds of times sharper than any steel blade.

might have used that material. Organic materials are materials that contain carbon. This means anything that has once lived: wooden posts, weapons, firewood, scraps of food, or bodies that were nourished by carbohydrates. Although radiocarbon dating is not totally precise, it can give a clear indication of the age of organic materials less than 30,000 years old.

Our scientists conclude from several bits of evidence that human-like creatures, different from the animal primates that came before, have been on the Earth for at least 1 million years. This is not a fact, but a theory, or general guess from a few facts that are available. A theory is not the truth, but as close to the truth as an interpretation of the facts can get. Newer theories replace older theories when more complete facts are discovered.

Scientists call this form of human ancestor by the Latin name *homo erectus*, or Upright Man, because his bones show that he walked upright. After Upright Man came another possible ancestor called *homo sapiens*, or Thinking Man. Modern human beings are called *homo sapiens sapiens*, or Thinking Man, the Wise. Thinking Man was our ancient ancestor, and he was also the ancestor of a parallel family line of cousins, Neanderthal Man, *homo sapiens neanderthalensis*, who no longer walk the Earth.

Neanderthal Man was short and stocky, physically strong, with large

bones and a thick brow. But he was not an animal, not an ape. In addition to his bones, the scientists have found all sorts of remains of the Neanderthaler's life, such as body ornaments and distinctive stone tools. He adapted and survived in Arctic-like weather for thousands of years, refining his skills and tools into a culture of his own. He made camps and ritual burial sites, the traces of which have been found all over Europe and western Asia as far east as Russia and as far south as Israel and Iran. These Neanderthal men and women lived in family groups, hunted, cooked their food, and honored their dead, just as people have always done. Then, suddenly, they disappeared from all over the world in a short period of time. What happened to them? Did they die of a sickness that our own ancestors survived,

The same human mind that would later create cathedrals and spacecraft began meeting the problems of living in the Ice-Age by using stone tools, weapons, and furs.

somehow? Did our own ancestors kill off these distant cousins? Nobody knows. They were followed by our own more recent ancestor, *homo sapiens sapiens* (Thinking Man, the Wise), another branch of the *homo sapiens* family tree.

The Stone Age

Forty thousand years ago, the descendants of *homo sapiens sapiens* lived like nomads. They had no permanent home, but traveled depending on the change of seasons, the migratory patterns of the animals they hunted for food, and the large climatic events, such as drought or the Ice Age, in which the northern parts of the Earth underwent an almost endless winter. What were these earliest of people like? Sometimes you see comical pictures of "cave men," extremely hairy people, hunched over, uttering grunts, and holding clubs. Men who believed that early man was not different from an ape drew these pictures. But there is not now, nor has there ever been, any evidence to support that belief. *Homo sapiens sapiens*, from the first day of his existence, walked upright. Although he had no written language, he spoke with a vocal system designed for musical expression. It would be unreasonable to suggest that his vocabulary was as limited as that of the dumb beasts. His tools, though simple, were practical, skillfully crafted, and increasingly refined.

Early people were, in fact, good users of stone. The use of stone for tools to provide food, clothing and shelter gave its name to this age of history. Early man's mastery of stone for tools was both good enough for survival and capable of beauty. One stone could sharpen another, and the sharpened stone became a spear tip, tied to a stone-whittled tree branch. The spear would kill an animal, which would give meat for cooking and, thanks to a stone knife, a hide for clothing, a screen to block the wind, a roof to stop the rain. Early man used stones to cut holes into animal bones and make needles to sew clothing, and tiny stones and bones were made into buttons.

The human Stone Age occurred during the last of the Earth's geological Ice Ages. At the time of their greatest expansion, the ice glaciers covered all of northern Europe (including the British Isles, Germany, Poland, and Russia). They covered North America, as far south as the Missouri and Ohio River valleys, Greenland, and Iceland. The global chill changed tropical central China into a wind-swept grassland, and the ice heaps had so

This ancient stone was given a sharp flaked edge for use as a hand-held cutter and scraper. In strong, experienced hands it was very effective.

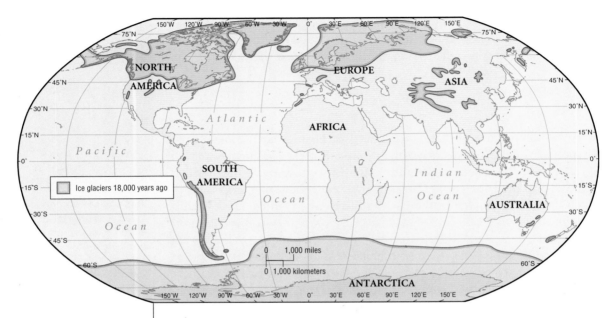

NORTH AMERICA

EUROPE

ASIA

Atlantic

AFRICA

Pacific

SOUTH AMERICA

Ice glaciers 18,000 years ago

Indian

Ocean

Ocean

AUSTRALIA

Ocean

0   1,000 miles

0   1,000 kilometers

ANTARCTICA

This map shows the extent of glaciers covering the earth about 18,000 years ago.

much water in them that the sea level dropped and showed land bridges between Asia and North America and between Asia and the islands of the East Indies. Stone Age man migrated across these land bridges and traveled into distant lands. Later, these lands were cut off by water when the glaciers melted and the seas rose. When the Ice Ages ended, a warm and fertile Europe and Asia were left, teeming with animal life, valleys, and plains where nomadic human beings could find good hunting and live well.

Stone Age man had many talents. He was a craftsman, creating the bow and arrow for better hunting. He was a naturalist, tracking animals. He was an inventor, making lamps from animal fat and twigs in order to work by night. And he preserved food through drying or smoking it over fire.

Even though survival was the main goal, Stone Age man showed a reflective nature, a desire for beauty, and a wish to create. Scientists have found, for example, a 30,000-year-old flute made out of a bird bone, a 23-ton elaborate house constructed from 400 mammoth bones, kilns around 24,000 years old to fire decorative pottery, and carved ivory jewelry even older. Yet the most stunning example of early man's artistic nature, a mysterious and lovely treasure, was found in the darkness of the Earth.

Man's First Artwork

The oldest paintings in the world are not in museums but on walls and ceilings in deep caves and rocky gorges in Europe, Africa, Asia, and Australia. Primitive and beautiful cave paintings dated from 30,000 to 11,000 B.C. depict a great variety of animals in simple, life-like forms: bison, horses, wild cattle, deer, mammoths, wolves, foxes, oxen, owls, and the woolly rhinoceros. The ancient artists also made stylized decorations, such as rows of dots or circles, and stencil outlines of their hands.

Discovery of this remarkable art began in the mid-1800s in southern France and northern Spain. Two of the largest, best-preserved collections are in Lascaux, France, and Altamira, Spain. Hobbyists and scientists continue to find more cave art. As recently as 1994, the oldest collection of all was discovered in Chauvet, France.

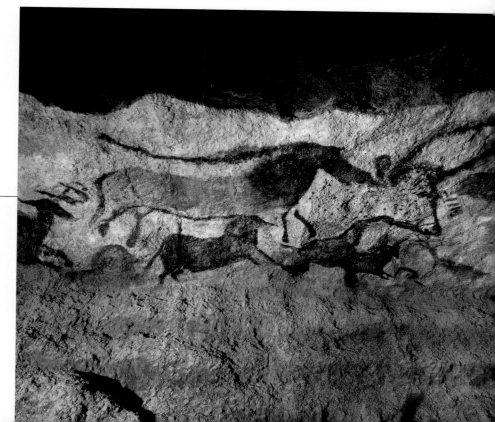

Reconstruction of cave painting of wild animals. Limestone caves at Lascaux in western France contain over 1,500 color paintings by ancient artists from more than 17,000 years ago.

The New Stone Age—Nomads Become Farmers

After generations of constant mobility, the human family began to settle down. When Stone Age people traveled with the hunt, they gathered and ate the plants they found growing in the wild. Around 9000 B.C., however, people living in the Middle East began cultivating the land to grow these grains themselves. Also, around this time, they began to domesticate and herd animals, such as sheep and goats, which could supply them with milk, meat, and clothing. Because they could grow food, people could finally grow communities, cities, and civilizations.

An early farming community was not very different from the temporary shelters of the nomadic hunters. It was a collection of single-family huts clustered near a large, open common area, sometimes with a surrounding wall to keep in animals and keep out intruders. Garden plots and grain fields clustered around the enclosure. Within the common area peo-

Map of the Near East locations of some of the earliest cities.

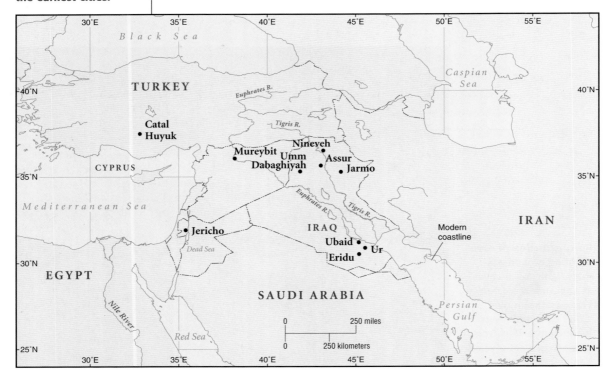

ple would mill the grain, milk the goats, weave baskets, and make pottery. These communities were small and simple, and the people could pick up and move to another area when the farmland was used up.

Once people learned how to cultivate and irrigate their farms, it became possible to build cities. The oldest known city in the world is Catal Huyuk, excavated from south-central Turkey. Catal Huyuk was built around 6150 B.C. This unique city looked like a single giant fortress, because the houses were built right up against each other with no streets in between. The citizens entered and left their houses through openings in the ceilings, and to get from place to place they walked across the roofs, using ladders for the differing heights. Such a city would have been difficult for an enemy to approach, let alone overcome.

Catal Huyuk in Turkey is an ancient city from 6800 B.C. whose residents once worshipped bull-gods and earned a living by trading obsidian blades made from local volcanic rock.

Cities Under the Sand

To look at modern-day Iraq, with its miles of desert sands spreading out to the Persian Gulf, it is hard to imagine this region was once farmland, and the home to the earliest great civilizations. Iraq, Syria, and Palestine form the area called the Fertile Crescent, a crescent-shaped belt of excellent farmland watered by the rivers and the rains from the Mediterranean. Iraq was once called Mesopotamia, literally "middle of the rivers." The land between the historic Tigris and Euphrates Rivers, was once rich with farms, bustling with industry, and overlooked by towering temples and huge carved statues.

Over time, river courses shifted and the silt deposits left behind pushed back the seacoast and dried the farmland into dunes. Though the Old Testament and the historical writings of the Greeks spoke of the ancient

Map of Mesopotamia showing Sumer and the chief cities.

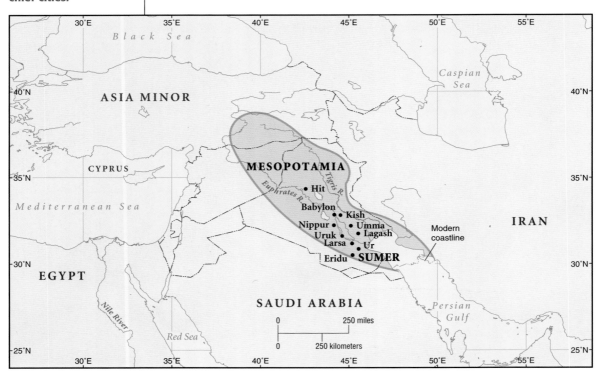

Mesopotamian cities of Babylon and Assyria, the sand held a secret that would not be revealed until archaeologists dug it up in the late 1800s. That secret was Sumer (SOO•mer), mankind's first civilization.

A civilization is more than a tribe and greater than a city. The word civilization means "the condition of life in cities." A civilization must have cities. But the word means much more. Unlike the simple life of the nomad, a civilization looks beyond the day-to-day. A civilization looks above, to God, with art and worship. It looks to the future, with education, sciences, and the development of resources. Also, a civilization looks back, telling the stories of where it came from. Sumer, which existed from nearly 4000 B.C. until about 2000 B.C., was all of these things. (Note: Keep in mind through this section on ancient history that dates are not certain before 1000 B.C., because the civilizations had incomplete records and ancient peoples used different methods to calculate the passage of time.)

Sumerian Religion

The True God gave to mankind the revelation of nature, its beauty and orderliness. Sadly, fallen human beings could not interpret it properly. They made gods of the forces of nature from their own imaginations. These forces they tried to trick, bribe, or placate with offerings and rules. Like all prehistoric peoples, the people of Sumer knew that there were forces greater than themselves. They worshiped these forces in the form of gods: gods of the Earth and sky.

To be nearer the gods of the sky, Sumerians built the **ziggurats**, solid structures in the shape of layered pyramids reaching hundreds of feet above ground. There are no interior rooms in the ziggurats, but outside stairways lead to the sacred temples located at their peaks, an attempt to touch the world of the sky gods. The gods of Sumer were thought to be heavenly landlords, for whom human beings were the field hands and slaves. All society was organized to serve and placate the angry gods.

Ziggurat: Solid, layered, stone pyramid structure.

Sumerian Inventions

From Sumer we have inherited that most fundamental invention, the wheel. Before Sumer, there is no record or evidence of the wheel. For example, the American Indians had no wheel—not until the Europeans brought it with them in the 15th century. Also, Sumer invented a plow to turn the heavy soil of the Euphrates valley, and pontoon boats to sail the rivers.

Sumerians also developed a legal code, a system of formal education for the young, remarkably effective medicine, and practical architecture of brickwork. Probably the most important legacy of Sumer was the invention of writing. Called **cuneiform**, meaning "wedge-shaped," this early writing consisted of symbols poked with a sharpened stick called a **stylus** onto soft clay tablets that were later baked or dried in the sun. The first samples of cuneiform were discovered, and efforts at translation made, as early as the 17th century.

Cuneiform: Wedge-shaped.
Stylus: A pointed stick used for writing on wax or clay.

With the digging up of the great sculptures and temples of Sumer in the mid-1800s came the discovery of many more whole and fragmented tablets. Serious translation efforts moved forward thanks to such intrepid researchers as Henry Rawlinson, an English adventurer, diplomat, scholar, and amateur archaeologist. During a series of dangerous exploits in the 1830s and 1840s, Rawlinson dangled from a mountain precipice to copy inscriptions on the rock face below.

Some historians suggest that writing emerged in agricultural society to try to simplify trade exchanges, a kind of accounting system. It is evident from the kind of writing seen on the tablets that Sumerian writing had reached a much more advanced degree. Writing was used for bills of sale, but also to maintain temple records, to honor kings, to teach children, and to tell stories. The Sumerian epic of Gilgamesh has been found on clay tablets in Ur, and a later version in Babylon, translated into the Babylonian language.

Cuneiform tablet, a record found in an office of ancient Babylon; written in a kind of writing made with tiny wedge-marks pressed into clay with a pointed stylus.

Life in Sumer

The cities of Sumer were ruled by kings who thought of themselves as gods and who were often buried with riches and even servants. The cities were built within high walls and had at their centers an upraised temple, which the people dedicated to a particular god who watched over them. Like the gods of the later Babylonians, Egyptians, Greeks, and Romans, the gods of Sumer were fickle and limited, rather like cartoon superheroes. The religion of the Sumerians had a sad fatalism—life was a gift but lacked purpose and fulfillment beyond this world. Even the hero Gilgamesh achieves nothing lasting in the end.

Gilgamesh

Gilgamesh was the name of a real and very powerful king of Sumer, but in the story he is a fictionalized hero, part-god and part-man. The epic poem, first preserved in 2600 B.C., is full of noble themes of love, friendship, bravery, and the search for the meaning of life. Ultimately, however, it is a tragic tale, for the hero does not find the hope he desperately seeks. Like the broken clay tablets on which *Gilgamesh* is preserved, this story is somehow incomplete.

As the poem opens, Gilgamesh is the strong and brave king of the city of Uruk, but he is such a bully that the citizens cry out to the gods to put him in his place. The goddess Ishtar hears their cry and creates Enkidu, a man as strong as Gilgamesh but wild and animal-like, with horns on his head. Enkidu lives in the forests outside the city and is a friend to the beasts; but he frightens a hunter, who seeks a way to trap Enkidu and bring him to the city. Gilgamesh sends one of Ishtar's priestesses out to the forest to tame Enkidu, and she does so, teaching him to speak and to understand the ways of men.

She also tells Enkidu about Gilgamesh, and, eager for the challenge, Enkidu comes to the city of Uruk and steps in Gilgamesh's way as the king tries to enter a house to choose a bride. The two giant men begin to wrestle, each one as strong as the other. Suddenly the fierce fighting stops. Gilgamesh emerges as the winner, and to the surprise of the townspeople, Gilgamesh and Enkidu embrace and declare each other the closest of friends.

The two embark on a series of adventures, including the defeat of a terrifying monster, Humbaba, as well as a great bull sent by Ishtar to kill Gilgamesh and destroy Uruk after the king refuses to be her husband. As punishment for killing the bull, Enkidu is stricken and dies. Distraught at losing his friend and facing his own eventual death, Gilgamesh sets off in search of eternal life.

He journeys to Utnapishtim, his ancestor who enjoys immortality on the far side of the Bitter River. But when Gilgamesh reaches the old man, Utnapishtim sadly can offer no hope, for he says it is only a special mercy of the gods that granted him eternal life. He does tell Gilgamesh of a secret plant that can restore youth, but after Gilgamesh pulls the elusive plant from the bottom of the river, a snake steals it.

Finally, Gilgamesh reaches the land of the dead, where he talks with Enkidu. He learns that some people, especially the fathers of many sons, enjoy reasonable comfort in their life after death, but that Gilgamesh himself, who would die with no one to mourn him, is awaited by the worst fate of all—living in dust and eating scraps that even dogs refuse.

Gilgamesh, king of Uruk, represented in a clay image made to seal documents by being pressed into a wet clay envelope.

Head of a king of Akkad, perhaps Sargon the Great. Created about 2250 B.C.

In spite of this fatalism, the accomplishments of the Sumerians were notable. The laws of Ur-nammu of Sumer formed the basis for the famous Code of Hammurabi, a great king who ruled Babylon in the Mesopotamia of later years. Today we even have the Sumerians to thank for such commonplace calculations as the 60-second minute, the 60-minute hour, and the 360-degree circle. Also, they traded their farm produce and sophisticated crafts for wood. With wood to make ships, they were able to expand their trading to Africa and India. From the ivory, gold, and precious stones they obtained from these far lands, they created magnificent jewelry and handcrafted beautiful instruments, such as lyres and harps.

What Happened to Sumer?

Sumer was troubled by constant battles between the cities and their kings, who had no real national government to keep peace. And, located as it was at the intersections of land and water and so successful in accumulating wealth and food supplies, Sumer became a target for invading tribes from the outlying areas.

One such conqueror was Sargon, one of the first great military leaders in history, who conquered Sumer in 2360 B.C. Sargon was an Akkadian, a member of a tribe living to the north of Sumer which was raised to city life by the more advanced Sumerians. The son of a shepherd, Sargon served in the palace of the king of Kish, a city in Akkad. He became king himself, and commanded a huge army for his time, some 5,000 men. (He was also the first to institute a military draft of all eligible young men to his army prior to launching an attack.)

Sargon devised novel battle plans. Instead of moving in a disorganized crowd, his soldiers fought in formation behind rows of shields, while his mounted warriors attacked along the sides of the battlefield from animal-drawn carts. With his new methods and conquering spirit, he eventually conquered all of Sumer, then moved back north toward the Mediterranean to add Syria to his possessions. He made Akkadian the language of all the Mesopotamian world, replacing the language of Sumer. When he died, he ruled the largest empire of his time. Sargon reigned for 56 years, and his empire lasted through the reigns of his son and grandson.

After the death of Sargon's grandson, the Akkadian Empire broke up. But the Sumerian way of life, its laws, beliefs, and culture, had spread to all of Mesopotamia and to the later empires of Assyria and Babylon, which inherited the civilization of the Sumerian city-states, explained below.

Likeness of a man worshipping the gods of Akkad, unearthed in the Palace of Sargon.

Egypt, the First Nation

While Sumer was reaching maturity, another civilization, Egypt, was born 1,000 miles to the west, across the Red Sea in North Africa. Drawing life from the world's longest river, the Nile, and its fertile valley, Egypt was perhaps the first nation-state in history. A nation-state is a unified government for all the people who speak one language and have a common culture. Egypt had become one people with a common language by 4000 B.C. They obeyed one king over all the Nile Valley and joined in great works. Today, on the western horizon outside the modern city of Cairo, stands the Great Pyramid, flanked by two other pyramids almost as large, and guarded by the great stone Sphinx, all silent witnesses to Egypt's fascinating past.

The earliest known settlers of Egypt are called the Hamitic (hah•MIH•tic) people, in 6000 B.C. Our name for them comes from their own name for the land, Khemi. These people farmed along the Nile Valley and its delta, the marshy plain where the north-traveling Nile empties into the Mediterranean Sea. The region was especially good for livelihood because of its warm climate and the annual flooding of the Nile, which spread rich silt over the nearby fields, renewing their fertility every year.

Early technology also lent a hand. The farmers used the invention of the *shaduf*, a long pole balanced over a forked stick, with a water bucket on one

Map of ancient Egypt showing the Delta, Memphis, Thebes, and the location of the pyramids.

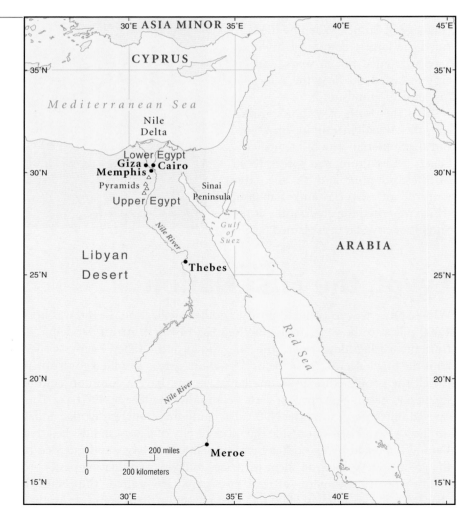

end and a counterweight on the other. They would dip the bucket into the river, then swing it around to pour the water into a nearby channel to flow downhill to water the fields.

From these early settlers, two kingdoms developed, one in the Lower, or Delta region, the other upriver to the south, called Upper Egypt. Possibly as early as 3500 B.C., King Menes (MAY•nays) united the two realms of Lower Egypt and Upper Egypt into one kingdom. The great achievements of his reign were said to include the development of water basins to irrigate the Nile Valley and the founding of the city later to be called Memphis, the capital of Egypt.

Surrounded by a forbidding desert, Egypt was somewhat more secluded, and thus safer from constant foreign invasion than Sumer. The Egyptian kingdom was so safe and stable that it lasted over 3,000 years. Historians divide Egyptian history into four periods: the Old Kingdom (2670–2198 B.C.), the Middle Kingdom (1938–1759 B.C.), the New Kingdom (1539–1100 B.C.), and the Late Period (1100–332 B.C.), when Persia conquered Egypt. These four periods encompass a total of 30 dynasties. A dynasty is a continuous family reign, generation after generation. Throughout their dynasties, Egyptian kings, called Pharaoh (Pharoah meant "The Great House," rather as we refer to "the White House"), ruled their land with special authority. As in Sumer, they were revered like gods. The people willingly gave their service to the pharaoh in exchange for his leadership and the magical protection they believed he brought them.

Lifting water from the Nile with a shaduf, an ancient tool for moving water to irrigate fields.

The World in Pictures

One way we have learned about the culture of ancient Egypt is through its writing, some of which still exists today. The art of writing may have been learned from travelers from the more established Mesopotamia. But since the Egyptian written language is so different from the Sumerian, the Egyptians probably developed writing on their own.

They also used different writing tools. In addition to carving on the walls of tombs and other buildings, the Egyptians invented the first paper. Using a shredded reed dipped into an ink made from minerals and water, the Egyptians painted on material called **papyrus** (pah•PIE•russ), which was made by stripping the papyrus reed, pressing and pounding the strips into flat sheets, and hanging the sheets to dry.

Papyrus: Paper made from pressed and woven reeds.

Hieroglyphic writing, from the tomb of a pharoah in Thebes, Egypt.

Egyptian writing was complicated. Not only did the hieroglyphics (hieroglyphics is a Greek word meaning "sacred writing") consist of several hundred little pictures which could mean all or parts of a word, but it also included alphabetic symbols and could be written left to right, right to left, or top to bottom.

Life and Death in Egypt

Because of the complexity of their writing, only 1 percent of the populace was literate, and the scribes who trained for years to write hieroglyphs were second in status only to the king. The primary occupation was farming, although there were also craftsmen, engineers, architects, artists, and laborers of various types. Egyptians honored family life and loved leisure. They drank beer and enjoyed banquets, music, and dancing. They kept their hair short and wore wigs, finely woven linen clothes, and makeup.

The Egyptians also believed in many gods. Ra, the sun god, was supreme, and from him sprang a whole "family" of other gods, who were in charge of natural elements, such as the sky and the Earth, or abstract

The Rosetta Stone

The hieroglyphs might never have been translated were it not for the Rosetta Stone. This huge basalt slab, recovered on the Nile Delta in 1799, was carved in both Greek and two forms of the Egyptian language, making it a kind of translation dictionary. But even then, it took many years for experts to translate ancient Egyptian inscriptions and documents.

The Rosetta stone; it is named for an Egyptian village in the western Delta where it was discovered by French scholars.

values, such as learning and justice. The gods were thought to take animal forms, and were often depicted with human heads on animal bodies, or animal heads on human bodies. They were seen as having human personalities, but animal appearances. The greatest gods were thought to be above animal or even human nature, but visible as animals.

The Egyptians' belief in a literal and physical life after death led to many unusual practices, such as the practice of mummification. Believing that

The Egyptians told many stories about their gods. One of the more famous ones goes like this: Geb, god of the earth, and Nut, goddess of the sky, had four children, named Osiris, Set, Isis, and Nephythis. Set was always jealous of his brother Osiris, who ruled Egypt. One day, Set tricked Osiris into lying in a coffin, then nailed it closed and threw the coffin into the river. Isis, who was wife and sister to Osiris, searched for him day and night, distraught and weeping. When she finally found the coffin, Set snatched it from her and chopped Osiris into pieces, scattering the pieces all over Egypt. Isis wandered over the countryside, gathered the parts of Osiris' body, and put them back together. Osiris and Isis then had a child, Horus, whom Isis raised in secret when Osiris left to become king of the Other World. Horus grew up and conquered his uncle Set to take his rightful place as king of Egypt.

the departed soul could return to the body, the Egyptians developed methods to prevent its decay. The word "mummy" comes from an Arab word for wax, since the preserved bodies, which had been soaked in salts and wrapped in linen strips, appeared wax-like. In the later years of the empire, Egyptians mummified animals they believed to be sacred, such as cats, **ibises,** and even crocodiles.

Ibis: A wading bird related to the heron.

The Mysterious Pyramids

The burials for kings, and later even for common people, were elaborate. At first when Egyptians were buried, a small stone building called a *mastaba* marked the grave. But in the Third Dynasty of the Old Kingdom, around 2750 B.C., an architect named Imhotep built the first pyramid for the pharaoh Zoser. This 200-foot step pyramid looks like a mastaba with successively smaller ones on top. In the temples in front of the pyramid, corridors and rooms held the treasures of the pharaoh to assure him an easy afterlife.

The successors of Zoser built even more spectacular pyramids, with designs that looked toward the gods of the night sky. Although the Greek historian Herodotus conjectured that the pyramids were built by slave labor, more recent scholars believe farmers and other free workers built them as something to do during the Nile's annual flooding and as an act of honor to the king.

The most spectacular pyramid, indeed the largest building in the world, is the Great Pyramid of the pharaoh Khufu, constructed during the Fourth Dynasty around 2571 B.C. Standing approximately 480 feet tall, this pyramid was the tallest man-made structure prior to the 19th century. With each of the four sides measuring 750 feet, the area of its base covers more than 13 acres—enough to enclose six football fields. As a testimony to the mathematical genius of the Egyptians, the base is a true square. More than

Egyptian Mummy, lying as it was found in its grave in the western desert of Egypt.

2 million stone blocks, most weighing 2½ tons and quarried from near the Nile, were used in its construction. Although today the pyramid appears rough, at one time it was covered with a smooth layer of brightly polished limestone and capped with marble. What a stunning sight for the ancient world!

Near the Great Pyramid in Giza (GEE•zah) are two others, also built in the Fourth Dynasty, for the pharaohs Kahfre and Menkaure. These three buildings mark the last of the most elaborate pyramids, perhaps because of the enormous expense of their construction. Oddly enough, no records show how the pyramids were built. Some have supposed the workers built ramps of Earth around the pyramid so that stones could be dragged to the top along the sloped paths. Without the invention of pulleys or the use of wheels, the workers must have used rollers, ropes, and human muscle.

Also in Giza is another mysterious monument: the Great Sphinx. The giant limestone figure, 240 feet long and 65 feet high, has a lion's body and a man's head. The statue was not named "Sphinx" until much later when

Pyramids of Giza.

the Greeks named it from one of their stories. The Sphinx was built to represent the sun god, Ra. Its face looks like the pharaoh Khafre, whose tomb it appears to guard.

The Pharaohs

Of the many pharaohs who guided Egypt through its history, a few stand out. One is Akhenaten, who ruled in the New Kingdom from 1353–1335 B.C. He changed his name from Amenhotep IV to Akhenaten to honor Aten, the god of the sun. While abandoning military conquests, Akhenaten attempted great social and religious changes within Egypt. He moved the capital from Thebes, where it had been since the Middle Kingdom, to a grand new city he ordered built and named for Aten, a city known today as Tell el-Amarna. Akhenaten then tried to change the **polytheistic** (many gods) religion of his people to a type of **monotheism** (one god), by raising Aten above all other gods and abolishing the temples and veneration of all the other gods. Upon the pharaoh's death, however, the nation resumed its traditional polytheistic religion and the capital was returned to Thebes.

Another outstanding pharaoh was Hatshepsut (hot•SHEP•soot), the mother of Thutmose III, who during the boy's childhood ruled for 15 years of the Eighteenth Dynasty. One of possibly two female pharaohs, she is

Polytheism: the belief in and worship of many gods.
Monotheism: the belief in and worship of one god.

Ancient portraits of two pharoahs, Akhenaten (left) and Hatshepsut (right).

sometimes depicted in statues as a man, beard and all. Hatshepsut kept a peaceful kingdom and built a number of monuments, including a beautiful temple, Deir-el-Bahri in western Thebes.

The Nineteenth Dynasty of Egypt began with the reign of Ramses and his successors, who returned military vigor to the kingdom. Fighting the Hittite people for control of Palestine, Ramses II led an army in the battle of Kadesh, only to be greatly outnumbered by Hittite-led troops from more than twenty Asian peoples. According to a tale recorded on Ramses' monument, the brave fighting of his army resulted in a draw, although history records a Hittite victory.

Eventually Ramses II signed what may be the world's first peace treaty with the Hittite king Hattusilis, who later gave one of his daughters to Ramses for his wife. The two empires lived peacefully for more than fifty years, and Ramses II gained a reputation as Egypt's most vigorous builder. In addition to revising the tombs and buildings of former pharaohs with his own name and likeness, Ramses II left such monumental constructions as the four statues carved from the rock at Abu Simbel.

Thutmose IV and Ti-O

Some 1,000 years after construction of the Sphinx, an Egyptian prince, Thutmose IV, was sleeping in its shade after hunting. The Sphinx told him in his dream to clear away the sand that nearly buried it, and that if he obeyed he would become king. Thutmose did as he was told, and due to the untimely death of his older brother he became king during the Eighteenth Dynasty, the first dynasty of the New Kingdom. The story of his dream is recorded on a stele, a stone marker placed between the giant lion's paws.

The great Sphinx was once painted in bright colors, while the pyramid of Khufu, shown behind it, was sheathed in polished limestone that gleamed and reflected the sun's rays for many miles around.

The Young King "Tut"

The pyramids and tombs contained vast storehouses of treasure, which was stolen time and again by clever tomb robbers. Despite the builders' best efforts—installing false doors and passageways going nowhere—the burglars outwitted them. Nearly all the tombs were stripped of their riches, often in the very lifetime of those who buried the kings. Tutankhamen (TOOT•in•COM•mon) (1333–1323 B.C.) was an exception; his burial chamber was untouched until it was discovered in 1922 by Howard Carter, an English archaeologist. The remains from the tomb included the king's mummy inside three nested coffins, the innermost one of solid gold and the outer two of gilded wood.

The **sarcophagus,** bore a beautiful mask of the dead king's head, depicting his face in gold, and around it the symbols of the king-

dom, the vulture and the cobra. The chamber also held jewelry, sacred writings, gilded furniture, clothes, weapons, and other objects. Though the achievements of this boy king were minor, he became known to all the modern world through the discovery of his tomb. His funeral possessions have traveled around the world, on display in museums.

Sarcophagus: A large, stone coffin. In Greek, the name literally means "flesh-eating stone."

Excavators remove objects from King Tut's tomb (left). The head of King Tut's sarcophagus (right).

Ancient Egypt is to us a mysterious place, with its fixation on death and the afterlife and its strange gods, tombs, and statues. Indeed, the Egyptians did not seem eager to extend their culture to other lands, nor to allow other ideas, from the Greeks and the Romans, for example, to shape their understanding of the world. In time, Egyptian civilization was superceded by the culture of the conquering Greeks and Romans, and lost completely to the Muslim conquerors out of Arabia. But this early civilization continues today in some ways. Their papyrus led to the development of our paper, manufactured from wood pulp. The Egyptians divided their year into 12 months and 365 days, as we still do today. They developed important mathematical formulas, such as how to find the area of a circle or how to make a true right angle, and they practiced a crude but scientific medicine. Egyptians also marked time with water clocks and sundials of various types. One surprising invention is the umbrella or, more likely in the mercilessly hot sun of the desert, the parasol.

Today we marvel at Egypt's pyramids, great-pillared monuments, mummified animals, two-dimensional, stylized art, and written language. Its exotic culture seems to have nothing in common with the Muslims and Christians who live along the Nile today. Egypt is distant also in time; it was already so old that even the ancient Greeks considered it ancient. Yet perhaps because of that distance, the majesty and mystery of the world's first nation-state have stirred the imagination of every civilization since.

Chapter 2 Review

Let's Remember   Write your answer in a single complete sentence.
1. What are the two divisions of the Stone Age?
2. What were the geographical conditions in which the Stone Age took place?
3. How many dynasties and years were there in the four periods of Egyptian history?
4. What is the Rosetta Stone and why is it important?
5. Who was the pharaoh who tried to change the polytheistic religion of Egypt to monotheism?
6. Who was Tutankhamen?

Ramses II wearing the double crown of Egypt: the tall crown of the Delta inside a short round crown.

Let's Consider   For silent thinking and a short essay, or for thinking in a group with classroom discussion:

1. Using the time of Christ's coming as the fixed point of history, describe the movement of time, backwards and forwards, B.C. and A.D.

2. In ancient history, dates before 1000 B.C are not precise because of the incomplete records and the different ways of calculating time. Imagine the problems of one civilization reckoning time according to solar calculations and another according to lunar calculations.

3. Three sciences study the past: paleontology, archaeology, and anthropology. Define the difference between history, which is the study of written records, and archaeology, paleontology, and anthropology.

4. What sort of people would have made the cave paintings? Discuss the characteristics that distinguish even the earliest creations of man from the instincts of the animals.

5. What depended upon the use of the wheel? The invention of the wheel in Sumer made what other technologies possible?

6. What numerous improvements became possible because of using Egypt's papyrus, instead of wood or stone or clay, to write on.

Let's Eat!

A Stone Age soup could have been made by putting water, meat, and wild onion into a leather container. Stones could then be heated in an open fire and dropped into the leather container to make the water boil.

The Mission of Israel

God Calls Forth a Nation

The early civilizations of Sumer, Egypt, and their successors developed in a similar fashion. Groups of families settled in an area, began to organize their common life, and as they did so, natural leaders emerged. These leaders rose to become kings and led cities or even nations. Religion was an important part of everyday life and involved the worship of many gods, from personal, household gods to cosmic personalities guiding the Earth, water, and sky. Pagan priests, acting on behalf of the people, appeased the unpredictable gods with sacrifices, and the people hoped for good fortune.

The nation of Israel, which emerged in the Mediterranean region during the waning days of Sumer, was an entirely different story. Israel existed because in some unexplainable way, God wanted this people for himself. God had a plan for this people and, through it, for the world. He began his nation Israel from a very strange origin: an elderly, childless couple, Abram and Sarai.

This couple did not remain in their native place. Trusting in the command of God, they moved to a foreign land to make their home

Sara and Abram had many mysterious adventures. See Genesis, Chapter 20.

among strangers and enemies. They did not reach out to multiple gods with prayers and sacrifices. Instead, the one, true God of heaven and Earth reached out to them.

So begins the story of Israel. Through that nation, all nations would find hope of eternal life through the Son of God, Jesus Christ.

At Haran, a city in Sumer, God broke into human history when he spoke to Abram, saying: "Go forth from the land of your kinsfolk and from your father's house to a land that I will show you. I will make of you a great nation, and I will bless you; I will make your name great, so that you will be a blessing. I will bless those who bless you and curse those who curse you. All the communities of the Earth shall find blessing in you." (Genesis 12:1)

Abram obeyed, took his wife Sarai and nephew Lot and all their possessions, and moved southwest into Canaan (KAY•nan), a region of Palestine to the west of the Jordan River. When Abram arrived, God made a spectacular promise, considering Sarai was barren and Canaan was occupied already, by the Canaanites. He told Abram: "To your descendants I will give this land."

God continued to make promises to Abram and tested his faith. Then God made a covenant with Abram, an "everlasting pact" to make Abram the father of nations and kings and to make Canaan their permanent possession. In exchange God asked only that he should be their God. He changed the man's name to Abraham, "Father of Multitudes," and his wife's name to Sarah, "Princess." In time God proved his word.

The Exodus

Exodus: A mass departure of a people from a place.

The second book of the Bible tells the story of the next period in Israel's history, the **Exodus**, or "going out." This dramatic story is even today retold every year in Jewish homes at a special prayer ceremony and family meal called the Seder (SAY•der). Comparing the biblical narrative with other records seems to show that the events of the Exodus took place during the Nineteenth Dynasty of Egypt during the reign of Ramses II.

At the end of the second millennium B.C., his capital city, the House of Ramses, was located in the north. The massive building Ramses did called for large numbers of workers and who better to pick on than the immigrant Hebrews?

But then, according to Exodus, the pharaoh (his name is not given in the Bible) was so threatened by the growing numbers of Hebrews that he ordered the killing of all Hebrew baby boys. One mother however, spared her son by placing him in a basket beside the river. He was found by a servant of the pharaoh's daughter and was adopted and raised in the palace. The pharaoh's daughter named him Moses.

When he grew up, Moses killed an Egyptian for striking a Hebrew, then, fearing punishment, escaped to Midian. In Midian he married the daughter of a shepherd and settled into life with her family. One day, while helping with his father's flock, he saw something amazing on the mountain above him. It was a bush that burned but did not disappear into ashes! Moses climbed the mountain and God spoke to him from the bush, telling Moses to lead the Israelites out of Egypt into Palestine, the "land flowing with milk and honey."

A bit reluctantly, Moses obeyed, and when the pharaoh refused to release the Hebrew slaves, God sent ten plagues upon Egypt. The final plague was the death of all first-born sons, except Hebrew babies. God "passed over" the homes of the Israelites who had placed the blood of a sacrificed lamb on their doorposts. And so the celebration to remember this event is called the Passover. Every year to this day, the Passover remembrance includes the Seder meal and the retelling of the sacred story of deliverance.

Moses then led the Israelites across the Red sea that miraculously parted, but it washed over the Egyptians who were pursuing them. On the far shore, the Israelites broke into a song of joy, whose deeper meaning about salvation from the slavery of sin and death would be revealed later on: "I will sing to the Lord, for he has triumphed gloriously; the horse and his rider he has thrown into the sea./ The Lord is my strength and my song, and he has become my salvation;/ this is my God, and I will praise him, my father's God, and I will exalt him."

Following Moses, Israel became a nation on pilgrimage as it crossed the Red Sea, leaving Egypt and marching to meet the God of all creation in the desert of Sinai.

To Covet: To desire that which belongs to another.

Bedouin: A nomadic Arab in the deserts of Arabia, Syria, or Northern Africa.

Moses presents the Ten Commandments, written by God, to the people of Israel. This painting, by Raphael from the early 1500s, reflects the strong identification of Catholics with the Jews as the people of God.

The Commandments

Moses and the Israelites lived in the desert for 40 years, a time of testing and trial. Though they had suffered as slaves in Egypt, they grumbled over their new difficulties on the way to the Promised Land. God, however, provided them with a special food called manna, and the Israelites journeyed south along the western edge of the Sinai Peninsula, which juts into the Red Sea.

At the southern edge of the peninsula, God summoned Moses to the top of Mount Sinai, and here he gave him and his people the Ten Commandments:

1. I am the Lord your God, and you shall not have other gods besides me
2. You shall not take the name of the Lord your God in vain
3. Keep holy the Sabbath Day
4. Honor your father and mother
5. You shall not kill
6. You shall not commit adultery
7. You shall not steal
8. You shall not bear false witness against your neighbor
9. You shall not **covet** your neighbor's wife
10. You shall not covet your neighbor's goods

The desert of the Sinai is not like the Sahara. More rocky than sandy, there are hardy trees and enough scrubby plants for the sheep and goats to graze. Today several thousand **Bedouin** (BEH•doo•in) still herd there. A substance like the manna described in the Bible can been seen today, though not the miraculous amount given to the Israelites. It is a flaky white material that comes from the sap of desert bushes that have been pierced by a certain type of insect.

These commandments, simple yet complete, made a tremendous advance in human civilization. They placed great demands on people in order to lead them to their true end, or purpose: union with a loving God through love of him and love of neighbor. The commandments talk about not just the outward action (like stealing) but also the thoughts that lead to this action (like coveting). They are meant to set God's people free not from human slavery, but from the slavery of sin. Though meant for the people as a whole, the commandments are directed to the individual.

The Ten Commandments are based on the knowledge of right and wrong that can be understood just through human reason. Because of this, they are principles not only for the religion of the Hebrews. Yet God revealed them to his chosen people in a dramatic display of thunder and lightning, and he inscribed them "with his own finger." (Exodus 31:18)

The Conquest of Canaan

The following book of Numbers tells how the Israelites moved from Sinai to the south of Palestine. There the Israelites proceeded to enter Canaan at Kadesh-Barnea, a city ruled by the Amorites. At God's command, Moses sent 12 men, one from each tribe, to scout out the area. They reported that the land was rich with produce but too formidable to take because of the high walls and the variety of opponents, including "giants," probably the native Anakim people.

The Israelites were afraid and angry with God. He punished the spies, and the people repented. But then, against Moses' warning, they tried to attack from the foothills, and were pushed back north to Hormah. The Israelites returned to the desert for 40 more years.

About the year 1200 B.C., Joshua succeeded Moses as commander-in-chief, and he took over Canaan. To the south, the Israelites conquered the town of Jericho

Joshua leads Israel to attack and destroy the city of Jericho at the Lord's command.

(this famous victory is recorded in Joshua 6). Joshua and his army turned north and conquered that region, too. The entire country was then divided up among the 12 tribes: Ruben, Simeon, Gad, Judah, Issachar, Zebulon, Dan, Benjamin, Asher, Naphtali, and the two tribes from Joseph, Ephraim and Mannasseh. The priests of the tribe of Levi were given no land but placed in charge of the holy places.

Phoenicia

The Greeks called the Canaanites of the Bible Phoenicians. Canaan means "land of the purple," and the Greek *phoinos* means "blood red." Both names referred to the deep purplish dye the Phoenicians produced from the native shellfish called a murex. Phoenicians were successful seafarers, merchants, **mercenaries**, and inventors of glass and glass-blowing.

The Phoenicians formed city-states occupying the coasts of modern-day Syria and Lebanon. They were independent at times, but usually ruled by one superpower or another. While under rigid Assyrian rule in the 9th century B.C., they took their civilization to colonies in other regions, the foremost being the city of Carthage in northwest Africa, near modern-day Tunis. The Carthaginian and Phoenician civilization was finally conquered by Rome in 146 B.C.

The Phoenicians' greatest legacy for humankind was used by them just as a tool for trade: the alphabet. Somewhere between 1500 and 1000 B.C., the Phoenicians developed a quick method of writing by simplifying Egyptian symbols. Noting that most languages have only a few basic sounds that compose words, they created a single symbol, a letter, to match each sound. The original alphabet contained 22 letters. Nearly all languages, except Chinese and Japanese and their derivatives, now use variations on this alphabet.

The Dreaded Philistines

After the conquest of Canaan came the period of the judges, recorded in the book of Judges, when wise chiefs and military heroes ruled the various tribes of Israel. During this time the Israelites did not enjoy the victories they had under Joshua. Instead, God used the peoples around them as a test of their faith. If they slipped back into polytheism—that is, the idol worship condemned in the First Commandment—God would hand them

A map showing Phoenicia and the division of ancient Palestine between the twelve tribes of Israel.

Mercenary: A soldier for hire.

Greek Inscription.

Phoenician Inscription.

Hebrew Script.

The Hebrew written language is a direct descendant of the Phoenician, because the Israelites adopted the writing of the Canaanite people when they entered their land west of the Jordan. Unlike most modern alphabetic languages, Hebrew is read right to left, like Phoenician.

over to their enemies. One such enemy was the Philistines, who dominated Israel for 40 years.

The Philistines, referred to by the Egyptians as the Sea Peoples, moved from the Aegean Sea region around 1200 B.C. and seized southwest Palestine. A sophisticated people of their day, they were known for their skills in metalworking, pottery, and the shipping trade. Their military might was also advanced. They were a formidable foe for the Israelites and were not defeated until the reign of King David.

But during the period of the judges, God raised up one special hero who would weaken their domination. From the book of Judges, Chapters 13 to 15, comes the story of this legendary hero, Samson.

The Legend of Samson

Manoah of the tribe of Dan had a wife who could have no children. One day an angel appeared to them and said she and her husband would have a son who would help free their people from the Philistines. The woman was to take no strong drink and to eat no unclean foods, and when the boy was born he was not to let a razor touch his head, as a sign of his consecration to God. It came to pass that the woman bore a son and named him Samson. As he grew his mother kept her promise, and Samson's hair grew long. Samson had incredible strength. One day he killed a lion with his bare hands. He grew up and was married. When the Philistines stole his wife and gave her to another man, he caught 300 foxes and, tying torches between the tails of each pair, set fire to all their fields and orchards. When the Philistines came after him, Samson took the jawbone of an ass and killed 1,000 of them!

Then Samson fell in love with a Philistine woman named Delilah, to whom her people promised a vast sum of money in exchange for finding out the secret of his great strength. Samson teased her and would not tell her the truth, until finally he could take no more of her complaining. He told her that his strength lay in his consecration to God and that if a razor touched his head, he would be as weak as any other man.

When he fell asleep that night, the treacherous Delilah called for someone to shave off Samson's seven locks of hair. The Philistines then grabbed him, blinded his eyes, and threw him into prison. One night while the Philistines held a huge, riotous party to celebrate Samson's capture, they brought the prisoner to the middle of the temple for their amusement. Samson, whose hair had begun to grow back, prayed to God for one last show of strength. He pushed hard against the two middle columns that supported the temple. In an instant the entire building collapsed, killing everyone, including the fallen hero, Samson.

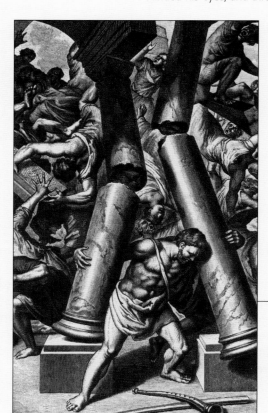

In revenge, Samson brings down the temple of their god upon the Philistine leaders for tricking, capturing, and blinding him.

Israel's First King

In time, the Israelites desired unity in their nation that the judges could not provide. They said that for this reason they wanted a king. The last judge, the prophet Samuel, did not approve. Samuel knew they wanted a king for the wrong reason, not to help them keep the covenant with God, but rather for power and prestige: "We too must be like other nations, with a king to rule us and to lead us in warfare and fight our battles" (1 Samuel 8:20). Finally Samuel relented, and at God's inspiration and with Israel's acclamation, Saul, son of Kish, of the tribe of Benjamin, was named king.

Saul had a tragic reign. He disobeyed God several times, which brought upon him the wrath of the prophet Samuel. God revealed to Samuel Saul's successor while Saul was still king. Saul also suffered from an affliction, described in Scripture as an evil spirit, which caused him to lose consciousness. He blamed this and other grievances on his best warrior, David, and plotted to kill him. Throughout his reign Saul was unable to defeat the troublesome Philistines, and in the end, when the Israelites were overcome at Mount Gilboa, Saul fell upon his own sword.

Upon learning of Saul's death, the Judahites,—the Israelites who lived in the southern part of the kingdom—declared David king, and Ishbaal, son of Saul, became king of Israel to the north. Seven years later, after Ishbaal's death, David was anointed king of all Israel at the age of 30. He reigned for 40 years as Israel's greatest king.

David, Hero-King of a Golden Age

The youthful David was the handsome youngest son of Jesse of Bethlehem. He was a shepherd boy who wrestled wild animals, killed a giant with a mere stone from a slingshot, and played music that calmed a crazed King Saul. As king (from approximately 1010–961 B.C.), David was a military master. He defeated the Philistines, the Moabites, the

In this painting by Bernardo Strozzi, David is shown using Goliath's own sword to cut off his head. David refused any other weapons but those he had used as a shepherd: his staff, his sling, and five smooth stones from a nearby brook.

Map showing David's kingdom.

Parable: A moral point told through a story.

Arameans, the Ammonites, the Amalekites, and the Edomites. Ultimately he extended his empire from Egypt to the Euphrates River, marking the golden age of Israel. David pushed the Jebusites out of Jerusalem and made it Israel's capital city, to be called the City of David.

To the outskirts of the city (according to God's command), he brought the Ark of the Covenant, and with a heart full of joy and love for God, he danced before it. (2 Samuel 6:14) In fact, to David—poet and musician— are attributed a majority of the psalms of the Old Testament. The covenant God made during David's reign, to establish his throne forever, had religious significance; Jesus of Nazareth, born to the House of David, would fulfill this promise.

In these years of peace and prosperity, David was favored by God and admired by his people. His battle against Goliath tells of the ultimate victory of right over wrong, no matter the odds. A second famous story about David teaches another truth: pride goes before a fall.

Because David was a man of power, he thought he could have whatever he wanted. So, when he saw a woman called Bathsheba and liked her, he took her for his wife though she was already married to Uriah (you•RYE•ah), a Hittite by birth. To cover his sin of adultery, David added another: he ordered the soldier Uriah moved to the front lines in a battle and the man was killed. Nathan, the prophet, shamed David with a **parable** that moved the king to sorrow for his sins. The parable was about a poor man who had one little lamb that was taken by a rich man even though he had many lambs of his own. The injustice of this act caused David to cry out against this greedy rich man: "The man who has done this deserves to die!" Nathan replied, "You are the man! Now, therefore, the sword shall never depart from your house because you have despised me." David suffered punishment when his child conceived with Bathsheba died. They had a second son, Solomon, who ascended to the throne after the death of David.

David's Son by Bathsheba—Solomon

The most important contribution of Solomon—whose vast wisdom, wealth, and wives were legendary—was the building of the first Temple. Solomon accumulated great wealth and built Jerusalem from a little frontier castle into a great city with fine buildings and palaces. But the Temple was the glory of all his building.

After Solomon died and his son Rehoboam ascended to the throne, the ten northern tribes of Israel **seceded**—that is, broke away—and appointed for themselves another king. Judah, of the south, retained only the lands of Benjamin and Judah.

To Secede: To withdraw politically from another nation.

The 11th chapter of Kings in the Old Testament explains that this division was Solomon's punishment for giving in to his foreign wives and worshipping their gods. Nearly 1,000 years after God called Abraham to the worship of himself alone, his people were still being pulled back to worship idols. The two kingdoms battled against each other until they were overtaken by two outside empires, Assyria (Ah•SEER•ee•AH) and Babylon.

Assyria, the Cruel

Assyria was a major civilization in Mesopotamia that grew out of the city of Ashur on the Tigris River, north of Babylon and east of the Hittites in about 1350 B.C., and lasted until 650 B.C. During its last years, the Assyrians had control over an enormous region, having conquered eastern Egypt, and all of Mesopotamia and Syria. They fought hard and developed into a ruthless warrior state.

Assyrians used the walls of their temples and palaces to show boastful battle scenes from their wars. These are scenes from the conquest of Arabia by their cruelest king, Ashurnasirpal, carved around 650 B.C.

Every Assyrian man was trained to use weapons and had to fight if summoned. The techniques they developed to lay siege and invade walled cities were highly efficient. The Assyrians used battering rams, scaling ladders, horse-drawn chariots, cavalry, bows, spears, and even giant slings. War, killing, and battles dominate their art, especially the stone-cut **bas-reliefs** on the palace walls of Ashur and Ninevah, their greatest cities.

The Assyrians were particularly bloodthirsty and even boasted of it. They did not just kill their enemies, but sometimes beheaded, impaled, burned, or even skinned them. The greatest—and cruelest—Assyrian conqueror was Ashurnasirpal, who celebrated his victory with the construction of a grand palace in Nimrud. He was succeeded by Tiglath-Pileser, whose forces swarmed into Israel in the 8th century B.C. The Assyrians defeated the cities of Israel but stopped at Jerusalem, the capital of Judah. This city the king left

Bas-relief: A fairly flat sculpture in which the design is raised slightly from the background.

alone for the price of a huge sum of money, which King Ahaz of Jerusalem ended up stealing from the Temple (2 Kings 16:8).

Tiglath-Pileser died in 727 B.C. and was succeeded by Shalmanaser V, who stopped an attempted revolt by capturing Samaria in 721 B.C. Sargon II finished the victory, thus ending the Israelite nation. The people of Israel were deported, some to the far reaches of Assyria (2 Kings 17:6), and the rest of Judah remained united but under Assyrian authority. The worst was yet to come: the invasion of Babylon.

Babylon, Successor to Sumer

Babylonians, adapting much of Sumerian culture, wrote on clay tablets and even had their own version of the Sumerian epic, *Gilgamesh*. They worshipped many gods and built ziggurats to reach them. It is likely that the Tower of Babel named in the book of **Genesis** refers to the ziggurat in the city of Babylon, the highest ever built.

Genesis: The coming into existence of something.

The Babylonian religion developed a new twist, reading the future to discover the gods' will. The pictures imagined from the patterns of the stars—the constellations—became linked with the fortune-telling of horoscopes. The Babylonians were so fixated on knowing the future that they even tried to read the livers of dead animals.

The second Babylonian Empire featured famous architecture, including an 11-mile wall around the city with a road on top of it and the 30-foot Ishtar gate with its bright blue, glazed brick decorations.

Hammurabi receiving the law from Shamash, the sun god.

Hammurabi was a great king of Babylon and lived about 1800 B.C. His most significant contribution to history was to create a list of 282 laws that all people of his kingdom had to obey. Just the act of writing the laws down had two good effects; it prevented the strong and rich Babylonians, and officials, from unfairness to the common man, and it discouraged crime by letting everyone know what was wrong and what the punishment was. Some of the 282 laws are quite a bit harsher than our laws today. Generally, if a Babylonian hurt someone's eye or tooth, he would have his own eye or tooth put out. Also, the death penalty was the punishment for many crimes, from murder, accidental manslaughter or kidnapping, to breaking into a house or bearing false witness in court

Overlooking the gate were the magnificent "Hanging Gardens," which were acclaimed among the Greeks' Seven Wonders of the World. Some remains have been found of the gardens, which seem to have been richly planted Earth terraces built on a giant step pyramid. The greatest achievement of Babylonian culture, and one that provided a just and well-run government, was its code of laws.

The great king of the Babylonian Empire was Nebuchadnezzar II, who expanded the realm from Elam to Egypt, including Syria and Palestine. He also oversaw the elaborate restoration of the ancient city of Babylon. And he attacked Jerusalem to prevent an alliance between Judah and Egypt. Later, when the Judahites attempted a revolt, he stormed the city and utterly destroyed it, burning the king's palace, all the houses, and even the Temple. The fall of Jerusalem, related in 2 Kings 24–25, took place in 586 B.C. All the

Above: How the Hanging Gardens of Babylon may have looked. **Below:** The Ishtar Gate, a main entrance in the walls of ancient Babylon, recently rebuilt.

Nebuchadnezzar casts Jews into fiery furnaces. He tormented the exiles to make them give up their faith in the Lord.

inhabitants of Jerusalem were deported, and thus began the period in Jewish history known as the Babylonian Captivity.

The Prophets

During the assaults on the nation of Israel, from within and without, God spoke to his people to give them courage, hope, direction, and sometimes punishment. He spoke his messages through prophets, who were holy men often serving as direct advisers to the king. The greatest of these included Isaiah, Jeremiah, Ezekiel, and Daniel. They are known as the "major prophets." There are twelve "minor prophets," from Hosea to Malachi, whose shorter books bring the Old Testament to a close. Some prophets do not have books named for them; Nathan was one and so was Elijah, prophet during King Ahab's reign.

The prophets delivered a consistent message to Israel, which could be summed up in the two great commandments: love God and love your neighbor. Repeatedly the Israelites would return to pagan worship, and the prophets would call them back to the covenant with the one, true God of Abraham and Moses (Jer. 10:1–16). When the Israelites fell into sin, breaking the commandments and ignoring the laws of Moses, the prophets urged them toward moral reform. Often they used the image of an unfaithful spouse to describe Israel, and God as the patient and forgiving husband (Hosea, Ezekiel 16).

Another strong theme is the need to care for the poor, especially widows and orphans (Isaiah 10:1–4). Yet, despite the woe and the warnings, the books of the prophets are shot through with a sense of love and hope: God is the Lord of history, the One who allows the rise and fall of nations for his purposes. He will not utterly abandon his children despite all their disobedience. He will send a Messiah to save them. In Isaiah's description of God's suffering servant and glorious Zion (Chapters 7–12, 52–53), we see the foretelling of Jesus Christ and of his final, reign overall.

Jeremiah, the Suffering Prophet

The prophet Jeremiah was born of a priestly clan in about 600 B.C. in a village near Jerusalem. God called him at the age of 22 to prophesy during the 13th year of the reign of King Josiah of Judah. After the scattering of Israel in 721 B.C., Judah found itself surrounded by powerful enemies: Assyria to the north, Egypt to the southwest, and a growing Babylon to the southeast. Under Josiah, the people returned to worship God alone, but when the king died and his son took the throne, they reverted to idol worship. As the prophet of God, Jeremiah preached severe warnings. For his unpopular message he was rewarded with scourging and imprisonment.

Still, he went on prophesying, and as recorded in Jeremiah 20, he even foretold the Babylonian capture. When he prophesied doom at the Temple, the priests and prophets seized him and called for his death. He was spared, but in 586 B.C. Jerusalem did fall, as predicted, to the Babylonians. During the time of exile, Jeremiah prophesied a new covenant that prefigured Christ's coming. Later he was taken away to Egypt and died there, as legend has it, at the hands of a fellow Israelite.

The prophet Isaiah being instructed by a seraph, one of the great angels assigned by God to guard the Ark of the Covenant. Painted in 1726 by Giovanni Battista Tiepolo.

Babylonian Captivity

The sorrow of the exile into Babylon is expressed in the Book of Lamentations and the hope of a new day in the prophetic books of Baruch and Ezekiel. Yet this time was not without gain for Israel. Exile brought the people to

Jeremiah, in Israel's darkest days, preached a final warning to the rulers, and to the people, to return to God, or they and all of Jerusalem would be destroyed.

The Handwriting on the Wall

D aniel, a Hebrew prince, served in the royal court of King Nebuchadnezzar and, like the patriarch Joseph, was renowned for his goodness and his accurate interpretation of dreams. One night during the reign of a later king, Belshazzar, a mysterious thing happened. The king was in the midst of a great banquet with laughter, music, and wine, when suddenly he saw a human hand appear in midair. The hand began writing unknown words on the wall of the palace. The frightened king searched for a magician or astrologer to interpret the words, but none could. Then the queen suddenly remembered Daniel, and the king quickly summoned the Hebrew prince to the palace. Daniel told him the meaning of the words: "*Mene* means God has ended your kingdom, *Tekel* means you have been measured and found wanting, and *Peres* means your kingdom will be divided between the Medes and Persians." Daniel's interpretation came true. King Belshazzar died that very night, and the city fell to the Persians in the morning.

repentance, devotion, and an ambition to preserve their faith through the writing of most of the Old Testament. Chief among these books was the Law, also known as the Torah, or the Pentateuch, the first five books of the Bible: Genesis, Exodus, Leviticus, Numbers, and Deuteronomy.

Two stories from the book of Daniel depict this deepening faith and foretell the end of the exile: the fiery furnace and the writing on the wall.

T hree Jewish youths with the melodious names of Shadrach, Meschach, and Abednego refused to bow down before a golden statue made by King Nebuchadnezzar. The king flew into a rage, and had his soldiers tie up the three youths and throw them into a white-hot furnace. Miraculously, the three did not die nor were they even harmed by the flames. Instead they walked around singing praises to God! Nebuchadnezzar called them out, and seeing that their clothes were not even singed, gave honor to God and made Shadrach, Meschach, and Abednego leaders in the province.

Persia, a Burst of Power

The Jewish exile did come to an end, and in less than 50 years. In 539 B.C. Babylon was conquered by the Persians, a sudden superpower that rolled across the whole civilized world west of China. By 400 B.C. Persia ruled the largest empire the world had known and the largest in the West until the emergence of Rome. Its conquests stretched from southeastern Europe, across all of Mesopotamia and Egypt, and as far into Asia as the Indus River in Pakistan. In terms of time, however, Persia lasted but a moment—little more than 200 years. Where did the Persians come from, and why did they grow and then fade so quickly?

The tiny state of Anshan in the Aryan region (modern-day Iran) was home to Cyrus II. This gifted general conquered the Medes, the people that had taken over Assyria for good in 609 B.C. With the former Assyrian Empire under his belt, Cyrus moved west toward Europe. He funded his army from the conquest of the wealthy Croesus, king of Lydia, and took

Map of the Persian Empire showing its extent and its major cities.

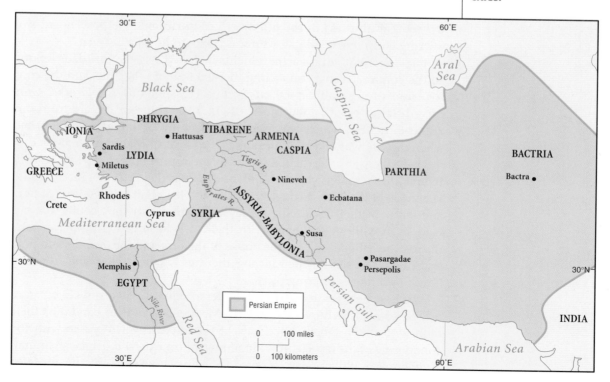

A morning service in a synagogue in Teaneck, New Jersey.

Babylon in a surprise attack. The Persians, though militarily strong like the Assyrians had been, were not so cruel. Their tolerance of the cultures of their conquered nations proved a blessing for the Jews and others and was no doubt a reason for the Persians' quick success.

Persian religion itself took one of three forms. The popular religion, like so many others, worshiped many gods. The magi, the name of a tribe that produced priests and astrologers, revered angelic beings and spirits. The royal court and the nobility followed Zoroastrianism. This religion, the religion of the kings, started with a prophet named Zoroaster (also written Zarathustra) in the 6th or 7th centuries B.C. He proclaimed two warring gods: one good god who was opposed by an evil spirit.

The Persians' cultural achievements included a system of roads linking all the empire, a canal connecting the Red Sea and the Nile, and the construction of a grand capital city, called Persepolis by the Greeks. Only carved staircases and a few of the original 100 columns remain from this grand structure, which was either accidentally or intentionally burned when the city was taken by Alexander the Great of Macedon in 331 B.C.

Under Persian rule, the Jews were able to return home. In 515 B.C., they rebuilt the Temple, which would be the worldwide center of worship. Having kept the faith through the Exile, the Jews had learned how to pray and study in their local cities. They had found that they could worship God, even without the Temple. In their own local gathering places they met on the Sabbath to read the books of the Law and the prophets, to pray and study. The site for their local gatherings is called *synagogue*, from the Greek meaning "gathering place."

The Jews held fast to their faith as Persia fell to Greece and Greece gave way to Rome. Jews moved all over the Mediterranean world and took their faith with them. Finally, the Israel of the ancient world ceased with the conquering of the last Hebrew kingdom by Rome in 63 B.C. Like all human kingdoms, it did not last forever. Its ideas, however, are the roots of modern Judaism, Islam, and Christianity. It can be said that despite its troubles, no other ancient nation had such an impact as Israel, which bore the revolution of monotheism against a world of deeply engrained polytheism for 2,000 years.

Chapter 3 Review

Let's Remember Write your answer in a single complete sentence.
1. What were the new names given to Abram and Sarai?
2. The Exodus probably took place during the reign of which pharaoh?
3. What were the Ten Commandments that Moses gave to the Israelites? (Name them)
4. The land of Palestine was divided up among how many Israelite tribes? (Name them)
5. What did the Greeks call the Canaanites?
6. In the 8th century, Jerusalem was saved from the Assyrians because King Ahaz did what?
7. The fall of Jerusalem in 586 B.C. and the deportation of the inhabitants is called what?
8. Who are the major prophets and the minor prophets?
9. What is the Pentateuch?

Let's Consider   For silent thinking and a short essay, or for thinking in a group with classroom discussion:
1. Can the "natural law," which is the knowledge of good and evil and can be understood by human reason alone, be known by all people and all religions?
2. How much do we depend upon the alphabet that was developed by the Phoenicians?
3. The summary of the Law is contained in the commandments to love God and to love your neighbor. Consider how different this is from the hundreds of rules that existed elsewhere, for instance the 282 laws of the Code of Hammurabi.
4. Consider the courage of the Jews who kept their faith alive as they studied and prayed in their local cities during the Babylonian captivity.

5. Consider what a hopeful and revolutionary message—monotheism— was given by the Israelites to the ancient peoples, all of whom worshipped many gods.

Let's Eat!

The Jewish Passover meal is a ritual still observed in Jewish families to this day. The meal replays the Exodus of the Jewish people from Egypt and consists of a roasted lamb and unleavened bread, bitter herbs and wine. It was this Passover meal that Jesus ate with his disciples that became known to Christians as the Last Supper, when the Blessed Sacrament of the Eucharist was instituted by Jesus.

Chapter 4 The Marvelous Greeks

Introduction

The land of the Greeks lies on a peninsula that reaches out into the Mediterranean Sea east of Italy. Long before the time of Christ, a remarkable nation arose in this beautiful setting of jagged mountains and crystal harbors. Ancient Greece was the home of adventurous warriors and traders, of **philosophers** who defined excellence and virtue, of poets who gave us stories of duty and love, of architects and sculptors who created works of timeless beauty. These Greeks called

Philosopher: Lover of wisdom.

Map of ancient Greece.

themselves Hellenes and their land Hellas. Our name for them and their land comes from the Romans, who referred to Hellas as *Graecia*.

We call ancient Greece the "Cradle of Western Civilization," which means that these Hellenes were the first people to grapple with important questions of the human spirit, such as how to recognize truth, determine justice and virtue, organize and govern society, and create beauty and order.

The Homeric Myths

The Greeks treasured their historic myths. These are stories, sung and later written down by Greek poets to explain the origin of their culture and to model for them the right way to think and live. The greatest poems of this oral tradition are by the poet Homer, *The Iliad* and *The Odyssey*. They tell stories from the Trojan War, a war that we know now only from his stories.

The Trojan War: The Legend

The famous Helen of Troy was the legendary cause of the Trojan War. Aphrodite, the goddess of love, had caused Paris (son of the Trojan king) to fall in love with Helen. Helen was married to a Spartan king but eloped with Paris to Troy. In response to this grave insult, the Greeks attacked the city of Troy. After ten years of cruel fighting, there was no winner. Great heroes died on both sides. Homer tells of the killing of the Trojan prince Hector by the Greek Achilles. Only the oaths of the Greek princes and their sense of honor kept them fighting on the wind-swept plains of Troy. Ultimately, trickery succeeded where brute strength did not. The wily Odysseus thought of a plan to get into the city. The Greeks withdrew from Troy, leaving a large wooden horse for the Trojans to find. Several Greek warriors were hiding inside the huge figure.

Sinon, a Greek spy, pretended that he had escaped just before being made a human sacrifice by his fellow Greeks. He told the Trojans that the key to victory was to possess the large wooden statue of the horse. When the horse was brought into Troy, the hidden Greeks emerged from it by night. They let waiting Greek soldiers into the city, and Troy was destroyed.

Greek warriors rush from a hiding place inside the great horse-idol to open the gates of Troy for the enemy Greek army waiting outside. Painting by Henri Motte.

These two epics became the guide for living for later Greeks, who believed that the events in these stories actually took place, and wanted to imitate the struggle for excellence, moral correctness, and devotion to family and city that Homer described.

The Greek City-State

As the population of Greece and its farm economy grew, the small cities and surrounding lands became independent political units. These are called city-states, because each city was an independent political country. While all Greeks considered themselves to be Greeks, they owed political loyalty only to the city-state in which they lived.

The two primary city-states of Greece were Athens, which dominated the north, and Sparta, which led the Peloponnese. It is hard to speak of one without the other, because they represented very different, even opposing, manners of living out the Greek way of life.

Sparta–A Military Oligarchy

Sparta was known over the world, then and now, as representing a type of military sacrifice and discipline. Its citizens were soldiers first, and its armies the best trained. But, this vigilance came at a high cost for the Spartans.

Sparta was not always a military dictatorship. It was a land of poets and artists before around 800 B.C. when King Lycurgus imposed his strict laws upon it. He turned a festive people who enjoyed life into an armed camp.

Childhood was short for both the girls and boys of Sparta. At the age of seven they left their home and lived in a military barracks where they were trained in physical fitness, discipline, and the ways of war. Boys hunted for part of their daily food and endured hardships to strengthen their mind and body. Spartan men were expected to serve the city until they were

Spartan warrior

The ancient Spartans of Greece lived in a valley called Laconia. Because they valued feats of arms more than fine speeches, Spartans were taught to use as few words as possible at all times. Using the fewest words possible is called "**laconic** speech." The practice was shown when King Phillip of Macedon sent the Spartans a letter: "If I come down to your country, I will level your great city to the ground." In a few days the letter came back from the Spartans. When Phillip opened the letter, he found only one word written on it—"If."

Oligarchy: Political rule by a small group.
Laconic: The use of very few words.
Monarchy: Inherited political rule by all of the people governed.
Democracy: Political rule by all of the people governed.

50. They could be allowed to start a household at age 30. However, women were married much younger, approximately at 14.

The Spartans were forced to be constantly on guard because they made slaves of the people they conquered in war. The slaves, called *helots* (helots means "the captured" in Greek), had a miserable life and always wanted to revolt. A secret police put to death any helots thought to be too independent or troublesome. When the secret police failed, the army would intervene.

A strong army was also needed for the wars of conquest that provided for the growing city and to get its way in the political and military affairs of Greece.

The Spartans organized themselves in an **oligarchy** (rule by the few). Judges, two generals, and a small council of elders made the decisions for all of the people of Sparta. Earlier in their political history, the Spartans had united two cities to form Sparta. Each had its own king. United Sparta kept the two kings as co-monarchs. Later, the two kings were also the generals. Rule by a royal family is called a **monarchy**. Because it still had its two kings, Sparta still thought of itself as a monarchy.

Athens—a Direct Democracy

The foremost city of Greece was Athens. Athens was organized politically as a **democracy** (rule by the many). Athens was a direct democracy, that is, every citizen (male adult with property, usually) had the right to vote in the assembly. They did not elect representatives (a representative democracy is the system in the United States).

In the Athenian system each citizen was a representative of himself and his family in the assembly, and ordinary citizens carried out roles in government such as being judges or administrators. The time not needed by a citizen to be a merchant or farmer, or run his own business, was taken up by the affairs of the city. It was the obligation of every citizen to serve in the army in time of war. Athens did have slaves for the most distasteful tasks, such as mining, but on a much smaller scale than Sparta. Unlike the Spartans, free-born Athenians farmed their own lands and worked at manual labor and crafts. And while Athens was willing to fight to protect its interests, it had no permanent standing army because, mainly, it sought to lead, not enslave, its neighbors.

The Athenian boys were taught how to become good citizens by learning how to read and write, how to speak persuasively, and how to do math-

Visible from far out to sea, the ancient temples of the Acropolis still rise over the city of Athens; once a fortified mountain, the Acropolis, or "high town," has always stood at the heart of the city.

ematics. They also learned of the history of Greece, including its military history, so that all of its male citizens could serve as army officers in time of conflict. Although their training was not as rigid as that of the Spartans, the Athenians had tremendous love of their democracy and fought very hard to defend their city and families.

Draco and Solon

An Athenian leader named Draco wrote the first laws of Athens. These laws carried such severe punishments, that we now call harsh laws **draconian**. This written law, though harsh, was an important step in protecting the rights of the ordinary citizen. Over time, however, ordinary farmers lost their land to rich moneylenders, and some people even had to sell themselves into slavery to pay off their debts. As a result, there was danger of rioting and the breakdown of law and order.

Draconian: Cruel, or harsh.

Solon (sometimes called "Solon the lawgiver") came into this very difficult social situation. Solon was a nobleman who was also a successful merchant, a noted writer, and a leader of government. Solon was First Archon from 580–570 B.C. Under the Athenian method of government, the First Archon shared power with the king (called the King-Archon), and a third ruler of lesser power, the Polemarch, or head military general.

Solon came up with a remarkable solution to the problem. He crafted and put into effect a skillful compromise that stopped the civil war that was brewing. He returned all lands that had been given for debts back to their original owners. He freed everyone who was paying off debt, and

Solon dictating the emergency laws which reformed society and saved Athens from civil war.

forbade people to sell themselves for debt. Solon made part of the legislature open to all citizens, but kept the highest positions for the wealthiest citizens. He didn't take the lands of the rich away and give them to the poor, but maintained the traditional social order of Athens.

Solon may well be remembered by his own summary of his political career: "I have thrown a stout shield over both parties, and as a result both sides have taken offense." While Solon's reform of the laws prevented the breakdown of order, the weakened nobles and strengthened workers continued to clash. In time, three factions emerged: the Plain (representing the nobility who resisted Solon's reforms), the Coast (mostly businesses and farmers who supported Solon's laws), and the Hill (farm workers and shepherds who did not think Solon went far enough).

Cleisthenes and the Establishment of the Council of 500

Cleisthenes created the final phase in the development of Athenian democracy around 500 years before the birth of Christ. The first written laws of Athens were Draco's harsh precepts. Then Solon modified those laws, outlawing the taking of farmers' lands because of unpaid debts and selling yourself into slavery to pay back debts. Now Cleisthenes made another major change, one that would last for many years. He composed a new constitution for Athens.

Although he made many changes, two were the most crucial. The first was to abolish the political power of the four old tribal divisions of Athens by replacing them with ten new artificial tribes, called *demes*. The demes were not related to the old families and did not have wealth or social status. In this way he established new loyalties, and he included many citizens who were previously "outsiders" because they weren't from the old tribes.

His second major reform was to establish the "Council of 500," which shared power with the assembly. Each new tribe provided

Aristides the Just

Aristides was a military and political leader in Greece in the turbulent times of the war against Persia. Despite the many difficult decisions that he faced, he was given the name "the Just" by his fellow Greeks. He was one of the ten generals in the famous battle of Marathon. After being exiled for political disagreements with powerful rivals, he was recalled to help defeat the Persians' second invasion. Aristides was also trusted to determine the amount owed to Athens by each of its allies to defend Greece against Persia. A story is told that when the Athenians were taking a vote on whether to send him into exile, Aristides came on a poor peasant trying to write something on a ballot. Aristides asked if he could help. The man did not recognize him and asked how to spell "Aristides." "Why do you want to vote for Aristides' exile?" the statesman asked. The poor man replied, "Because he is always being called 'the Just.'" Aristides wrote his own name on the poor man's ballot.

Map of ancient Greece, with its colony cities on the shores of Asia Minor, and their neighbors in the Persian Empire, Sardis, and the provinces to the east.

50 representatives to the council, and the council proposed laws to the assembly and enacted the laws that were passed by the assembly. The council also appointed ten generals, one from each tribe. The assembly still consisted of all citizens, which then meant all adult males with some property.

The effect of the changes of Cleisthenes, which were to last 200 years, was both to reduce the power of the nobles and to balance the power of the assembly by creating a governing body of representative democracy (the council members represented their tribes, and not just themselves). This added stability to the government and stopped one faction or person from controlling the government.

The problems that caused Cleisthenes to develop this somewhat complicated government of ten tribes, an assembly of direct democracy, and a representative Council of 500, were similar to those that the American founders had. And their solutions were similar in many ways: two assemblies of lawmakers, generals appointed from the assemblies, and top leaders with powers limited by a written constitution. The American experiment should be seen as a continuation of the democratic tradition begun by these ancient Greeks.

War with Persia

At this time (roughly 500 B.C.) the Greek cities of Ionia (on the western coast of Asia Minor) were part of the Persian Empire, the most powerful government on Earth. It is hard to overestimate the power of the Persians. The empire stretched from the Asian grasslands and the mountains of Armenia to the river valley of Egypt. Its center and capital was in modern-day Iran. This vast area, with millions of people, paid tribute to the fabulously wealthy Persian king, who knew nothing of the mainland Greeks.

The Athenians ran up against this great power when they sided with the Ionian cities that revolted from Persia. After marching to the aid of their former colonies, the Athenians burned the Persian city of Sardis to the ground and returned home.

The Persian king, Darius, was outraged and vowed revenge. He sent a **flotilla** of ships with soldiers aboard to Greece to crush the rebellion. At this point, events looked very dark for the Athenians.

Flotilla: A fleet of small ships.

The Battle of Marathon

The Battle of Marathon is one of the famous battles of history, deserving to be mentioned along with the Battle of Hastings (1066) when the Norman, William the Conqueror, defeated the Saxons in England, with the defeat of the Spanish Armada by the English (1588), and with the defeat of Napoleon at Waterloo (1815).

The Athenians, without the help of the Spartans or any one else except for the small city-state of Plataea, were badly outnumbered. The Persians landed on the coast of Greece near Athens on the plain called Marathon, and the two sides prepared for battle.

Miltiades, the Athenian general, placed the larger part of the Athenian force at the flanks (ends) of the line and attacked the Persians at a dead run. The metal armor of the Greeks protected them from the arrows of the Persians, and the Athenians defeated the Persians in sharp hand-to-hand fighting, finally turning the flanks (ends) of the Persian lines to the center and crushing them in a pincer (encircling) movement. Many of the fleeing Persians were killed when they were forced into nearby swamps.

The battle of Marathon, where Athens defeated the Persians in a desperate battle.

After the victory at Marathon, the Athenian army ran home as quickly as it could to protect the city from the Persian fleet and the remnants of the Persian army. They feared that traitors in the city would surrender to the Persians before the army returned. The modern-day running event called the "marathon" recalls the distance and place of this famous ancient run.

Pheidippides' Marathon Run

Pheidippides' first task was to run the 140 miles to Sparta and ask for their help in beating back the first Persian invasion. This feat he accomplished over hilly and rough roads in two days. He also ran back to Athens with the disappointing news that Sparta could not help right away because of religious observances. The legend of Pheidippides tells that he fought in the battle, then raced the 26 miles from Marathon to Athens after the victory over the Persians. He gasped out, "Rejoice! We win!" Then Pheidippides fell dead, completely spent from doing his duty.

Thermopylae and the Brave 300

The Persian King Darius was, of course, even more enraged when he learned of this defeat and organized a massive invasion of Greece that, this time, would not fail. But Darius died before the invasion could be organized. It fell to his son, Xerxes, to lead the huge invasion force. The Persian forces lashed boats together to make a temporary pontoon bridge at the Hellespont, the narrow passage of sea between Asia Minor and Greece. Later reports claimed that it took Xerxes' huge forces a full seven days and seven nights to cross into Greece. Xerxes expected a full surrender to his overwhelming forces. His first surprise (one of many on his ill-fated campaign) was that the Greeks chose to fight, and organized to meet the Persians.

It fell to the Spartans to block the advance of the Persians into central Greece at Thermopylae (Thermopylae means the "Hot Gates") where the mountain pass was so small that the Persians could not employ their superior numbers and the Spartans' greater skill at hand-to-hand fighting could be put to good use. The Spartans numbered just 300 and were led by King Leonidas. This small group prevented the Persian army from advancing. The attitude of the Spartans was expressed by one of their soldiers. When told that the arrows of the Persian archers were so numerous that they blotted out the sun, he replied, "That's good, we'll get to fight in the shade."

What the Persians could not accomplish by force they eventually gained by treachery. They purchased information of a hunters' path that would place them behind the Spartans and endanger their positions. When Leonidas heard that the Persians were advancing along this path, he chose to defend the pass to the last with his royal guard of 300 men, sending away the rest of his forces to fight another day. By choosing to stay and defend Thermopylae, Leonidas was giving the Greek cities an additional several days to organize their navy to oppose the Persians.

As expected, the Persians attacked the 300 with all their might. The brave 300 fought with their swords and in hand to hand combat. Two days later, the fighting had stopped. The Spartans were together in death, with several thousand Persians killed and two precious days gained for the defense of Greece. Years afterward, a grateful people erected a monument to their memory with these words to commemorate them:

> Go tell the Spartans, passerby,
> That here, obedient to their word, we lie.

The battlefield of Thermopylae, where a small Greek force led by the King of Sparta held a pass against the entire Persian army for a brief but crucial time in 480 B.C.

Victory over the Persians

After the Persians had fought their way past the Spartans, they approached Athens to burn the city. Rather than join the Persian Empire, the men, women, and children of the city fled south to the Peloponnese or across the straits to the island of Salamis. After sacking Athens, Xerxes was determined to punish Sparta, too. To do so, he had to pass through the narrow strait of water that separated Athens from the island of Salamis. The ships of Athens and its allies guarded this passage.

Because the waters where the battle was fought were narrow, the greater numbers of the Persian ships could not all be used. Also, the sturdy Greek ships had the advantage over the larger and less maneuverable Persian ships. The Greeks rammed the Persian ships with their own ships and then boarded the ships and fought hand to hand. The result was a Greek victory.

Themistocles was actually responsible for this surprising victory in a number of ways. He persuaded the Athenians to invest in building a large fleet of ships with money from a big silver mine. He came up with the strategy of fighting the Persians on sea at the favorable location of Salamis. He also kept the Greek allies together so they could fight as a group against the Persian fleet. And, last but not least, he was the general who directed the Greek forces to a victory.

The Golden Age of Greece— The Leadership of Pericles

After this decisive defeat of the mighty Persian fleet at Salamis, Athens organized its

An Oracle at Delphi Speaks— "Wooden Walls Will Save the City"

The Greeks consulted the oracle at Delphi to find the best way to defend Athens against the Persians after they fought past the Spartans at Thermopylae. They believed that the priests at Delphi spoke for the gods. The oracle said, "Wooden walls will save the city."

Themistocles, the Athenian leader, understood the oracle's puzzling message to mean that Athens should abandon the city and meet the Persians on water, defended by "the wooden walls" of Athens' ships. This resulted in the battle of Salamis, the great victory over the Persians that took place in the narrow strait between northern and southern Greece.

In the sea battle off the island of Salamis in 480 B.C., the warships of Greece, led by the Athenian navy, gained a complete victory over the Persian fleet.

Stone bust of Pericles, the young politician who led Athens when it first flourished as an empire after the defeat of the Persians. Created about 500 B.C.

The Parthenon, the principal temple on the Acropolis of Athens, built between 447 and 438 B.C. Originally a giant statue of Athena Parthenos, or the Virgin Athena, stood within.

allies into the Delian League, keeping the treasury on the god Apollo's sacred island of Delos. For several years the Delian League did indeed defend the area from the Persians. Then Athens transferred the treasury behind its own walls, saying that the island was not safe. Athens also forced all the Delian League member-cities to pay tribute to it, so that it was a group of allies in name only. In fact, after the defeat of the Persians, it was an Athenian Empire. Also, Athenian citizenship was made more restrictive—both parents had to be Athenians to make someone a citizen. No new immigrants could become citizens. This limited the number of Greeks that benefited from Athens' Empire and limited Athens' benefits from new arrivals.

Athens also made its government more democratic during this time—the assembly of the people became the primary legislature. The assembly elected ten generals who ruled Athens. From among their number the generals then elected a chief political leader. In 461 B.C. they elected Pericles, who dominated Athenian politics for the remaining 33 years of his life from various elected positions.

Pericles began an ambitious public building program. Chief among these was the temple of Athena Parthenos (the Maiden). It was called the Parthenon. It was built on the Acropolis, a high hill of stone, overlooking the city. The sculptor Phidias designed the Parthenon. Its architect was Ictinus and its master builder was Callicrates. These men, working together with many other artists and workers, built what has been called the most beautiful building ever. Its proportion and line are exceptional, with its columns giving a sense of strength and beauty at the same time. The Acropolis was originally a fortress; Pericles' buildings turned it into an artistic treasure. The Acropolis also contained several other temples and huge statues. The temples could be seen for miles out at sea.

Other arts flourished under Pericles—so many, and with such beauty, that this period is called the Golden Age. Sculptures of beauty and proportion that captured the character and human spirit of their subjects were also created during this time. The greatest Greek sculptor was Phidias, who was in charge of building the Parthenon and also sculpted the large statue of Athena inside it. Phidias sculpted another large and famous statue, one of Zeus at Olympia, where the Olympic games were held. Phidias' Zeus at Olympia, bigger even than his Athena, was called one of the Seven Wonders of the Ancient World.

The Seven Wonders (clockwise from top): the Temple of Artemis at Ephesus, the Hanging Gardens of Babylon, the Lighthouse of Alexandria, the Pyramids of Egypt, the Mausoleum of Halicarnassus, the Colossus at Rhodes, and the Zeus at Olympia.

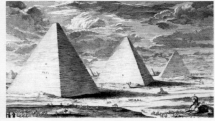

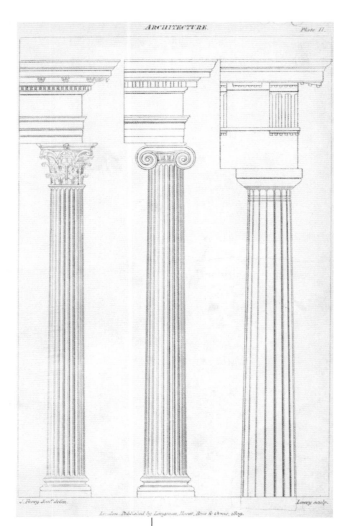

ARCHITECTURE.   Plate II.

An illustration of three orders of Greek columns: Corinthian, Ionic, and Doric.

Classical Greek architecture developed into three major styles or orders. These were three separate sets of rules for architects. The "Dorian" order had a simple, fluted column, with a simple round "capital," the stone cap at the top of a column. The "Ionian" had capitals carved like scrolls. The "Corinthian" had more ornate capitals carved in the shape of flower petals.

The dramatic arts of comedy and tragedy also flourished under Pericles. Greek comedy, whose most famous author was Aristophanes, caricatured and joked about many subjects in Greek life, from war to politics. Greek tragedy was developed during this period also. It tried to find meaning in human suffering, exploring the beauty in life even when death and pain occur. The three most notable authors of Greek tragic poetry were Aeschylus, Sophocles, and Euripides.

The Peloponnesian War

In the midst of Athens' political, economic, and artistic success, trouble was brewing. Sparta was naturally alarmed over Athens' growing power and ambition. So when Athens clashed with city-states in the southern peninsula of Greece, Sparta came to their aid. Athens wanted to rule all of Greece and did not avoid war with Sparta.

Thus Pericles led Athens into a ruinous war with the cities of the Peloponnese led by Sparta. Sparta invaded the north and laid waste to the farm country around Athens. Even worse, a plague broke out in the overcrowded cities. Athens lost a great part of the population, including Pericles himself, who died of the plague in the second year of the war he had begun. Eventually, a truce with Sparta was made.

Alcibiades and the Defeat of Athens

Even after this painful lesson the Athenians were anxious to use war to broaden their empire. When an enemy of Syracuse on Sicily, an island south of the toe of Italy, asked for help, Athens was willing to help to increase its empire. Unfortunately, Alcibiades, a general of Athens who had his wealth taken away by the assembly, escaped to Sparta. And he told Sparta about Athens' military weaknesses for the campaign in Sicily. And so the Athenian ships were caught in the harbor and defeated by the Spartan fleet. Famine and disease further weakened the Athenians. Finally the troops were attacked and slaughtered by the Spartans and the men of Syracuse.

Athens lost most of its fighting force at Syracuse. Constant raids by Sparta followed this horrible defeat. After years of this difficult and expensive war, Athens was exhausted and was forced to surrender. In the year 404 B.C., Athens agreed to pull down the walls protecting the city and join the Spartan alliance. It must have seemed a fate only slightly better than death for this proud people who had ruled an empire only a generation ago.

Above: Greek warrior in full armor, from a wall painting of the 4th century B.C.

Left: A shield-wall of Greek hoplites (heavy-armed soldiers) faces an attack of enemy chariots—a tribute to the gods carved in 525 B.C. on a wall of the Siphnian Treasury in Delphi.

The Retreat of the Ten Thousand

After the end of the Peloponnesian War, many young Athenian men felt betrayed and angry at the defeat of their city. One such young soldier was Xenophon, who answered a letter from an older friend to come to Asia Minor and join him in a Greek regiment. The 10,000 Greek soldiers, most of them young and inexperienced, were going to help a Persian prince named Cyrus to take the Persian throne from his brother.

Xenophon, the valiant Athenian general.

Cyrus was slain in battle. The Greeks found themselves alone and in the heart of a hostile continent. They tried to make an agreement with Tissaphernes, the victorious Persian general. Tissaphernes called the Greek officers to a meeting under a flag of truce, and than treacherously slew them all. The young Greek soldiers were terrified. In their despair, when all seemed lost, a leader was found.

Xenophon said to himself: "Who is left to do this? Who other than I? Am I not an Athenian, used to taking responsibility for the city when I vote? I am old enough to take command of myself, I am old enough to take command of others." He summoned the assembly and explained that the only hope lay in their weapons and strong right arms. He himself, he said, was willing to follow another, if anyone would come forward, or to lead if necessary. They acclaimed him their leader and began at once to make preparations for their retreat. All the baggage that could be spared was burned. They set out at night, crossed a broad river, and ran into the first attack of the enemy. Xenophon tried to repel the attack; the Persians cut them off from the coast of the Mediterranean. They were forced north. Soon the winter weather brought snow and ice. Buffeted by storms, drenched and blinded by snow, they struggled on through snow six feet deep. The able-bodied carried many sick and wounded. The column kept formation as well as they could, while the enemy harried them from the rear. At the last pass out of the mountains they found their way blocked by wild mountain tribesmen. With the resolve that was now their habit, the strongest of the column ran at the wild men and drove them off. The column finally came to the edge of the mountains and saw far below them, shining in the distance, the blue water of the sea.

The men cried with pleasure, "The sea! The sea!" and ran and stumbled down the slope toward the plain below. Then with a sudden impulse they stopped and set themselves to gather stones. Where they had first gazed upon the sea, they raised a monument. The remnant of the 10,000 had forced their way to safety.

A count showed that about 6,000 of the original ten had made it. In true Greek fashion, the healthy and sound voted to wait for the ships that the wounded would send back to them. Relief arrived soon and the survivors went home. Their fame spread throughout Greece and their glorious march became an inspiring legend to be celebrated ever after.

Socrates, Plato, and Aristotle

Socrates was a Greek philosopher (or "lover of wisdom," in the Greek language) who lived during the Peloponnesian War and the defeat of Athens. He believed that the purpose of men's lives is to understand what is right and good, and then to do it. This, he said, was virtue.

His method of teaching and the depth of his questions were unique. He would not teach by speaking what he knew, but rather "pulled the truth" from his students by patient questioning. He searched to know the truth about the basic questions of man's life—how he should live and

One summer Socrates, the philosopher, built himself a house. His neighbors were surprised by the size of the house; it was by far the smallest in the neighborhood.

"Why have you built such a tiny box for a house," they said, "when you are one of the most famous men in all of Greece?"

"I have little reason," replied Socrates, "but small as it is, I will be happy if I can fill this house with true friends."

The House of Socrates

Socrates, the Athenian philosopher, intently awaiting a student's reply. An ancient Roman bust.

The Death of Socrates.

Plato points up to the heavens while Aristotle gestures downward to this world, in a detail from *The School of Athens* by Raphael.

Apology: A formal defense, or justification, of one's actions.

what his responsibilities were. Perhaps his questions made some in Athens uncomfortable. At any rate, in the defeated city his enemies found sympathy for their attacks on the old man. Falsely charged with corrupting youth, he was condemned to death by public trial. Refusing exile, he obeyed the court, and instead drank poison hemlock.

Socrates' death did not stop his influence, however. His brilliant student, Plato, wrote many books about Socrates' conversations, or dialogues, with his students. In Plato's account of Socrates' trial, The **Apology** *of Socrates,* the old man tells his judges that he would rather die than stop asking questions and calling men to virtue, "for the unexamined life is not worth living."

Plato's *Republic* asks the questions: "What is justice?" and "How should men live together in society?" Plato says that all men live as if chained in a cave, able to see only shadows thrown on the walls, and think that the shadows are reality. The man who wants the truth must free himself from those chains and climb out of the cave into the sunlight and look directly on the Truth. Such men will understand justice and live as men are supposed to live. The *Republic* is still read by people today who want to understand what is true and good.

Another great philosopher who studied with Plato and followed the tradition of Socrates was Aristotle. Aristotle believed that we learn the truth about the world by observing it and making logical conclusions from what we see. In this he is the father of modern science. He also taught that God was "the unmoved mover," that is, God alone has the power to act as he wills, for there is no power over God.

Aristotle composed lectures on logic, science, theology, ethics, and politics. Until modern times, his works were accepted as the final authority on many questions. Even in the modern world, all philosophy must grapple with the questions and answers developed by Aristotle in Greece many years ago.

Hippocrates, the Father of Medicine

The first great doctor whom we can name was Hippocrates (406 B.C.) For many generations his family had practiced medicine, and the people believed that the family was descended from Asclepius, god of healing, a physician named in Homer's poems. Hippocrates once and for all separated the study of the human body from superstition, declaring that the body is a part of nature that men must learn to understand. He knew very little about the structure of the human body, though he had some correct ideas about the role played by the heart and the brain. But he discovered that each part of the body has a specific function, and that sickness can be treated only by finding out which part of the body is not doing its proper work. One of his discoveries was that certain diseases might be traced by listening to the sounds in the chest, the beating of the heart and the pumping of the lungs. He investigated what herbs and exercise could be used to bring each unhealthy part of the body to health, and founded a guild of physicians, each swearing an oath to heal, to poison no one, to abstain from any evil use of his arts, to perform no abortions, to keep patients' secrets to himself, and to do no harm. The Hippocratic Oath was taken by all doctors on entering their profession, until the end of the 20th century that saw the horrible legalization of abortion.

Alexander the Great (356–323 B.C.)

Having exhausted themselves in the bitter Peloponnesian War, the Greeks were easily conquered by King Philip of Macedonia, a country just north of Greece. His plan was to lead the combined Greek and Macedonian forces against Persia and put an end to its ambitions to conquer the Greeks.

But he died before these plans could be carried out, and it fell to his young son, Alexander (born in 356 B.C.), to complete them. Alexander was just 20 when he assumed the throne. What followed was an amazing

Above left: An ancient European coin showing the caduceus, a symbol of professional medical doctors—a staff entwined with two snakes. It was originally a symbol of inviolability, carried by ambassadors and heralds.
Below: Hippocrates, the father of medicine, from a painting by Justo de Gante in the 15th century.

Alexander the Great at the decisive battle of Issus, a plain in southern Turkey, as shown in an ancient Roman mosaic created in the 1st century A.D.

series of military victories. During the next 13 years Alexander defeated the Persians and conquered the Egyptians, Babylonians, and parts of India. He established a great new city, including a center of scholarship, in Egypt. This city he called Alexandria.

Alexander died young in 323 B.C., but the huge territory that he conquered became "hellenized." That is, it took on Greek (Hellenic) culture—dress, language, and habits. And though the empire he created did not hold together after his death, the influence of Greece remained.

Archimedes and the Scientists of Alexandria

The scientists of Alexandria and Syracuse advanced the study of science during this time. Aristaeus calculated the distance of the moon and sun from the Earth and Ptolemy created a map of the heavens.

Archimedes was a scientist from Syracuse who wrote many works on mathematics, geometry, and mechanics. The king of Syracuse had paid a large sum to a sculptor for a new crown. The crown was an irregular shape, and the king feared that the sculptor had used less gold than he claimed. He asked Archimedes to solve the problem. After many days, the scientist saw the solution when he got into his bath and the water ran over the side. The crown would displace an equal quantity of water, which could then be

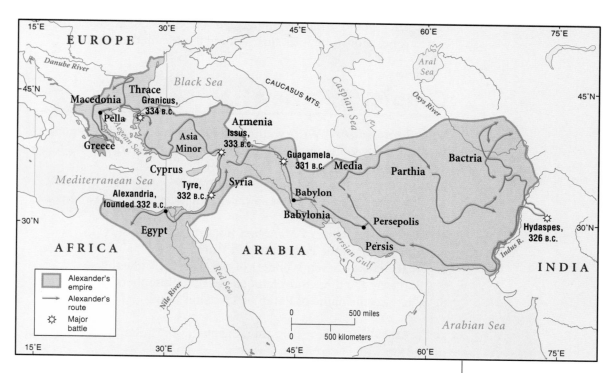

Map showing the marches of Alexander's army and the extent of the Greek Empire he created.

weighed and compared to the weight of gold. He was so delighted that he ran naked through the city shouting, "*Eureka!*" (I have found it).

The Greek Legacy

Just as furniture fills a house, the thoughts of the Greeks furnish the mind of the modern world. Ideas like logic, justice, and progress come from the Greeks. So does our democratic government. Modern science owes its method to the Greek philosophers, and the beauty and proportion of Greek art and sculpture have inspired and informed artists ever since. The public buildings of the Greeks still inspire awe and are imitated today. Greek tragedy reveals the worth and beauty of human life amidst suffering and pain. In short, the Greeks left us an incredibly rich deposit of culture. This legacy was spread from Egypt to India by Alexander. As we shall see, it remained for another conquering people, the Romans, to spread the legacy of the Greeks even farther. Before the advance of the Romans was halted, they would bring the influence of the Greeks to England, modern-day Europe, and the peoples surrounding the Mediterranean Sea.

Chapter 4 Review

Let's Remember   Write your answer in a single complete sentence.
1. What two peoples invaded the Greek peninsula and began the history of ancient Greece?
2. What are the two great epics written by the Greek poet Homer?
3. Why were Greek city-states so called, and what were the two main city-states?
4. Why was the Battle of Marathon important?
5. Who fought in the Peloponnesian War?
6. What were the Seven Wonders of the World? (Name them)
7. Who were the three most famous Greek philosophers?
8. What was the name of Philip of Macedon's son?

Let's Consider   For silent thinking and a short essay, or for thinking in a group with classroom discussion:
1. Why is Greece, and not Sumer or Egypt or Israel, called the Cradle of Western Civilization?
2. Think of all the writing, arts, and drama that flourished in the Golden Age of Athens and imagine that nothing so beautiful had ever existed before in the world.
3. Consider the teachings of the Hippocratic Oath, which insisted that doctors had, above all else, to practice healing.
4. Consider what a revolutionary idea it was to have government by a democracy and not by a powerful tribe or king.

Let's Eat!

Since ancient days, the Greeks and all peoples of the Mediterranean have enjoyed a simple combination of flat fried bread wrapped around grilled or roasted meat; cucumbers were available and might have been added. Today, we can enjoy this ancient food as a gyros sandwich or a stuffed pita; it is usually eaten with tomatoes, onions, and a cucumber sauce.

Eternal Rome

Chapter 5

About 700 B.C. a small group of families lived in small huts on top of a hill near a river in central Italy. They spoke the Latin language, and the small village they were in was called Rome. By 100 B.C., from these most humble beginnings, the Romans ruled the entire Mediterranean world, from Spain to the Caspian Sea. The Roman conquest united the Mediterranean world for centuries under one language, one set of laws, one system of roads, and one ruler.

Ancient coin of the Roman Empire, bearing the image of Emperor Augustus Caesar. Found in Jerusalem, Israel.

Geography

Rome is located in Italy, a peninsula off Europe, to the north of the Mediterranean Sea. On the map Italy looks like a large boot about to kick a triangular football. The island that looks like the football is Sicily. The northern boundary of Italy is the huge mountain range called the Alps. These high peaks cut the peninsula off from northern winds and snows, leaving it a warm and sheltered land, sunny and mild—ideal for living. Down the center of Italy is a chain of mountains, the Appennines, which contains several extinct volcanoes and one active volcano near the foot of the boot, called Vesuvius. The volcanic ridge extends into Sicily where Mt. Aetna is also active.

On the eastern side of the peninsula is the Adriatic Sea, and on the western side is the Mediterranean itself. These two warm seas keep the temperatures of Italy temperate and even. The

85

Map of Italy, showing mountains, rivers, and some important cities.

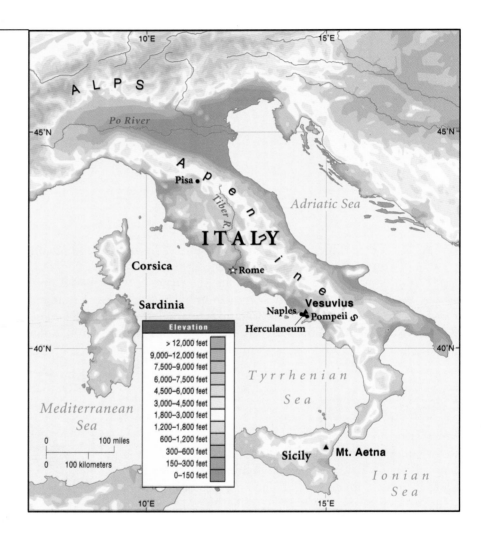

north of Italy is a wide and fertile valley watered by the Po River, flowing eastward into the Adriatic Sea. The two long coasts are different: the eastern coast is abrupt, rocky, and swampy where flat; the western coastal slope is broad and has small rivers. It was the best farmland in ancient times. To the west the Arno River passes the cities of Florence and Pisa; the Tiber flows through Rome. To the south, on a great bay beneath the slopes of Vesuvius, is the city of Naples and the buried ancient cities of Pompeii and Herculaneum.

Humble Beginnings

Legend has it that the city of Rome was founded about 753 B.C. The legendary founder of Rome is Romulus, who gave his name to the city and became its first king. The story relates that Romulus himself chose a hundred advisors, called senators (elders), from the original families of Rome. These advisors formed a council called the Senate. Ever after, Romans called their government "The Senate and People of Rome." They wrote their name as SPQR—*Senatus Populusque Romanus.* These original families were called **patricians** (fathers). Families that came to Rome later were called **plebeians** (people). Fathers were very important in Roman culture. Under the Roman system, the father of a family had absolute power over his family, including his adult sons. He literally had the power of life or death over them. In practice, however, his power was moderated by his advisors, which included his senior adult relatives.

Patrician: A person of noble birth, an aristocrat.
Plebeian: A person of low birth, a commoner.

The Roman Republic

Kings ruled Rome in its early years. During this time the kings ruled with the assistance of the land-owning farmers, who also served as armored

Romulus and Remus

In this famous story about the founding of Rome, Romulus and Remus were set adrift by their mother upon the Tiber River in a small basket, to save them from wicked enemies. As they drifted to the bank, they were found and suckled by a she-wolf and guarded by a woodpecker, in the woods where future Rome would be. In time, they grew to manhood and returned to Alba Longa, their home city, to avenge their mother. Then they set off with a band of young friends to find a new home. Romulus killed Remus over a petty quarrel. Romulus then founded Rome near where he and his brother were raised, and his friends gave his name to the new village—Rome.

This statue was created about 500 B.C. to show how Rome's founders, Romulus and Remus, were suckled by a she-wolf.

Horatius at the Bridge

The Tiber River as it flows through Rome today.

Horatius was a young and strong soldier of Rome. The Etruscans, a neighboring people, attacked Rome and were about to cross the bridge across the Tiber and enter Rome when Horatius told his fellows to chop down the supports to the bridge quickly, while he and two companions would hold off the advancing enemy. With so small a space to advance, and the skill, strength, and courage of the three Roman soldiers, the Etruscans were kept on their side of the bridge. Finally, the Romans destroying the bridge shouted that they were almost finished, and that the three brave defenders should return to the Roman side. At this Horatius dismissed his friends and carried on alone, fighting furiously until the bridge collapsed. Rome was safe, but all who watched from the Roman side were sure Horatius would perish in the swirling waters with his heavy armor. A huge cheer for Horatius went up from both sides as he came to the surface, and with almost superhuman effort, swam to the Roman bank to be pulled to shore by his friends. Horatius' courage is remembered to this day.

The Sixteen Days of Cincinnatus

Cincinnatus had been a wealthy general of Rome. But bad fortune had reduced his wealth, and he had turned to tending his farm in the hills outside Rome. In those days there was honor in working one's own farm. While Cincinnatus worked his own fields, the army of Rome was trapped and defeated by northern tribes. No one was left to defend Rome from the enemy but boys, old men, and the few guards of the city. In desperation the leaders of the city sent a delegation to Cincinnatus and they found him at his plow. After they explained the emergency at hand, Cincinnatus came to the city to meet with the leaders of Rome. They explained that they would make him absolute ruler of Rome so that he could deal with the terrible threat. It took 16 days for Cincinnatus to organize his small troop of men and defeat the enemy. Given the threat involved, it was an amazing feat of leadership. But what came next revealed the great character of Cincinnatus. He reported the defeat of the enemy to the city leaders, laid down his spear and shield, and simply returned to his plow. Cincinnatus has been admired by many over the centuries for his citizenship, with no ambition for honor, glory, or riches. The officers of the American Revolution called themselves the Society of Cincinnatus, and the city of Cincinnati, Ohio, was named for him.

foot-soldiers when needed. The last king, Tarquinus, was cruel and immoral. His crimes finally became too much to bear. In 509 B.C. the patrician families, led by Lucius Junius Brutus, ancestor of the assassin of Julius Caesar, expelled the king and put the Roman republic in its place. They formed a "Senate" of the leaders of the patrician families. The Roman Senate elected two rulers or "consuls" each year. Both consuls had to agree on whatever action would be taken. The term of only one year, which could not be repeated, limited their power. But many experienced ex-consuls in the Senate could guide the actions of the consuls.

A True Story of the Geese that Kept Guard Over Rome

Rome was under siege. An army of tall, fierce, golden-haired warriors from the tribes of Gaul (now France) had swept down upon the city and defeated Rome's soldiers. The barbarians were beating on the gates of the city. Fierce battles were fought in the streets of the city itself as the tired Roman soldiers retreated with their families to the fortress on top of the Capitol Hill. The Gauls were not only strong, they were fearless and fought with a kind of madness that terrified the Romans. At last the Romans were safe in their fortress, for who could think of climbing the steep rock and the high walls on its top? But when the men and women looked down from those high walls at the burning homes they had left behind, they saw that the Gauls kept up their assaults. They settled down to a siege of the Capitol. Weeks went by and the Romans could not break out or the Gauls break in. But the Romans inside grew very hungry. Many times they looked at the sacred geese of the Temple of Juno and thought that it might not be so great a crime to eat these fat, gray birds. But to kill them would be a sacrilege. One night, a brave young Roman named Manlius was supposed to be on watch, but he fell asleep near the Temple of Juno. A strange sound came through his troubled dreams and woke him up suddenly. He sprang to his feet and grabbed his spear. He recognized the sound at once. It was the hissing of the sacred geese. What had upset the birds? Manlius ran to look inside the temple compound and he came face to face with a Gaul. The leader of the Gauls had led his men up the rock and to the walls where they joined the temple. Manlius saw that the first man already had his hands on the parapet to haul himself over. Manlius struck at those hands and hurled the man back down the hill.

Louder and louder the geese clamored. The other Romans woke from sleep to see what it could be. They found Manlius defending the walls alone. With shouts and spears they rushed to his rescue and in a few minutes all the Romans were awake and the Gauls beaten back and scrambling down the rock the way they had climbed up.

A relief depicting the sacred geese of the Temple of Juno.

Attending a historical reenactment, a Roman standard bearer wears a bear's pelt and carries the shining *signum*, the insignia of his military unit.

This early Roman republic saw abuses against the common people, the plebeians, by the patrician class and their supporters. Plebeians were not given enough land to make a living and were often forced to work off debts by becoming the servants of the wealthy. In 494 B.C. matters came to a head when the plebeians withdrew from Rome and demanded a hearing for their grievances before they would return to work. This resulted in the creation of a "tribune," someone who had the power of a magistrate in Rome. The tribunes could intercede on behalf of a plebian in the Roman courts, and had the right to stop (veto) government actions they felt would damage the plebeians. In this way the Roman Republic found a way to satisfy the political desires of the patrician classes as well as those who worked and lived a common life.

Rome Extends Its Empire

The War with Carthage: the Punic Wars

Rome became more powerful and the ruler of Italy. Its growing commerce and influence brought it into conflict with the other major Mediterranean power at this time, the city of Carthage, located on the northern coast of Africa.

The Roman name for the Carthaginians, *Punici* (Phoenicians), comes from the Phoenician origins of Carthage. The rivalry between Rome and Carthage flamed into war in 264 B.C. over the island of Sicily. Each of these cities wanted to be the supreme power and so an all-out, extremely destructive war took place on land and sea. Several major cities on Sicily were totally destroyed, causing untold misery to the Sicilians. Rome suffered enormous losses, estimated at 100,000 soldiers and 500 ships. For more than 20 years the war dragged on. Eventually, Rome defeated Carthage in 241 B.C. in a decisive sea battle off the western coast of Sicily. The terms imposed by Rome were harsh: Carthage had to leave Sicily, return all imprisoned Roman soldiers, and pay to Rome a large sum of money over ten years. Sicily became a province of Rome, and was ruled as a foreign territory. Thus the First Punic War came to an end.

Carthage was a strong and proud city, and soon regained strength and proceeded to conquer southern Spain. Hannibal, son of the Carthaginian ruler Hamilcar, who had led Carthage into Spain, refused to accept the limitations imposed by the Romans. Hannibal was determined to crush the power of the Romans, and chose the strategy of attacking Italy by land. In order to do so, he would have to start in Spain, move north across Gaul (modern-day France) and enter Italy from the north by crossing the daunting Alps. This came to be known as the Second Punic War.

In the beginning of his tremendous undertaking,

Hannibal's campaign went well. He picked up allies in Gaul and successfully crossed the Alps with thousands of men, mules, and elephants—an amazing achievement. He also succeeded at first in fighting the Romans in Italy.

But, Rome would not make peace. Roman generals avoided direct battle with Hannibal, and some 16 years of fighting finally wore him down. Eventually, he was confined to the extreme south of the peninsula. Rome ended his attack of Italy by attacking Carthage. Hannibal returned to his native city to direct the defense, but was defeated by Roman forces at Zama in 202 B.C.

When Hannibal's 16 years of pillage and destruction were over, Rome committed itself to extending its empire. To the north in Italy, Gaul (France), and Spain, Rome fought many battles against the Gallic tribes. There was constant fighting to keep and enlarge the western provinces. In the east (Greece and Macedonia), Rome made many allies and was content to allow the local peoples to rule themselves, as long as they did not rebel against Roman domination. When they did, Roman armies arrived to make an example of them.

The Third and final Punic War against Carthage ended when Rome totally destroyed the city in 146 B.C. Rome leveled Carthage to the

Hannibal brought African fighting elephants from Spain across the Alps to support his army in attacking the Roman legions. This painting is from Italy, painted centuries later in the 16th century A.D.

The Oath of Regulus

The Roman General Regulus was captured by the Carthaginians in battle. The leaders of Carthage said they would let Regulus return to Rome with a proposal to end the war, if Regulus would give his word as a Roman to come back to imprisonment in Carthage should he fail to broker a peace.

Regulus did return to Rome, but he would not enter the gates. "No longer am I a citizen or a senator of this great city. I will neither enter her walls nor take my seat in her Senate." A delegation from the Senate came out to seek his advice. He said: "It is to no purpose to ransom those who have surrendered while they still hold their weapons. Let them be left to perish. Let war with Carthage go on until Carthage be conquered."

Then he prepared to return to Carthage. His wife and children begged him not to return. The Senate offered to send another in his place. He refused to break his oath, put his affairs in order, and left for Carthage, where he died in prison. "I am spent with battle and near death," said noble Regulus, "and what will the peoples think of Rome if her generals will not keep their oaths?"

ground and sowed salt into its fields so that no crops would ever grow there again.

From Village to Empire

In the 500 years it took for Rome to grow from a village by the Tiber River to the supreme power of its world, many changes had taken place. At first the Roman soldier had been a farmer who took up arms when needed. In later Rome, full-time soldiers were often noncitizens who served for 25 years and then were given citizenship, some money, and a farm. These soldiers tended to be loyal to their generals, who would provide for their retirement, more than to Rome and its people.

Many of the defeated men, women, and children who had opposed Rome were sold into slavery and worked the large farms of the patricians. No longer able to make any profit from their small holdings, many common farmers moved to Rome where they were dependant on the government for food, which was handed out daily.

The government of Rome also provided free entertainment for the common citizens. These entertainments were called the "Games," and were held in a large stadium called the "Circus," because it contained a racecourse for horse and chariot races. The Games took the form of popular chariot races and athletic contests, but also included the spectacle of men fighting animals to the death, and gladiator fights. The gladiators were mostly slaves who were forced to fight and kill each other for the amusement of the Romans. It was possible for a gladiator to earn his freedom, but much more likely, he could only escape this brutal slavery by an early death.

The patrician classes that governed Rome as members of the Senate had changed also. Once patriotic men, many became selfish and greedy as the wealth of the Roman conquests passed through their hands. As the senators became more concerned with their own success than with the future of all Romans, Rome became weaker. It was not enemies outside its borders that caused this weakness, but the loss of the virtues of courage, loyalty, and fortitude among the people.

Slaves had fought to the death in Rome, but always in private funeral services; later, private slave-duels became a public entertainment, demanded by the corrupt Roman mob in the days of the empire.

The Rise of the Caesars

The Start of the Civil Wars

Gaius was Julius Caesar's given name and Julius was his family name. Caesar was the name of his branch of the Julian family. He was called Julius Caesar to honor both families.

As more and more land and wealth came into the hands of the patricians and the knights, who were a class above the common man (or plebeians), there was increasing friction between the upper and lower classes. The patricians no longer needed the common farmer for defense, so the lower classes lost their bargaining power and privileges. Eventually, war broke out between generals and their private armies, all claiming to represent either the rich or the poor. For 100 years the rule of law was overturned by civil war and tyranny. Powerful men killed their rivals and used poor excuses to condemn others as traitors, take their family's money, and give their offices to friends. The Senate was too weak to control this turmoil.

Julius Caesar

Gaius Julius Caesar was a senator from a patrician family who allied himself with the rulers of Rome and pleased the people by paying for elaborate spectacles at the Circus.

Crossing the Rubicon—Julius Caesar on 10, January 49 B.C.

The term "crossing the Rubicon" means to take an irreversible step. This term came into our language when Julius Caesar and his army crossed this small river, the official border of Italy, on their way to Rome. Roman law and tradition strictly held that no governor of a province could enter Italy with his army. To cross the Rubicon would mean to defy the Senate and replace the Roman Republic with a rule by Caesar and his army. It would mean plunging Rome into a bloody civil war.

Julius Caesar crossing the Rubicon River.

Eventually he was elected consul and was given command of Gaul. Julius Caesar conquered Gaul for Rome and even made a raid into England. This was the first broadening of the Roman Empire for many years and was an impressive feat of generalship.

Caesar moved against his rivals and brought his army over the Rubicon River to take control of the city. He became **Dictator** of Rome. His rule lasted several years. Caesar reduced debt payments for the poor, resettled many poor and former soldiers with land in the provinces, and granted citizenship to non-Latin Italians and people whom Rome had conquered in Gaul. He also doubled the pay of Roman soldiers.

Despite the benefit of his strong leadership, the patricians feared Caesar's contempt of the Senate and the system of the old Roman republic, which they cherished. He took many honors to himself, ignored the Senate, and was even accepting the honor of divinity like the Eastern kings. This proved too much for the Senate. Several senators plotted together and attacked him with their daggers on March 15 (the **Ides** of March), 44 B.C. His old friend, Marcus Junius Brutus, descendant of the Brutus who drove out the last king, was among those who killed him. Caesar recognized him as one of the assassins, and sorrowfully reproached him: "Even you, Brutus?" ("*Et tu, Brute?*")

Dictator: A person who rules absolutely with no checks on his power.

Ides: The middle day of the month in the Roman calendar.

Our word emperor comes from Augustus Caesar's title as commander in chief of Rome's armies, *Imperator*. All successive rulers of Rome took his family name as their title and mark of authority: *Caesar*. From Caesar come the titles of European monarchs, *Czar* or *Tsar* in Russia, *Kaiser* in Germany.

Pax Romana: The Roman Peace

Map of the Roman Empire at the time of Caesar Augustus.

When Julius Caesar was murdered, his adopted son Octavius (later called Augustus) gained control of Rome. Although he retained enormous pow-

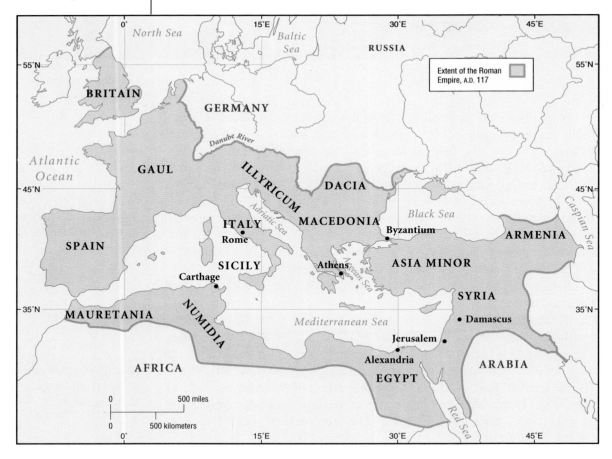

ers, he shared the rule of the vast empire with the Senate. By giving the Senate its due, he made himself more acceptable to the patricians who helped him to rule the vast Roman holdings. This system was to function for roughly 500 years.

Roman rule during this period extended over a huge part of the globe. The empire incorporated all the lands around the Mediterranean Sea, and stretched from the Atlantic Ocean to the Caspian Sea. The Roman Empire brought to these lands law and order, local governing counsels, paved roads, orderly commerce, good food, hot baths, sanitation, and Roman citizenship. Also, local men of wealth or talent could reach high positions in the Roman world. Many from the provinces became senators and even consuls. This achievement is perhaps the greatest feat of government the world has ever known.

Portrait of Julius Caesar's adopted son, Augustus.

The Slaves of Rome

The economy of Rome depended on slavery. In a time when there was no mechanization for cultivating fields, mining minerals, or building roads, and with Romans serving in the army or other civil service, slaves filled the gap. The menial work around the home as well as higher skills such as the education of children, intricate crafts, and business management often fell to slaves too. The state itself owned slaves for building public works. Gladiators, who were cruelly forced to fight one another to the death in public spectacles, were slaves as well.

Estimates are that one-third of all those who lived in Rome were slaves. They were mostly captured enemies and the sons or daughters of slaves. Although slaves could not win freedom, masters could free their own slaves as a reward for good service. Upon their death, many slave owners freed their slaves. This process was called "**manumission**" and made the slave into a "freedman." Freedmen were lower in rank than Roman citizens but higher than slaves. Some, who were well educated and skilled in government, business, or the arts, became wealthy and influential.

Manumit: To free another from slavery.

The Persecution of Christians

The early Christians had been troubled frequently by persecutions and abuse from local governors and mobs, and in A.D. 205, the Emperor

Christian martyrs in the Circus Maximus. An undated engraving of a painting by Jean Léon Gerôme.

Saint Sebastian, Christian martyr, in death. Painted by Gerrit van Honthorst about 1623.

Septimus Severus ordered all people in the empire to sacrifice to him as the divine emperor. Local governors used that excuse to kill and imprison Christians. But the empire had taken no official position about Christians as such. But then in A.D. 250, in response to the reverses that Roman armies were experiencing, many Romans looked to the refusal of the Christians to worship the Roman gods as treason and the Emperor Decius began an official persecution of the Christian religion. Bishops, priests, and deacons were the obvious targets, and many were arrested, tortured, and killed. Known Christians and those who refused to worship the Roman gods were also put to death. The Roman games had long since included the gory spectacle of condemned prisoners being consumed by lions. This was the fate of many Christian martyrs who would not worship Roman gods.

In A.D. 302, the Emperor Diocletian ordered the worst persecution yet, one that took the lives of 10,000 martyrs. However, only a decade later, in A.D. 313, the Emperor Constantine converted to Christianity and made it a legal religion of Rome. This immediately and radically changed the status of the Church. Christian worship was encouraged, beautiful churches were built, and the work of

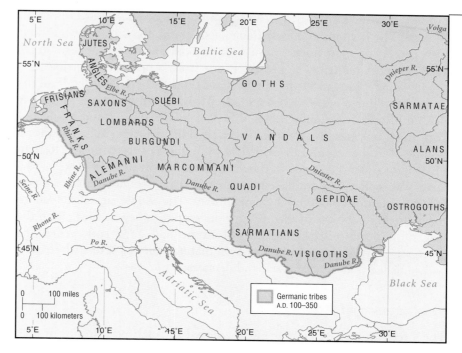

Map of the boundaries of the many Germanic tribes in Europe between A.D. 100 and 350.

bishops was financially supported. For the next 200 years while Rome remained the ruler of Italy, the church flourished with official support. But when the Roman rulers wanted to use Christianity to unite the empire, there began a long struggle to keep the spiritual Church independent of civil rulers.

The Decline of the Roman Empire

From roughly A.D. 250 to 500, the strength and willpower of the Roman Empire declined, until finally Rome was ruled by Germanic tribes from the north. The empire had grown too large to be properly run. The people were ruinously taxed to pay for the huge armies needed to defend the borders, and the armies themselves found it harder and harder to recruit soldiers. The Romans and their Italian armies did not want to spend their lives protecting their huge frontier. Non-Roman armies were hired from various Germanic tribes to protect Rome from other German tribes and the invading Huns, and from the Persians on the eastern border. If all the payment to the tribes were not met, they would turn on Rome. Turn they did, and Rome was finally defeated by Germanic tribes. Rome could not keep them out, because its army was a shell of its former self. The moral decline of Rome was also evident. The willingness of the common Roman or Italian to spend 25 years in the army, to earn only a "grub-stake" and a farm, was replaced by an idle city population that depended on bread and entertainment provided by the government. The Senate lacked the will to make the hard choices needed to save the empire. They had forgotten the task of leadership. The character of Rome had gone soft. When the moment of crisis came, the will of steel that had carried it to such heights had vanished in a thousand self-indulgences.

The Legacy of Rome

The Greek way of looking at life, expressed through philosophy, drama, art, architecture, politics, and science was learned by the Romans and then passed on to future peoples of the world. But Rome also communicated its own cultural legacy to the peoples of its empire. Rome made the rule of law, not the whim of a dictator, the model for effective and just government. All Roman citizens, from the highest to the lowest, were expected to obey the law. Roman law courts tried to apply the law justly to all who came before them. The great orator and philosopher, Cicero, made his name as a lawyer.

The Roman rule of law and way of government was a great teacher of civics to all the nations within the empire. The Roman Empire, with roles and responsibilities for administrators and citizens, from emperor to lowliest footsoldier, inspired all the lands that would later govern themselves. The Roman Republic and the best of the empire would forever be a shining example of civic spirit, rule by law, and the courage that enables citizens to do their duty for the good of all.

Chapter 5 Review

Let's Remember   Write your answer in a single complete sentence.
1. What does SPQR mean?
2. The Punic Wars were between which rival cities?
3. Who was Hannibal?
4. Who were the opponents in the Roman Civil Wars?
5. Why did the Roman senators want to kill Julius Caesar?
6. What was the Pax Romana and how long did it last?
7. Who was Diocletian?
8. Approximately how long did the decline of the Roman Empire last?

Let's Consider   For silent thinking and a short essay, or for thinking in a group with classroom discussion:
1. The mythic origins of Rome and the verifiable history of Rome.
2. How much the Roman Empire, and the Western civilization afterwards, owed to the Greeks.
3. How the government of Rome was set up to balance power and to ensure the common good.
4. How the geographic location of Rome established it as central to the whole Mediterranean world.
5. Why Christianity spread so rapidly throughout the Roman Empire.
6. What was happening in Rome at the time of Christ's coming.
7. The life of a Roman patrician or plebe.

Let's Eat!

The Romans put a sauce called *liquamen* on almost everything they ate, much as ketchup or soy sauce are used today. *Liquamen* is a very salty fishy-tasting sauce, similar to anchovie paste, and can be found in supermarkets. Try this authentic Roman side-dish for dinner: Put 1 large package of frozen green beans in water; add 1 Tbls. anchovie paste, 2 Tbls. Olive oil, 1 T. coriander seeds, 1 t. cumin, 1 small leek, chopped. Boil together and serve.

Chapter 6 Christianity: A Gift from God

The Hinge of History: The Life of Christ

"In the sixth month, the angel Gabriel was sent from God to a town of Galilee called Nazareth, to a virgin betrothed to a man named Joseph, of the house of David, and the virgin's name was Mary." (Luke 1: 26–27) So begins the most awesome event in all of human history, the story of the **Incarnation**, when God became man in the person of Jesus Christ. Jesus, fully God and fully man, was born in Bethlehem, the hometown of King David, in Judea about 2,000 years ago. His birth came to be seen as the fulcrum of time itself. For many centuries, dates have been counted either back from his birth and labeled B.C. (B.C. means Before Christ) or after his birth and denoted A.D. (A.D. means *Anno Domini*, Latin for "the year of the Lord"). Because of a possible miscalculation of ancient calendars, modern historians now believe Jesus' birth may have taken place as early as 4 B.C. Nevertheless, the year 2000 was celebrated worldwide as the 2,000th anniversary of the defining event, the Incarnation.

> **Incarnation**: The uniting of divine and human natures in Jesus Christ

> **Shepherds searched out the holy infant in Bethlehem after angels proclaimed his birth. A 17th century painting by Bartolomé Esteban Murillo.**

The World at the Incarnation

Jesus was born into a world within a world, a Jewish Palestine dominated by the Roman

Empire. The nation of Israel collapsed under the Babylonians in 597 B.C., and the Jewish people were scattered. Those who returned from exile to Palestine were ruled in turn by the Persians, the Syrians, and then the Greek Empire under Alexander the Great.

In 47 B.C., the Roman general Pompey appointed as governor of Galilee a young Jewish leader, who had been educated in Rome; within ten years he became king of the whole region. His name was Herod.

Aqueduct: A structure which diverts water from one source and carries it to another.

Devoted to the spread of Greek culture at the expense of Jewish sensibilities, Herod built theaters, stadiums, and the city of Caeserea Maritima and its great six-mile **aqueduct**, which channeled fresh water from a tunnel dug through Mount Carmel. As famous as he was for his building enterprises, he was as well known for his cruel grasp for power, which led him to murder three sons, two wives, and other people who threatened him politically. The massacre of the innocent first-born sons in Judea, recorded in the Gospel of Matthew, is an example.

Under this bloody ruler, five main factions of Jews quarreled with one another. The Herodians just wanted comfort and peace under the Roman government. The Zealots, on the other hand, sought to evict Rome from Palestine by force. The Sadducees were the religious authorities. The

The Scroll of the Rule, an ancient document of the Essenes.

A Buried History

The greatest contribution of the Essenes was not to be discovered until many years later. In the year 1947, in the Qumran region near the Dead Sea, a shepherd boy accidentally discovered hundreds of ancient Essene manuscripts. These scrolls, containing parts of nearly every book of the Old Testament, had been tucked into clay jars and buried in caves during the Roman assault in A.D. 70. The scrolls have been of great interest to biblical and historical scholars because they shed light on the lives of the Qumran monks who kept and hid the writings. The scrolls also reveal Jewish thought at the time of Christ. In addition, the biblical manuscripts are remarkably consistent with the Hebrew Scriptures which have been studied throughout the centuries. This answers people who say the Bible has been changed through history. In fact, the old Scriptures are the same today.

Pharisees saw themselves as keepers of the law, and they judged harshly others who followed it less strictly. The Essenes were also devoted to the law but kept a lower profile with prayer and study.

There were also common people, faithful Jews awaiting the Messiah, and among these were Mary, the mother of Jesus, and his foster father Joseph, a carpenter. The brief and powerful life of Jesus, his miraculous words and works, notorious death, supernatural resurrection, and establishment of a world-changing religion could not have been foretold from his humble beginnings. If so, perhaps more would have been written about Jesus by outsiders.

Instead, what we know of his earthly life comes almost only from the four books of the Gospels: Matthew, Mark, Luke, and John. The Gospels were written by those who knew him or who knew his apostles within a generation after Jesus. The Evangelists, or Gospel writers, were: Matthew, a tax collector and one of the Twelve apostles; Mark, an early convert and companion of the apostles Peter and Paul; Luke, a Greek **Gentile** (non-Jew), physician and companion of Paul; and John, an apostle.

Gentile: A person who is not Jewish.

According to the evangelist Matthew, Jesus' birth in Bethlehem was celebrated only by a nearby band of shepherds to whom a chorus of angels appeared in the sky. Later, some magi came "from the East," to honor the king whose coming was made known to them by a special bright star. Warned in a dream of Herod's plan to kill the child, Joseph fled with his family to Egypt, then some time later returned and settled in Nazareth in Galilee.

The baptism of Christ.

For thirty years Jesus lived a hidden life. The Gospels say nothing about this time. Then, Jesus' cousin John the Baptist suddenly departed for the desert, where he put on rough clothes and ate wild food. Behaving like an Old Testament prophet, John preached repentance, baptized people, and announced the near arrival of the Messiah. Jesus came to him for baptism. Because John knew who Jesus was, he reluctantly immersed him in the Jordan River and only after Jesus insisted that he do it. Then, a voice from heaven (sounding like thunder to those who stood nearby) declared Jesus to be the beloved Son of God.

Jesus then went into the desert for forty days, where he faced and overcame the devil in a trial of temptations. When Jesus left the desert, he called twelve men to be his disciples, most of them uneducated fishermen. He began to journey throughout the region preaching to the people, individually and in great crowds, about the kingdom of God. This kingdom, he said, was a spiritual rather than a political kingdom. Such a profound message took time to sink in, even for his closest followers.

It was Peter, the leader of the Twelve, who was the first to call Jesus the long-awaited Messiah and the Son of God. When he did, Jesus revealed his plan for Peter: he was to be the rock upon which Jesus would build his church (Matt. 16:18). Jesus gave Peter the keys of the kingdom, an allusion to the second-in-command in David's kingdom of Israel. Since Jesus' kingdom was spiritual, this authority was profound and referred to the power to forgive sins (Matt. 16:19).

Jesus' first miracle was at a wedding, where at his mother's request he made the bride and groom happy by quietly seeing to it that there was enough wine for the celebration. From there he worked many wonders: healing lepers and other sick people, expelling demons, restoring eyesight and hearing, calming a storm at sea, walking on water, multiplying food for the crowds, and raising people from the dead. He spoke to his countrymen in parables, using examples from everyday life to explain deeper truths. Jesus attracted many disciples, but was also rejected by many, especially when he taught of the need to eat his body and drink his blood (John 6:66).

The marriage feast at Cana.

Jesus also offended the Jewish leaders by appearing to break the letter of the sacred laws, such as Sabbath rest, in order to reveal the need to follow the spirit of the law. Jesus called the Pharisees **hypocrites**—accusing them of making demands upon others that they would not keep themselves. He also angered them by saying he was God (John 10:30, 13:14). In their pride and unbelief, they accused Jesus of blasphemy and plotted to arrest him.

Hypocrite: A person who pretends to be virtuous but who is not.

After three years of public ministry, Jesus was betrayed to the Jewish authorities by Judas Iscariot, one of his own trusted apostles. Brought first

The Last Supper, the First Eucharist

One of Jesus' last significant actions was to celebrate the Passover with his apostles. This was no ordinary Passover meal; this was the first Eucharist and, further, at this event Jesus commissioned his apostles to be his priests. They were to wash others' feet as he washed theirs (John 13: 1–17), and to break bread and offer wine in his name, a supernatural bread and wine that was, and would continue to be in every Mass, his own body and blood (Matt. 26:26–28).

to a religious trial, then to a secular trial before the Roman official Pontius Pilate, Jesus was condemned to death, whipped, beaten, and mocked, and finally nailed to a cross between two criminals. Then, three days after he died, he rose leaving the burial cloths on the floor of the tomb and moving aside a huge stone that blocked the entrance to the tomb. For the next forty days, Jesus appeared to his disciples in bodily form at various times and places. Leaving Peter and the apostles to establish the Church on Earth and to spread the good news of salvation, and promising to his followers the aid of the Holy Spirit, Jesus ascended bodily into heaven.

The Church—A Perpetual Gift

Jesus expressed his intention to establish a church (Matt. 16:18), but when did the Catholic Church actually begin? When Jesus was born? When he called the apostles? Or when he declared that Peter was the rock? The event sometimes called the birthday of the

When Christ suffers on the cross and gives up his life in agony, only the women disciples remain as witnesses. Painting by Eugène Delacroix, 1853.

Church actually occurred after Jesus' Resurrection, on the Jewish feast of Pentecost (Greek for "50th"), celebrated 50 days after Passover.

On the Pentecost following Jesus' Ascension, while Jews from around the world gathered in Jerusalem, the apostles and Jesus' mother and close relatives were praying together in a house in the city. Suddenly the room was filled with the sound of a great wind, and fire appeared over the head of each person. Filled with the power of the Holy Spirit, the disciples went out into the crowds and spoke about Jesus and the meaning of his life, death, and Resurrection. Miraculously, the people could understand the disciples in their own various languages.

The first Christians were eager and bold. Even Peter hardly resembled the same man who fearfully denied the Lord three times (Matthew 26: 69–75; Mark 14:66–72; Luke 22:54–62; John 18:15–18, 25–27). The young Church attracted more and more followers, and the apostles, under the leadership of Peter, appointed deacons to tend to the new converts. The Christians lived a common life centered on the Sunday liturgy and the teaching of the apostles. They shared property and daily meals, and just as in a family, the stronger members cared for the weaker.

The First Sermon

"Then Peter stood up with the Eleven, raised his voice, and proclaimed to them…'You who are Israelites, hear these words. Jesus the Nazarene was a man commended to you by God with mighty deeds, wonders, and signs, which God worked through him in your midst, as you yourselves know. This man, delivered up by the set plan and foreknowledge of God, you killed, using lawless men to crucify him. But God raised him up, releasing him from the throes of death, because it was impossible for him to be held by it… Therefore let the whole house of Israel know for certain that God has made him both Lord and Messiah, this Jesus whom you crucified…' Now when they heard this, they were cut to the heart, and they asked Peter and the other apostles, 'What are we to do, my brothers?' Peter said to them, 'Repent and be baptized, every one of you, in the name of Jesus Christ for the forgiveness of your sins; and you will receive the gift of the Holy Spirit. For the promise is made to you and to your children and to all those far off, whomever the Lord our God will call.' He testified with many other arguments, and was exhorting them, 'Save yourselves from this corrupt generation.' Those who accepted his message were baptized, and about three thousand persons were added that day." (Acts 2:14, 22–24, 36–41)

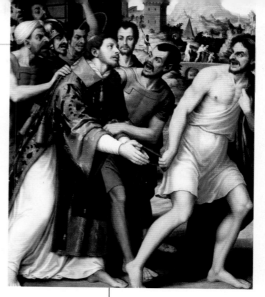

Yet the growing Church proved a threat to the Jewish authorities, who condemned the new religion and even ordered the stoning death of Stephen, a young deacon. Stephen was the first **martyr**; he died rather than deny his faith. The witness of Stephen and other martyrs did not cause the Church to disappear, but instead strengthened it in two ways. First, someone who would die so courageously for his faith stirs up the faith of others. Second, when Christians were being hunted in and around Jerusalem, they took the Gospel to the distant regions to which they fled.

None reached more of the world with the story of Christ than a man who had once been a persecutor himself: Saul, better known as Paul. Saul, a leading Pharisee from Tarsus in Asia Minor and a Roman citizen, was also the disciple who did the most to lead the Church from being a kind of sect, or group, within Judaism, to an entirely new religion open to Jews and non-Jews alike.

The leading of St. Stephen to his martyrdom. Painting by Juan de Juanes, 16th century.

Martyr: A person who chooses to die rather than to deny his faith.

The Apostolic Age

The first 100 years A.D. are called "the Apostolic Age," referring to the lives and leadership of the original apostles. This age included the writing of the entire New Testament—the four Gospels, the Book of Acts, the 21 Epistles, and the Book of Revelation. It also included the rapid spread of the new faith, aided by the peace, unity, and organization of the Roman Empire.

The Christian Scriptures

When the first Christians gathered to read the Scriptures, what they had was the Hebrew Scriptures. The first book of the New Testament to be written was probably Paul's letter to the church in Thessalonica, in about A.D. 52. As for the Gospels, there is some debate. Tradition has held that Matthew's came first, but some recent scholars think Mark may have been the first to write his account in about A.D. 60. Soon after came Matthew's and Luke's versions (in about A.D. 70–85). It appears they may have referred to Mark's shorter Gospel and added their own stories and inspired reflection. John's Gospel was the last to be composed, in about A.D. 96.

A lid, decorated with martyrs and saints, from a chest used to keep bodily remains for veneration. It shows the four evangelist symbols: man (Matthew), lion (Mark), ox (Luke), eagle (John). Made in Italy in the 14th century.

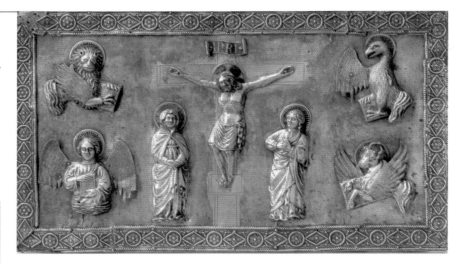

Canon: Standard; the list of books considered as truly inspired by God.

The word "canon" comes from the Greek word meaning "standard" or "measure." When used to refer to the books of the New or Old Testament, it means the books that have been declared by tradition and the teaching authority of the church to be divinely inspired and authentically reliable in recounting salvation history. The Bible as we know it was fully formed by A.D. 397.

St. Athanasius proposed the New Testament **canon** in A.D. 367. The New Testament canon is made up of 27 books declared to be authentic and divinely inspired. This list was formally confirmed by bishops' councils at Rome in A.D. 382 and at Carthage in 397. The councils also confirmed the Old Testament canon.

The infant Church was centered in Jerusalem and in Antioch, the city where Jesus' followers first came to be known as "Christians." The safety and ease of travel over the well-designed Roman roadways allowed the disciples to spread the "good news" throughout the world, and the intellectual heritage from Greece prepared the way for free discussion of new ideas. Even the widespread use of two languages, Latin and Greek, made it easier for the missionaries to communicate.

Poor people and slaves were the first to embrace Christianity. Just as Jesus fulfilled the Jews' hope in the Messiah, he fulfilled the deepest yearnings of non-Jews who were not satisfied by the superficial emperor worship of Rome, or the gods of the popular mystery religions such as Mithras, the Persian god of light, or Sol, the sun god of Syria. The pagan religious celebrations of life after death in the return of spring each year were for the new converts a mere foreshadowing of Christ's final overcoming of death by the Resurrection.

In time, teachers and philosophers such as Iranaeus, Tertullian, and Origen thought and wrote deeply about Christian belief and philosophy.

Circumcision, Baptism, and the New Covenant

One of the most hotly debated matters of the early church was resolved in the time of the apostles. All Jewish males were required to be **circumcised** in infancy; it was a sign of the covenant between God and man. With so many new converts who were Gentiles (non-Jews), the question of circumcising the male converts became a matter that threatened to divide the new faith. It was Peter who finally decided the question. Speaking with the guidance of the Holy Spirit, as he did in the first sermon, Peter said that circumcision was not required of the converts; they were to repent, be baptized, and live in Christ. Baptism became the new sign of the covenant between God and man, and infant baptism of both baby girls and baby boys came to take the place of the Jewish rite of circumcision for baby boys.

To Circumcise: To cut off a male's foreskin.

This appealed to the educated culture of Rome. Yet it wasn't just intellectual arguments that won over believers. Converts were attracted by the joy of the Christians, their courage, and the way they cared for widows, orphans, prisoners, and one another in close-knit communities. According to Tertullian, the pagans used to observe, "See how those Christians love one another!"

The *Didache*

The oldest Christian writing besides some of the books of the New Testament, was the "Teaching of the Twelve Apostles," known by its Greek name, for "teaching," the *Didache*. Written by an unknown author in Syria at about A.D. 60 or later, the *Didache* consists of 16 chapters of church guidelines and moral teaching. It covers liturgy, prayer, the Sunday obligation, community rules, and even the Church's first definitive and formal condemnation of abortion. The *Didache* was influential in the early Church, but the complete manuscript was lost for 800 years. A monk in a monastery in Constantinople found an 11th-century copy of the manuscript in the 1800s.

By the 3rd century, Christianity had spread throughout the whole Mediterranean region. Missionaries also traveled out of the empire into present-day Iran, Iraq, and the country of Armenia, which became the first Christian kingdom in history in A.D. 301.

As for the apostles' own journeys, tradition holds that Peter traveled to Rome, John to Ephesus, James to Spain, Bartholomew to India and Armenia, Simon and Jude to Persia, Thomas to India, and, less certainly, Andrew to Scythia and Epirus, Matthew to Ethiopia or Persia, and Philip to Phrygia. The New Testament records only the death of James (Acts 2:12), who was beheaded by King Agrippa I in Judea in A.D. 44. It is believed that all the apostles were martyred except for John, who died in old age after his exile in Patmos.

Peter was the first pope. The word "pope" comes from "pappas," the Greek word for "father." At first, all bishops were called "pope," but over

The martyrdom of Peter in Rome.

The Bones of St. Peter

St. Peter's Basilica in Rome is erected over the tomb of the Prince of Apostles. Beneath the main altar of the basilica the bones of St. Peter lie. It is certain that Peter lived in Rome, and tradition, supported by numerous accounts, claims that St. Peter died there in the 60s by being crucified head-down. The site of his martyrdom death was probably the Circus (a huge oval arena) or Gardens of Nero on the Vatican, since so many other gruesome activities of Nero's persecution took place there. Peter was buried in the pagan cemetery on the slope of Vatican hill, a site near his martyrdom. For a time the remains of Peter lay with those of St. Paul, who was also martyred at approximately the same time, in the catacombs along the Appian Way at

the place where the 4th-century Church of St. Sebastian now stands. The bones were probably taken there in the 200s to protect them during another persecution when Christian burial-places were desecrated. Two hundred years after that, the bones were returned to their original burial site, and in the 4th century, Emperor Constantine built the first church of St. Peter over the original site. The present basilica was built in the 17th century incorporating the ruins of the 4th-century church. Although tradition held for centuries that the altar of Constantine's church was built over the tomb of St. Peter, there was no archeological excavation until the 20th century. In the 1940s Pope Pius XII authorized archaeological study and excavation under the main altar of St. Peter's Basilica. There, surrounded by Christian graves and many ancient inscriptions asking the prayer of St. Peter, was found a funerary niche built by Pope Anicetus (155–166) for St. Peter's remains. In this niche they found the bones of an elderly, powerfully built man, which after they were carbon-dated to the 1st century, were declared by Pope Paul VI in 1968 to be the bones of St. Peter.

time, only the Bishop of Rome retained the title. "Bishop," or *"episkopos"* in Greek, means "overseer" or "shepherd." Peter wrote his epistle from Rome (referred to by the code name "Babylon"); he was killed under the Emperor Nero, as was Paul. The 4th-century bishop and historian Eusebius recorded the traditional story that Peter believed himself unworthy to die like the Lord, so he asked to be crucified upside down. After the fall of Jerusalem in A.D. 70, Rome became the center of the Church.

Christians Under Siege

In an empire that tolerated many religions, Christianity was despised. Why? For one thing, the Christians would not make sacrifices to any of the Roman gods, including the emperor. (The Jews likewise refused to perform pagan sacrifices, but their historical practices, "the ways of their fathers," were respected by Rome.) For another, Christians met before dawn on Sunday, and night-time gatherings were forbidden by the authorities who feared political plots. Christians would not fight in wars, and they would settle their legal affairs through their own bishops rather than Roman courts. Even the Mass, at that time called an "agape" or "love feast," was completely misunderstood by the Romans, who thought the Christians were immoral, or even cannibals!

A fragment of a stone casket, the remains of a burial in early Christian times. In Rome Christians made use of underground burial halls called catacombs.

As a result, Christianity was declared illegal, and Christians at various times and places were arrested and sometimes killed. Persecutions were sporadic, breaking out in various times and places, until A.D. 249, after which a worldwide persecution began. Although this historical period is sometimes called the Age of Martyrs, Christians have given up their lives rather than deny Christ throughout the life of the Church and into the present day, with the 20th century witnessing more martyrdoms than in any previous century!

The Persecutions

A series of persecutions took place over the first centuries of Christianity:

A.D. 64   Rome was severely damaged by a fire; the emperor Nero put the blame on the Christians who were viewed widely as "haters of humanity" for their refusal to sacrifice to the gods. Large numbers of Christians were crucified and skinned alive. Peter and Paul were among the martyrs; Peter was crucified upside down, and Paul was beheaded.

The Colosseum, built in Rome between A.D. 72 and 82, just after the destruction of the Temple of the Lord in Jerusalem. Some of the building stone probably came from the destroyed Temple.

A.D. 65–249   During these years, isolated local persecutions, fairly infrequent, took place when Christians were blamed for any natural disasters that occurred, as though the gods were angry because the Christians did not sacrifice to them. Many of them died in the Roman games. Audiences gathered in the Colosseum to watch as Christians and other "criminals" were trapped in a center arena with wild, hungry animals that attacked and devoured the unarmed people. Those who survived the lions' jaws were killed with the guards' swords.

A.D. 250   The emperor Decius began his first general persecution. Those who failed to produce a *libellus*, a certificate proving that the bearer made sacrifices to the gods, were put to death. Many Christians died throughout the empire.

A.D. 253–259   Valerian continued the widespread persecution, particularly singling out bishops. Roman soldiers even cut the bishops down with their swords as they celebrated Mass.

A.D. 303–306   Diocletian unleashed the last general persecution, and his junior emperor Galerius was especially vigorous in carrying it out. Christians died in great numbers and often after cruel tortures, such as being burned alive. Ending in the West in A.D. 306, the persecution was officially called off in 313 with the Edict of Milan, when Constantine legalized Christianity as a religion.

The Matter of Faith

In the midst of intermittent persecutions through the first three centuries, Christians also enjoyed long periods of peace. During these times they had to work out internal struggles over the beliefs and practices of their new religion. The Jewish Christians argued over whether certain Jewish rituals needed to be observed in the new covenant. Converts brought with them ideas from former religions that had to be absorbed into Christianity or rejected. Even the philosophical debates of the Greeks raised questions that the early Church had to address.

Perpetua's "Day of Victory"

One of the earliest writings by a Christian woman is the prison diary of a 22-year-old noblewoman, Vibia Perpetua. In the year A.D. 203 Perpetua and some Christian companions were arrested in Carthage for refusing to offer pagan sacrifices. The darkness and heat of the prison and the cruelty of the soldiers frightened Perpetua, and she also worried about her infant son. "Such cares I suffered for many days," she wrote, "and I obtained that the child should abide with me in prison; and straightway I became well and was lightened of my labor and care for the child; and suddenly the prison was made a palace for me, so that I would sooner be there than anywhere else."

Perpetua's father begged, cursed, and even tore hair from his beard to get his beloved daughter to give up her resolution. He tried to frighten her with warnings that her baby would die if she died. Yet Perpetua's faith remained strong. She wrote: "Father, said I, 'Do you see this vessel lying, a pitcher or whatsoever it may be?' And he said, 'I see it.' And I said to him, 'Can it be called by any other name than that which it is?' And he answered, 'No.' 'So can I call myself nought other than that which I am, a Christian?'"

Finally Perpetua and her companions received their sentence, to be thrown to wild animals in a public spectacle. A fellow Christian wrote, "Now dawned the day of their victory, and they went forth from the prison into the amphitheater as it were into heaven, cheerful and bright of countenance; if they trembled at all, it was for joy, not for fear." One of Perpetua's companions was her slave, Felicity, who had just given birth; since she was no longer pregnant, the Romans permitted her to be executed. First whipped, then mauled by a wild cow, Perpetua and Felicity shared the kiss of peace with their friends before dying by the sword.

For example, the Gnostics (Gnostic comes from the Greek, meaning "to know") thought the material world, including the human body, was bad. When certain Gnostics came into the Church, they rejected the authority of the apostles and claimed to have "secret teachings" from Jesus that confirmed their belief that the divine Jesus was not really a man.

In contrast, another belief called Monarchianism held that Jesus was human and divine, but somehow "less God" than the Father. Such false beliefs are called **heresy**, which means a denial of a truth of the faith by a baptized Christian. **Orthodoxy** means adhering to the tradition of faith as handed on by the apostles.

Heresies of the Early Church

Today it is hard to imagine a time when the Church did not universally believe that Jesus is true God and true man, that the Trinity is three Divine

Heresy: The denial or perversion of a truth of the faith.

Orthodoxy: The belief in and practice of the truth of the faith as handed down by Christ and his apostles.

The round apse of a Catholic Church in Turkey at the ancient city of Sardis, built in the 4th century A.D. The altar was in the apse, where Mass was offered.

Persons in one God, or that the forgiveness of Christ extends to all people, not a select few. Yet these were topics of critical discussion and even fighting in the early Church. As educated people began to convert, it became important to express the Christian faith in careful, clear philosophical language.

Even though some groups broke away, the debates allowed the Church to deepen her understanding of the apostles' teaching. Keeping the Church united in faith became the work of the bishops, those appointed to succeed the apostles, under the leadership of the Bishop of Rome, successor to Peter.

The central mysteries of the faith are difficult—perhaps impossible—for man to fully explain. Trying to reason through these profound truths gave rise to heresies that attempted to explain Christ and the Trinity in simpler ways. In its councils, the Church's bishops acted decisively to end heresies and uphold the truth.

Does Heresy Matter?

Is arguing over heresy mere quibbling or is something more at stake? Heresy is not trivial, for what is at stake is our salvation. The early Church understood that what heresies claimed struck at the very root of what the Christian Gospel claims. If Jesus is not fully divine nor totally human, then, among other consequences, the sacraments are meaningless. Yet Jesus said: "I am the way, the truth and the life, and no one comes to the Father but through me." The sacraments are the way for us to come to the Truth and the Life in him. Ideas matter because they determine how we live and what we do. This is why the Church was and is so concerned with correct doctrine.

The heavenly coronation of Mary by the Holy Trinity—Father, Son, and Holy Spirit.

The Apostles' Creed

Although the present form of the Apostles' Creed first appeared in the 6th century, it can be traced in one form or another back to apostolic times. The creed can be found in a document from around A.D. 200, containing the Roman baptismal liturgy. This creed seems to have been a baptismal creed summarizing the teachings of the apostles. It was given to the converts when they were baptized. Each line was asked in the form of a question to which the convert gave assent, indicating he both understood and believed.

In the early Church, the bishops agreed on the creed. The earliest date of the Apostles' Creed is unknown. The Nicene Creed was formalized in A.D. 325. This is the creed we recite even up to today at each Sunday Mass. Recently, the bishops exercised their teaching authority by putting out, under the direction of the pope, a new universal catechism.

Worldwide Persecution

Decius became emperor in A.D. 249, and in an effort to strengthen Rome and his own leadership, he ordered everyone to return to the old religion and make sacrifices to the gods and to him. If someone could not produce a *libellus*, that person would be executed. A *libellus* was an official document proving that the bearer of the document had sacrificed to the pagan gods. Some bishops and their followers were killed, some went into hiding, and some did not sacrifice but paid sympathetic officials to produce a *libellus* saying they had. Others simply gave in and sacrificed.

From 261 to 300 there was peace, but Galerius, a junior emperor (called a caesar) under Diocletian, determined to stamp out Christianity. Issuing edict after edict, he harassed the Christians more and more, ordering churches and even the Scriptures to be destroyed. In 304 the familiar requirement to sacrifice or die resulted in cruel tortures and executions throughout the empire. Whole Christian communities were destroyed.

Yet Galerius could not eliminate the Church. In 305 Diocletian resigned, and the caesars of the West, Constantius Chlorus and Maxentius, stopped the persecution there. Finally in 311 the dying Galerius proclaimed that

Christians in the East would be allowed to meet and to celebrate the liturgy. Christianity was legal throughout Rome for the first time in 250 years.

Internal troubles began again when the Church had to deal with the matter of believers who had denied their faith. Should they be forgiven or permanently excluded? The disagreement led to a **schism**, or splitting off, of a strict group called the Donatists in North Africa, who thought the Church would be weakened by forgiving the fallen, especially bishops and priests. The rest of the Church decided that all could be forgiven after a period of penance. Years later St. Augustine, a bishop in North Africa, tried to bring the Donatists back into the Church. He explained that the sacraments are valid (i.e., true and imparting God's grace), even if the minister is unworthy, because the true minister is Christ himself.

Schism: A divison or split.

An Emperor Converts: The Church Under Constantine

After three centuries marked by so much difficulty and torment for the Church, a most surprising thing happened. By the end of the 4th century, the most hated religion in the Roman Empire became its official religion. The man responsible for the transformation was Constantine the Great, senior emperor of Rome from A.D. 306 and sole emperor from 324 until his death in 337. Constantine was not the emperor to declare Christianity the state religion, but he did more than anyone to prepare the way for that declaration.

Constantine was born about A.D. 280 to a Christian mother, St. Helena, and Caesar Constantius Chlorus, who restored tolerance of Christians in his region in 305. Succeeding his father in 306, Constantine defeated Maxentius, his rival in the West, in A.D. 312. This event is associated with his conversion to Christianity, although Constantine was not baptized until the end of his life.

In A.D. 313 Constantine met with Licinius, emperor of the East, in Milan. Together they signed the Edict of Milan, which granted full religious freedom and the return of property to the Christians. Throughout the next 25 years, the political status of Christians continued to improve. Coins bearing pagan symbols now included Christian symbols. Churches that had been damaged were restored, and grand new churches were built with public money.

Even civil laws began to reflect Christian morality and practice. Sunday was observed as the official day of rest. Masters could no longer kill their slaves, nor could the families of slaves be broken up. Sins against marriage, such as adultery, were punished more severely. Priests and bishops were relieved from the obligation of military service.

Constantine's desire for unity in the empire extended to the churches as well. An Alexandrian priest named Arius (instigator of the Arian heresy) began teaching that God the Father "created" Christ, so that the Son was not fully God. The division between those who held the full divinity of the Son and the Arians who denied the Incarnation, split the Egyptian church; Christians even fought each other violently. To settle the riots and help the desperate bishops, Constantine assembled the first ecumenical council, or worldwide meeting of bishops. The leading

The Cross That Won the West

Constantine, who possessed Britain and Gaul (France), took arms against Maxentius, who occupied the capital city of Rome. Marching with his soldiers toward the city, Constantine suddenly saw a vision. In front of the afternoon sun there appeared a cross, bright with light, and the words "By this sign, conquer." Immediately Constantine had his soldiers decorate their shields with the symbol he had seen, the Chi-Ro, a cross made from the letters of the name "Jesus" in Greek. (See picture.) They faced down Maxentius' army at the Milvian Bridge across the Tiber River, and as the enemy soldiers retreated, the bridge broke, causing Maxentius and his army to fall into the river and drown. Constantine had won Italy.

Ancient Roman sculpture of Emperor Constantine, created about A.D. 307–337.

defender of the Incarnation and the divinity of Christ was St. Athanasius, another Alexandrian theologian.

The Council of Nicea met in 325 to hammer out the first creed, or formal statement of belief. This creed summarized and clarified the teachings of the apostles, especially on the nature of Christ as "begotten not made" and "one with the Father," and was eventually revised into the Nicene Creed we recite today in the Sunday liturgy. The Arian heresy had failed to win the day, but the determined Arians continued to spread their teachings for some time, despite the council's decision. St. Athanasius suffered exile and attack for his defense of the Truth.

Map of Constantine's empire—showing the provinces and the two capitals, Rome and Constantinople.

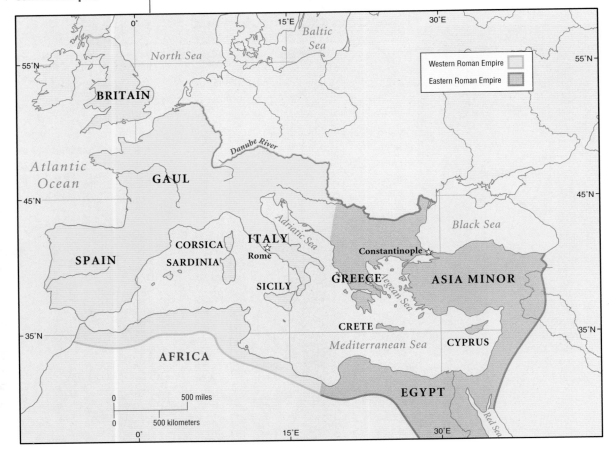

Constantinople, the Roma Nova

In 327 Constantine founded a new capital he called Roma Nova (New Rome), later named Constantinople (city of Constantine). The new city was built on the site of the ancient Byzantium (modern-day Istanbul, Turkey), and was more centrally located for access to the whole empire. There Constantine built the first central church of the empire, the cathedral Hagia Sophia (Hagia Sophia means Holy Wisdom, in Greek). Having given his Lateran palace in Rome to the Bishop of Rome, Constantine symbolically placed the leadership in the West in the hands of the Church.

Seventeen centuries later Constantine's city, still flourishes; now known as Istanbul, from a Greek phrase adopted by the Turks who conquered it, which meant "to the City."

After Constantine's death in A.D. 337, the empire suffered various divisions through the feuding of his sons and their successors. In 380, in an effort to unite Rome in one religion, the Christian emperor Theodosius decreed Christianity as the official and only recognized religion of the empire. Ten years later he ordered all pagan temples to be closed. Many people converted, but not for the same reasons as they did during the age of martyrs. Being a Christian was now most helpful, if not actually required, in order to have a successful and comfortable life and prestigious position in the Roma Nova.

Also, the dominance of the Roman Empire was weakening under continued attacks by surrounding peoples called "barbarians," from a Greek word meaning "foreigners." Two leaders who emerged during this era were among the most influential Christians of all time: St. Jerome and St. Augustine of Hippo.

St. Jerome

St. Jerome was born Eusebius Hieronymus in 331 in Dalmatia, the region known today as the Balkans, and he was taught the Roman classic writers,

Ascetic: Austere self-denial of physical things for spiritual reasons.

such as Virgil, Cicero, and Horace. Raised a Christian, he was also attracted to a new movement known as **asceticism**. Asceticism is a life of rigorous self-denial for the purpose of growing like Christ. Ascetics did such things as fast from food, go without sleep, live a life of voluntary poverty with few material comforts, and spend many hours in prayer and reading Scripture. Some ascetic Christians even moved to the desert to live in small communities or, more radically, as hermits.

One night Jerome had a dream in which he was condemned at the judgment seat of heaven with these words: "You belong to Cicero, not Christ!" (Cicero was a famous Roman writer, whose style was imitated for centuries by young writers.) Jerome immediately abandoned the Roman writers and left for the Syrian desert to take up Scripture. Distracted in prayer, he decided to discipline his mind with a difficult undertaking: the study of Hebrew. St. Jerome became the first Latin Christian to learn the ancient language of the Old Testament.

St. Jerome, the great theologian and scholar of Hebrew, in his study. Painted by Marinus van Reymerswaele between A.D. 1540–1550.

St. Jerome wrote many books and treatises, but his greatest contribution by far to Christianity and the Western world began when he was serving Pope Damasus. It was then that the scholarly priest undertook to translate the Bible from its original languages. The Old Testament in use at the time was not based on Hebrew, but on a Greek translation called the Septuagint; because of several variations, the text was corrupted and unreliable. Pope Damasus wanted St. Jerome to sort through the variations and come up with one standard Latin version. That wasn't good enough for St. Jerome. With his expert knowledge of Hebrew and Greek, he started at the very beginning and translated the four Gospels. Twenty years later, with the help of two learned Roman women, St. Paula and St. Eustochium (mother and daughter), he completed the entire Bible in Latin. It was accepted after some controversy as the standard and reliable translation and given the title *Vulgate*, which in Latin means "popular."

St. Augustine

St. Augustine was born in 354 in Thagaste, a small city in Latin-speaking North Africa, now modern-day Algeria. His mother, St. Monica, became a renowned Christian saint, and his father Patricius was a Roman official and a pagan who later converted to Christianity.

Sent from his hometown to be educated in Madaura and then Carthage, Augustine studied the Roman classics and became a master of rhetoric, the art of speaking and writing. But his education did not preserve him from immoral living; unmarried, he lived with a woman for 15 years and fathered a son. Hungering for truth and wrestling with his conscience, Augustine was drawn to the Manicheans, a Persian sect that combined elements from Christianity and pagan religions. They believed that good and evil were equal powers engaged in an ongoing struggle, and they thought that matter was evil; rejecting the Old Testament, their beliefs about Christ were also odd and unorthodox. After nine years in the sect, Augustine began to have doubts. He moved to Milan to teach; there, he encountered St. Ambrose, a brilliant Christian bishop. St. Ambrose helped Augustine to see that the Manichees had misrepresented the Church and the Scriptures.

St. Augustine, A.D. **354 to** A.D. **430.**

As an adult, Augustine had resisted studying the Scriptures, but now he began to accept their clarity and authority. Augustine's conversion was almost complete; only one question remained: his immoral relationship. Should he marry or forsake marriage for a chaste life of complete devotion to God? One day, while praying and weeping in a garden, he heard a child's voice say, "Take and read." Augustine opened a book of St. Paul's epistles, and his eyes fell on the following passage in Romans 13: "…let us conduct ourselves properly as in the day, not in orgies and drunkenness, not in promiscuity and licentiousness, not in rivalry and jealousy. But put on the Lord Jesus Christ, and make no provision for the desires of the flesh."

In that instant Augustine's anguish ceased, and he embraced the call of chastity. In A.D. 387, St. Ambrose baptized both Augustine and his son. Augustine and a little company of friends and relatives began a type of simple community life of prayer and contemplation, but their joy turned to sorrow with the death of Augustine's mother, St. Monica, whose constant prayers he credited for his conversion. Soon after, Augustine's teenage son also died.

Augustine moved to Hippo, a major seaport in North Africa. In 391 at a Mass in the cathedral, he was surrounded by the congregation and brought to the bishop to be ordained a priest. In 395, recognized for his gifts of oratory, knowledge of Scripture, and admirable character, he was made bishop.

St. Augustine was widely known for his defense of Christianity against two major heretical groups, the Donatists and the Pelagians. In doing so, he developed several major teachings of the Church. The Donatists had long ago separated over the issue of bishops who weakened during persecution. To them, St. Augustine argued that sacraments are valid even if the minister is a sinner, and that the Church is holy even though it consists of saints and sinners. He also taught that once baptized, a person need not— nor cannot be—rebaptized and that there is no salvation apart from the Church, which is the mystical body of Christ. From St. Augustine we have the understanding of the four "marks" of the Church: one, holy, catholic, and apostolic.

In his attacks on Pelagianism, St. Augustine developed the Church's teaching on original sin and the necessity of grace, reflections that earned him the title "Doctor of Grace." He also wrote *The City of God*, a monumental work that showed the superiority of Christianity over paganism, which still had some strength in the West. St. Augustine wrote an astounding amount, including more than 100 books, 200 letters, and 500 sermons. St. Augustine's thought was the most influential in the West until St. Thomas Aquinas in the 1200s. As Roman Africa collapsed under the attacks of the Vandals, Augustine's health also declined. He died in 430, when the barbarian tribe fell upon his city of Hippo.

Beyond The Roman Empire

In *The City of God*, St. Augustine wrote that the Church was the one true city that would continue into eternity, even while the City of Man—that is, the various countries and empires in history—would rise and fall. He wrote this at the dawn of the 5th century, when the world was in a tumult. Weakened and split between two emperors, in the East and the West, Rome was besieged on all sides by a half dozen different plundering foreign armies. The well-armed Goths invaded the city of Rome in 410, and 20 years later the Vandals crossed into Spain, covered North Africa, and turned north again toward Italy. The Huns swept west and south from Asia, and the Franks descended through western Gaul (modern-day France).

The rough invaders were fierce; the words "barbarian," "Vandal," and "Hun" came to be synonyms for the kind of viciousness and destructiveness with which they fought. Fear was great, even among Christians, as churches and public buildings alike were torn down. Yet the City of God did stand. The strength and organization of the Church guided the West through the "end of the world" and into a new age.

The Last Emperor of the West

With their power all but gone, the Romans joined forces with one barbarian tribe to fight another. In 451, the Romans and the Visigoths, a Germanic tribe, defeated the Huns in Gaul, preventing Attila's forces from taking over Europe. In just 25 years, however, the last remains of the Western Roman Empire disappeared. The Germanic king Odoacer organized a rebellion against Rome in 476 and deposed the last Western emperor, Romulus Augustus.

This map shows the main barbarian invasions that harassed the Roman Empire, and their routes and dates.

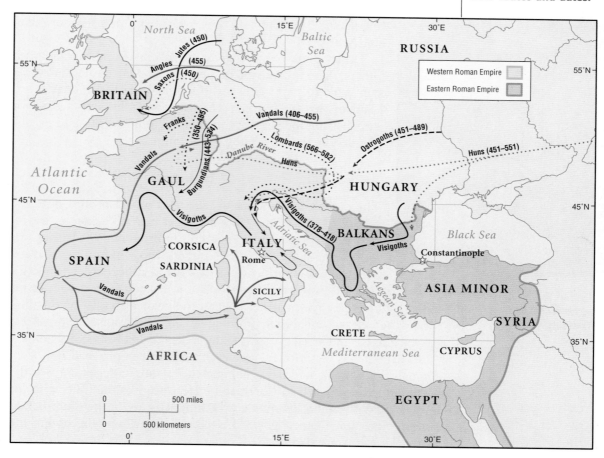

Monasteries and Missionaries

By the 5th century, many individual Christians had left the busy world for a quiet life of purity, prayer, and study. This practice started in the East and then took hold in the West. Those who withdrew from the world for a life of pious solitude were called hermits or anchorites. One of the best-known hermits was St. Anthony of Egypt (251–356). He and the other hermits who lived near each other for safety and to share the Eucharist became known as the Desert Fathers. Their devotion to God inspired people to seek their wisdom, and through the years many imitated their rigorous ways of life. Some lacked all moderation and good sense; these went to bizarre extremes. One radical fellow, named Simeon, moved to the Syrian Desert in 423, built a platform on a six-foot pillar, and lived on the top of it.

Others preferred to share a life of prayer and sacrifice with others; these became the first monks. St. Martin of Tours was a converted Roman soldier who founded the first monastery in Gaul in the 4th century. This monastery became a base for evangelizing the peasants, many of whom had clung to paganism despite the conversion of the empire.

One of the monasteries of Meteora, in Thessaly, Greece.

St. Patrick, Patron of Ireland

The monastic life began to take hold in Ireland too, after the arrival of one of the Church's most beloved missionaries, St. Patrick. Born to a Christian family in Britain in 390, Patrick was kidnapped at age 16 by Irish pirates who sold him into slavery. The next six years he lived a hard life as a shepherd. During this time of enslavement and isolation, Patrick grew devout in his faith. Inspired to escape, he traveled either to Britain or Gaul—on this, history is not clear—and began training in the faith and Scriptures. He returned to Ireland a bishop, succeeding Ireland's first bishop, Palladius.

St. Patrick was victorious where even a mighty empire had not been. Though the Romans had never conquered Ireland, under St. Patrick the island largely converted to Christianity. He won over the Celts with his love of the natives and his simple preaching. His use of the shamrock to describe the Holy Trinity led to the three-leafed clover's becoming the national symbol of Ireland.

Legends about St. Patrick abound, and it is hard to separate fact from fiction. But his legacy was soon evident. By the 6th century, Irish monks were traveling throughout Western Europe converting pagans and rebuilding after the barbarian attacks. Monasteries were founded in Gaul, Switzerland, Belgium, and Italy. These monks followed the strict model of the Irish missionary monk St. Columbanus (550–615).

St. Patrick is shown here at the end of his life, as a great missionary bishop to the Irish. Yet he had come to Ireland kidnapped and enslaved: a Christian boy alone, owned by pagans in a pagan land.

At the same time a new and distinctly Western monasticism was born. This came about through the *Rule of St. Benedict.* The rapid spread of these monasteries allowed the Church to preserve classical culture and build a new civilization on the ruined Roman Empire.

St. Benedict and His Rule

St. Benedict of Nursia (480–550) did not set out to found a religious order, let alone to spread monasticism far and wide. Born in Nursia, Italy, St. Benedict attended school in Rome but left the corrupt city as a teenager to live as a hermit in a remote cave in Subiaco, Italy. His holy example attracted followers, and eventually 12 small communities established themselves in the area, each with a leader chosen by St. Benedict.

St. Benedict's humble mountaintop monastery became the Abbey of Monte Cassino in Lazio, Italy. Shown as it looks today.

In 525 St. Benedict moved to a mountaintop located between Rome and Naples, Monte Cassino. There he established what would become one of the most famous and influential of all monasteries. St. Benedict then set to writing his Rule for religious life, an inspired combination of freedom and discipline, structure and flexibility, fellowship and solitude. The Rule was simple— St. Benedict himself described it

The Father of English History

A historian known as St. Bede the Venerable (673–735) recorded the missionary travels of St. Augustine. St. Bede wrote more than 40 works on history, Scripture, and grammar, and wrote *Historia Ecclesiastica,* his masterpiece on the history of England from 55 B.C. to A.D. 731. The tomb of St. Bede the Venerable is in Durham Cathedral in England.

Left: The tomb of St. Bede the Venerable in the Galilee Chapel at Durham Cathedral, built during the 12th century in the city of Durham, England. Right: Detail of a manuscript by a Benedictine monk and scholar, the Venerable Bede.

as a "rule for beginners," and it was common sense living, not bizarre and not too demanding.

For example, St. Benedict's monks were each to have their own bed (as opposed to sleeping on straw on the ground or stone floor). Not only that, they were to have a mattress, two blankets, and a pillow; they were allowed up to one pint of wine a day; and the daily meal included a choice of two cooked dishes. The monks were to spend their days in a balanced schedule of prayer, study, exercise, manual labor, and rest. They were to live a chaste life in common under obedience to an "abbot" (Latin derivative of the Aramaic *abba,* meaning father). The extreme asceticism of the early monks had attracted relatively few persons, but many more Christians could live according to the more moderate Rule of St. Benedict, and they did. Monasteries began to sprout up across western Europe.

The Reluctant Pope

One man who promoted the late 6th century monastic movement was a wealthy Roman nobleman who became a monk himself and then one of the most noteworthy popes of history, Pope St. Gregory the Great. The son of a Roman senator, Gregory was chosen to be the prefect of Rome, a high civil office—but as a Christian he forsook his life of prestige. He spent his wealth to found seven monasteries, one of which he founded on his own estate and later joined himself.

In 578 he was ordained a deacon and the next year he was made an ambassador to Constantinople. From 585 to 590 St. Gregory served as abbot of his monastery, and he was widely respected as a holy leader. In 590, the priests and people of Rome unanimously elected him pope, despite his protests.

St. Gregory became a true father of Rome, both by defending the city from the threat of the Lombard invaders and by feeding the city-dwellers who were suffering famine brought on by a plague. He was also the first to send monks out of Rome to evangelize barbarians. One monk he sent was St. Augustine of Canterbury, the "Apostle of England." St. Augustine became the first archbishop in England, and he appointed bishops over London and Rochester from his see at Canterbury.

Not all the monks' students went on to become priests. Many accepted "minor" orders, which gave them the legal rights of clerks (clergy) without the duties and disciplines of priests. In the cities, the bishops also ran schools, but the monasteries taught the country people.

The earliest monks set off to leave the "world"—that is, what they thought to be the temptations to sin in everyday life. Even the Christian Empire was not Christian enough for them. In later centuries this changed. Christians built a new world under Christ, under the papacy, and under the Church.

Gregory the Great, pope in a dark time, seen busy with his enormous workload. He was one of the most effective of all the popes. Painting by Carlo Saraceni, about 1590–1620.

Chapter 6 Review

Let's Remember   Write your answer in a single complete sentence.
1. What do B.C. and A.D. mean?
2. What are the four Gospels that tell of the life of Christ?
3. Who was the leader of the apostles to whom Jesus gave the keys of the kingdom?
4. What is the event that Christians call the birthday of the Church?
5. What was the apostolic age?
6. In what city were Jesus' followers first called Christians?
7. What was the Didache?

8. Who was Constantine?

9. What Mediterranean city was called the New Rome?

Let's Consider   For silent thinking and a short essay, or for thinking in a group with classroom discussion:

1. What happened during the hidden life of Jesus, before he began his public ministry?

2. In what ways did Jesus express his intention to establish a church as his gift to the world?

3. How radically did St. Paul change after his conversion and how much of a surprise was it to everyone?

4. How different was the love of Christians in caring for their widows, orphans, and one another from other practices in the ancient world?

5. How rapid was the expansion of Christianity all over the known world?

6. Why were the heresies of the early Church so strongly suppressed?

Let's Eat!

St. Monica might have fixed this recipe; it was a favorite food throughout the Roman Empire in the early days of Christianity. It is called *Ova sfongia ex lacte* (eggs and milk) and is like an omelet or scrambled eggs: Beat 8 eggs together and add a cup of milk and 2 T. of olive oil (or melted butter); mix thoroughly. Fry in a pan like an omelet and serve topped with honey and a little pepper.

Chapter 7 Byzantium and the Rise of Islam

The Byzantine Empire and the Church

From the first centuries of Christianity, the Church began to develop two personalities: East and West. These had two separate languages: Greek and Latin. Greek was the language spoken in the East, and Latin in the West. Their development was at first mixed with the cultures and histories of the two empires of Rome. In the Eastern Empire, the Church was run by the four patriarchates, the sees of Alexandria, Antioch, Constantinople, and Jerusalem. In the West there was one, the see of Rome. (A "see" is the seat or central town of a bishop.)

Because there was no central government, the West separated the moral and spiritual rule of the Church from the political rule of the state; in the East, the emperor had moral, religious, and political authority. When the West was collapsing at the end of the 5th century, the Church evangelized the barbarians and thus created the post-Roman world of the Middle Ages. Meanwhile, the East survived as the Byzantine Empire until the 15th century. The four eastern patriarchs allied themselves with the Imperial power and suffered its misfortunes along with its rewards.

Roots of the East

Several great men guided the East in the early centuries, including St. Athanasius (see Chapter 6). Another was St. Basil the Great (A.D. 330–379), one of the fathers of Eastern monasticism. Born into a saintly family in Cappadocia, St. Basil and his brother, St. Gregory of Nissa, and a third

St. Basil the Great, monk and bishop of the early Church in Asia Minor; St. Basil is especially venerated among eastern Catholics. This is an 18th century painting, now in the Dominican monastery in Dubrovnik.

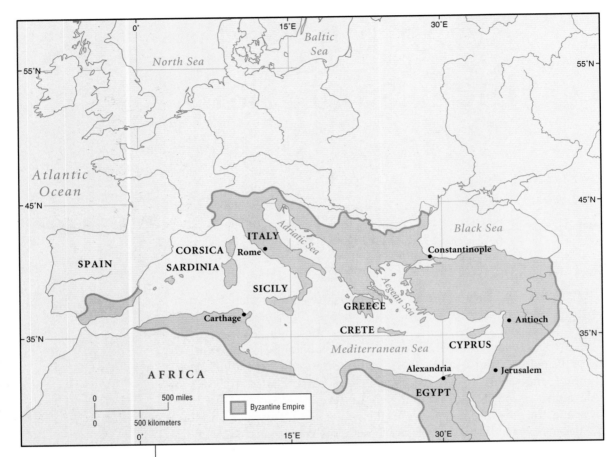

Map of the eastern Roman Empire in the 500s showing Constantinople and the three ancient patriarchal cities of the east: Jerusalem, Antioch, and Alexandria.

Arianism: The heresy that denied the full divinity of Christ.

man, St. Gregory of Nazianzus, joined together to form a monastic community in northeast Asia Minor. Known as the Cappadocian Fathers, these three created the rule followed by later Eastern monasteries.

After a few years of living as a monk St. Basil was summoned home by his bishop, who ordained him in 364. St. Basil was made bishop of Caesarea of Cappadocia in 370. At this time, **Arianism** had split the Eastern Church. (Arianism was the heresy that said that Christ was not divine. This heresy troubled the West in the fifth and sixth centuries when the Arian Goths and Vandals invaded.)

The orthodox St. Basil was soon battling with the emperor Valens, who was an Arian. St. Basil resisted Valens' bribes and threats and remained an orthodox Christian. Meanwhile, the saint's popularity soared. St. Basil was noted for his love for the poor, to whom he gave clothes, food, education, and medical care.

A huge crowd mourned St. Basil's death in 379. Two years later his orthodoxy was confirmed at the Council of Constantinople, where the Nicene Creed affirmed belief in Christ's divinity.

St. John Chrysostom

The East also produced one of the world's greatest preachers, who earned the nickname "Chrysostom," or "golden mouth." St. John Chrysostom (A.D. 550–407) was born in the Christian center of Antioch and raised by his widowed mother, a Christian. St. John was so gifted that he even stopped a widespread panic, saving many lives. In A.D. 387 riots broke out when Emperor Theodosius passed a new tax, and the angry people stormed through the city, damaging the statues of the emperor and his family. When order was restored and the people awaited in terror the punishment of the emperor, St. John calmed them with his sermons "On the Statues," producing a "silence…as deep as though not a single person was present." Eventually through the intercession of the bishop, the people won pardon from the emperor.

St. John Chrysostom, 4th-century bishop of Constantinople, from a 19th-century mosaic by Edward Burne-Jones.

St. John Chrysostom was named Bishop of Constantinople, and his troubles with the Eastern Empire began. His ascetic ways, his harsh discipline, and his attempts to reform the comfortable clergy made him an enemy of the Empress Eudoxia and some Church leaders. He was deposed by a synod of Eastern bishops and then exiled by Eudoxia's husband, Emperor Arcadius. Days later, fearing a popular uprising, the emperor allowed St. John to return.

St. John Chrysostom remained officially deposed, but he defied the order and still acted as bishop. The Emperor Arcadius was furious. In A.D. 404 the emperor's soldiers stormed an Easter Mass and killed worshippers and those being baptized. St. John again was exiled. Driven off to the Armenian mountains, set upon by countryside marauders, and in poor health, he nevertheless continued to minister, writing more than 230 letters and welcoming the numerous Christians who traveled to see him. In 407 he was ordered to a more remote location. St. John died en route, in the city of Pontus.

Justinian the Great, emperor of the Byzantine Empire, shown in an ancient mosaic from the walls of San Vitale, a church in Ravenna, Italy.

History of the Byzantines

The Byzantine Empire—also called the Eastern Roman Empire, or the Greek Empire—was officially born in A.D. 395. That year Emperor Theodosius (the one who made Christianity the national religion of Rome) died, leaving the leadership of Rome to his two sons: Arcadius and Honorius. Arcadius ruled the Eastern half from the capital of Constantinople. His lands included: Syria, Asia Minor, Pontus, Egypt, Thrace (Bulgaria), Greece, Macedonia, and Crete. The other son, Honorius, ruled the empire to the west from Rome.

The greatest emperor of the East was Justinian, who reigned from 527 to 565. His mighty army recovered lands in North Africa, the Balkans, Italy, and southern Spain. Justinian sought to unite his empire with a massive reform of the Roman laws called the *Corpus Juris Civilis*, or Code of Civil Law, based on the principles of Roman law and Christian teaching. This codebook became the foundation for the laws of the European countries to come.

Another of his accomplishments was the rebuilding of the late Constantine's magnificent cathedral, the Hagia Sophia, which had been destroyed during a political revolt in Constantinople in 530. Justinian hired two prominent architects who created a design that took 10,000 workers and five years to complete. The new church featured exquisite mosaics and soaring domes, which would be imitated in churches throughout Europe.

Justinian's wife, Theodora, was a clever and brazen woman. When Justinian met her, he was a senator and she was an actress in the city cir-

The ancient Cathedral of the Divine Wisdom (Hagia Sophia in Greek) as it stands today in Istanbul, Turkey. Built in the 6th century, it was converted into a mosque by Muslim conquerors.

Theodora, co-ruler with Justinian of the Byzantine Empire, shown with her court. From a mosaic created in the 6th century.

cus, the Hippodrome, where her father was the bear-keeper. Justinian himself had arrived in Constantinople as a poor Christian peasant boy sometime around 500, but rose to power under his uncle, who became Emperor Justin I. Justinian appealed to his uncle to change the law that forbade the marriage of a senator to an actress, and Justinian and Theodora were married in 523. Four years later Justin I died, and Justinian and Theodora were crowned emperor and empress.

Justinian gave his empress her own palace and great authority. Theodora was known to be cruel to her enemies, but she was also politically prudent in ways that Justinian was not. When a riot turned into a revolt, threatening to overwhelm the royal couple, she refused the leave the palace and said she would rather be buried an empress than a commoner. She thus encouraged Justinian to remain, and when his soldiers went out again to stop the revolt, they succeeded.

After Justinian's death, the prosperity and stability of the empire suffered from constant uprisings of the Lombards in Italy, the Visigoths in Spain, and the Persians in Syria, Palestine, and Egypt. In 627 Emperor Heraclius stopped the Persians before they reached Constantinople. He reestablished the seat of the empire, but the show of strength was short-lived. In another 100 years the Islamic invasion dealt the Byzantine Empire an even harder blow.

Muhammad and the Muslims

The Story of Muhammad

Mecca: The central holy city of the Muslim religion and the destination of Islamic pilgrims.

In the year A.D. 570, a boy named Kuthon ibn Abdallah was born to a poor but respectable family in **Mecca**, in the land of Arabia, the large southwestern peninsula of Asia between the Red Sea and the Persian Gulf. The story is that when the baby boy was presented to his family, his grandfather called him "Muhammad," which means "praised." From that time on, the boy was known by that name, although its meaning would not be realized until many years later. More than any other individual, Muhammad would change the history of his desert homeland.

The Legend of the Kaaba

The story of Abraham from the Old Testament more or less makes up the first part of the story of the Arabian people. According to the Old Testament book of Genesis, Sarah could not believe she would conceive a child in her old age. So she allowed her Egyptian slave Hagar to behave as a wife to Abram, and Hagar became pregnant and bore him a son, Ishmael. After God made a covenant with Abram and changed his name to Abraham, Sarah became pregnant and gave birth to Isaac. Sarah was alarmed that her son, being the second born to Abraham, would have to share the inheritance with Ishmael; Abraham was caught in the middle, because he loved both sons. But God told Abraham: "Heed the demands of Sarah, no matter what she is asking of you; for it is through Isaac that descendants shall bear your name. As for the son of the slave woman, I will make a great nation of him also, since he too is your offspring" (Gen. 21:12–13). Abraham sent Hagar and Ishmael away into the wilderness with bread and a skin of water. After wandering far into the desert, the mother and child ran out of water, and the boy began to weep from thirst. God took pity on them and opened in the desert a well of fresh water, from which they drank. *(Up to this point, the stories are the same for both religions; the Arabian legend continues the story in this way)*: Abraham heard of the miracle and came at once to build a temple near the well, called the Kaaba, in which he placed a black stone he received from his father, a stone that was said to have come originally from the Garden of Eden, where God had given it to Adam. Hagar and Ishmael made their home near the Kaaba, and many years and descendants later, a city grew up around the temple and the miraculous well. This city was Mecca, the holiest of cities for the descendants of Ishmael, the Arabs.

Abraham sends away Hagar and Ishmael.

Muhammad lost both parents when he was still very young. Muhammad's father died before the boy was born, and his mother died when he was six. The orphan was taken in by his grandfather for two years, and then went to live with his uncle, Abu Talib. Muhammad grew to be a hard and honest worker. As a boy he tended sheep, and as a young man he drove the camels that traveled in caravans carrying Arabian goods to be sold throughout the Byzantine Empire.

Muhammad's skill and reputation grew so that a wealthy widow, Kadijah, hired him to lead her caravans. She was impressed with his looks and natural leadership. Kadijah was 40 years old and had three children. Yet she sent a servant to ask the 25-year-old Muhammad if he would marry her, and he agreed. They lived happily together for the next 15 years, raising children and becoming wealthy merchants in Mecca.

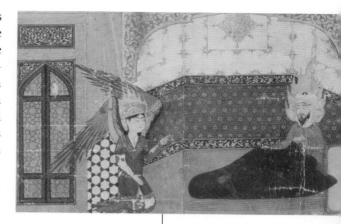

Muslim image showing how Muhammad received the Qur'an from heavenly messengers.

But Muhammed became dissatisfied. While traveling in caravans and mingling in the marketplaces, he had learned the teachings of the Jews and the Christians. Their morality contrasted with the wickedness of his Arab brothers. The Arabs had remained pagan, worshipping idols at Mecca and

Each year millions of Muslims from all over the world visit Mecca, where they perform a prayer ritual centered on the Kaaba, a draped, cube-shaped stone building in the courtyard of the great mosque. The Kaaba still contains the black stone, believed by scientists to be a meteorite.

Muslim pilgrims gather around the Kaaba (the black cube in the middle) to perform Friday dawn prayers at the Grand Mosque in Mecca, Saudi Arabia.

As in Jewish prayer, Muslim men worship separately from women.

other holy sites, or had abandoned religion altogether, taking up gambling, drinking, mistreating their wives, and other abuses. He felt a spiritual restlessness among his people, and he believed they needed a leader, a prophet, to steer them toward the truth.

Muhammad began to spend hours secluded in a cave on the mountain of Hira to pray and meditate about these concerns. One evening he reported an uncanny experience. While he was in prayer, he heard bells and then a loud voice commanding, "Read!" When the startled Muhammad replied that he could not read, the voice recited some words, which then appeared on a flaming scroll that Muhammad, though illiterate, was able to read. Shaken, he stepped outside the cave, where a brilliant angelic form appeared above him and identified himself as the angel Gabriel.

Muhammad said later that he was so terrified he thought he was losing his mind. He ran down the mountain and home to his wife to tell her what had happened. Kadijah believed the experience was real, as did a wise Christian woman of the city to whom she related the story. She encouraged Muhammad to return to the site and continue to pray. For two years Muhammad heard nothing more from God (Allah in Arabic), but just as he was about to lose hope, he again experienced what he believed were further revelations from Allah. The visitations were traumatic for him, causing him to sweat, sometimes faint, or even go into convulsions.

In A.D. 613, three years after Muhammad's first encounter, he began to preach publicly, gathering a few followers—mostly family members—and many critics. At first his message was simple monotheism: "There is no God but Allah, and Muhammad is his prophet." The Arabs knew Allah as one of the pagan gods; now Muhammad proclaimed Allah as the only God. Muhammad preached a basic morality, encouraging his listeners to give up idolatry, lying, stealing, and drunkenness.

Christianity considers Muhammad's religion to be heretical. Over time Muhammad created a new religion by combining elements from different religions—mainly Judaism and Christianity—with his own imagination. With regard to Judaism, Muhammad saw himself as the last prophet, on the order of Isaiah, Jeremiah, and Ezekiel. Drawing from the Christians, Muhammad taught that charity toward the poor and weak was required for holy living. He also promoted his favorite ideas of reform. For example, he allowed his followers to continue the Arabian practice of polygamy, the taking of multiple wives, but no more than four at any one time and suggested that they be treated equally. But, he exempted himself from his own rules and had many more than four wives. Muhammad called the new religion Islam, meaning "submission to Allah," and its followers Muslims, or "true believers," literally, "those who submit." Submission here means abject and total surrender, as to a conqueror.

In A.D. 622, the leaders of Mecca feared the growing power of Muhammad and his followers, so they plotted to kill Muhammad. Learning of the plot, the prophet fled by camel; this night flight, the *Hegira*, is marked as the most important date in the Islamic calendar. In the same way Christians mark time, according to the birth of Christ, the Muslims calculate time from A.H., *Anno Hegira*, the Year of the Flight.

Muhammad arrived safely in Yathrib, and from that time the city became known as Medina, the City of the Prophet. No longer the humble and ridiculed preacher of Mecca, Muhammad soon established himself as supreme ruler of Medina. His authority was not just political but social and religious as well. His laws, some of which were borrowed from Christianity, demanded care for the poor and orphaned, forbade the practice of killing unwanted babies, placed a ban on drinking alcohol, and ordered an annual month-long fast (Ramadan).

From his position of civic leadership, Muhammad now took a different approach to spreading his religion. He decided that the best way to unite the Arab world in the belief of Islam was by war, or more precisely by a **jihad**—a holy war. To fund his army, the prophet-turned-warrior-king used his knowledge of trade routes from his days of driving camels. Muhammad and his men raided goods from traveling caravans, and from the loot obtained by their plundering, they could afford to challenge Mecca in a series of skirmishes.

In A.D. 630, Muhammad's army finally attacked Mecca, but they met no resistance. The outnumbered Meccans simply surrendered. Crying "Allahu Akbar!" ("God is most great!"), Muhammad rode into the courtyard of the **Kaaba** shrine, placed his hands on the black stone, and ordered that the stone idols of the shrine be destroyed. Since then, the Kaaba has been the

Saved by the Web

One legend tells how Allah intervened to protect Muhammad. When the prophet and his friend Abu-Bakr first left the city they hid in a cave, where they remained for three days. Immediately after they entered the cave, a spider appeared and began weaving a web across the entrance. When the Meccan soldiers came upon the cave, they decided no one could have entered it and left the web intact, so they went on.

Hegira: The night flight of Muhammad and the date around which the Islamic calendar is centered.
Jihad: A Muslim holy war.
Kaaba: The temple Muslims believe Abraham built and placed a black rock given to Adam from God.

The practice of daily prayer, five times daily, facing the shrine of the Kaaba, dates to the year A.D. 624. When Muhammad first arrived in Medina he yearned to unite Jews and Christians into the religion of Islam, so he had his followers pray while facing the holy city of Jerusalem. Some say that when the Jews resisted his efforts to convert them, he angrily ordered Muslims to face the Kaaba instead. Others say Muhammad had a revelation from God that his followers should face the Kaaba, and it was the Jews who grew angry. In the end, the Muslims drove out two of the three Jewish tribes from Medina and, as a punishment for suspected treason, he executed all 609 men of the third tribe.

spiritual center of Islam, and no statues or pictures, which Muslims consider idols, have been allowed in a place of prayer.

Although he returned once again to Mecca, Muhammad lived in Medina until his death in A.D. 632. By then, Muhammad had acquired four of the ten wives he was to eventually marry. The youngest and most memorable of his wives was just 16 years old. The daughter of his longtime friend Abu-Bakr, Ayesha was six years old when Muhammad married her, though she didn't live with Muhammad until she was nine. According to traditional stories, Ayesha was a strong-willed and spoiled girl. When Muhammad gave her a pearl necklace from a caravan raid, then regretted that he didn't share it with his fellows or even his other wives, Ayesha stubbornly refused to give it back. Legend also has it that she was extremely jealous of the memory of Muhammad's first wife, Kadijah. Yet in the end Muhammad favored Ayesha, and he died with his head in her lap.

The Qur'an

His followers believe that Muhammad received revelations from God for 22 years, beginning in A.D. 610. Muhammad was illiterate, which was not unusual for that time. Instead of writing, he proclaimed his teachings to his followers in the public square, and various believers recorded his words. These sermons, or ***suras***, number 114 and, combined, make up the Qur'an ("Reading"), the holy book of Islam.

Many of the *suras* resemble moral teachings and commandments from the Old or New Testaments. This teaching from the Qur'an on generosity,

Suras: The sermons within the Qur'an.

for example, is familiar to Western readers: "A kind word with forgiveness is better than almsgiving followed by injury. Allah is Absolute, Merciful! " But others simply retell primitive Arabic sayings that call for the brutal killing of opponents. Still others reflect a utopian version of Muhammad's own cultural fantasy. In *sura* 45, heaven is charmingly depicted as a delightful garden in which beautiful maidens who never grow old wait perpetually upon the faithful Muslim men with rich foods and wine.

The Qur'an was first compiled under Abu-Bakr, Muhammad's successor. Abu-Bakr told the scribe Zaid ibn Thabit to collect all the scraps, notes, and remembrances from Muhammad's sayings. Zaid then checked the notes with various believers to agree on what Muhammad actually said. He wrote down the *suras,* organized from longest to shortest, and presented the book to Abu-Bakr.

This copy of the Qur'an was written and illuminated by hand for the Sultan of Morocco in the 18th century.

Yet some problems arose over the meanings of words and the accuracy of the various copies made from the original. Late in life, Zaid was asked by the Caliph Othman (who ruled Islam from A.D. 644 to 656) to oversee a "once and for all" version of the Qur'an. Twelve scholars worked to produce the Qur'an that is used today. The reading *in Arabic* of the Qur'an is considered the only valid one; therefore, the Qur'an has no official translation into other languages.

Beliefs of Islam

Although there are divisions within Islam, Muslims share common beliefs. They believe in God, good and bad angels, the Qur'an, prophets, judgment, and predestination—that is, that God has already determined what will happen to people. (The Shiite sect, however, rejects predestination.) They follow what are called the five pillars.

Belief in one God (Allah). Muslims view the Christian belief in the Trinity (Three Persons in one God) as polytheistic and our sacred Scriptures as corrupted. They believe that Jesus is merely a prophet and not the Son of God. They claim Muhammad is the greatest of the prophets, greater than the "prophet Jesus."

What Do Christians Today Think about Islam?

Along with Judaism and Christianity, Islam is one of the world's three great religions. As a monotheistic religion with a heritage traced to Abraham, Islam shares some beliefs and history with Judaism and Christianity. Muslims also are to be admired for a serious moral code, for their anti-abortion stance, their frequent and reverent prayerfulness, charity, and humility before God. There are, however, some serious differences in theology and practice. Islam is not a sacramental religion and has no priests. There are no sacraments and no magisterium and no tradition of saints. There is also a higher regard for women within Christianity. Christians venerate Mary, who is the model for all Christian women. Islamic women have nothing that resembles the status of Mary as the Mother of God and as the First Apostle, though Mary is highly praised by Muhammad in the Qur'an as a righteous woman. Islam encourages a warlike spirit, and recommends conversion at the point of the sword through Holy War. Christendom has had to fight off Muslim invasion time and time again, as late as A.D. 1688. The new militancy of Islam throws our theological differences into ever sharper relief.

Prayer five times a day. Prayer can be done anywhere and in private, although prayer in an assembly is desirable. Muhammad did not like bells, but a caller, or *muezzin*, a man who calls the faithful to prayer. When Muslims pray, they adopt special postures, including kneeling, and they face Mecca, or more precisely, the Kaaba shrine.

Almsgiving, or giving to the poor, is necessary for salvation.

Fast of Ramadan. In remembrance of Muhammad's original revelations, Muslims fast from pleasures, including food and drink, from sunrise to sunset, every day for one month, during the ninth month of the Muslim year.

Pilgrimage to Mecca is required once during a person's lifetime. Only Muslims may enter the city of Mecca.

Spread of Islam

Caliph: A successor of Muhammad.

After Muhammad's death, his friend Abu-Bakr was elected the first **caliph**, or "successor." Although the majority in both Mecca and Medina accepted his leadership, some tribes rebelled, and the new caliph fought them for

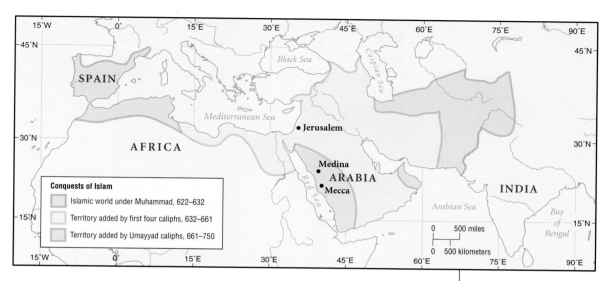

two years to bring them into unity with the others. Abu-Bakr then attacked neighboring Persia (modern-day Iran), and under the command of the Qur'an to "make war on the infidels" (unbelievers), called for a jihad. The "infidels" were the Christians.

The Dome of the Rock

One of the distinctive landmarks of the Jerusalem skyline is the Dome of the Rock, an Islamic mosque built on the site of the former temples of Solomon and Herod the Great. When the Muslims conquered the city in 638, Caliph Omar himself helped clean up the site, which had been for years a city dump. In 691 the famous mosque was completed. The limestone rock sheltered within the mosque has special religious significance for Muslims. They believe, for example, that the rock was where Abraham nearly sacrificed Isaac, as well as a place of prayer for all the great prophets and where Muhammad ascended to and returned from heaven.

Upon his death, Abu-Bakr was succeeded by Omar, a popular military leader. From A.D. 634 to 644, the Muslim army continued its takeover of Persia then moved west to conquer Egypt and Syria. The city of Jerusalem was occupied in A.D. 638 and has remained a Muslim stronghold ever since, except for one century during the Christian Crusades.

Murdered by a vengeful Persian slave, Omar was succeeded by Othman, who was slain by soldiers who resented his favoritism of his relatives. The fourth caliph was Ali, a relative of Muhammad, who at the age of 12 had been the first male to accept the teaching. In 661, a member of the new and strict sect, the Kharijites, assassinated Ali. The violent deaths of their leaders and the civil division of Islam did not stop the Muslims. The Islamic invasion continued into the 8th century. From Persia the armies moved east into Sind (today's Pakistan). To the west they conquered the rest of North Africa, and to the north, they battered the weakened Byzantine Empire and almost seized Constantinople. The Islamic conquerors took over and continued the Byzantine civilization of their conquered lands. They substituted Muslim ideals and Muslim law for Christian ones, but respected the ancient Greco-Roman heritage and learning, and merely added Arabic language and customs to the already civilized life of their new empire. The Islamic Middle East kept the Byzantine civilization of the once-Christian lands and allowed it to continue and grow, without its Christian direction.

In 711, the Arabs crossed the Straits of Gibraltar from Morocco in North Africa and advanced into Spain. From there the armies crossed the Pyrenees Mountains into France, but in one of the most decisive battles in history, the Muslims were halted near Tours, 150 miles from Paris, by the Frankish leader Charles Martel. If the Muslims had won, it is likely they would have overrun Europe, replacing Christianity as the formative religion of the West.

By the 9th century, the Muslim Arabs had expanded their conquests into India, western China, and the Malaysian and Indonesian islands. In a little more than 100 years after the death of its founder, Islam covered half the known world and seriously threatened Christendom with violent warfare.

Why was Islam so successful? For the Arabs, the Muslim religion provided a strong national identity, especially in the way it tied ancient Arab history to the creation of the world and the great patriarch of faith, Abraham. Secondly, and most importantly, the victory of Islam was a military feat. Each success gave momentum for future success, and seemed to prove that God was indeed with Islam. Muslim soldiers were emboldened

Charles Martel in the Battle of Tours.

The King Who Saved Christian Europe

Charles Martel (688–741) was ruler of all the Franks. His quick and effective military style earned him the nickname "the Hammer." After a series of battles against neighboring tribes from Germany, he took on the Spanish Muslims (sometimes called the Saracens) who had moved into southern Frankish territories and were approaching Tours, a city on the Loire River. Charles' army met the invaders near the town of Poitiers. In the great battle that ensued, the Muslim leader of Spain, Abd-er-Rahman, was killed, and the invaders fled in the night. In 739, the Muslims advanced again into the Burgundy region up to Lyons, but, once again, Charles drove them out of the kingdom, this time for good.

by religious passion. "Allah is with us!" they cried, as they rode into foreign lands. For them even failure meant success; their religion promised that a soldier's reward for death in a holy war was heavenly bliss. Also, unlike Christianity or Judaism, Islam was not difficult. Nobody had to interpret the faith in their daily lives. There were no mysteries, nothing beyond human understanding. It was a simple religion of clear rules for personal conduct and religious observance.

When the Muslims conquered a land, they did not at first force their Islamic religion upon their subjects, although they did charge a heavy tax to non-Muslims, a payment for tolerance of religious diversity! Many people found it helpful to convert. The social and political atmosphere strongly favored Islam, and few, in the heresy-torn Christian lands, were able to resist that force.

Islam's Golden Age

Through the years different Islamic clans held the caliphate. In 750 the Abbasids took it by revolt and held it for 500 years. This age, particularly the 9th through 11th centuries, marked the peak of Islamic civilization. It was a time when European culture was dormant except for the work of the monks. With an empire stretching from Morocco to India, a standing army to control the trade routes, a strong agricultural economy, and tax revenue from conquered peoples, the caliphs had the stability and wealth to encourage culture. In 762, the Caliph Al-Mansur moved the capital to Baghdad, a new city he built on the Tigris River atop the ruins of an ancient Babylonian city. Drawing on Byzantine civilization's architecture and engineering, Baghdad became one of the grandest cities of the medieval world and the center of the empire's advances in literature, mathematics, astronomy, medicine, art, and architecture.

One of the most famous writings from this period is *The Thousand and One Nights*, better known as *The Arabian Nights*, a collection of some 200 stories including "Aladdin and the Lamp," "The Flying Carpet," "Sinbad the Sailor," and "Ali Baba and the Forty Thieves." The actual origin of the stories is unknown; they were based on folk tales gathered from throughout the East. The setting of the stories is a desperate tactic of a clever young woman to save her life.

Another kind of literature that thrived under the Islamic Empire was poetry, long appreciated in the Arab culture. Poets were considered either gifted or even possessed by genies, or powerful spirits. Around the 11th or

Omar Khayyám's poetry
(translated by Edward FitzGerald)

On our powerlessness over time:
The moving finger writes, and having writ
Moves on; Nor all your piety nor wit
Shall lure it back to cancel half a line
Nor all your tears wash out a word of it.

On the joys of romantic love:
A book of verses underneath the bough,
A jug of wine, a loaf of bread—and thou
Beside me singing in the wilderness—
Oh, wilderness were paradise enow!

Scheherazade and the *Arabian Nights*

Once upon a time there was a wealthy king who ruled over Arabia, called King Schariar. All was well in the kingdom until he made a terrible discovery. The wife whom he loved and trusted had betrayed him. Shocked and broken-hearted, he immediately ordered her execution. Yet this was not enough to erase his bitterness. He decided no woman could be trusted and so all would be punished. Each day he would marry one of the young women of the kingdom, and the following morning he would have his new bride killed. The terrible executions took place day after day, as family after family sorrowfully gave up their daughters to the bloodthirsty king. The grand vizier, second in command over the kingdom, did his best to shield his own daughters from their sure fate. One day, his wise and beautiful eldest daughter, Scheherazade (pronounced Sha-Hare-a-ZAHD), volunteered to be the next bride. The vizier tried to talk her out of it, but she persisted. "Do not fear, father, for I have a plan," she told him. "If I succeed, I shall save not only my life but that of the other maidens in the kingdom." To carry out her plan she asked that her younger sister, Dunyazade, be allowed to spend the night in the palace. The vizier reluctantly agreed.

The wedding took place, and late that night Dunyazade entered the royal chamber. "What is it?" King Schariar demanded. "Oh my king," began the girl, "all my life my sister has entertained our family with the most wonderful stories. Knowing that in the morning

"The Flying Trunk" scene from the *Arabian Nights*, Hans Christian Andersen's version of the ancient and anonymous tales.

she will be killed, I would like to ask her to tell one more tale, so that I might remember her by it." The king agreed, and Scheherazade began her tale.

The young woman's deep brown eyes shone with wonder and her hands danced as she transported the king to a magical world of a poor boy, a lamp, and a powerful genie. Through the night her melodious voice filled the room with fantastic adventures. She told of grand palaces, jewels beyond counting, carpets lifting into the air, evil magicians, and beautiful princesses. The king, his imagination utterly seized, drank in every word. When the first light edged through the curtain of the royal chamber, Scheherazade suddenly stopped, midsentence. "What?" said the king. "Don't stop now! What happens next?"

"I must end the story," the clever Scheherazade said with a sad voice. "The dawn is here, and with that, my execution."

"No, no!" he replied. "You must go on and finish the tale tonight. I can put off your execution until tomorrow."

And so that night she picked up the story where she had left off, but again the next morning she stopped in the middle of another even more exciting adventure. The king had to hear the end of it too. So once again, he postponed her execution.

The stories continued this way night after night, and lasted for 1,001 nights. By then, Scheherazade had won the heart of the king, who regretted his evil deeds and grew to love his wise and good bride. Scheherazade was allowed to live, and so, too, did her tales, known as *The Thousand and One Nights*.

One of the most famous Islamic physicians was Ibn Sina, born in A.D. 980 and known in Europe as Avicenna. His masterwork was a five-volume medical encyclopedia titled the *Canon of Medicine,* which translated the Greek medical writings, but also organized and summarized all medical knowledge up to his own time. The *Canon* was the main textbook for medical students in the Near East and Europe for centuries. Ibn Sina was also a prominent philosopher, the "prince of philosophers," who led the Islamic revival of the Greek classical thinkers, especially Aristotle.

12th centuries, Omar Khayyam wrote some of the greatest poetry. A Persian astronomer and one of the leading mathematicians of his day, he is best known as the author of the *Rubaiyat,* Arabic for "quatrain," or four-line poetry. The West came to know Khayyam's poetry in the 19th century, when the English writer Edward FitzGerald gave a rhymed translation of 100 of the 1,000 quatrains

Khayyam was also an expert in a form of mathematics known as algebra, from the Arabic *al-jabr,* which means "re-joining." Algebra uses symbols—usually letters of the alphabet—in place of numbers in mathematical operations. During the 9th century, Arab mathematician Muhammad ibn Musa al-Khwarizmi further developed algebra, which had first been invented in A.D. 280 by a Greek mathematician, Diophantus of Alexandria. Translations of al-Khwarizmi's work brought algebra to Christian Europe in the 12th century. Al-Khwarizmi also popularized the use of zero in mathematics. His name gave us the word "algorithm." The English word "cipher," which means "zero," comes from the Arabic *sifr,* or "empty."

Medicine, too, advanced during this period. From the study of the Greeks and their own experimentation, Muslim surgeons knew how to remove diseased tissue, amputate limbs, and even remove cataracts from the eye. They cauterized wounds, which means applying heat or chemicals to stop bleeding. The Arabs were advanced in dental health as well, and emphasized cleaning teeth with powders or rinses applied with a softened stick, perhaps the world's first toothbrush.

The Islamic contribution to art was unique. Unlike the Greeks and Romans with their realistic sculptures, and the Europeans of the Middle Ages with their portraits of saints, the Muslims believed creating art in the

Carved woodwork decorates the walls of a Muslim school, using Arabic script and intricately carved patterns to avoid creating images. At the Bou Inania Medrassa, in Fez, Morocco.

likeness of a person was offensive to God. Therefore, images of Muhammad and other people can be found, but never displayed in mosques. All depictions of Muhammad himself are recognizable by the absence of a face; he is always shown with no human features, a blank.

Islamic religious art consisted of calligraphy, or beautiful writing, colorful geometric designs, and abstract mosaics. In place of religious statues, the Muslims excelled in the creation of elaborate rugs and other decorative crafts. They also developed a grand and distinctive form of architecture, of which the Alhambra in Granada, Spain, is a majestic and stunning example.

The Islamic world borrowed from and carried forward the forms and learning of Byzantine civilization to a golden age of Islamic civilization in the 12th century. Then, the ideas of the greatest Muslim philosophers seemed to the religious authorities to be losing the path of Muhammad, leaving the way of true believers. *Sharia* law, Muslim religious law, was used to stifle further development and it progressed no

A patio of the Alhambra of Granada in Spain, built in A.D. 1350.

further in any area. Western science, technology, arts, and political freedom passed it by. The Islamic countries remained essentially unchanged, both as a culture and a civilization, from late antiquity until they met the modern European countries in the 19th century.

Chapter 7 Review

Let's Remember   Write your answer in a single complete sentence.
1. What was the name of the great Byzantine preacher whose name meant "golden mouth"?
2. What is another name for the Byzantine Empire?
3. What is contained in the Kaaba in Mecca where Muslims from all over the world come to pray?
4. How do Muslims calculate time?
5. What is the name of the book that records the sayings of Muhammad?
6. What are the five pillars of Islam?

Let's Consider   For silent thinking and a short essay, or for thinking in a group with classroom discussion:
1. How much of the early Christian world was lost to the conquering Muslims?
2. Why did Islamic culture stop growing and developing after its "golden age"?
3. Why did the Muslim religion and culture spread so rapidly?
4. What is the status of women and children in a polygamous society?
5. Why did tolerance became a quality of the West?

Let's Eat!

By Muslim law, alcohol—wine—was not to be drunk, so the Muslims developed coffee to drink instead. The name coffee, however, means wine, even though it is not wine. Turkish coffee is very stong and sweet, almost a hot, black syrup.

Chapter 8 # Europe: The Middle Ages

The Middle Ages (approximately A.D. 500–1453) was the age of castles and kings, knights in armor, monks and cloisters, ballads and romance, poets and pilgrims, crusaders and saints. It was a time of the Church as a world power, and of a little poor man, called St. Francis of Assisi. Although superstition and ignorance were widespread, these centuries were illuminated by soaring intellects: John Duns Scotus, Abelard, St. Albert the Great, and St. Thomas Aquinas among the educated. Midway between the classical age of Greece and Rome and the classical revival, known as the **Renaissance**, stand these Middle Ages, a unique and formative period in Western civilization.

> **Renaissance**: A rebirth, or revival, of artistic and intellectual activity.

The Dark Ages (A.D. 500–1000)

The beginning of the Middle Ages is called the Dark Ages. The Dark Ages were so called because little was known about them. The unity, organization, government, education, and high culture of the Roman Empire had been disrupted and lost. Even though the memory of such institutions was kept quietly alive in the monasteries, the marks of civilization themselves had all but disappeared by the 6th century.

But these 500 years produced, under the leadership of the Church, a new civilization with a distinctly Christian culture. We call it Christendom.

This era also gave birth to **capitalism**, an economy based on the free exchange of goods and services that has lasted to the present day; and it gave us political organizations of national assemblies and parliaments.

> **Capitalism**: an economic system characterized by the private ownership of property and the free exchange of goods and services in a competitive marketplace.

Feudalism: A political system in which a vassal works for a lord in exchange for land and protection.
Chivalry: The moral code of conduct of knights.

The political and social chaos of this period brought about **feudalism** as a political system, with its moral code, known as **chivalry**.

Even more amazing, the entire continent of Europe, a huge mix of clans and loyalties, was united in faith because of the missionary zeal of great and heroic saints.

Charlemagne of France, Emperor of the West (742–814)

Charlemagne was the king of the Franks and ruler of the largest and most powerful realm in Europe. Idealized in legends and in portraits as a giant of a man with flowing blond hair, he was, in fact, large and strong, but not especially tall; and his hair was more auburn than blonde. His large eyes were striking, and he spoke clearly and intelligently. Charlemagne was a prayerful and devoted Christian and generous to the poor. He wanted to bring his people back to the peace and prosperity of the Roman past. He loved his children and kept them near him even when they were grown.

In 771, Charlemagne had to intervene to protect Rome from a Lombard invasion. Defeating Desiderius, the Lombard king, Charlemagne became king of the Lombards and extended his empire further by adding Lombardy (northern Italy) to Frankish Gaul and Germany.

For the next 33 years Charlemagne fought the Saxons, a pagan Germanic tribe in the northeast, until their defeat in 804. He thus added to his kingdom most of modern-day Germany. Meanwhile, he expanded his empire in every other direction—east to Austria, the modern Czech Republic and Hungary; northwest into Brittany, the northwest French peninsula between the English Channel and the Bay of Biscay; southwest into Spain; and south into Italy as far as Rome.

The tribe of the Goths made this statue of Charlemagne to hold relics of his body for veneration. Created sometime after A.D. 1349.

Charlemagne Christianized what he conquered . Mostly this was easy because the monks and missionaries had been busy evangelizing the West. Charlemagne, a guardian of the Christian faith, believed religious unity was necessary for political unity in his young empire.

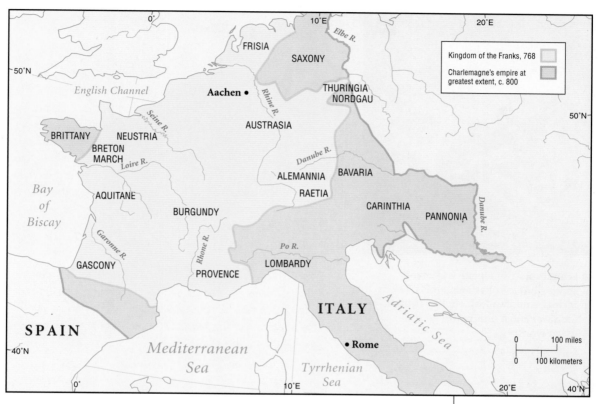

Map showing the development and extent of Charlemagne's Empire.

But some of the conquered pagans, notably the Saxons, stubbornly resisted conversion. So in 786 Charlemagne ordered the beheading of 4,500 Saxons who refused to be baptized. This was a terrible deed—the worst of his otherwise noble reign—and it resulted in a war of nearly 20 years until the Saxons' final defeat.

Charlemagne's legacy was not just military but civic. He ushered in a period of cultural revival that would later be called the Carolingian Renaissance. Eager to restore education to the West, the king invited scholars to his palace in Aachen, where lively discussions were held on classical subjects such as mathematics, rhetoric, and astronomy. Charlemagne himself learned to speak Latin and to read Greek, and he encouraged literacy among all his subjects.

A scene from the legend of Roland, who was one of Charlegmagne's 12 principal commanders. He lies dying after an ambush and battle with Muslim warriors.

The Song of Roland

One of the popular medieval epic poems based on the exploits of Charlemagne is *The Song of Roland*, a romantic tale of a brave nobleman and nephew of Charlemagne who was betrayed by his stepfather, Ganelon. Lured by the jealous Ganelon into a surprise ambush of Muslim warriors in Spain, Roland and his faithful friend Oliver found their company greatly outnumbered. The Franks fought bravely, but their defeat was sure. At length Roland blew a horn to summon the help of his king. When Charlemagne first heard the blasts of his horn, Ganelon, who was at his side, tried to convince the king it could not be Roland. But when the blares of the horn grew quiet, Charlemagne understood what had happened, and he hurried his army to the rescue.

He arrived too late. Oliver had been killed, and Roland, after mourning his friend like a brother, likewise fell. As he died, Roland prayed to God to take his soul. While Charlemagne's troops pursued the Muslims, the king found his dead nephew on the battlefield, and he tore his beard with grief.

The Holy Roman Empire

Tribunal: A court of justice.

In 800 Charlemagne's leadership of a Christian world was formalized. After enemies in Rome had driven Pope St. Leo III out of the city, Charlemagne gave the pope refuge and later was judge of a **tribunal** which ruled that Leo was in the right. On Christmas Day, the pope returned the favor. He crowned Charlemagne emperor of a new entity: the Holy Roman Empire.

Though Charlemagne was said to be surprised and unhappy with the crowning, he accepted it and ruled for 14 more years; upon his death he handed over the empire to his one surviving son, Louis the Pious. Called "the Pious" for his high moral standards and generosity to the Church, Louis did not have the authority of his father, and in 840 he gave up the throne. His four sons fought over the empire and after a battle in which one was killed, the remaining three—Charles, Louis, and Lothair—signed the Treaty of Verdun in 843 that divided the empire into three parts.

Charles's region would become France, and Louis's would be the future Germany. Between the two regions and extending south into Italy, the ancestral homeland of the Franks along the Rhine River and the imperial lands of Lombardy and Rome, was the share given to the eldest brother, Lothair, who was to be called the emperor. The three regions would continue to call themselves the Holy Roman Empire. When Lothair died and left no heirs, his land went to Louis. For the remaining years of the Holy Roman Empire, the Germans would attempt to dominate Italy, but without success.

Invasion and Conversion of the Norsemen

From ancient times people had lived along the coasts of the cold northern lands of Scandinavia—Norway, Denmark, and Sweden. By the time of the Middle Ages there were three principal tribes: Norwegians, Danes, and Swedes. They spoke a Germanic language and were related to the tribes that had invaded and conquered the Roman Empire. Together they formed a people called the Norsemen, or

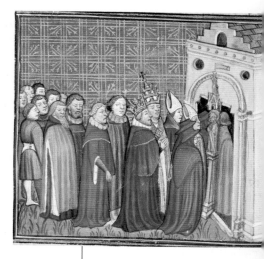

Charlemagne and his court enter in solemn procession to celebrate Mass after his coronation as emperor.

Beowulf: Hero and Epic

The Dark Ages produced a particularly memorable piece of literature, of special interest to English speakers. The epic poem *Beowulf*, which dates to the 8th century, was written in the oldest known form of English, called Old English, or Anglo-Saxon. It is the most important sample of Anglo-Saxon writing, and it is the oldest epic of the Teutonic tribes.

A terrible monster called Grendel, half-man and half-devil, has been terrorizing the Danes. Every night he emerges from his watery lair, crosses the fens (northern Europe swampland), and invades the hall of King Hrothgar. He seizes some thanes (knights) and takes them home to devour them. Beowulf, a prince of the Geats from southern Sweden, gathers some companions and sails across the sea to the rescue.

In a great battle in Hrothgar's hall, Beowulf wrenches Grendel's arm from his socket, and the monster goes away to die. Grendel's mother then comes to the hall to avenge her son's death, and grabs another thane. Beowulf chases her into her sea cave and kills her.

Beowulf sails back home, where he is made king of the Geats. He rules in peace into his old age, when a cup belonging to a dragon is stolen and this dragon begins to destroy the land. Beowulf helps to kill him and then dies of his wounds—a hero to the last.

Northmen—also known as Vikings—who had become skilled seamen, great merchant traders and explorers, and ferocious warriors.

Envying the rich lands and comforts of their southern neighbors, bands of Viking pirates terrorized Europe for 200 years, beginning with their first invasion of England in 787. If the barbarians of the 4th and 5th centuries were cruel, history shows the Vikings to be the most violent and destructive of all—murdering, looting, and burning down churches, monasteries, and entire villages. The fortified castles typical of the Middle Ages were first constructed as a defense against these terrifying invaders.

Within 100 years of their first invasion, the Vikings had taken nearly all of Britain. They posed a constant threat to France as well. Traveling up

To the Ends of the Earth

The Vikings developed the most effective sea vessels of ancient times. The fast-moving longboats enabled them to explore farther than anyone had ever gone. In 870, Vikings traveled northwest to a fertile island they called Iceland. Then in 982 one of the great Viking explorers, Eric the Red, sailed farther west to the icy country he named Greenland, to entice future settlers. In 1000 his son, Leif Eriksson, a convert to Christianity, headed to Greenland to spread the Gospel. Having heard of a land even farther west, he continued to North America, where he was the first to establish a settlement, the settlement of Vinland, named for its grapevines. The exact location of Vinland is unclear—scholars debate whether it was New England or the Labrador coastal region of Canada. We do know that during this era Vikings landed in Newfoundland, Canada, because of a Norse settlement found in 1963 that has been dated to approximately A.D. 1000.

An 8th-century Viking ship leaves its home base at Dawn Ladir Cliffs, Norway, on an expedition to gather slaves and trade goods by plunder.

King Alfred and the Cakes

After a great battle between the Danes and the English, the English army scattered. King Alfred was alone as he fled through the woods. He happened upon the home of a woodcutter, and he asked the woman there to give him something to eat and shelter for the night. Not recognizing the ragged fellow as her king, she agreed to feed him if he would watch the cakes cooking on the hearth.

Alfred meant to watch the cakes, but then his thoughts about the war and his army distracted him. He forgot all about them, until the hut filled with smoke from the burning cakes! The woman came in and yelled at him: "You lazy fellow! See what you have done!" King Alfred missed his supper but not the lesson: You are never too great that you can disregard the little things.

Alfred, King of Wessex, the Saxon king who battled and then converted the Danes who were invading England. Painting by Pierre Duflos, 1780.

rivers in their easily maneuvered longboats, they invaded Paris three times, once with a fleet of 700 ships. They occupied the western coast of Europe, and later sailed to the Mediterranean and made a kingdom in Sicily and southern Italy.

Beginning in the 8th century, groups of Swedish Vikings descended south to Russia (from the word "Rus," which means "Red-haired") and founded Kiev. In 907 the Viking Oleg of Kiev launched a fleet of 2,000 ships against Constantinople. The trade treaty Oleg exacted from the Byzantine emperor made Kiev one of the major commercial centers in the Middle Ages.

But the terrors did not last forever. Over time, the Vikings became Christianized and absorbed into European culture. In Britain, a Saxon king in Wessex resisted the Danish invasion. After constant battles between the Danes and Saxons, the Saxon king, Alfred the Great, worked out an agreement in 878 whereby each would respect his own territories. Part of the bargain was that the Danes would convert to Christianity.

In France, king Charles the Simple made a similar arrangement with the Viking Rollo in 911. Charles's bargain was that if Rollo and his people

Duchy: The territory of a duke or duchess.

would stop their attacks and become Christian, they could have a large northern territory with Rollo as duke. This land became the duchy of Normandy (named for the Norsemen), which developed into the most powerful **duchy** in France. Meanwhile, the Scandinavians of Kiev converted to Christianity under Vladimir in 988.

The Middle Ages (A.D. 1000–1453)

The Great Schism in the Church (1054)

Patriarch: Supreme father of bishops in the Eastern Orthodox Church.

The Muslim invaders eliminated the old Christian centers in Syria, Israel, and Egypt. This was a disastrous loss. The new Arab Empire completely separated the Church in the East from that in the West, and challenged each half in different ways. The East saw one Christian capital after another come under Muslim rule, until only Constantinople and its bishop, called the **Patriarch**, remained. The West, dominated by the Christianized Germans, was able to keep out the Muslims. Now that the East had only one patriarchal see, a new kind of rivalry emerged between Constantinople and Rome.

The two cities, Rome and Constantinople, could not have appeared more different. Rome had been attacked and damaged by so many invaders, and afflicted by plague, famine, and social disorder, that it barely resembled its former grand self. Constantinople, on the other hand, remained a strong and gloriously rich city, crowned by the beautiful cathedral, the Hagia Sophia. Constantinople's glories were among the reasons that Russia chose the Eastern form of Christianity. Eastern clerics looked down on Western churchmen as uneducated and unsophisticated. What could poor, unwashed sons of Germanic barbarians or their vanquished subjects explain to the theologians of Byzantium? And what right had the Pope of Rome—ruler of a bedraggled little ruin of a city and subject to barbarian captors—to command the last free patriarch in the East, heir to the authority of Antioch, Alexandria, and Jerusalem? The Pope in Rome and the Patriarch in Constantinople took opposite sides of a church dispute, each claiming superior authority over the whole church. The patriarch and the pope mutually **excommunicated** one another in 1054.

To Excommunicate: To cut off a person from the sacraments of the Church.

Yet Constantinople and Rome stood alone in defending Europe against its enemies—Islam and the barbarians of north and east. Tragically, the schism of the churches further divided the heirs of the old Roman world and left East and West to fight each alone.

Feudalism

During the Dark Ages there emerged a completely different type of societal organization, called feudalism.

The word "feudal" comes from the Germanic *feod*, which means "fee." The fee was a gift given by a superior or lord to his **vassal**, who was a high-ranking soldier, or knight. In exchange for the fee, the vassal would promise his military service and loyalty to the lord. Sealing this exchange was a solemn contract called a feudal oath.

At first the fee, or **fief**, was a basic provision such as food, clothing, and shelter, or a gift related to warfare, such as a knight's armor or weapons. In later years the fief was a piece of land, and the vassal was not so much a soldier as a nobleman and landowner. As the vassals accumulated lands, they too became lords, exchanging oaths with their own vassals, to whom they distributed portions of their land.

At the bottom of this pyramid was the largest segment of the population, the peasants. Not being knights, they could not make feudal oaths. They lived and worked as **tenant farmers** under the protection and control of their overlords. Some peasants were freemen, but most were serfs, bound by law to the land and the occupation or work of their fathers.

The word **serf** comes from the Latin *servus*, or slave, but a serf was not actually a slave. A serf had to do unpaid work on the lord's land, the manor, and he could not leave the manor without permission. But he had rights; for example, his portion of the land could not be taken from him as long as he did his duty.

An early form of feudalism first existed among the Germanic tribes in the days of Rome. A tribal chieftain

> **Vassal**: A person who has sworn allegiance to a lord.
> **Fief**: A piece of land.
> **Tenant farmer**: A person who lives on and farms land owned by another and who pays rent to the owner of the land.
> **Serf**: Someone who is bound by law to the land and the servile class of his father.

Peasants working on vines.

had around him a special band of soldiers, referred to as *comites*. The *comites* gave the chieftain protection and loyalty and in return received generous rewards from the loot taken in war. (The Latin word *comites* became the French *comte* and the English "count," and gave us the name "county.")

"Equal opportunity," "rags to riches," or "pulling oneself up by the bootstraps" did not exist in the Middle Ages. People's fortunes were determined by their families. If you were of a noble family, you were a noble; if you were born to a serf, then you were a serf.

Two problems prevented feudalism from being a more stable and lasting form of governance. First, because a lord had vassals in his military service, he tended to use them, which meant continual outbreaks of small wars. (Today the word "feud" refers to extended conflicts between families or clans.) Second, vassals began to gather so much land and men that they became more powerful than the king. This is what happened and led to the breakup of the Holy Roman Empire, because Charlemagne's descendants lacked his power and skill to keep the vassals in line.

Knights and the Code of Chivalry

The English word "knight" comes from the Anglo-Saxon *cnecht*, meaning a boy or a personal servant. Knights were actually warriors on horseback, the cavalry of medieval times. To become a knight, a boy from a noble family would begin training as a squire (from the French word for "shield bearer"). A good squire would be knighted at age 21, or sometimes younger, in a religious ceremony. In the ceremony, the bishop would slap the knight on the cheek. In some places today, this tradition is echoed in the Church's Sacrament of Confirmation, when the bishop gently slaps the cheek of the person being confirmed as an awakening to live out the faith.

Early knights wore coats of "mail," small iron rings linked together, and they carried large shields for protection. Full plate armor and smaller shields came into use only in the 15th century. Though the armor looked stiff, a knight could actually move easily because of the links of rings. A knight's chief weapon was the double-

Three knights from the 15th century, displaying different styles of military armor and weapons.

edged sword, but his weapons also included the horse-lance, pointed sword, short ax, mace, and dagger.

Knighthood was not just about warfare, however. Knights swore to live by a moral code known as chivalry (from the French word for knight: *chevalier*). Chivalry is a Christian code of behavior, with both the virtues and the acts of mercy. Under this code a knight devoted himself first of all to God and to defending Christianity; he would be brave, loyal, honest, and merciful to his defeated enemies. Knights were to be kind and gentle to all, especially the weak. They held women in high esteem, protected them, and treated them with great courtesy. Personal integrity and faithfulness to your promises determined "honor," the highest value of chivalry.

The Church in Feudal Society

Churchmen, called "clergy," made up the third class in feudal society, being neither peasants nor nobility. Lower clergy—parish priests and monks—prayed, administered the sacraments, and tended to people's spiritual and temporal needs. They provided education, refuge, and social welfare for the poor. Higher clergy—bishops and abbots—had the status of nobility

The Legend of King Arthur

King Arthur may or may not have lived in history, but he certainly lived in legend in England. His story was told by the Briton tribe (from which we get the name for the island, "Britain"). According to some accounts, Arthur was not born but was mysteriously cast up by the sea. When he became king he gathered pure and noble warriors like himself into a council called the Round Table, where each knight was equal to the other knights. Arthur's enchanted sword, Excalibur, offered special protection to his people. According to legend, Arthur did not actually die, but was miraculously taken to an island to await his future rule of Britain.

King Arthur and his Knights at the Round Table. An early engraving.

The Heroic Hildebrand

One pope who fought against the right of kings to appoint bishops was Pope St. Gregory VII (ruled 1073–1085). Pope Gregory was born with the name Hildebrand in northern Italy in 1020. An educated and pious monk, he served Pope Gregory VI and then Leo IX. As he grew in popularity among the people of Rome, Hildebrand also grew disturbed by the corruption within the Church, with the buying and selling of church offices and the leadership of immoral men. He believed that the main source of the corruption was lay investiture, which was when the emperors and kings, rather than the pope, appointed bishops. When Hildebrand became pope, taking the name Gregory VII, he banned the practice.

This angered the young king of Germany, Henry IV, who depended on the support of the German bishops to keep the nobles in line. If he could no longer reward men with clerical appointments, he could lose power in Germany. So in 1075 the match between pope and king began.

When Henry made a clergy appointment in violation of the order, St. Gregory threatened to excommunicate him. Henry gathered his bishops to file protest, and Henry himself wrote a letter calling St. Gregory a "false monk." St. Gregory then excommunicated Henry and ordered that no one in the kingdom should obey him. The German nobles told Henry that he had to get the ban lifted, or he would be replaced. Henry had no choice but to go to St. Gregory to beg forgiveness.

The nobles at first tried to prevent Henry from meeting with the pope, but in 1077 the king crossed the Alps—the mountains dividing German and Italy—and stood, barefoot and in rags, in the snow outside the castle in the mountains where the pope was staying. Henry waited there for three days until the pope came out, forgave him, and lifted the excommunication.

Henry IV, the German Emperor, doing penance before the door of the pope at Canossa.

and were sometimes made vassals; they protected and administered their land just like any count or baron. Most remained independent, loyal only to God and the pope, but others swore allegiances to counts or kings. This led to divided loyalties, with noblemen claiming the right to name their own men as bishops or abbots, when only the Church had that right. Kings and emperors quarreled with the pope and his representatives over who should "invest," or install a bishop into office. This conflict, called the "**investiture** controversy," lasted for many years in Europe.

From the heart of the Church beat the rhythm of daily, weekly, and yearly life for nobleman and peasant, clergy and king. There was the Sunday Mass each week, and through the year numerous saints days and feast days, sometimes with elaborate processions and, of course, feasting. Popular devotions to Mary and the saints flourished; the rosary, Stations of the Cross, and Passion plays were among the practices born during the Middle Ages.

In an age when most people couldn't read, the story of salvation was told in pictures: stone statues, painted walls in the churches—and beginning in the 12th century, stained glass windows—depicted scenes and figures from the Bible, from Adam and Eve to the Resurrection of Christ. The holy words of Scripture and prayers of the Mass, resounding from the priest's pulpit and the altar, were also memorized. The liturgy itself was a splendor for the senses, with rich and colorful vestments, the smell of incense, the chant of choirs, the sonorous bells calling all to worship. For entertainment, Bible stories were retold in "mystery plays" acted out in the churchyards or on raised platforms in the streets.

Another feature of medieval life was the pilgrimage. People of all classes would leave their homes to travel, usually on foot, to pilgrim sites: Marian shrines, holy wells, and holy cities, such as Rome and Jerusalem. Reaching their destination, the pilgrims would offer prayers of thanksgiving or petition at the tombs of the apostles, or the sites of Jesus' passion, death, and resurrection. The journey itself, usually difficult and dangerous, was an act of faith and penance. Although not at all as hard as medieval travel, modern-day pilgrims still continue this pious tradition, visiting the ancient places as well as more recent shrines commemorating Mary's miraculous appearances in Lourdes, France; Fatima, Portugal; and Mexico City.

Investiture: The act of establishing in office a bishop.

The Angel Gabriel asks Mary to be the Mother of God. From the Life of Christ, Lancet Window at Chartres Cathedral, France; built about A.D. 1150.

The Crusades: "God Wills It!"

From as early as the 3rd century, Christians had been making pilgrimages to the Holy Land. Even after the Muslim occupation in the 7th century, pilgrims were allowed relatively safe passage. But at the dawn of the 11th century, the Seljuk Turks, an Islamic tribe that later founded the Turkish Empire, fought the Byzantines in Asia Minor and seized a large region. They then began a campaign to keep Christians out of Muslim territory. Pilgrims were harassed and killed, which roused the anger of the West against the Muslims. The Turkish attack on the Byzantine Empire led the emperor to seek help from the pope, Urban II.

In 1095, at the Council of Clermont in France, Urban addressed a great crowd with a plea: Let Christians take up arms in a holy war to win back Jerusalem, and so reunite with their brothers in the East. His call, "God wills it!" was met with enthusiasm by the ordinary folk, spurred on by faith, and it promised them relief from the struggles of serfdom. The knights, too, embraced the call for military conquest. So began the First Crusade, named for the Latin *crux*, or "cross." During the next two centuries there would be eight major and a few minor crusades.

In the end, after more than 200 years of warfare, the Crusades did not win possession of the Holy Lands which remained firmly in Muslim hands. Only the First and Sixth Crusades achieved substantial successes, but even those gains did not last. The military efforts also failed to achieve the popes' goal of reuniting the Eastern churches with Rome. To the contrary, unity was less likely than ever as animosity ran high between East and West. The conquest of Constantinople by traitorous crusaders in the Fourth Crusade had the further effect of weakening the Byzantines, who were badly prepared for the attack and eventual overthrow by the Turks in the 15th century.

The Crusaders land at Damietta, an Egyptian town in the eastern Nile Delta.

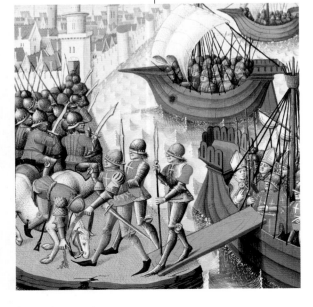

The Crusades did bring about significant changes in the West, however. During the Crusader years, the Europeans were exposed to Islamic culture which was more technically advanced than that in the West. Interest in Arab products, such as sugar, and cotton, opened up markets for trade, and this trade increased the importance of the Italian port cities of Venice and Genoa (JEN•oh•ah). Coins stolen from the Muslims were circulated, which boosted trading and helped transform Europe into a money-based economy.

The Crusades also took their toll on the feudal system. The cost of the military effort drained the resources—possessions and people—of the feudal lords. As their power diminished, the power

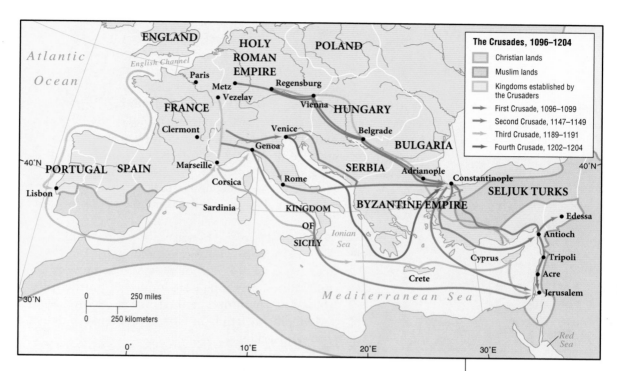

The Crusades, 1096–1204

Christian lands

Muslim lands

Kingdoms established by the Crusaders

First Crusade, 1096–1099

Second Crusade, 1147–1149

Third Crusade, 1189–1191

Fourth Crusade, 1202–1204

Map of the first four crusades, showing Christian lands and Muslim-dominated lands (whose populations were often still mostly Christian).

of the kings increased. The authority of the popes also increased as they commanded armies in the name of a Christian ideal.

The Rise of Towns and the Changing Farm

Changes in farming brought a period of greater wealth and cultural achievement. One of these changes was the invention of a simple farm machine: the wheeled plow. With this plow, the serfs could farm more land, produce more crops, and have more to trade with other manors. Some of the extra crop they could use to buy their freedom.

The farmers' markets, where goods were traded or sold, grew into busy population centers. More food and trade meant more people, just as large cities today continue to draw outsiders looking to make a living. Of course, large is a relative term; even a large medieval town such as London had only 35,000 inhabitants in 1377. Towns gave peasants freedom from feudal lords because a town could receive a charter directly from the king. And the king was only too happy to cut back the power of his vassals.

The New Merchant Class

In towns, people set up shops to offer services and became tailors, butchers, bakers, shoemakers and so on. Craftsmen—the cloth weavers, glassmakers, masons (stone builders), coopers (barrel makers), cobblers (shoe menders), and carpenters—began to organize in groups called **guilds**. The guilds were a type of early labor union, with rules and fees. The guilds established levels of expertise, beginning with the apprentice, or student, and ending with the master. They controlled prices and policed their own, seeing to it that the reputation of the guild was maintained.

Guild: A group of merchants or craftsman dedicated to protecting and furthering their individual trade.

One of the most important persons for this new merchant class was the banker. Money was needed as a standard and convenient form of exchange, and it largely replaced the bartering of goods. Banks could also make loans with money, and loans could enable merchants to start new businesses. The most successful bankers in Europe were located in northern Italy; these international bankers, such as the Medici (MED•eh•chi) family in Florence, became as rich and powerful as kings.

Most of the merchants did not have tremendous wealth and power. They formed a kind of middle class, enriching medieval life with their goods, building fine houses, and in some cases sponsoring the highest art form of the Middle Ages, the soaring stone cathedral.

The walled city of Carcassonne, in France, has been restored to show how parts of medieval Europe appeared in those centuries.

Cathedrals: Heights of Worship

The flowering of the High Middle Ages was best seen in its glorious churches, the major art form of the era. Two styles of architecture emerged between the 11th and 15th centuries: Romanesque and Gothic.

These cathedrals, called Romanesque because they resemble Roman buildings, consisted of heavy blocks of stone, strong columns, multiple arches, and sometimes domes. The stone ceilings reached upward in curved vaults shaped like half a barrel. Narrow aisle windows let in soft light, while the paintings, sculptures, and tapestries filled the churches with sumptuous color. Romanesque cathedrals were usually made in the shape of a cross, with the altar area (the apse) facing east, toward Jerusalem. This style dominated Europe until the mid-12th century.

In 1140, the Abbot Suger (sue•ZJAY) of France completed a renovation of his church at St. Denis, and a revolution in church architecture was born. This later style, which almost immediately replaced the Romanesque, came to be called Gothic, a name that incorrectly associates the medieval buildings with the barbarian tribes of the earlier centuries.

Unlike the heavier, darker Romanesque churches, the Gothic style featured tall pointed spires, intricate stone carvings on the outside walls, ceiling vaults with many cross-cutting "ribs," immense, open interiors, and windows everywhere that filled the church with light. Relying on skeletal structural supports outside the building, called "flying" buttresses, to hold up the roof, Gothic cathedrals could reach fantastic heights, symbolic of the worship that believers sought to give God.

Two of the best examples are Chartres (SHART•ruh) Cathedral in France, completed in 1224, and Cologne Cathedral in Germany, not completed until 1880. England developed its own variation of Gothic design, called English Gothic, best represented by the cathedrals of York and Bath. The 19th century saw a revival of Gothic design for churches, and many great American churches were built in imitation of medieval cathedrals.

The cathedrals of the Middle Ages were true houses of worship, large enough to fit a town's whole population at a single Mass. They sometimes took centuries to complete. Yet centuries later they still stand, the first true civic projects in the world, built for the common good with the money, time, and effort of all classes, from the wealthy sponsor and the skilled architect to the laborer who carried the stones.

Once a church was too high—the record 500-foot central spire of Beauvais Cathedral in France collapsed 20 years after the church's completion in 1272. But generally they were successful feats of engineering and awe-inspiring to the present day.

Chartres Cathedral, France.

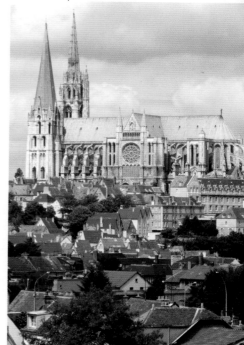

England in the Middle Ages

William the Conqueror (1027–1087)

William I of England rose from both shame and nobility to become one of the greatest leaders in the history of Europe. His principal achievement, known as the Norman Conquest (1066), led to the early formation of England as one of the first nation-states in the Middle Ages. A nation-state is a kingdom united by one language and culture and under one government.

Succession: The act of inheriting the throne of kingship.

History in Pictures

The 231-foot Bayeux Tapestry, commissioned by William's half-brother Bishop Odo, tells the story of the Norman Invasion in a series of 72 needlework scenes. The tapestry is considered a better history than the contemporary written records. Originally hung in Bayeux cathedral, it is now at the museum of Bayeux, France.

William was born to Robert, duke of Normandy, and his mistress, the daughter of a tanner (leather maker). Because William was illegitimate and had no automatic right of **succession**, Robert made his barons promise to acknowledge William as the rightful duke upon Robert's death. But, when the duke died in 1035, the barons killed young William's two guardians and the boy went into hiding. At age 15, now a well-trained knight, William assumed the duchy. In 1047 he proved himself an able ruler by defeating a rebellion with the help of the French king, Henry I. In the year 1052 or 1053 William sought to improve his station by marrying Matilda of Flanders. The marriage held political possibilities—both Matilda and Edward, king of England and half-Norman cousin to William, were descended from Alfred the Great—but it was also a happy union.

Two stories tell of William's wish to extend his Norman power to the land across the channel. It is said that in 1051 William visited King Edward (called "the Confessor") in England and charmed his childless relative into naming William his successor. Some years later, Harold, Earl of Wessex and the expected successor to Edward, was shipwrecked in Normandy. William released him on condition that he make a sacred promise to help William succeed to the English throne.

In January 1066, Edward died, and Harold was named king. William was on good terms with the pope, and received his permission to invade and claim the throne. Landing on England's coast in September, William's troops defeated Harold and the Saxon English on October 14, 1066, at the Battle of Hastings. William moved on to defeat troops in London, and was crowned king in Westminster Abbey that Christmas.

Though William faced several rebellions, he put them all down and by 1070 had full command of England. In 1072 he conquered Scotland, and years later defeated his own son Robert, who attempted to usurp Normandy in William's absence. William spent most of his energies on England. A just and decent ruler, he allowed some English governance to remain, such as the courts, but he also introduced practices from the European continent, such as the feudal system.

To aid administration he prepared in 1082 the *Domesday Book*, a complete survey of people, property, and lands in the country. Such a complete record was unique for its time and a great help to William's administration.

After a life of success, William died in an unglamorous way. Having grown quite fat in his old age, he injured his large stomach on the saddle-

horn of his horse, and died of the injury in 1087. Besides his children, two of whom succeeded to the throne, William left a profound legacy. He organized four diverse peoples—Saxon, Celtic, Danish, and Norman—into the beginning of a unified English nation.

Henry II and St. Thomas Becket of Canterbury

Henry II, great-grandson of William the Conqueror, ruled England until 1485. Henry II's chief contribution to his country was establishing the common law, even now a component of the legal system in modern England and the United States. This law attempted to standardize punishments for crimes no matter where in the country they occurred or by whom committed, whether a noble or a freeman.

Henry's centralizing of power had its benefits, for it freed the busy king to engage in the constant travels, battles, and other activities he enjoyed. Having married Eleanor of Aquitaine in France, he became ruler of French lands, and spent much time there. Henry had in his royal court, however, at least one serious challenger, someone who would overshadow the king's reputation by becoming a saint.

Thomas Becket (or Thomas à Becket) was an educated young noble who served the archbishop of England. Then, because of his great reputation, he was recommended to the post of chancellor and became an advisor to the king. By all accounts Becket served the king well, and the two became friends. Upon the archbishop's death six years later, Henry II gave the holy chair of Canterbury to Thomas, thinking it a clever political move to have a faithful underling his one real rival for power, in the Church's high seat. Things did not turn out as Henry expected.

Thomas seemed a changed man when he assumed the role of archbishop. Suddenly he was pious, he was priestly, and he was a strong leader of the Church. Soon he disagreed with Henry II over various church-state issues, such as the treatment of clergy accused of crimes. For a time Thomas was exiled in France, but he returned, only to another dispute with the king. One night in his court, the impetuous King Henry burst out to his knights, saying: "Will no one here rid me of this troublesome priest?" Four of them took him at his word, and they hastened out to Canterbury. On December 29, 1120, while Thomas knelt in prayer at a side altar, the knights murdered him with their swords. Immediately the story came to light, and King Henry was punished for his crime with a public beating. St. Thomas was promptly declared a martyr and a saint, and Canterbury became a popular pilgrimage site. The site where he was murdered is marked in Canterbury Cathedral and can be seen by visitors today.

King Henry II and His Interesting Family

King Henry II of England was also known for his difficult marriage to the spirited and cultured Eleanor (1122–1204), whom he married to acquire the French territory of Aquitaine. Since Henry was already count of Anjou, he ended up ruling more of France than did the French king, Louis VII. But because Eleanor had divorced King Louis VII of France prior to marrying Henry, there were ongoing battles between the two countries.

Eleanor was a fascinating and politically ambitious woman for her time—queen of France at age 15 and then of England at age 32. She married Louis VII, but grew tired of him. "He is more of a monk than a king," she said. She managed to have the marriage annulled in 1152; two months later she married Henry, who was her junior by 11 years. Henry and Eleanor had many children together, including two sons who would succeed their father. They were Richard I and John, and their characters and legacies were as different as could be. Eleanor advised both of them in turn, and at times stood against her own husband, who refused to share power with them.

When Henry died, Richard took the throne. Called Richard the Lion-Hearted by his people, he was a dashing and courageous soldier, who engaged in many rather expensive adventures, including the Third Crusade, which drained the royal treasury. Not much of his time was spent in England, but he was no less loved for it; he figures favorably in a great number of English legends.

After Richard died from a battle wound in 1199, John I became king, and he was one of the worst England ever had—so much so that no later English king has been named John. He was the villain in the Robin Hood tales. But because of him, a great document was born, one that would have significance for years to come and for miles beyond England's shores: the *Magna Carta.*

Robin Hood

The best bowman in England shot his arrow, and it struck a hair's breadth from the center of the target. Then a stranger stepped forward, dressed in tattered scarlet clothes. He drew back his bow and shot his arrow so true it knocked a feather off the other's shaft before landing dead center. The sheriff of Nottingham who had called the contest declared the stranger the winner, but he did not know to whom he awarded the golden arrow as prize. It was, in fact, his sworn enemy, the good Robin Hood.

Robin Hood, legend's favorite outlaw, was a green-clad forest-dweller who stole from the rich and gave to the poor, rescued damsels in distress, gathered a motley band of good-hearted men, and faithfully served King Henry and his successor, King Richard, who was mostly away in the Holy Land. Robin Hood's merry adventures, told and retold in story, play, and film, recalls the lively Christian spirit of the age, tweaking the noses of English nobles and clergy who were Christian in name only.

Robin Hood with his horn and bowman.

The Magna Carta (1215)

John taxed the people heavily, and because of his battles with the Church, his country came under a ban from Pope Innocent III. For six years no sacraments, not even weddings, were celebrated in England. Then, when John needed the pope's help to fight France, he turned England over to the Church, which placed on the people another huge tax burden. The barons rebelled.

In 1215 John was forced to meet the nobles in a meadow called Runnymeade on the Thames (TEMS) River. There he signed the Magna Carta, the "great charter," which granted certain rights to John's vassals, including a general council of barons, the first parliament, to influence the king's rule. The Magna Carta did not overturn the royal government, but it established the principle of limits on government. Later, however, because it limited the payments of vassals and established a general council, it led to the principle of no taxation without the consent of the governed. This in turn led to the cry of the 18th-century American colonists: "No taxation without representation!"

The Great Council established by the Magna Carta in time evolved into the modern British Parliament (from a French word meaning a conference) and was a model for other law-making bodies in the West, including the federal Congress and state legislatures of the United States.

Rebuilding the Church: St. Dominic and St. Francis

In the late 12th century two men were born. They shed a new light upon the struggling Christian world. Dominic, a nobleman from Old Castile, Spain, and Francis, the son of a well-to-do cloth merchant in Assisi, Italy changed the world with their preaching.

St. Dominic (1170–1221), born Domingo de Guzman, was an educated priest working in his local diocese in Osma, Spain, in 1203 when his bishop, Diego, called him to southern France. Bishop Diego and others were preaching to the Albigensians, also called Cathars, who were followers of a Christian heresy who believed that matter was evil and so denied Christ's Incarnation and the sacraments. St. Dominic's preaching and personal holiness won over many converts, but in 1208 disaster struck. First, Bishop Diego died, leaving Dominic without support. Then a papal representative for the region was murdered, and Pope Innocent II ordered a crusade against the Albigensians. This Albigensian Crusade, as it was

The Holy Preacher: St. Dominic

Before the mother of Dominic conceived him, she had a dream that she would give birth to a dog who leaped from her womb and ran through the whole earth, setting it on fire with a blazing torch that the dog carried in its mouth. The emblem of the Dominicans is a running dog with a torch in its mouth. The Dominicans were lovingly tagged the *domini canes*, the "Dogs of the Lord" because they went through the world "barking" the sacred knowledge of God.

St. Dominic confronting the Albigensians.

called, proved to be savage, and St. Dominic risked his life as he continued to preach.

In 1214, a good man named Simon de Montfort allowed St. Dominic to take refuge in his castle near Toulouse, and this became Dominic's base for his new order, which won approval from Pope Honorius III in 1216. Unlike monks who enjoyed a certain status and security in their monasteries, the Order of Friars Preachers (the Dominicans) were to be **mendicants**, or beggars. They would own no property and live on alms, trusting God to care for them as he did "the flowers of the field and the birds of the air" that Jesus spoke of in Matthew's Gospel.

Mendicant: A beggar.

The world was ripe for such an ideal. During the next four years Dominican houses for men and women were founded throughout France, Italy, and Spain. St. Thomas Aquinas, for example, was an Italian Dominican. Three centuries later, Spanish explorers spread the order to East Asia and the Americas. St. Dominic's order has been one of the most vital and formative in the Church, and remains active to the present day. The saint himself traveled until his dying day; he became ill on his way to Hungary and died in Bologna on August 6, 1221. He was canonized in 1234.

St. Francis of Assisi: "The Little Poor Man"

St. Francis with the stigmata in the upper church of the Basilica of San Francesco, Italy.

Francisco Bernardone (1181–1226) of Assisi, in Italy, was planning to be a soldier when he was wounded in battle. While he recovered, Francis spent long hours praying in the churches. He gave away his belongings to the poor. He also started giving away his father's goods. This was too much for his father, the respectable Pietro Bernardone; Pietro brought his son to the bishop of Assisi for a hearing. To everyone's shock, Francis stripped off his clothes—which he said were the property of his earthly father—and announced his new life of total dependence on his heavenly father. Dressed in a rough brown robe, hastily provided by the scandalized bishop, Francis set out at once to rebuild the old ruined church of San Damiano with his own hands, because it was there that Francis heard the voice of Christ telling him to rebuild his Church.

St. Francis' joy, simplicity, and unselfishness made him as attractive in poverty as he had been in wealth. "The Little Poor Man," as he was called, was soon leading a band of men devoted to prayer and aid to the poor. St. Francis sought the pope's approval of a new order of monks. Innocent III was prepared to deny the request until a dream convinced him otherwise. In his dream he saw the cathedral church in Rome, St. John Lateran, starting to crumble; holding up its walls was St. Francis.

St. Francis had his disappointments, too. He dreamed of converting the Muslims, but was turned back by ill health during the crusaders' attack on Damietta, Egypt, in 1219. Though St. Francis did not get to evangelize the Muslims in Egypt, he had a chance to meet with their ruler, the sultan, who came away quite impressed by the holy friar.

Upon his return to Europe, St. Francis found that his order had grown rapidly and that his rule needed revision to suit its increased size. With Pope Honorius III's approval of the revision in 1223, St. Francis turned his attentions to solitude and prayer. The following year he received the **stigmata**—bleeding wounds that appeared mysteriously in his hands and feet like the wounds of Christ. St. Francis' health began to decline, and on October 3, 1226, at the age of 44, he died. In a decisive testimony of his holiness, St. Francis was declared a saint just two years later. His ideal of

Stigmata: Miraculous bodily wounds resembling those of the crucified Christ.

A Patroness of TV: St. Clare (1194–1253)

She was beautiful, noble, and destined for a happy marriage and motherhood. But a secret love drew the lady Clare, ever since she heard the preaching of the cloth merchant's son, Francis Bernardone. In 1212 at the age of 18, St. Clare slipped out of her castle in Assisi at night and met St. Francis in his little chapel of the Portiuncula (por•chi•UNC•oola). St. Francis cut short her long golden hair and gave her a rough tunic to wear in place of her fine robes. By the light of the brothers' candles, St. Clare gave her life and heart to her one beloved, Jesus Christ.

At first St. Francis found a home for St. Clare in a Benedictine convent, but soon she had her own band of followers, including her sisters and her widowed mother. The women moved into a convent at San Damiano and formed the Order of the Poor Ladies, later called the Poor Clares, with St. Clare as abbess. For the remaining years of her life, St. Clare lovingly

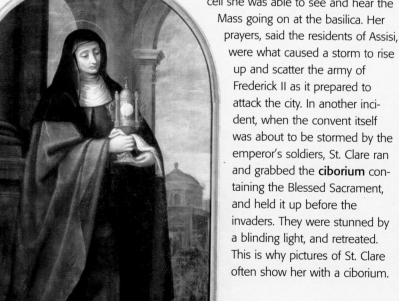

guided her fellow nuns—as a mother—and awaited approval for her strict rule of gospel poverty. In 1253 Pope Innocent IV finally approved the rule; St. Clare died two days later. Like her spiritual father St. Francis, her canonization came soon, just two years after her death.

St. Clare is the patroness of television, because it happened that alone in her cell she was able to see and hear the Mass going on at the basilica. Her prayers, said the residents of Assisi, were what caused a storm to rise up and scatter the army of Frederick II as it prepared to attack the city. In another incident, when the convent itself was about to be stormed by the emperor's soldiers, St. Clare ran and grabbed the **ciborium** containing the Blessed Sacrament, and held it up before the invaders. They were stunned by a blinding light, and retreated. This is why pictures of St. Clare often show her with a ciborium.

Ciborium: A closed vessel for keeping the consecrated wafers of the Eucharist after Mass.

holy poverty was so popular, that, to this day, it remains a vibrant way of life for thousands of priests, religious sisters and brothers, and lay people.

A New Way of Learning

In the early Middle Ages, people seeking education came to the monasteries or to cathedral schools run by the bishops. In the later period, the growth of towns and a new capitalistic economy led to a new place of learning, known as the university. Our modern universities, offering bachelor's, master's, and doctoral degrees in various subjects, are direct descendants of these first universities.

Today young students study a collection of separate "subjects," including mathematics, reading, writing, spelling, history, geography, foreign language, science, and physical education. In the Middle Ages, education was quite different. Students did not study individual subjects, they were instead introduced to and immersed in the liberal arts. Young students (seven years of age) studied the **trivium** (*trivium* is Latin for "the three roads"): grammar, logic, and rhetoric. Grammar was the Latin language and its literature; logic was orderly thinking; rhetoric was the art of speaking and writing. Next came the **quadrivium** ("the four roads"): arithmetic, geometry, astronomy, and music. These seven made up the liberal arts. After learning the trivium and quadrivium, advanced students went on to the higher disciplines of philosophy, medicine, or law. The highest study—the queen of sciences, the queen of the liberal arts—was theology, the university's central focus.

It took time for universities to develop. At first teachers simply traveled from town to town to give paid lectures in Latin (the language of the educated). Then students gathered around certain teachers and sought more formal training. The students and teachers organized themselves into centers of learning, most developing a particular specialty. The major university centers were Bologna, Italy (law), Paris (theology), and Salerno, Italy (medicine); in England they were Oxford and Cambridge (philosophy). The University of Paris became the model for later universities throughout Europe.

Trivium: A course of study in grammar, logic, and rhetoric.
Quadrivium: A course of study in arithmetic, geometry, astronomy, and music.

A professor at one of the great universities of Europe leads a seminar discussion in the 14th century.

St. Thomas Aquinas

It was 1239, and the Holy Roman Emperor Frederick II, fighting again with the pope, was excommunicated. To retaliate, the emperor moved his troops into the famous Benedictine monastery of Monte Cassino, where the 14-year-old Thomas of Aquino, Italy, had been sent to study. Thomas then moved to Naples, where Frederick had founded a new university. In 1243 Thomas decided to become a priest in the Order of Friars Preachers, the new order founded by St. Dominic. At Naples Thomas learned about the writings of the ancient Greeks, rediscovered by Islamic thinkers. Influenced by this study, St. Thomas Aquinas went on to revolutionize Christian theology and to become a doctor of the Church. He is known as "the Angelic Doctor," one of the intellectual giants of all history, and the greatest mind to emerge from the Middle Ages. It is ironic that the "Angelic Doctor" had once been called a "dumb ox" by his boyhood teacher who was exasperated by the student's silence.

Statue of St. Thomas Aquinas, by Jacopo della Quercia, dating from around A.D. 1400 in Lazio, Italy.

St. Thomas traveled to Paris, where he studied under the revered St. Albertus Magnus, a German scholastic philosopher and a Dominican. Ordained in Cologne, St. Thomas received his doctorate in theology in 1257. Two years later he was sent to Rome, where he taught at a Dominican school, and wrote numerous theological **treatises**. It was in Rome that St. Thomas began his masterwork, the *Summa Theologica* (*Summation of Theology*), a full and systematic explanation of Christian philosophy.

Treatise: A well-organized, written argument.

In 1269 St. Thomas was summoned back to Paris to judge a fierce intellectual dispute between two groups of Christian thinkers. On the one hand were the followers of Averroes, a 12th-century Islamic philosopher who, supposedly based on Aristotle's thought, placed human reason over God's revealed truths, those acquired through faith. On the other hand were those who rejected the pagan Aristotle altogether and favored faith over reason. Using clear and brilliant arguments, St. Thomas showed the errors of both. He showed that faith and reason are not in conflict, but partners in the search for truth, with faith guiding reason and reason serving faith.

Then, without warning, St. Thomas suddenly stopped writing. Late in 1273, while he was busy lecturing and working his way through the *Summa*,

Poor Scholars in the Middle Ages

Roger Bacon, an English philosopher and scientist, was also a Franciscan monk. He was an early researcher in the study of optics, and he is considered one of the leading figures in the development of science during the Middle Ages.

A story about Bacon illustrates a common challenge to poor scholars in the Middle Ages. In 1266 Pope Clement IV, whom Bacon had met as a cardinal during his studies at Oxford, asked Bacon to send him his writings. Bacon had no money for parchment or copyists. He solved the problem in a clever way in a letter to the pope: "As a monk I for myself have no money and cannot have; therefore I cannot borrow, not having wherewith to return; my parents who before were rich, now in the troubles of war have run into poverty; others, who were able refused to spend money; so deeply embarrassed, I urged my friends and poor people to expend all they had, to sell and to pawn their goods, and I could not help promising them to write to You and induce Your Holiness to fully reimburse the sum spent by them (60 pounds)." The pope could hardly refuse!

St. Thomas began receiving some profound visions during prayer. These encounters so affected him that he announced: "Such secrets have been revealed to me that all I have written now seems like straw." He never finished the *Summa*. In a short time his health began to decline, and while he was on his way to the Council of Lyons in 1274, St. Thomas fell ill and died. He was canonized in 1323 and named a doctor of the Church in 1567.

A Stricken World

One day in 1347 an Italian trading ship left port and headed home to Venice from the Black Sea. But before the boat docked, a mysterious and horrible disease had killed many of the sailors on board. Fearing contamination, the port of Venice turned the ship away, so it continued on to other ports in Italy and along the Mediterranean, spreading disease everywhere it docked. As the cargo was unloaded in Naples, Genoa, and Marseilles, so were common rats and their fleas, the sources of the bacterial infection that had killed the sailors. Within days the infection spread through the towns, and in a few months the disease had reached all of Europe. Within two years one-third of the population of Europe had died; one half of the population of England died.

This disease was the bubonic plague, or Black Death. Two weeks after being bitten by an infected flea, a person would develop swellings in the armpits or groin, called buboes, and pools of blood would collect under the skin in black patches. Fever, thirst, and delirium would follow, and then almost certain death within days or even hours. Only one-fourth of infected people survived. The disease killed the young and the old, the poor and the rich. Some monasteries and villages were wiped out to the last person; other regions, such as Poland, were mysteriously untouched.

Without knowledge of the deadly bacteria (which would not be identified until the 19th century), the people were helpless to stop its spread. They had no antibiotics to kill harmful organisms as we do in modern times. Some people closed themselves off in their city homes, while others fled to the countryside. Many good priests stayed and ministered to the sick and dying and were themselves afflicted. Many feared it was the end of the world. Then, almost as quickly as the plague started, it stopped.

By 1349 the epidemic had run its course. It would recur in isolated areas every 10 or 20 years, only to disappear again.

A plague patient, surrounded by physician and helpers. Woodcut, 1512, from "Fasciculus Medicine" printed by N. de Antwerp.

The strange affliction had a curious effect on society. There was an end to optimism in art and philosophy, because death and the after-life obsessed the painters and sculptors. The sudden deaths of so many people—including half the populations of London and Florence—meant fewer people to work the farms. Those who were left had more power to demand freedom and money from landowners. This led to a rapid end of serfdom.

The horror of so much death and disease shook the confident faith of the Middle Ages. The few runaway priests who had abandoned their stricken people returned to fill church offices left vacant in the death-cities. The result was a kind of spiritual plague that spread through the church.

From Feudal Kingdoms to Nations

The growth of towns, the opening of the East by the Crusades, the Black Death, the beginnings of exploration—all these worked together in the later days of the Middle Ages and moved most of Europe from feudalism into stronger central governments. Three great nation-states formed around feudal kingdoms, bringing regions together to share a common language, a common code of law, and allegiance to a strong central monarchy. They were England, France, and Spain. Italy remained divided among many city-states and Germany was divided among hostile princedoms. Each nation began to develop its own strengths and character. The kingdoms were becoming nations.

Chapter 8 Review

Let's Remember Write your answer in a single complete sentence.
1. Charlemagne was king of what Germanic nation before the Holy Roman Empire?
2. Name the liberal arts.
3. The Great Schism of 1054 divided the Western Church from whom?
4. Chartres Cathedral is an example of what style of architecture?
5. What was the Black Death?

Let's Consider For silent thinking and a short essay or for thinking in a group with classroom discussion:
1. What would have caused the Norsemen to turn from trade to savage plundering?
2. Why was chivalry a Christian code of behavior?
3. Why were the Crusades fought?
4. Why was the Magna Carta important?
5. What were the qualities of Sts. Dominic and Francis?

Let's Eat!

A Medieval Pastry: Crispels. Modern and easy recipe for Crispels. Buy in the frozen section a package of phyllo leaves. Cut the layers into circles with a biscuit cutter. Quickly fry in Crisco vegetable oil until golden and crisp. Drain on paper towel. Drizzle honey over all and serve warm.

Chapter 9 Europe: The Renaissance and Its Consequences

The Fracture of Christendom

Medieval men and women thought of themselves as citizens of their own kingdom, but also of a greater culture and civilization that included all the many kingdoms of Europe—Christendom. Christendom had fought wars against the Islamic invaders, seen the flowering of thought and art in the 1200s, and lived through the terrible plague years of the 1300s. In the 1400s and 1500s, Portuguese and Spanish sailors discovered the lands of Africa and the Americas and made Europeans aware of them. It seemed that Christendom was about to extend its culture into the entire world.

But a disagreement about principles can shatter a civilization and fragment its culture. The Catholic Christian culture of Europe was almost broken apart by such disagreements. Fortunately, the different versions of Christianity held common Christian principles, and encouraged new approaches and solutions to practical problems. European civilization, powerful because of its sciences and technologies, spread throughout the world and affected all other cultures: Africa, Asia, and the Americas. Exploration led to trade and conquest. By the 20th century, Western culture controlled the entire world. Religion, politics, and the arts, all underwent changes between the 15th and the 18th centuries, as Europe changed from its Christian medieval culture to modernity. Christian Europe did not stagnate and stop developing after

A medieval astronomer measures the motions of stars and planets while two assistants take notes.

181

its achievements in the high Middle Ages. The fundamental principles of Christian culture gave birth to new ideas and forms in science, politics, and morality. From these developments came the world culture we inhabit today, that form of European civilization called "modernity."

Modernity: Christian culture since the Renaissance.

Modernity is essentially a Christian development and is characterized by (1) science (the West's reliance on the physical sciences for answers to humanity's problems), (2) human rights (the West's protection of the rights of the individual and the political systems that ensure those rights), and (3) tolerance (the freedom of religion that allows many faiths and philosophies to exist within the West). These three—science, human rights, and tolerance—are the result of the Christian principles seeking for Truth, for Justice for all mankind, and for Love of neighbor.

Secularism: Rejection of religious concerns.

Through the centuries, because of the tragedy of sin, the principles of truth, justice, and love have been less evident than they should be. Often deformed into materialism instead of science, violent revolution instead of justice, and a godless **secularism** in place of love—a secularism that tries to solve the problem of tolerance by ignoring God and religion altogether. A deformed Christian culture is found in materialism, revolution, and secularism.

The Search for Truth

Jesus promised his followers that "you shall know the Truth, and the Truth shall make you free." Truth and freedom stand at the head of Christian culture's goals. Pursuit of the truth about God and man required a pursuit of the truth about the physical world that God made and that mankind inhabits. And life in heaven could well depend on the freedom of an individual to do what he knows to be right and what God is asking of him. Human political institutions had to be questioned and continually reformed, just as human conceptions of physical realities had to be refined, if God's truth was to be found.

Phenomena: Occurrences perceptible by the senses.

In the 14th century St. Thomas Aquinas's great synthesis of Christian and Greek philosophy was challenged by William of Occam (1290–1350), an English university professor. Occam's challenge of scholastic thought, called nominalism, implied that an explanation of the universe's laws more simple than Aristotle's or the Greeks' was needed. The truth would have to be found through more careful observation of nature. Over the next three hundred years, "natural philosophers" gave several explanations of the motion of the heavenly bodies and other **phenomena** of nature in the effort to improve on Aristotle.

The Renaissance

Scholars generally refer to the great wave of creativity that began in Italy in the 1400s, and spread to all of Europe in the next century, as a renaissance, a rebirth. The learning and artistic inspiration of the ancients was thought to have been reborn. The sculpture of Ghirlandaio, Donotello, and Michelangelo, the painting of Botticelli, Raphael, and Michelangelo, the inventions of Leonardo da Vinci, and the architecture of Bernini and Boromini made Florence and Rome centers of beauty for the ages.

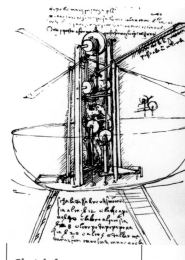

Sketch for a helicopter by Leonardo da Vinci.

The visual arts joined the search for truth in an effort to render people and scenes realistically. The Italians led the way in this search. The names of Michelangelo, Leonardo, and Raphael have come to stand for the highest accomplishment of visual art in our civilization, but their achievement owed much to their predecessors. Early in the 15th century, Piero della Francesco published a book on the principles of **linear perspective**. Perspective shows the lines of the visual world according to a vanishing point, where parallel lines appear to the eye to meet in the distance. His work established the laws of vision for his succesors. Perspective transformed Western painting into a realistic and mathematical science. Perspective drawing allowed architects and engineers to view the finished product before scale models and drawings were started.

Michelangelo's famous statue of Moses.

Linear perspective: The illusion of depth by drawing parallel lines converging at a point in the distance.

Anatomy: The structure of a plant or animal.

Frescoes: Paintings created on fresh, moist plaster.

The Last Judgement, painted by Michelangelo on the ceiling of the Sistine Chapel in the Vatican.

All the great master painters of the 15th and 16th centuries studied human **anatomy** in order to learn to draw the human form accurately. Michelangelo Buonarroti was a sculptor more than a painter. He loved his beautiful *Pieta* that still greets visitors to St. Peter's in Rome. Visitors still marvel at his *Moses,* and the *David,* carved for the town hall of Florence. Reluctantly, he turned from sculpture to create his greatest paintings, the **frescoes** of the Sistine Chapel in Rome. On the ceiling he depicted scenes from the Old Testament. Years later he painted a gigantic *Last Judgment,* with his own features on the flayed skin of St. Bartholomew, near the hands of the Savior. He died in 1564, in Rome.

Michelangelo's contemporary was his fellow Florentine, Leonardo da Vinci. Leonardo was both a great painter and a student of science. He recorded the anatomy of birds and human beings, and came up with many inventions based on his studies of mechanics and anatomy. His inventions were too far ahead of his time and remained only sketches in his notebooks, until the last century. Two of his paintings are world famous, the portrait called the *Mona Lisa,* of a beautiful Florentine noblewoman, and the superb *Last Supper,* now carefully protected in a Milan museum because it is deteriorating.

Luther and the Protestant Revolt

The on-going battle against corruption in the Church itself brought a schism within the Latin Church of the West during which three popes scandalously claimed the authority of the See of Peter. In 1414–1417, the Council of Constance had to decide which of the three was, in truth, the rightful pope. The council chose Martin V over his rivals. But the schism resulted in a loss of authority for the papacy and a general mistrust among Christians of many papal claims. Heretical revolts against the Church broke out in Bohemia, Germany, southern France, and northern Italy.

The Fall of Constantinople (1453)

In 1453 the great city of Constantinople fell to the Turks. No one in the West could believe it. Constantinople had always withstood attack, and could not fall! But fall it did, and with it the defense of the eastern approaches to Europe. The fall of the city meant the end of the Byzantine

Empire and the last claim of imperial authority. The Turkish threat to Europe was only briefly stopped at the siege of Belgrade, where the troops of John Hunyadi, a Hungarian general, and St. John Capistrano won the day. The Turks would invade again and get as far as Vienna in 1529, and again be stopped at Vienna in 1683.

Among the refugees fleeing to Italy and Western Europe from conquered Byzantium were scholars and teachers, who brought with them the books and ideas of the ancient Greek world. New ideas and long-lost texts were suddenly the talk of the West. In Germany, a young Catholic inventor, Johannes Gutenberg, perfected a printing press using movable type. This printing press was able to make many copies of a book, and quickly made books available to everyone. Gutenburg's Latin Bible (1455) was the first book printed in Europe. The Gutenburg press then published a *Turk Calendar*, a list of cities that the Turks would likely conquer and upon what expected date the fall would take place. It warned merchants and missionaries what the safe border of Christendom had become. In England, in 1484, William Caxton also made a press and printed a collection of stories about the legendary King Arthur, *Le Morte D'Arthur*, by Sir Thomas Malory.

Johannes Gutenberg in his workshop showing his first proof sheet.

The siege of Constantinople.

The threat of Islam was finally halted in the 1490s by victories over the Muslim kingdom of Granada in Spain and the startling discoveries of Portuguese and Spanish explorers. The two Christian kingdoms on the Iberian Peninsula, Castile and Aragon, were united by the marriage of their young monarchs, Isabella of Castile and Ferdinand of Aragon. Together they attacked the Muslims of Granada and completed in the 700-year-old effort to drive the Muslim conquerors out of the peninsula. Thus ended the long struggle called in Spanish the *Reconquista*.

While the Christian armies were besieging Granada, Queen Isabella was presented with a plan to get around the Muslim-held lands blocking the trade route to the Indies. The scheme was to sail west across the unknown ocean. This seemingly impossible western route was presented by Christopher Columbus, an Italian seaman. The queen's geographers doubted Columbus's proofs. They said that Asia was farther away than he claimed. Isabella at first turned him down. Finally, when Granada surrendered to her armies, she gave him three small ships and a crew. In 1492 Christopher Columbus discovered for the Spanish crown a sea route not to Asia, but to the Americas. The geographers were right; Asia was much farther away, but in its place was a land that would change Europe.

Columbus's ships: the *Niña*, the *Pinta*, and the *Santa Maria*.

Within 30 years, the Spaniard Hernando Cortez (1521) conquered the great Mexican Empire of the Aztecs. Next came the conquest of the Inca Empire by Francisco Pizarro (1533). Both these conquests poured tons of gold and silver into the treasury of Spain.

Meanwhile, writers and thinkers such as Thomas More of England (later St. Thomas More) and Desiderius Erasmus of the Netherlands became internationally known for their writings on justice and political order. More's book about a perfect society, *Utopia* (No-place), gave its name to impossible and dangerous ideals of political organization.

The debates and books on spiritual and temporal matters only made the quest for truth more urgent. Where was the truth of a just political order to be found? In tradition and established authority? In individual inquiry? In the opinions of experts, or popes, or kings? In the experience of ordinary men and women? What made for right action, or wrong? How should men of power behave? In the world of the Italian city-states, fighting and jostling for advantage with their neighbors, the Florentine statesman and political philosopher Niccolò Machiavelli (1469–1527), in his book *The Prince*, announced that traditional morality could no longer be counted on. Machiavelli claimed that princes had to act through power if they wanted to conquer. Only might could make right, he concluded.

Martin Luther

Niccolò Machiavelli

In the confused questioning of all tradition that afflicted the start of the 16th century, a German monk and university professor, Martin Luther, got into the quarrel almost by accident. Public debates at the university were ordinary and frequent, and on October 31, 1517, Luther announced he would debate a number of issues with any other university men. He nailed on the church door of Wittenburg, his university town, 95 "theses" (or positions on the issues), that he would defend in debate. Over the following year, the "university debate" attracted both Church and State authorities, until Luther was cornered into taking positions that set him against the Catholic Church and its whole history. Finally, the emperor of the Holy Roman Empire, Charles V of Spain and Austria, called a **diet**, or a parliament, of the empire to meet at the German city of Worms. Luther was asked to explain or **recant** (take back) his opposition to the Church. But Luther could not be moved. He uttered the famous sentence, "Here I stand, I can do no other." He was excommunicated.

In the years that followed, Luther and his followers formed a rival church organization. The Catholic Church judged them to be heretics. Luther's followers were called "Protestants," because they had made a public "protest." Soon after, other "protestors" joined the revolt with their own versions of religion. Ulrich Zwingli in Zurich, Switzerland, denied the

Diet: A German parliament.
Recant: A formal retraction, or taking back, of what one has said.

reality of supernatural grace through the sacraments of the Church. And John Calvin, once a Catholic theologian at the University of Paris, was invited to Geneva, Switzerland, to reorganize the city government. There he denied the traditional organization of the Church under its bishops and rejected the reality of the sacraments. Calvin proclaimed that God predestined those chosen for salvation. The teachings of Calvin were carried to Scotland and the Netherlands. In England, King Henry VIII, once honored with the title of Defender of the Faith for his attack on Martin Luther, abandoned his loyalty to the pope when the pope wouldn't annul his marriage. Henry declared the church in England independent of the pope, and made himself, as king, the head of the English church. St. Thomas More opposed this break with the Church and was beheaded by Henry. Henry's daughter Elizabeth I made England a bulwark of the Protestant revolt, setting England against the Catholic nations of the continent. Many Catholics were tortured to death in England for their faith, and it was death to be a priest in England during Elizabeth's reign and for years after. Calvinist ideas became part of English thinking although the English church never became completely Calvinist.

Convocation of bishops at the Council of Trent.

In Europe, the lands governed by the House of Habsburg (Spain, Austria, Italy, and the Rhineland, comprising the Holy Roman Empire of Charles V) and the larger part of France (governed by Francis I of the House of Bourbon) held to their Catholic allegiance. The peoples of northern Europe became Protestant, and the peoples of southern Europe remained Catholic. Christendom was so divided in religion and politics that war between the two religious positions consumed Germany and the Low Countries. Europe was be tortured by wars of religion for more than two hundred years.

The revolt of the Protestants resulted in a new council of the

Western Church. Pope Paul III called the bishops of all Europe to meet in the Italian town of Trent in 1545 where they met intermittently until 1563. This meeting was called the Council of Trent. The council considered the questions and complaints raised by the Protestants and responded with a reform of the church organization and a catechism of all that a Catholic could or should believe. The Catechism of the Council of Trent served the Church for four centuries.

Science

Tragically, in the pursuit of truth, European thinkers split the Church into competing churches and set nation against nation. Just as modernity began in a controversy over what is true, so modern science came about because of a search for the facts.

Modern science began by asking about the motion of the stars. Until the 1500s, traditional astronomy had accepted the model of the Greeks, summarized by Ptolemy. The Ptolemaic model assumed that the Earth was stationary, around which the heavenly bodies moved in circles—the moon, the planets, and the sun closest to the Earth, the fixed stars in patterns at the outer edge of the universe. This Earth-centered universe is what appears to the naked eye. A very complicated mathematics was needed to account for the motions of the planets as they appeared to the viewer. These mathematical problems first caused the older model to be questioned. The first to challenge that model with a more simple explanation of planetary motion was a professor at the University of Krakow in Poland, Nicolaus Copernicus (1473–1543). In the year of his death, 1543, Copernicus's theories were published by his friends in *On the Revolutions of the Celestial Spheres*. The book was brought to him on his last day and placed in his dying hands. He had been reluctant to publish because he knew that his ideas disturbed many people. Copernicus challenged the 1,200-year-old authority of Ptolemy's Earth-centered model of the universe and Aristotle's even older view of why bodies fall to the ground. His challenge to ancient authority required a complete change in mankind's concept of the universe. It is rightly called the "Copernican Revolution."

Nicolaus Copernicus was a priest, medical doctor, and astronomer. In 1543 he wrote a book which proposed the theory that the Earth and the planets rotated around the sun, and not around the Earth.

Heliocentric: Having the sun as the center.

Copernicus opposed the Ptolemaic model with a **heliocentric** theory. The sun, he said, is unmoving and at the center of circling planets. The Earth, he said, was itself a planet and moved in a circular orbit around the sun, with the moon circling the Earth. The Copernican model demanded two important changes in outlook. First, the size of the universe was vastly greater than imagined before. And the stars were so far away that they only seemed not to be moving. Second, there had to be another explanation for falling bodies, for why objects drop to the ground. Aristotle had explained that falling bodies were returning to the center of the universe, the Earth. But if the Earth was not the center, a new explanation was needed. The answer had to wait until the late 1600s when Isaac Newton came up with the concept of gravitation.

Copernicus's model of the universe, now seen as a solar system, was not totally accurate. The mathematics was as complicated as Ptolemy's because Copernicus believed in perfect circular orbits. But it was more convincing than the older model, and succeeded in making the sun, not the Earth, the center. Removing the Earth from center of the universe caused great shock. Western science would have to reexamine all its assumptions.

Elliptical: Having the shape of a curve (ellipse).

Copernicus's astronomy was improved by the theories of Johannes Kepler, a German astronomer who replaced Copernicus's perfect circles with **elliptical** orbits. But it was an Italian, Galileo Galilei, who proved that Copernicus's sun-centered model was right, and gave Western science a mathematical and observational basis. At age 17 Galileo entered the University of Pisa to study medicine. He happened to observe the swinging of a lamp hung from the high ceiling of the cathedral. He noticed that every swing of the lamp always took the same time to complete its arc, and concluded that the principle of the pendulum might be applied to clocks.

Galileo turned his attention to mathematics and motion. He disproved the Aristotelian claim that bodies of different weights fall at different speeds. He also showed that a body falls in a parabolic, not a straight, path. These discoveries indicated the motion of the Earth and led to his interest in the astronomy of Copernicus and Kepler. In 1609 he learned of the invention of the first telescope. He built an improved model that allowed him to observe the sky. He found that the surface of the moon is rough, not smooth as had been thought. He discovered that the Milky Way is composed of a collection of stars seen crowded together. He also discovered the moons of Jupiter, the spots on the sun, and the phases of Venus. These astronomical discoveries gave him the proof he needed to accept the Copernican theory of the sun as the center of our system.

Galileo's remarkable success in convincing the learned public of the certainty of his positions brought him enemies. Certain ideas of the ancient Greeks—Aristotle and Ptolemy—had become almost doctrinal for some Christians. Copernicus's model seemed to strike at the heart of Christian teaching; the literal sense of biblical miracles seemed threatened. A papal prohibition on teaching the theories of Copernicus was announced. Galileo's enemies began court proceedings against him before the Inquisition. In a famous letter to his patrons, he reminded the authorities that it had been the practice of the Church to interpret Scripture allegorically when it seemed to conflict with scientific discoveries. Further, "It would be a terrible detriment to souls if people found themselves convinced by a proof of something it was then made a sin to believe." The danger grew for several years until at last, in 1632, he published his *Dialogue on the Two Chief World Systems—Ptolemaic and Copernican.*

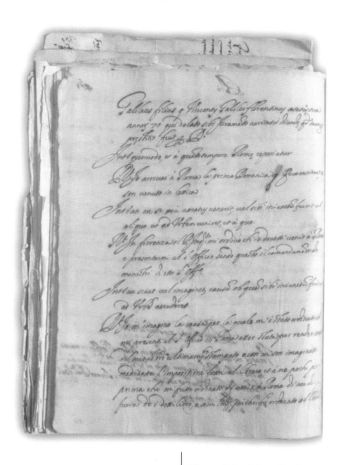

His rejection of Aristotelian and Ptolemaic ideas could no longer be denied. The Inquisition found him guilty of holding and teaching the Copernican theories. The pope himself commuted the sentence to house arrest, and the aging scientist withdrew to his estates for the last eight years of his life. In his house he worked out the application of the pendulum to clockwork, recorded his last telescope observations showing that the moon wobbles from side to side as it passes around the Earth, and rewrote the argument of his *Dialogue Concerning Two New Sciences* on the principles of mechanics.

Galileo's two greatest contributions to Western science were the importance of mechanics, a measurable and mathematical science, and the value of close observation in experiments. He created the modern idea of an experiment, an observed reaction under close controls.

The original handwritten pages of Galileo's book, *Dialogue on the Two Chief World Systems—Ptolemaic and Copernican.*

Literature

In the verbal arts, the search for truth led to new ways of describing character and creating realistic human figures in realistic lifelike situations. Two great masters of realistic storytelling were Miguel Cervantes of Spain, author of the epic novel *The Adventures of Don Quixote,* and William Shakespeare of England.

Cervantes

Miguel de Cervantes Saavedra was Spain's greatest literary genius. He invented the psychological short story in Spanish, and authored plays, poems, and other novels. His fame rests on his literary accomplishments, but he thought of himself as a soldier and civil servant.

Born in 1547, little is known of his youth, but at age 22, he fled Spain to avoid punishment for a fatal duel. He joined the Spanish contingent in the great sea Battle of Lepanto against the Muslim Turks. The Triple Alliance—Venice, Spain, and the papacy—stood alone against the greatest invasion of Christian Europe since the 8th century. In 1571, the Christian fleet, commanded by the Spanish Don John of Austria, met a massive fleet of Turkish galleys at Lepanto at the mouth of the Gulf of Corinth. Cervantes's bravery was noted by Don John. Cervantes remained more proud of his part in Lepanto than of any other achievement in his full life. He was wounded twice in the chest, and was permanently maimed in the left hand by a chance shot from the Turks—"to the greater glory of the right," he said.

While returning to Spain in 1557, Cervantes was taken prisoner by Muslim pirates and sold into slavery at Algiers. For 23 years, he was a prisoner of the Turks in Algiers. His several attempts to escape only brought him cruel punishments and torture. At last, his freedom was purchased by the Brotherhood of the Most Holy Trinity, a society dedicated to freeing Christian slaves from the Muslims.

Returned to Spain, he was too old to seek military appointment, and turned to literature. In addition to writing a number of successful plays, he served the royal government for fifteen years as a naval quartermaster, taking part in the outfitting of the fleet and troops for King Philip II's planned invasion of England in 1588—the Spanish

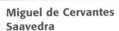

Miguel de Cervantes Saavedra

Armada. Then he withdrew from civic life to write, and in 1605 published *Don Quixote de la Mancha*. The book was an immediate success.

Cervantes never made much money from his novel, but it won readers all over Europe. An English translation, appearing in 1612 before the author's death, was the first of hundreds of translations into other languages. Cervantes died at home on April 23, 1616.

William Shakespeare

By the greatest coincidence, on the same day that Miguel Cervantes died, another great writer of the century also died in his bed—William Shakespeare of England. Shakespeare's plays and poems are known as the most skillful characterizations in literature. His works, like those of Cervantes, have become part of world literature through translation into every European language.

Shakespeare was born in 1564 in the town of Stratford-upon-Avon in central England. His father, a successful tradesman and landowner in his county, was elected to several local offices. Later in his life, he suffered financially, possibly because of a refusal to abandon the Catholic faith in

Sculpture of Don Quixote and Sancho Panza.

Don Quixote

This tragicomic romance tells of an old and penniless country gentleman, Don Quixote, who is determined to live a life of knightly adventure like the characters of romance he has spent years reading. Armed in old and rusty armor and accompanied by his practical and unimaginative groom, Sancho Panza, Quixote transforms the mean and poor circumstances of his journey into the settings of noble romances. A simple barmaid becomes, in his imagination, the Lady Dulcinea, a flock of sheep becomes a Saracen army, and a line of windmills becomes a host of giants. Sancho rescues him repeatedly from his confusions, and at last is himself converted to a more forgiving and loving heart by the absurd chivalry of his old master.

Monument to William Shakespeare, in Westminster Abbey.

Protestant England. Although it will never be known for sure, Shakespeare was probably a Catholic, which he kept secret from the authorities because it was forbidden to practice the Faith in Elizabeth's England.

In 1582, at the age of 18, William was married to Anne Hathaway of Stratford, a woman eight years older. The couple had a daughter, Susanna; two years later they had twins, Hamnet and Judith. Stratford did not offer much chance for employment to William, and so he left his family with his father and went to London where he could practice his literary talents.

A master of both comedy and tragedy, he began his career with imitations of Roman comedy and tragedy, *Titus Andronicus* and *A Comedy of Errors*, and then a series of history plays that explore the death-throes of medieval England and the birth of the modern nation-state—*Henry IV, Henry V, Richard II,* and *Richard III.* Among other things, he asked: What is the cost to the monarch who chooses to rule in the Machiavellian fashion, ruthlessly? What is the cost to his people? A series of romantic comedies followed—*A Midsummer Night's Dream, The Merchant of Venice, As You Like It,* and *Twelfth Night.* Shakespearian comedy explores the effect of love on human behavior and the inevitable inability of love to solve all problems. The romantic comedies were followed by a series of tragedies, his greatest works, *Hamlet, Othello, King Lear, Macbeth,* and *Antony and Cleopatra.*

In Shakespearian plays, the subject of tragedy is presented as choices between personal loyalties and ambition for power. Personal weaknesses bring about the tragic end of the characters. A group of fairy-tale "tragicomedies" was his final creation, of which *The Tempest* is considered the greatest.

The very successful and honored poet retired from London in 1610 to Stratford. He died in the home of his daughter, Judith, on April 23, 1616. The realism of his characterizations and his exploration of human motivation transformed European literature. As his character Hamlet remarks, the purpose of theater is "to hold the mirror up to nature."

Justice

In those days, the center of political authority seemed as elusive as authority in religion. The traditional authority of monarchs was being questioned. In the 17th century, England underwent Europe's first violent

The Tempest

In *The Tempest*, Prospero, a great wizard, who was once the duke of Milan, is living in exile on a magical island, served by a spirit, Ariel, and a half-human monster, Caliban. Prospero's beautiful daughter Miranda accompanies him in his island exile. In a great storm, the ship bearing Prospero's enemies is wrecked on the island, and the young Prince Ferdinand of Naples sees and falls in love with Miranda. To test him, Prospero puts him to work at hard tasks. Ferdinand perseveres. The enemies are made to confess Prospero's virtue, and Miranda and Ferdinand are united. The spirits of the island are freed, and Prospero renounces his magic in words suggesting Shakespeare's own retirement from the literary world.

Ferdinand and Miranda in a production of *The Tempest*.

revolution when King Charles I and his supporters were defeated in 1642 by an army loyal only to the elected Parliament. The parliamentary victors beheaded King Charles in 1649 and declared the end of the English monarchy. Oliver Cromwell, general of the parliamentary army, declared himself Lord Protector of a commonwealth, a republic (1649–1658).

England's monarchs were restored only after ten years of Cromwell's military dictatorship. At Cromwell's death, Charles II, son of the slain king, was given the throne. But the old way of monarchy was again set aside when England's Parliament deposed Charles's brother James II, a Catholic, in favor of his Protestant sister, Mary, and her husband, William of Orange. England's unwritten constitution, limiting the powers of kings and of government itself, was the result of this revolution. The elected Parliament would now be the judge and superior of monarchy, and over the next century would take over more and more of the monarch's powers. The Constitution of the United States of America owes its existence to England's unwritten constitution.

Further imitation of this revolt against traditional monarchy resulted in both the American War of Independence in 1774–1778, and the dreadful French Revolution of 1789, with its attack on Christianity and the Church, and the execution of hundreds of innocent aristocrats and others. The

A mob of revolutionaries storm the Bastille prison in order to free its prisoners. This was the watershed event of the French Revolution.

French nightmare was repeated again in the Communist revolutions in Russia and elsewhere in the 20th century.

The search for a just government unleashed both dictatorships and injustice as well as fostering the best of democratic republics.

Secularism

It is hard to see that the secularism of today's West began in the principle of love. But efforts to pass laws of tolerance, ensuring the safety of dissenters and non-Christians, were first begun in England out of concern for the just treatment of minority faiths and believers. Toleration as a political principle was slow to come. England did not pass reforms that gave Catholics the vote and rights as citizens until the late 19th century. France and other European nations passed back and forth on the toleration question. No state, Protestant or Catholic, attempted toleration until the birth of the United States. By the latter half of the 20th century, the European nations tolerated many forms of religious expression, but this distinguishes Western culture from Asian and Islamic cultures.

The Protestant revolt created Protestant governments that were more intolerant of dissent than the Catholic governments were. In England, for instance, Catholics were deprived of the vote, of the right to attend university, and to worship freely; priests were put to death. Heavy taxes were laid on Catholics to force their conversion. Protestant groups that were not the established Church of England were also punished, though not as heavily as the Catholics. The Quakers were subject to fines and public humiliation for almost a century. Jews were heavily taxed and ineligible for public office.

Whipping Quakers.

Everywhere, Protestantism unleashed a multitude of sects and churches. No state of Europe was free of a variety of religious groups. The states that had some form of republicanism or democracy were not able to claim that one state church would be right for everyone. And so they were forced to tolerate all religions in some way.

It is not hard to see how tolerance of all faiths can go to the position that all religions are equally right and true. And if all are equally true, then all are equally false. But this has happened in today's world. Governments today try to avoid any favoritism for religion itself and adhere instead to the religion of strict secularism. Secularism is based on the belief that the discoveries of science are proofs of a strictly materialist universe. Secularism is a danger because it rejects the first principles of Western culture—Christianity and the Church.

Western civilization has proved it can grow with every change in culture and absorb civilizations and cultures from the rest of the world. Other cultures have been influenced and reshaped by contact with the West. Our material success and political stability have been the envy of the world. The question of the next century will be whether Western culture is again strong enough to find an answer to its own materialism and overcome its secularism.

Chapter 9 Review

Let's Remember   Write your answer in a single complete sentence.
1. What was the date of the fall of Constantinople?
2. Who printed the first moveable type printed book?
3. What two famous writers died on April 23, 1616?
4. Why was the Council of Trent called?
5. What was the Copernican revolution?

Let's Consider   For silent thinking and a short essay or for thinking in a group with classroom discussion:
1. What was the effect on Europe of the huge influx to Spain of gold and silver from the Americas?
2. Compare the older icons with the later realistic human figures in painting.
3. What would it have been like to be captured into slavery, as Cervantes was?
4. How important was balancing human rights and tolerance with the claims of faith and security?
5. How different would American government be if we had chosen a monarch instead of the English model of parliamentary government?

Let's Eat!

Rice Pudding in the Middle Ages was just like it is today. Rice pudding was eaten in Italy (where it was heavily flavored with almonds) all the way to England where it was a popular dish in Shakespeare's time. In fact, Shakespeare alludes to eating rice pudding in *A Winter's Tale*. Here is the recipe in the language of Shakespeare. Can you translate it? "Boyle your rice, and put in the yolkes of two or three Egges into the Rice, and when it is boyled put it into a dish and season it with sugar, synamon and ginger, and butter, and the juice of two or three Orenges, and set it on the fire againe." (Hint for today's cooking: bake it for an hour at 325°.)

Chapter 10 China: The Middle Kingdom

T he ancient name of that region we call China is Chung Kuo (QUO), meaning the "Middle Kingdom" because the Chinese thought that their land was the center of the world. The Chinese acknowledged no other civilization than their own, and for thousands of years they met no civilized neighbors. Everything around ancient China was barbarian territory, at least as far as they were concerned.

Over the centuries, China expanded from a small kingdom along the Yellow River to its present huge size. The forms and ideas of its civilization affected the rise to civilization of all its neighbors. The enormous country of modern Communist China, or the People's Republic of China as it is now called, includes more land than the United States. China's neighbors on the north are the states of Mongolia and Russian Siberia. The large province of Manchuria was briefly independent during the 20th century but is now again part of the territory of the People's Republic of China. China's neighbors on the east are the

Examples of the geographical diversity in China.

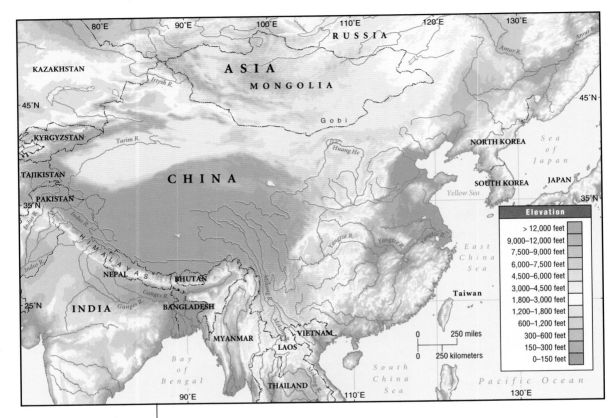

Map of modern China and its neighbors.

Archipelago: A group of islands.

two Republics of Korea on the peninsula, Japan on the island **archipelago** across the Sea of Japan, and the Republic of China on the island of Taiwan. On the south, China borders the Southeast Asian nations of Vietnam, Thailand, Bhutan, Nepal, and India. Its western neighbors are India and Pakistan.

China stretches from the cold northern plains of Asia to the tropical jungles of southeast Asia. Within this one country lie some of the tallest mountains in the world (the Himalayas), the worst deserts (the Gobi), the wildest and most dangerous rivers (the Yellow River and the Yangtze River), fertile lowlands and barren plateaus, snow-swept steppes, and tropical jungles.

Two great rivers cross almost the whole expanse of China from west to east—the Yellow River in the north, and the Yangtze River in the south. Civilization in China grew up along these two rivers. The valley of the Yellow River, where Chinese civilization began, is rich farmland, with deep, but dry, topsoil. In the beginnings of China's history, the Yellow River Valley grew abundant grain crops, such as millet and wheat. However, annual floods caused much hardship for the farmers and cities along the river, as they still do. The valley of the Yangtze, which is much farther south, is semitropical and surrounded by beautiful mountains. Rice growing made it a wealthy region. Farther south in China, tropical plants and flowers grow among the many farms and neatly ordered towns.

To the north lie the frozen plains and semidesert hills of Mongolia, once home to primitive tribes and nomads. The emperors of China built the Great Wall to try to keep out the fierce horsemen of Mongolia. On the western borders of China are two formidable natural boundaries: the Gobi Desert and the Tibetan Mountains. The thousands of miles of desert to China's west made travel difficult in the past and cut off almost all contact with the Mediterranean world until modern times. The great Silk Road, a caravan route stretching from the capital, Changan, across the desert wastes from oasis to oasis, connected China to Persia, and brought treasured silk to the Mediterranean world in return for Western gold. China's geography and vast distances isolated her from contact with other civilizations. Mistrust of strangers was so great that at times all foreigners were forbidden to set foot on Chinese soil.

China and the Culture of Asia

China has as many people as its diverse geography. It influences the culture of all of Asia. The Confucian moral code was followed by all of China's neighbors. The political culture of Asia has been heavily influenced by the Chinese governmental system, in particular the Chinese insistence on advancement by merit and the separation of government offices from inherited wealth. Chinese artistic styles and designs became the standard for beauty in the Far East. Chinese poetry gave its humanism and simplicity to China's neighbors. The Chinese written language is the basis for many Asian written languages, including Japanese, Korean, and Vietnamese.

The languages of China are very different from the Indo-European family of languages. Chinese words have one syllable; Indo-European words may have many syllables. Chinese is not an inflected language; that is, the meaning of the word doesn't change by adding syllables. Chinese has no plural nouns and no verb tenses. That is why the English spoken by some Chinese can sound like, "You go store yesterday. Buy four loaf bread." There are several dialects spoken in China. The written Chinese language is based on small drawings that represent ideas or things, rather than sounds. These drawings can represent many different dialects and languages, because they stand for ideas, rather than sounds.

Ideogram: A picture or symbol in a writing system to represent a thing or idea.

These drawings are called characters, or **ideograms**. People who read and write Chinese learn about 2,000 ideograms. Ideograms stand for simple ideas; these are linked to form more complex characters representing complex ideas. It is easier to begin reading languages that are written with phonetic letters, like our language. The written languages of Japan, Korea, and Vietnam are based on Chinese characters. The characters are the same but the spoken languages sound completely different.

From around 500 B.C., highly literate civil servants carried out government. After 200 B.C., these officials were chosen according to their score on a very difficult civil service examination. This created a rule by the most capable, called **meritocracy**. The civil service exam was a test of understanding the Confucian texts, written in very old Chinese characters.

Meritocracy: A government in which the most qualified and most talented people govern.

Although the civil service examination was open to all social classes, preparation and study for it cost a lot of money; only about 5 percent of the applicants were accepted into the Chinese civil service. This meant that few who were not sons of the wealthy could qualify for the examination. Of course, many who were not accepted were still very able; they became teachers, musicians, and minor officials.

In traditional Chinese writing thousands of complex characters are painted with precise brush strokes.

This Chinese system—a strong central government, national officials chosen by merit, and Confucian education for any who could undertake it—became a kind of model for government throughout Asia. Chinese government was imitated by Japan, and many promising Japanese students were sent to China to study. Inspired by the Chinese cultured civil service, other less powerful Asian nations created classes of their own.

Chinese Dynasties

The Chinese divide their history into eras, named for the principal ruling families or dynasties. Chinese history is said to begin with the Five Emperors, mythical rulers like gods, who invented civilization. The first historical **dynasty** was called Shang.

Dynasty: A powerful family that holds its power for a long time.

The Shang Dynasty (1766 to 1022 B.C.) The Shang dynasty kings were considered to be gods or godlike, and ruled a strict society, where each class or rank of person had to obey the group above it, up to the king. When they died, the Shang kings were buried elaborately with human sacrifice: officials, servants, and horses joined their king in a fancy grave. The Shang dynasty was based on an agricultural civilization located in the

A map showing the spread of China during the rule of four principal conquering dynasties.

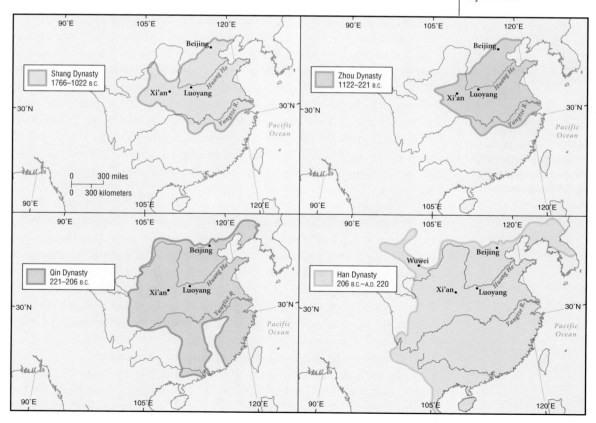

Oracle bones from the 14th or 13th century B.C., marked with early forms of Chinese writing. Shang dynasty.

Yellow River plain in northeast China. The use of bronze for tools and household items also developed during this time. Where bronze metal-working began is not known, but Chinese bronze work and Mediterranean bronze work occur at approximately the same time. This period was called the Bronze Age by early European paleontologists. Written Chinese was developed at this time; this early version of the language has been found written on bones, called "oracle bones." Shang fortune-telling was based on reading the cracking of the oracle bones when they were thrown into the fire. These oracle bones were saved as sacred objects in the royal palace libraries; there they keep a record of the earliest Chinese writing.

The Zhou Dynasty (1122–221 B.C.) This 900-year period may be divided into two periods. In the first, Zhou kings ruled the land through their own families and other aristocrats who supported the Zhou; they ruled by developing a system of roy-ally appointed local leaders who were directed from the central court. The Zhou Empire extended from the Pacific Ocean to the mountains of the west, and included both the Yangtze and Yellow River Valleys. The ability of the king to rule the whole country broke down. As a result, each local ruler controlled only his own piece of land. Because these several regions were in constant battle with each other, this second half of the dynasty was called Warring States. This period produced the great thinkers responsible for the development of Chinese philosophy. The most important was Confucius.

The Qin Dynasty (221–206 B.C.) The Qin reign was only one man and a brief reign by his son, a two-man dynasty. The Qin period was so disrup-tive and terrifying, and so harmful, that it brought about a rebirth of Chinese love of tradition and sense of purpose. In order to make the war-ring states adopt a loyalty to "China" instead of to their local state or par-ticular clan or king, the Qin king, Zheng, killed regional leaders and local royalty. He then recruited administrative talent from throughout China and assigned them tasks. He also moved the officials around China to pre-vent them from building up personal power in any one area.

Zheng unified central China by standardizing money, language, and the laws of all the land in central China. He also standardized the length of the axles of carts. On unpaved roads, carts could travel only where the worn

Confucius (551–479 B.C.)

onfucius was an aristocrat from the small state of Lu. He developed an ethical system that praised individual education and proper behavior toward one's parents, peers, superiors, and others. In his philosophy, a person became worthy of a great position, not by birth to a noble parent, but by individual merit. Confucius taught that respect for one's elders and obedience to one's superiors was the first moral principle. Confucius took on a small band of students, who followed him from Lu to other states, and who secured for him his first government post when he was already old. He devoted his old age to collecting and writing down the great poetry and ideas of the Zhou past. Confucius is directly responsible for collecting *The Book of Songs* and the *Spring and Autumn Annals*, a history.

ruts in the dirt matched their axle length. By standardizing that length, he promoted trade between the former warring states. But his use of peasants to build his great projects killed so many that there were fewer carts to travel the roads.

Zheng accomplished one of the wonders of the world: he built the first Great Wall. The Great Wall begins on the east coast, at the Yalu River, and continues for 3,000 miles over the mountains and deserts to the sands of the western Gobi Desert. The first Great Wall was built with terrible cost in human life. Thousands of peasants, or political trouble-makers were made to work on the wall, ramming Earth into frames to create bricks and hauling great stones from quarries. The first Great Wall ran from the coast inland for more than a thousand miles.

Zheng's peasant labor armies were also made to dig a canal, linking rivers and lakes, so that shipping could move between

Photo of the Great Wall of China showing the very difficult terrain the Chinese army had to defend.

the Yangtze and Yellow Rivers. The Grand Canal took almost as many lives as the Great Wall.

The Burning of the Books

Confucian thinking was considered harmful by Emperor Zheng. It could lead to questioning his policies. He outlawed all philosophical discussion and forbade his subjects to praise the past or criticize the present. All books other than official documents were to be burned. But the scholars refused to give up their books. They hid them from the emperor's troops. In 212 B.C. Emperor Zheng ordered 460 scholars, the greatest and most famous intellects of all China, buried alive as a warning to those who would defy his orders. A great bonfire of books was then set ablaze on top of their mass grave.

No one was safe in Zheng's Empire. His army officers were regularly purged to ensure their total loyalty. When he began to build his tomb, a huge structure covered with Earth to form a pyramid high enough to be seen for miles across the plain, the officers feared that he would order them all killed when he died.

Perhaps to their surprise, another monument Zheng created, the Terra Cotta Army, did not take human life. The Terra Cotta Army consisted of 8,000 full-size, realistic portrait sculptures of his soldiers, and were buried near Zheng's burial place. These clay statues look like his guards and officers. Each statue was created to be buried with the dead emperor in the place of its living original. Archeologists did not discover the army of statues until the 1950s. It stood 2,000 years or more beneath the farmland that surrounded the emperor's tomb.

Part of the clay-statue army discovered in Emperor Zheng's grave; it was created to accompany him into the afterlife.

The Han Dynasty (206 B.C.–A.D. 220)

During a period of political instability following Zheng's death, his son attempted to succeed him on the throne. The result was civil war and chaos. Liu Bang, a commoner, won the command of the army, and united central China. He proclaimed himself emperor, and was generally accepted by a tired people who had known enough of tyranny and civil war. It was the first time in Chinese history that a commoner had become emperor. Liu Bang was the founder of the Han dynasty. The Han gave their name to all ethnic Chinese from central China, who called themselves Han. The name is used to this day, much as Europeans in the medieval era called themselves Romans.

In an attempt to loosen the tight hold of the central government, Liu Bang allowed some local aristocracy to go back to their land and represent the king. He also made laws that followed Confucianism, rational principles of behavior. Confucianism set out broad rules of conduct: how peasants should relate to the king, king to peasant, son to parents, parents to children. In practice, Confucianism was more flexible than the tight laws of the Qin period.

The Han dynasty united all of central China by another education rather than regulations. The philosophy of the court (Confucianism) and the written Chinese language were taught throughout China. Eventually, all of urban and rural China was included in this educational system. Passing the national exam was a way for the poorest peasant to join the leadership class in China. Also, local differences in language and local customs gave way

The Story of Kwang Hung

A poor boy named Kwang Hung was very fond of books and loved to study. But he was too poor to buy lamp oil for his studies. He worked for a magistrate who paid him in books instead of money, which delighted him. But the books were of little use to the poor boy, who was free to study only at night and had no money to buy oil.

At last he thought of a solution. He lived in a closet room beside a tavern, and the tavern was well lit with lamps all night long. Kwang made a little hole in the wall, and by moving his book back and forth in front of the hole, he caught the light that came through and was able to go on with his studies. When the examinations were held, he so distinguished himself that he was recommended to the emperor for a high appointment. He served in many important posts and at last Kwang Hung became first minister of the empire.

over several hundred years to a standard "Han Chinese" culture, led by local officials of the central civil service.

The Han dynasty established trade routes with countries of the Mediterranean, crossing thousands of miles of desert and mountains. Chinese porcelain and tea were considered priceless by the Mediterranean peoples. But the greatest export was silk, a fine cloth made from the cocoon web of a silkworm.

A white marble head of Buddha. Tang dynasty.

The Tang Dynasty (A.D. 618–907)

After the breakup of the Han dynasty, there was a period of several hundred years before strong Tang rulers were able to unite central China. The Tang were able to go even farther, conquering areas around China, including important trade routes to Europe that were north of central China.

Buddhism had been brought to China from India during the Han dynasty, in the fourth and fifth centuries A.D. At first, Buddhism grew slowly in China; Buddhist writings were in Sanskrit and translation into Chinese characters was very difficult. Buddhism gained its greatest hold on China during the Tang dynasty.

Because Confucianism is more of a philosophy of life than a religion, many religiously inclined Chinese were attracted to Buddhism. Buddhism teaches that the world is an illusion, and it is necessary to escape the trials of the world to reach heavenly detachment, called **Nirvana**. The Chinese pagoda, with its many stories and curved roofs, was developed as a representation of the several heavens, or levels of detachment, and was part of a Buddhist temple.

Nirvana: The ultimate state of detachment of the soul in which it is freed from all things that enslave it.

regent: One who rules in place of another.

Empress Wu, the only woman to ever officially to hold the throne, took power in A.D. 690 during the Tang dynasty period. With her beauty and wiles, she married first one emperor and then his grown son after his father's death. She then poisoned her young husband and ruled as **regent** for their infant son. After killing three of her own sons, and deposing the fourth and last, she declared herself a man, crowned herself emperor, and set about reforming the imperial bureau-cracy that had grown soft and corrupt. She ruled wisely, and extended the territory of the empire south and north. Those who opposed her she put to death. She made Buddhism the official religion of the realm and lavished fortunes

Bhuddist figures from the Tang Dynasty found in the Longmen Caves of China, a place overlook-ing the Yi River, where more than 100,000 statues of Buddha and his disciples were carved into a cliff in A.D. 494.

on its monasteries. Empress Wu is credited with continuing the prosperity of the Tang dynasty by conquering China's neighbors, but then installed her own despots in some areas. Another woman, Tz'u-shi, who named herself Wu after her famous historic predecessor, ruled in the name of her sons and grandsons in the last days of the Chinese Empire, at the end of the 19th century A.D.

The Song Dynasty (A.D. 960–1279) At this time China's culture was more advanced than any in Europe. The Han, the Song, and the Ming peri-ods are regarded as the high points of Chinese culture. Because this was an era of general peace, China could put energy into developing government, trade, and technology. The technology of shipbuilding, bridge building, and of course the tools of war reached a high level. Song culture produced delicate poetry and luxurious living. The poets of the Song are considered the models of classical Chinese literature.

The life of the wealthy was one of ease and beauty. Even the poor were relatively well off, and there was little social discontent. Almost 300 years of cultural achievement allowed advances in medicine and science unknown to the rest of the world. This golden age came to an end through internal dissention. In the last two generations of the Song, the rulers were so wealthy and so idle, that their desire for luxury became twisted vice. The merchants and military grew to despise their rulers and long for the lost days of the Tang dynasty. Song poetry reflected the boredom of the point-less life of the ruling classes. China was ripe for a foreign invader.

Foot Binding

A Song emperor so much admired the way one of his wives danced on her toes, leaving prints in the snow like the prints of a deer, that he ordered all his wives to have their feet broken and bound so that they could all walk on their toes. This fashion-driven cruelty was required of all upper-class women and continued well into the 20th century.

The Yuan Dynasty—Rule of the Mongols (A.D. 1279–1368) Until 1279 China had been isolated and relatively free of outside influences. But then in 1279 the Mongols crossed the Great Wall and conquered China. Their dynasty lasted a little less than a hundred years. Led by their famous leader, Genghis Khan, the Mongol armies swept over China, Tibet, Russia, and eastern Europe. But Chinese influence over the Mongols proved stronger than the Mongol influence over China.

The Mongols were masterful horsemen; they used their horses to charge, attack, and conquer. While their skills in war were superior, their skills as governors of the territories they conquered were poor. The Mongols were nomadic people who traveled from place to place, killing or enslaving the peoples who lived on the land they wanted. The northern Chinese met this terrible fate when the Mongols rode against them.

GENGISKAN

Genghis Khan

Genghis and Kublai Khan

After the conquest of China, Genghis Khan (1215–1294) and his highly disciplined cavalry rode across western Asia and Eastern Europe as far as Poland without serious opposition. Only the death of Genghis made the Mongol armies in Poland turn around and head back to China to choose his successor. All Europe might have fallen to Genghis's armies otherwise. After Genghis's death they turned to southeast Asia and conquered those lands. With these areas and Persia, Tibet, and south Russia, the Mongol Khan controlled more land than any man in history.

His grandson, Kublai Khan (1215–1294), extended the reach of the Mongols even farther into southeast Asia, bringing Chinese influence to Vietnam. The Italian traveler, Marco Polo, visited the court of Kublai Khan in China and returned to Europe with stories of inventions and wealth no one would believe: tales of cities without crime or sewage in the streets, tales of black rocks dug from the hills that burned with hot flame, tales of books printed from blocks that could make many copies in an hour, tales of floating palaces and elegant dinners where the diners ate with long sticks of ivory and never touched the food with their fingers.

Later, the Mongols learned that it was more profitable to squeeze wealth from the Chinese than to kill them. Ultimately, the Mongols adopted the Chinese system of administration. The Mongols promoted extensive improvements in building, roadway, and agricultural. Trade with Europe increased, despite the long routes over land and sea. As a result, Chinese innovations such as printing methods, gunpowder for both cannons and fireworks, porcelain production, and medical techniques were introduced to Europe during the period of the Mongols. However, the ethnic Chinese (the Han people) were never allowed to enter the higher levels of government.

The Ming Dynasty (A.D. 1368–1644) Disease, Chinese opposition, and fighting among themselves eventually weakened the Mongols, and their rule fell apart. The Chinese regained power under the leadership of a commoner who took the name Prince Wu (Hong Wu). He called his dynasty Ming. For 300 years, one dynasty ruled and China knew stability and peace. Under the Ming, division between rich and poor became less sharp. The Ming emperors encouraged agriculture and technological development, and Chinese art achieved the form it would carry into modern times. Slavery was abolished. Farmers were relieved of crushing taxation. They were allowed to seek a better life and to move when serfdom was ended. The standard of living rose to new heights and the Ming dynasty was looked back on by future centuries as a golden age.

In foreign trade, China was able to exchange its own common materials for far more valuable goods because Chinese manufacturing techniques and artistic designs were much more advanced than those of other countries. The Mongols blocked Chinese trade routes through the northwest, so the Chinese used their seaports to the south to trade with India, Persia, and Africa. The Ming sent out huge fleets to explore the coastal routes to the south, bringing back trade goods from as far away as Zanzibar and the African coast. Chinese legend reports that Admiral Zheng De sailed his fleet of giant ships, some 400 feet long with nine masts of bamboo sails, to Sumatra and Borneo and then across the Pacific to the coasts of an uncharted land of "fiery mountains at the feet of the dawn." Will evidence someday be found that Chinese explorers reached our Pacific coasts or at least Hawaii?

The later Ming emperors grew afraid of the growing influence of foreigners in the ports of China, especially the Arabs, who taught Islam among the poorest classes of the cities. They closed Chinese ports and

Above: Animal-shaped vessel from China created 13th–14th century. Right: Porcelain covered jar created A.D. 1368–1644.

forbade the foreign trade their predecessors had encouraged. No non-Chinese could enter the kingdom without the severest penalty.

At the same time, the countries of Europe were sailing eastward. Portugal reached Asia, the Indies, and finally China. The Ming administration tried to keep the Portuguese out of China, but they bribed their way in and eventually set up profitable trade with China. The Spaniards and the Dutch soon followed.

It was during the Ming dynasty that Catholic missionaries entered China with the Portuguese traders. When the first Catholic missionaries arrived, they found remnants of a Christian church in the oldest Chinese cities, descendants of Chinese converted by Nestorian Christians from Byzantium a thousand years before. Portuguese Jesuits were particularly successful in learning the Chinese language, spreading the learning of the West, and making converts. By 1650 there were over 150,000 Catholics in China.

Matteo Ricci

The job of evangelizing China was given to a young Italian priest by his Jesuit superiors. Young Matteo Ricci was full of the zeal of Christ and eager to bring the liberation of the Faith to this rich and vast empire, so orderly and so respectful of learning and tradition. His own talents in science and mathematics won him the respect of a Chinese official in Canton, who gave him a pass to the capital at Beijing. Father Matteo had to learn to speak the elegant Chinese of the court and to adopt Chinese dress if he wished to be taken seriously. The Chinese knew only the roughest seamen and merchants from Europe; they thought of all Westerners as barbaric, unclean, and uneducated.

Confucianism and Buddhism alike have little use for gods or powers other than the human will, but Father Matteo was able to show his educated audiences that their ideas of right and wrong came from a Supreme Being, the Lord of heaven. Finally, he gained an audience with the emperor, after 16 years of trying, and only then because the clock he had brought from Italy caught the fancy of the emperor.

Ricci and his fellow Jesuits had assembled a church of 150,000 in some 40 years of evangelizing. To aid their work, they produced a translation of the liturgy and of the Scriptures into Chinese so that the Chinese could read and pray in their own tongue. This translation was called the Chinese Rite. In that era, when controversy with the Protestants over liturgy and Scripture in the European vernaculars was troubling the Church, a translation into Chinese, no matter how useful, was suspect. Authorities in Rome worried over allowing this vernacular, when others closer to home were not allowed it.

Unfortunately, the vernacular rites were finally not approved by Rome, and as a result, the Chinese government banned Christianity. The emperor ordered all foreign missionaries killed or exiled. The presence of thousands of Christians in China today began with a second wave of missionaries in the 19th century.

The Ching, the Last Dynasty of Old China In the 1600s the Ming dynasty fought a long war with invaders from the north, the Manchus, and lost. The Manchus took the name Ching dynasty for themselves. They held China until the 20th century. The Ching Manchus made harsh laws to keep the native Han Chinese from rebellion. Throughout the 19th century, Chinese emigrated in large numbers to new homes all over the world. They set up businesses or took jobs as common laborers. Every major city of the world has its Chinatown, where Chinese families have settled.

The Ching Manchus ordered that all Han men must wear their hair in a long braid (a queue) at the back of the head. All Chinese who emigrated to North America and anywhere else had to keep their queue—or never return to China. Men with long queues became the image of a "Chinaman" for Westerners in the 19th and early 20th centuries.

The long, braided hairstyle forced on all Han Chinese men by the Ching Manchu Dynasty.

Modern China, Born in Agony

Modern China cannot be understood without some knowledge of the country's story for the last 200 years, a troubled and terrible period in Chinese history. The last days of the Ching were marred by civil war and foreign invasion from the West. Western trade was limited to two or three seaport cities, where the emperor's officials thought they could control the rapid spread of European influence. Christian missionaries, particularly Protestant missionaries, followed the merchants and took their message inland, beyond the port cities. The mass of the Chinese people was already dissatisfied with alien Manchu rule. In the first half of the 1900s, China was hit by a series of natural disasters, floods, and droughts that caused mass famines and misery to the poor and middle classes. Many Chinese slipped past the Manchu border guards and port authorities and emigrated to the islands of Malaysia and Indonesia. China was ripe for civil war and uprising, and the Westerners added to the problem by selling opium, an addictive narcotic drug grown in India, to the Chinese. Efforts to ban opium failed, but a British shipment of the drug was seized by the police and burned. War between Britain and the imperial army left the government troops humiliated and the weakness of the Manchu power became clear to all Chinese.

In 1845, a new religion was founded by Hung Hsiu-ch'uan, a peasant who had been evangelized by Protestant missionaries. He declared himself a second son of God, the successor to Jesus, and offered his followers freedom from restrictive traditional ways, and communal ownership of property. To the starving poor of China, his primitive communism was very appealing. Thousands flocked to his cause. He called his religion Taip'ing, Great Peace. A revolutionary state was proclaimed in 1851 and the imperial forces were routed. The new political movement and religion gained ground through all the south of China. The Manchus were unable to fight back. Resistance to the advancing religious fanatics fell to local militias, fighting for their traditions and homes.

The largest civil war in world history, the Taipeng Rebellion, involved millions of combatants all over China. It wasted the economy, and split the country into several territories only loosely controlled by the Ching emperor, under the orders of local warlords and militia. Taipeng and its founder seemed victorious. But when his promised land reform failed to materialize, the factions within Taipeng failed to cooperate, and the move-

ment was broken after a defeat by Western-led militia. Plundering gangs of robbers and local warlords, called Nien, terrorized the countryside. The imperial government put down these bandits, and a second rebellion, the Nien Rebellion, was also defeated in bloody and destructive battles.

Because of the famine and constant civil war, thousands of Chinese laborers took ship to the Americas or the British-controlled islands of Southeast Asia in search of money to send home to starving families. The railroads of the American West were built by Chinese "coolie" labor.

Western help had been given to both sides, rebels and Manchus, because Westerners wanted a disunited China. And so China turned radically anti-Western. The empire was left to a boy, and his mother quickly seized power for herself and her allies. She was Tz'u-shi, the second woman in Chinese history to take command of the empire. She renamed herself Wu after her predecessor.

Meanwhile, the pseudo-Christian claims of the Taipeng movement caused both the Manchu government and the common people to grow anti-Christian. This anti-Christian feeling sprang from a sense of the danger to their own tradition and identity, and from the Christian support of the poor and oppressed against the official and gentry class. Christianity, with its constant awareness of the poor and social justice, sowed dissension and friction in the already disintegrating Chinese society.

China wanted Western industry and Western investment, however. And the great industrial powers of Europe all demanded the cheap labor of China for their new railroads, mines, and factories.

In 1900, a political movement called the Righteous and Harmonious Fists, known to Europeans as the Boxers, rose in rebellion, attacking foreigners and Chinese Christians and threatening all Westerners in the country. The Boxers cut off Beijing from the sea and western centers on the coast, and besieged the European and American legations inside the walls of the Forbidden City, the imperial palace, for eight long and hard weeks. The Dowager Empress Tz'u-shi sided with the Boxers and ordered her armies to attack the European port cities. A European armed force relieved the siege and almost captured the dowager Empress. She admitted defeat on August 15, 1900 and died a year later. The real power of the Chinese emperors was broken forever.

The Manchu government was forced to abolish many of its laws against foreign influence. Missionaries were again permitted free access to the interior; Chinese students were encouraged to study abroad in Europe or the United States. They formed several revolutionary societies demanding a republic and an end to the old monarchy that had lasted for thousands of years.

Sun Yat-sen was a commoner, educated in Hawaii and Hong Kong. He returned to China in the last years of the Manchu reign, and organized a political movement among the educated intellectuals living in the big cities. He advocated nationalism and socialism. For many years no one listened to him while the imperial government struggled to hold onto power. But the last emperor was forced to abdicate and declare a republic in 1911. Years of civil war followed, as first one faction then another tried to establish a permanent regime. Then Sun Yat-sen reorganized his earlier movement, the Kuomintang, or Nationalist Party, to include the Communists, and was proclaimed president in 1924. With their support, the Kuomintang began to subdue the provincial warlords and other political opponents. Then Sun fell ill with cancer, and died in 1925. General Chiang Kai-shek took control of the Kuomintang, and expelled the Communists in 1927.

Two Manchu ladies.

The Communists, led by Mao Tse-tung, Chou Enlai, and Lin Piao escaped the Nationalists and marched across China to safety in the far northwest, near Mongolia, where the Nationalist troops could not get at them. The escape is known as the Long March and remembered by the Communists as a heroic flight.

Chiang Kai-shek was never able to consolidate all the warlords into the Nationalist government, and the Republic of China was helpless before the invasion of the Japanese army in 1937. The war against Japan was devastating to China, but it united the vast country in an effort to expel the hated foreign invader. The Nationalists fought the Japanese occupation with American aid. The China-Japan war became part of a larger conflict when Japan attacked the United States at Pearl Harbor in 1941. Finally after eight long years of dreadful war and huge loss of life, China saw the last of the Japanese troops leave her territory.

The joy of victory was short-lived. The Communist armies in the far northwest had grown

Sun Yat-sen and his wife.

and perfected their fighting abilities during the combat with Japan. They moved on Chiang Kai-shek's Nationalists immediately after the Japanese were no longer a threat. By 1949, the Communists, supported by the Soviet Union, were masters of all of China, and the Nationalists had retreated to the large island off the eastern coast, Taiwan. American support for the Nationalists helped stop the Communist advance at the water's edge and allowed the Nationalists to form a government on Taiwan that they continued to call the Republic of China. The Communists called their new state the People's Republic of China. It was a regime of absolute tyranny and totalitarian control of every aspect of life of the Chinese, as bloody and destructive as that of the first emperor, Zheng Qin Huang Di.

Modern China was born in a long agony of disasters and civil conflict. Its history was influenced by contact with Christianity, both Catholic and Protestant. Christianity is once again swiftly growing there. But brutality, a stamp of Communism, still exists. There is, for example, no respect for individual human life in China, especially seen in forced abortion, infanticide, concentration camps, and public executions—often of

Christians. No matter how much trade exists between China and the United States, the Communist threat to the West lives on.

Chapter 10 Review

Let's Remember   Write your answer in a single complete sentence.
1. What was the Great Wall intended to do?
2. Who was Confucius?
3. What is an ideogram?
4. Who was Genghis Khan?
5. When did Christianity come into China?

Let's Consider   For silent thinking and a short essay, or for thinking in a group with classroom discussion:
1. How is our language different from the Chinese ideogram?
2. How did the various dynasties rule over the centuries?
3. What went into making the Great Wall?
4. How long did it take the Christian missionaries before they could speak with the emperor?
5. How does disregard for the importance of individual human life throughout all of China's history manifest itself?

Let's Eat!

The Confucian philosophy of cooking says that the elements of the universe are being combined, and it is important that cooking should be done with beauty and harmony. Women and men especially are encouraged to undertake the art of cooking.

A very simple Chinese recipe is Egg Drop Soup: Bring 2 cups of chicken broth to a boil. Beat 2 eggs with 2 T. of soy sauce. Drizzle the egg mixture slowly into the hot liquid. Add chopped spring onions. Serve hot.

Chapter 11

Japan: Land of the Rising Sun

The people of Japan call their country Nippon, meaning "Land of the Rising Sun." Our name for Japan comes from the Chinese pronunciation. When the Japanese used Chinese characters for the name of their country, Nippon, they used the Chinese characters for "sun" and "source." In Chinese, those characters would be pronounced as JIH-PEN. Europeans, learning the name from Chinese speakers, called it—Ja-pan.

Japan is a necklace of islands that runs north to south across from the coasts of Siberia, China, and Korea. West of Japan is the Sea of Japan. It separates the Japanese islands from the Asian mainland. East of Japan is the vast Pacific Ocean.

Only a very small part of Japan is hospitable. Today, Japan's over 100 million people inhabit the 15 percent of the country that is flat and fertile. The other 85 percent is mountainous, forested, and scenic. The mountains were formed from volcanoes, some of which are still active. The most famous is Mount Fuji, a beautiful, imposing volcanic mountain near Tokyo.

The soil from the volcanoes of Japan is rich, and the Japanese have learned how to get the most food from it. The largest crops are rice (a staple of the Japanese diet), tea, soybeans, and fruit. In addition to its own abundant and intense agriculture, Japan is a major market for food and agricultural products from other nations. Abundant fish

Mount Fuji (also called Mt. Fujiyama)

are harvested from the waters around the islands both for Japanese consumption and to sell to other nations.

The northernmost of the four main islands is called Hokkaido. Sapporo is its capital. The island is known for its beauty, including active volcanoes, hot mineral springs, and unspoiled lakes and forests. Its weather is cold and snowy in the winter and cool in the summer. Hokkaido is a favorite vacation spot for Japanese today.

To the south of Hokkaido lies the Island of Honshu. Honshu is by far the largest of Japan's islands and is home to the nation's capital, Tokyo. Honshu is heavily populated and currently produces much of Japan's world-class heavy industry (cars, boats, industrial machinery, etc.) and high-tech industry (electronic consumer goods and industrial components and instruments).

The inhabitants of Honshu benefit from an unusual feature called the Inland Sea. It is a waterway between the southeastern part of Honshu and the northern part of the next island in the chain, Shikoku. It creates numerous small coves and a waterway that is screened from the Pacific Ocean.

Typhoon: The hurricanes of the Pacific Ocean.

Shikoku is the smallest of the four major islands. Its mountains and valleys make agriculture very difficult. The Pacific side of the island is pounded with torrential rains and storms in the summer. Snows beset this beautiful land with its lush vegetation during the winter, and torrential rainfall during the spring and especially the summer. These harsh rains sometimes escalate into destructive **typhoons** in the Pacific Ocean.

The southernmost of the four main islands in the chain, Kyushu, is the third largest. It has a mountainous central region with coastal plains around it. The climate is subtropical, with heavy rain. The northern part of the island houses industry while the southern part produces abundant rice, potatoes, citrus, livestock, and fish.

Because its islands are volcanic, Japan also experiences many earthquakes. Some release just a small amount of energy and cause inconvenience, while others are terribly destructive. Because their homes have

The island of Kyushu, Japan. This view is typical of Japanese cities. Note the volcano in the background.

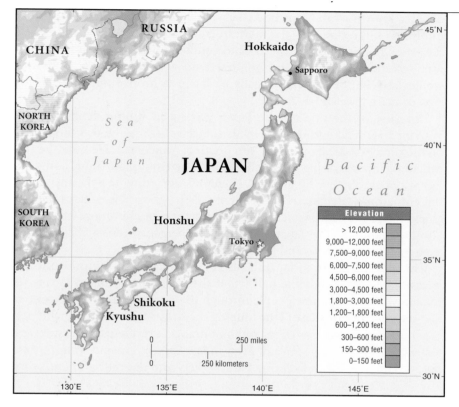

Topographical map of all the Japanese Islands with color scale keyed to elevation.

been repeatedly destroyed by storms and earthquakes, the Japanese have learned to work together as an inventive and courageous team, ready to rebuild as often as necessary.

Japanese Prehistory and Legend

The earliest inhabitants of Japan came to the islands in three waves: the first, Stone Age Caucasians from Siberian Russia, the second oriental farmers, and the third, also oriental, a group that migrated into the south and began the process of nation building that produced Japan. Around the 3rd century A.D., the tribe living in the Yamato Plain in central Honshu established itself as the dominant power in most of Japan. They founded a dynasty known as the Sun line that would give Japan her emperors, in unbroken succession into the modern era, even when other families held the actual political power. The Yamato family claimed that their family line was descended from the sun goddess who gave them three items that would later be the imperial regalia of Japan: a bronze mirror, a bronze sword, and a jeweled necklace.

The first of the line to rule Japan was called Jimmu Tenno (Divine Warrior). He held authority over his subjects, because he was thought to be the direct descendant of the sun goddess Amaterasu. He bore the title **mikado,** emperor of Japan, which means "The Honorable Gate," a title like Egypt's pharaoh, or "Big House." Therefore, according to this story, all of the emperors of Japan are descendants of the gods. His cousins became chieftains of the clans, which were not exactly tribes but more like associations of families. The Japanese clans have become industrial companies such as Toyota, Mikasa, and Mitsubishi.

Mikado: Emperor of Japan.

The oldest religion in Japan is Shinto, the worship of nature gods and ancestors. Shinto holds the belief that the gods who founded Japan will remain with the Japanese people through the imperial line. Shinto continued the ancient practice of worshipping the spirits believed to inhabit natural phenomena, such as rivers and mountains. It reverences ancestors and fosters prayers to them for aid. Even today, Shinto remains an important part of Japanese life in fostering natural piety and reverence for ancestors.

Shinto priests prepare offerings for a ritual in Kyoto, Honshu, Japan.

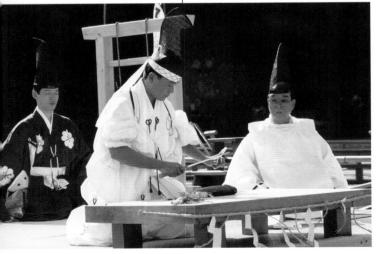

Influence on Japanese Culture

The nearest mainland countries were the little kingdoms of Korea, civilized by the Chinese and very wealthy in the eyes of poor Japanese. Japanese clans began to raid Korea and try to conquer it. What they saw in Korea of Chinese culture struck the Japanese raiders as superior to their own culture, and they began to imitate it. In that way, Chinese civilization first began to come into Japan. The king of one of the Korean kingdoms sent a number of gifts to the Mikado. Among them was an invaluable book, the *Thousand Character Classic*, written in

Chinese script. It was a guide to learning and reading Chinese characters.
Aside from a handful of men who
were able to read Chinese, the
Japanese were illiterate. The mikado saw
that the book would be very valuable to
him if he could read it. He sent to Korea for
a scholar who might be able to teach the
Japanese to read and write. The arrival of the
Korean scribe Wa-ni in A.D. 405 was a new dawn
for Japan. Chinese script became the first official
written language of Japan.

Writing Japanese in Chinese characters is very difficult.
The two spoken languages are completely different. Ideograms, or characters are very suitable for noninflected languages,
but not for inflected ones. Unlike Chinese, Japanese is an inflected language. It uses added syllables to indicate the meaning of a word in a sentence, as does Latin, Greek, or English. (We add -s to indicate more than
one, plural. We add -ed to indicate past tense to a verb, and so forth.)

In the 9th century the Japanese found a solution to the problem. A
Japanese monk named Kobo Daishi, who had learned both Chinese and
Sanskrit, the alphabetic writing of India, created a Japanese **syllabary** that
was appropriate to his own language.

Another import from Korea was Buddhism. A powerful minister of the
king sent for Korean monks to teach the court about their religion. The
ruling clans, however, feared that Buddhism would interfere with the worship of the emperor, a part of the traditional religion of Japan, Shinto. A
foreign religion might offend the gods, spirits, and divine ancestors. This
conflict between Buddhism and Shinto was a violent one.

Buddhism was finally allowed into the country when the crown
prince, Shotoku, decided that he would use China's great civilization as
his model for remaking Japanese society. His father gave him the power
to rule in the emperor's name and retired to his palace while his son
ruled the kingdom. To change his country, Shotoku began a truly revolutionary instruction: he insisted that his nobles learn and observe the
ethical laws of Confucianism. Shotoku, a hero of Japanese civilization,
began to borrow culture, something never before done in world history.
No other people had assimilated the forms and ideas of an alien culture
as Shotoku's Japanese did.

**Heian-period fan,
painted with Japanese
calligraphy, from the
late 12th century.**

Syllabary : A set of
written characters each
one representing a
syllable.

Statue of the Bhudda in Japan.

When the two religions, native Shinto and foreign Buddhism, came in conflict, and they did, the issue was solved by division of authority. Buddhism was first in philosophical or religious matters; Confucianism was first in secular policy, and Shinto would continue to direct court ritual and popular religion.

Under Shotoku's direction, Japanese who were skilled in the arts or Buddhist studies were sent to China to complete their studies. When they returned after 10 or 20 years of training at the Chinese court, they were given important government posts. Shotoku changed the life of Japan and gave to the imperial court its ceremony and philosophy. He died at the age of 49, the most powerful man in the realm, never attaining the imperial throne for himself. He was always just the crown prince.

The Heian Period (A.D. 794–1185)

The full flowering of the use of Chinese culture in Japan occurred during what is called the Heian period. An elegant court, modeled on imperial China, created poetry and music, artworks, and elegant calligraphy (the writing of characters in a beautiful and decorative way). In 793, a new capital city was built near Nara in the center of the Yamato plain, and named Heian-kyo, Capital of Peace.

Heian-kyo was the first true city in Japan. Its layout copied the Chinese capital city at Changan. It was rectangular, three miles long, and two and two-thirds miles wide. At its center sat the imperial palace. Parks and broad avenues, set at right angles, made it a lovely city. It came to be called simply, Kyoto, the capital.

While assimilating Chinese styles, Japanese artists portrayed their subjects with more realism and individual character rather than as idealized figures. Japan's oldest surviving portrait of an individual is the sculpture of the great Chinese monk-missionary Ganjin. It shows him as a wizened old man, wrinkled and worn, but meditating and tranquil of mind.

Japanese classical literature found its form only the century before Heian. In 760, an anthology of 4,500 poems, claiming to be from antiquity but actually from the preceding century, was issued. It was the *Man'yoshu*, the *Ten Thousand Leaves*. Most of the poems are short five-line poems called waka. A few are long poems, or choka. But the long poem does not work well in the language and was not a favorite of Japanese poets. The age of poetry that began in Heian was perfected by the Man'yoshu. A courtier was expected to be able to compose and recite a waka on command for any occasion, and to compose long poems for formal recitation when needed.

A hundred years later, in the 10th century, prose romances became fashionable reading, and women writers made names for themselves by mastering the form. Sei Shonagun's *Pillow Book* (1002) is now recognized as a masterpiece. The greatest prose work of the period was by another court lady, Murasaki Shikibu. It is called *The Tale of Genji* (ca. 1015).

While the arts at the court flourished, the administration was weakening. The imperial family came to rely on the Fujiwara family to help them govern. The Fujiwara gradually replaced the emperors as the real rulers of Japan and confined the royal family to its palace in Kyoto. But Fujiwara courtiers could not stand up to the growing power of the warrior clans from the provinces who began to make themselves the masters of Japan and scorn court life in the capital.

Two warrior clans came to rule the imperial family through marriages and military force. They were the Taira and Minamoto. The story of their long feud and struggle for control of the emperor is the subject of the long

Scene from *The Tale of Genji.*

The Revenge of Yoritomo

The Minamoto found favor at court and were given honors and wealth by the emperor. But the Taira surprised the Minamoto family in the night and slaughtered all the family except one small boy, Minamoto Yoritomo. The guards were going to kill this last of the Minamoto line, when he spoke up and said, "My mother and father are dead, and who but I can pray for their happiness in the next world?" The grandmother of the Taira was moved by his filial piety and remembered her own son who died as a boy. She begged for Yoritomo's life, and he was spared on condition of a distant exile.

Yoritomo was banished to Idzu, at the farthest end of the island. He was kept under close guard and his guards were told to kill him when he reached thirteen years. A faithful servant raised him and taught him martial arts in secret. When he was thirteen, he was so submissive and seemingly helpless that the lord of the Taira allowed him to live. Yoritomo bided his time.

He thought to arrange a marriage and thus ally himself with a powerful clan; but to avoid notice, and to secure the favor of the mother, he decided to marry the ugly daughter. He sent her a letter proposing marriage, but his servant had ideas of his own and gave the letter to Masago, the beautiful daughter.

That night the ugly sister had a dream of a pigeon flying to her with a box of gold. She told her dream to her sister, who said, "Let me buy your dream, little sister, and I will give you my golden mirror in exchange." The homely sister sold her dream for a mirror. She had hardly said yes when the servant appeared and gave the beautiful sister the letter from Yoritomo.

The two eloped, and Masago became Yoritomo's wife, aiding him in his quest for revenge and restoration of his house. The two of them set about collecting an army of followers and friendly lords, disturbed at the growing power of the Taira. The head of the Taira clan heard of this army and laughed, "For an exile to plot against the Taira is like a mouse going against a cat."

The laugh was soon Yoritomo's, for his forces routed the Taira on the battlefield at the Fuji River. The two sides halted for the night before the battle on either side of the swift and deep river. In the night, two of the Taira warriors thought to slip into Yoritomo's camp and assassinate him. They tried to cross the river through the wide shallows on their side, but their splashing stirred up the great flocks of ducks that were resting there on their migration north. The sound of the birds flapping and quacking woke the Taira troops, who thought they were being surprise-attacked by their enemy. In the confusion, many ran for safety and some fought their own men in the dark. In the morning, the Taira force was dead or fled from the field. The last of the Minamoto had won a bloodless victory.

Yoritomo and his beautiful wife Masago left the capital and built a new city for themselves and their followers at Kamakura, in a valley facing the open sea. Roadways were cut through the mountains to give access but be easily defended. Yoritomo and his wife made their own court more beautiful and attractive than the emperor's in Kyoto. Yoritomo died in his bed in 1199. The Minamoto family now took control of the capital and the imperial court lost control of the country.

Yoritomo releases wild cranes.

story-sequence, the *Heike Monogatori* (ca. 1250). Stories from that conflict became subjects of Japanese drama, both the Buddhist stylized drama, the No, and the popular *Kabuki* melodramas.

The Shogunate Period

The now powerless emperor, placed on his throne by Yoritomo and the Minamoto, was forced to turn to Yoritomo to subdue the other warrior-chiefs and bring peace to the country. In 1192, Yoritomo received a special title, **shogun**, or Supreme General, and with it the right to rule for the emperor. The office of shogun became the principal power in the land. The emperors, though always born of the ancient Sun Line, were mere figureheads without power or even enough wealth to keep up their palaces.

> **Shogun**: A military ruler of Japan.

The period of the shoguns brought with it a measure of peace and prosperity. However, there was a constant struggle between noble families for control of the country. Each powerful clan wanted to rule Japan in the name of the emperor. In the warfare, many lords died. Their orphaned

Samurai armour.

The Samurai

A system of loyalties from the ruler to the nobles and on down to other warriors was established by Yoritomo. The "code of the warrior" went along with this "lord-client" relationship. The warrior, or Samurai, was totally dutiful to his lord or master. His loyalty was absolute; a samurai would unflinchingly die rather than face dishonor. The courage of the samurai may be compared to that of the Spartans. Although the military skill of the Samurai was legendary, they were much more than warriors only. They were trained in writing and in politics as well.

The samurai were also drawn to a sect of the Buddhist religion known as Zen. Zen Buddhism stresses self-enlightenment through meditation and physical and mental discipline. Zen was blended with elements of the traditional Shinto religion to provide moral and artistic guidelines for the tough, yet loyal, and artistic samurai that ruled Japan.

Samurai: A member of a Japanese feudal warrior class.
Ronin: A mercenary samurai without a ruling lord.

Haiku: A form of poetry that compresses a complex idea or image into three unrhymed simple lines.

samurai became **ronin**, or lordless samurai. They hired themselves out as warriors or wandered the country simply taking what they needed.

Traditional Japanese Arts

Influenced by the natural beauty of Japan, the Shinto religion's appreciation of nature, and Buddhism's contemplative balance, Japanese artists developed very striking and unique Japanese arts: flower arranging (*ikebana*), growing and pruning miniature trees (*bonzai*), poetry (**haiku**), and the traditional tea ceremony.

Traditional Japanese flower arranging (*ikebana*) developed from Buddhist temple offerings. These artistic arrangements using natural flowers and other plant materials came to be used in the homes of the upper classes and to be recognized as an art form. The arrangements expressed the traditional Japanese idea of the balance of heaven, Earth, and man, using the plants to convey a personal thought or feeling.

Traditional Japanese poetry conveys a vivid thought or emotion in a stylized verse with definite rules. Poetic ideas are linked to natural objects, such as mountains, grass, or rain. The thought must be compressed into a very few words, suggested rather than stated. The Japanese poetic form best known in the West today is haiku, which consists of three unrhymed lines of five syllables, seven, and five syllables again. In haiku, enduring patterns of nature are often

Sesshu and the Mouse

Sesshu (1420–1506) was one of Japan's great artists. Originally, Sesshu studied to be a monk. However, he was so busy drawing that he neglected his studies. As a punishment, his teacher tied him to a pillar at the temple. Sesshu's tears created a puddle at his own feet and, using only his toes, Sesshu drew a mouse. Legend has it that the mouse was so lifelike that his teacher, upon seeing it, gave permission to Sesshu to study painting.

Shiki sansui by Sesshu Toyo, created around A.D. 1500.

Pruning a bonsai.

compared to momentary perceptions. The reader is challenged to find the meaning of the juxtaposition of permanent things and transient things.

The Zen monk, Basho, wrote one famous example of haiku:

This ancient pond here:
A frog suddenly plunges:
Plop of the water.

Japan's most cele-
brated haiku poet,
Basho, pauses to share
the midautumn festival
with two farmers.

Understanding such a poem requires visualizing the scene. Think of the oldest pond you know or can think of. Imagine yourself standing beside it, seeing the lichen on the trees and rocks, the color of the dark stones, the sense of ancient times, and men of prayer and thoughtfulness who have stood, like you, beside these waters. As you are drawn deeper and deeper into the contemplation of the deep water, a frog suddenly jumps in. You do not see him; he is too quick. But the sound of his hitting the water breaks your reverie, and in that moment the music of the rippling water reminds you that the ancient touches the now.

Sometimes the haiku can be used for moral perceptions as well. Another by Basho:

When a thing is said,
The lips become very cold
Like the autumn wind.

"When a thing is said," not just any thing, but a cold thing, cold enough to chill the lips that spoke it. How often do we regret having said an unkind

Woman performing
the Japanese tea
ceremony.

word almost as soon as we have said it? Here, Basho thinks of that moment of regret as a cold autumn wind, turning the lips, and the heart, cold with sadness, and perhaps a little fear.

The tea ceremony or chanoyu takes place in a small, out-of-the-way room set aside for tea. Honored guests arrive to take part in what is more than simply a social occasion. The gathering is a chance to purify the soul by appreciating nature. The ceremony is also an opportunity to appreciate the gardens surrounding the tearoom, the ceramic bowls used in the ceremony, and its decorative flowers. The tea ceremony, introduced from China, developed into its present form in the mid-1800s. It became an important form of social communication among the upper classes. The slow motions of the tea server, and the attention of the guests to every gesture reflect the Japanese attitude to existence.

The 1500s: The Portuguese Bring Trade and Christianity

In 1549, after some initial trading contacts, the Spanish Jesuit Francis Xavier (who later became the patron saint of missionaries as St. Francis Xavier) came to Japan with Portuguese merchants. His missionary activity was a spectacular success. St. Francis Xavier spoke enthusiastically about the spiritual understanding of the Japanese people and their openness to the Christian faith. Within two years there were thousands of Japanese Christians. Portuguese traders supported the missionary activity of their countrymen.

In 1590, Toyotomi Hideyoshi completed the military unification of the country. He opposed the tolerance of foreign missionaries. He saw the growth of Christianity as a foreign threat as well as a power play by his rivals among the samurai lords. Samurai lords of the island of Kyushu supported the Christians and their Portuguese backers. Hideyoshi's opposition hardened into total banishment of Christian missionaries. He made Christianity a crime punishable by death. Hideyoshi tried to crush the fruitful beginnings of the Japanese Church by crucifying 20 Japanese Christians alongside six of their European brethren. St. Paul Miki and companions, the martyrs of Japan, met death on a hill near Nagasaki on February 6, 1597.

Hideyoshi blows his great war trumpet at dawn before his victory at Shizugatake, 1583.

The desire to keep Japan pure from outside influences and therefore under the total control of the Shogun brought about further oppression of the Christian church. Thousands of Christians were killed. Others were forced to stop public worship.

The Tokugawa Shogunate

In 1603 another powerful ruler, Tokugawa Ieyasu, a descendant of the Minamoto Shogun Yoritomo, emerged as the ruler of all Japan after Hideyoshi died. He moved the capital to Edo, the site of modern-day Tokyo, on the eastern shore of the island of Honshu. The emperor's court remained at Kyoto. It was totally without power and preserved as an institution only because Shinto depended on the divine emperors of the Sun line.

The Tokugawa shoguns continued to isolate their country, forbidding contact with all foreigners and persecuting the Christians who remained. Japan was frozen in a class and caste system that left no room for mobility or change. The events of the 17th and 18th centuries in Europe and the rest of Asia passed Japan by. In the mid-19th century, it was without the industry or technology that made the European countries world powers.

Commodore Perry Opens Japan

In 1853, the United States sent Commodore Matthew C. Perry to Japan to pressure for trade. Faced with overwhelming military power, Japan opened its ports to the United States, and shortly thereafter to Russia, France, Great Britain, and the Netherlands. While Japan enjoyed the benefit of foreign contact, a group of young nobles rallied around the young emperor. He was called Meiji, meaning Enlightened Rule. Leading revolts around

Matthew Calbraith Perry (1794–1858). From an undated photo by Mathew Brady.

the country, the young nobles returned power to the emperor in what was called the Meiji Restoration.

The emperor's restoration was not what the young aristocrats had expected. Instead of returning the country to the way of the "ancients," which tolerated no outside influences, Meiji did the opposite. He banned the samurai class and the privileges of the nobility and created a modern army drafted from the common people.

He also allowed the practice of Christianity. The Japanese Christians had managed to keep their little church alive under persecution for over two centuries—all without the benefit of priests or any help from the outside. When Christianity became legal again, the small but brave community of Catholic Christians that had endured in quiet faith was able to worship freely in the open again.

Meiji invited representatives from the Western countries (England, France, Germany, Portugal, the Netherlands) in order to learn a different way of government from them. He established a Western-style constitution with a prime minister and democratic elections.

Meiji ordered the building of industrial factories on the European model and, like his ancient predecessor, Crown Prince Shotoku, he began to remake Japan. As a result, the economy of Japan, along with its industrial and military power, grew overnight. Japan had a fully equipped modern army by the end of the 19th century, barely 50 years after Commodore Perry's sailing into Tokyo harbor.

Many Japanese emigrated in the last half of the 19th century and the first half of the 20th. They found new homes in the United States, and in the Spanish-speaking countries of Central and South America. Japanese students traveled to Europe and America to study in the universities, and Japanese artists were warmly received. The past of Japan lingers on in not so pretty ways in the tradition-bound ranks of the army, still bound by the code of the samurai, Bushido.

Japan wanted to imitate the Europeans in other ways besides industry and politics. Japanese politicians wanted the wealth of an empire. In 1905, Japan fought a naval war with its new steel warships against Russia, and forced the tsar's army to surrender; Russia had to cede the island of Sakhalin, north of Japan, to the mikado's government. In the 1930s, Japanese nationalists, fearing American and British power, and worried that China in its long civil strife would damage Japan's commercial interests in Asia, declared war on China, and within two years overran much of eastern China. Japan had learned western technology and organization, but it had not changed its old code of ruthless warfare. The Japanese committed atrocities in China that turned all the world against them. A secret pact with Nazi Germany helped Japan to dominate parts of Asian. By the 1940s, Japanese military power grew so strong that Japan challenged the United States and England, and continued the invasion of China, in its quest for total domination of East Asia. On December 7, 1941, the Japanese fleet attacked the United States naval base at Pearl Harbor, Hawaii. After a long struggle, island by island in the South Pacific, Japan's armies finally were pushed back to the home islands.

On Kyushu is the city of Nagasaki. Nagasaki and Hiroshima, a city not far away on the southern tip of Honshu, were destroyed by the first atomic bombs dropped on August 6, 1945. While it is tragic that innocent people died in these bombings, most notably in the large community of Catholic Christians in Nagasaki, the dropping of the atomic bombs led to a swift end of World War II. Hundreds of thousands of lives, both American and Japanese, were spared by the dropping of the atomic bombs because the planned invasion of allied land troops was not carried out. The Japanese had planned, if invaded, to execute thousands of prisoners of war. Japanese women and children had been drilled to resist an invading force, and, like their men, they would have fought with sharpened bamboo sticks to the

Modern Tokyo at night, looking north to Chou-Ku.

very end. Japan surrendered on September 2, 1945—the end to its dream of world conquest.

Today Japan is a constitutional monarchy. The emperor holds a ceremonial position, and the country is a democracy ruled by an elected parliament. Japan's industry and technological science add to the well-being of all the world.

Chapter 11 Review

Let's Remember   Write your answer in a single complete sentence.
1. What do the people of Japan call their country?
2. The emperors of Japan come in unbroken succession from which line?
3. What does mikado mean?
4. Who was St. Francis Xavier?
5. Who was Commodore Matthew Perry?

Let's Consider   For silent thinking and a short essay, or for thinking in a group with classroom discussion:
1. How would living on a series of islands affect the sense of a country's unity?
2. What might have happened in Japan had Christianity not been suppressed under Hideyoshi in the 16th century?
3. Ponder the division in Japanese art of Earth, Man, and Heaven.
4. Ponder the bravery of the Japanese Christians in keeping the faith for 200 years.
5. How did the rapid development of Japan, both for good and bad, in the 20th century come about?

Let's Eat!

One of the main foods of Japan is fish. Sushi and sashimi, two very popular Japanese fish foods, can now be purchased in American supermarkets and in the many Japanese restaurants in America. Some folks get mixed up with the terms sushi and sashimi. Sushi means "seasoned rice" and sashimi means "sliced raw fish."

Chapter 12

India: The World of the Rajas

India is so large that, historically, it has always included several kingdoms. The Indian subcontinent today contains three separate independent countries: Pakistan, India, and Bangladesh. Sri Lanka, an island, is a fourth independent nation. The subcontinent was divided between two countries when the British gave India its independence in 1948: a Muslim state and a Hindu state. The territory of Muslim Pakistan was split into eastern and western portions by a thousand miles of India, inhabited by Hindus. The eastern territory of Pakistan then declared its independence from the western, and took the name, Bangladesh.

The Geography of India

The subcontinent of India is surrounded by seas on three sides: the Bay of Bengal lies to the east, the Arabian Sea to the west, and the larger Indian Ocean to the south. The large island of Sri Lanka (Ceylon) lies off the southern tip of the mainland.

India is composed of four fairly distinct geographic regions: the mountainous north and northeast of the Himalayas and their foothills, the fertile plains watered by several rivers including the Indus and Ganges, a rocky triangular plateau south of the fertile plains called the Deccan, and a coastal plain on the southern tip called Tamil Nadu. The northern half of India contains two great river valleys: the Indus, which flows west into the Arabian Sea, and the Ganges, which is the sacred river of the Hindus; both rivers rise in the Himalayan Mountains.

Women collect water in pots, carried on their heads, in the desert in Rajasthan, India.

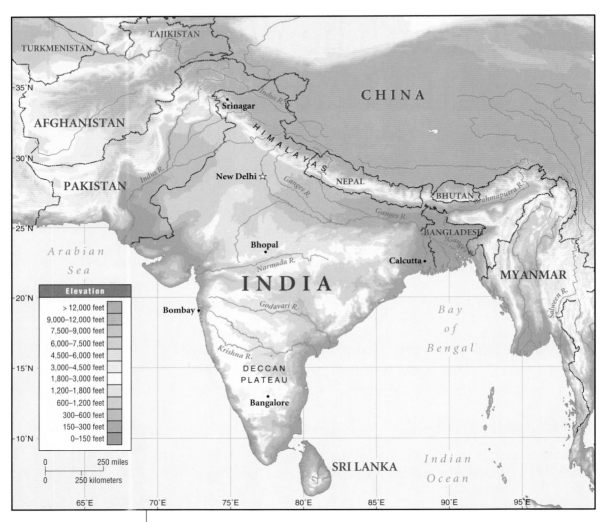

Map of India.

Monsoon: Heavy seasonal wind and rain

Most of India is tropical in climate with seasonal **monsoon**s, heavy rains that occur during the summer in the north and the winter in the south. These heavy downpours cause floods that are often ruinous to the farmlands along the great rivers. Up on the central Deccan plateau, the enemy of the farmer is prolonged droughts. Famines have struck India from the earliest times, caused by these extremes of climate. The country, however, is blessed with forests of trees and bamboo, as well as a variety of mineral deposits, including iron ore, coal, silver, copper, and zinc.

There are also mountain ridges across the subcontinent, that divide the country roughly in two parts: the north and the south. Perhaps this is the reason that the languages of the northern part of the country derive from Sanskrit, an Indo-European language like Latin and English, while the languages of southern India derive from Dravidian, an older language once found throughout the Indian subcontinent.

The Beginnings of India

Ancient Indus River Civilization

One of the four first civilizations of mankind grew up along the banks of the Indus River, a watercourse longer and mightier than the Tigris-Euphrates Rivers, and far more treacherous. The Indus rises in the Himalayan Mountains of Nepal and rushes south and then west over 1,000 miles to the Arabian Sea, leaving tons of silted soil from the highlands along the banks as its violent floods subside. Around 2600 to 1900 B.C., it was home to a civilization that built large cities along its banks. Three of

The Many Languages of India

Modern India recognizes many different languages as legal. Because of so many languages it conducts most of its business in English.

Map of Indus civilization.

Remains of the granaries of Harappa, Pakistan.

those cities have been unearthed by archeologists in the past hundred years: Harappa, Mohenjo Daro, and Dholavira. Harappa and Mohenjo Daro are now in Pakistan; Dholavira is across the border in India. Harappa, built beside the Ravi River, a tributary of the Indus, is the name given to all this first Indian civilization.

The Indus valley culture shows a surprising regularity in its city plans and forms. Mohenjo Daro and Harappa could be twin cities, laid out by the same architect. These ancient Indus cities were built according to a central plan or design, with straight, north-south thoroughfares and almost identical dwellings for all classes of society. The courtyard-style houses opened onto narrow alleys of regular, straight, grid-like intersection. Houses had toilet drains, and there were public toilets on each of the five city mounds. Each house had a bathing platform. The bath water ran off into a common waste channel to the river. A bath was taken by pouring water over the body, not by a tub or a shower. Daily bathing—atop a raised bathing platform—is obligatory in Indian society to this day.

Mohenjo Daro and Harappa, are hundreds of miles apart, yet very similar. Most notably, both are built on five mounds of brick, lifting them above the floods of the Ravi and Indus. Between the mounds, a canal or dry avenue allowed flood waters to pass harmlessly by the city. The very thick walls of the island-mounds were in some areas 45 feet thick. One of the mounds held a citadel of palace and government buildings on its platform top. Towers and gateways into the citadel wall were reached by a ceremonial ramp. Another mound held storehouses, workshops, and barracks for laborers. Private homes rose on two other mounds; public buildings, including a large bathing pool, were situated on the last.

But the cities seem to have had no fortified city wall. Were these cities never afraid of invasion? The five mounds could have been easily attacked, one at a time. Were they built to hold off the flood waters of the rivers, a greater foe than a human army? The force of the floodwaters might have raced between the five sections of the city and yet not taken down the mounds. If this was so, fighting men would have fought off invaders in front of the city.

The remains of elephants have been found in these ghost cities. This indicates that using elephants for work, warfare, and transport in India is at least as old as these Indus valley cities. Depictions of an elephant deity have been found inscribed on ancient seals and tablets of clay.

Harappan civilization also developed a written language. Unfortunately, its ideograms are not intelligible to modern scholars. They are not like the writing of Mesopotamia or the later writing of Indian peoples. Only fragments of this writing survive, inscribed on clay shards that may once have been part of larger clay tablets, like those of Sumer.

All the cities of the Indus seem to have been abandoned at about the same time, not invaded at all. Perhaps a massive flood or series of floods ruined the farmland with salts or mud beyond the ability of primitive farmers to repair them. The bodies of many people were unearthed in the ruins of Mohenjo Daro by the first archeologists. Recent discoveries indicate that the dead bodies are from a plague, or perhaps a massive flood, that so devastated Mohenjo Daro that its citizens simply left the city forever. The refugees then set up smaller villages over the mountains to the east in the valley of the Ganges River and became the ancestors of the modern Indians. They took with them their Indus culture, its cooperation, its gods, its farming technology, and its love of cleanliness and daily baths.

Harappan Stone tablets, containing pictographic writing, found at the archeological site of Mohenjo-Daro. (ca. 2500–1700 B.C.).

The Aryan Conquerors

In a pattern that was being repeated in Greece, Europe, and the Middle East, aggressive northern tribes from the Asian steppes pushed into India around the year 1500 B.C. They were part of the people who overran and conquered Persia. They brought their Indo-European language, fast chariots, and bronze weapons into northern India. Eventually they conquered it through unrelenting warfare. They called themselves *Aryas*—meaning "Noble People." These *Aryas* tribes found an advanced thousand-year-old agricultural civilization along the Indus River. The original Indus farmers were called Dravidians. Because India is a large subcontinent, with mountains and rivers that divide it, the original Dravidian culture remained strong in some southern areas. The original Dravidian language is the basis for the languages of southern India.

Language, for most nations a powerful unifying force, is not so for India. Because of the conquest, the many languages of India are not just dialects of the same language, but are based on two different language families. To solve the problem, modern India uses English as the common language of government and education.

The society of India today has many elements that can be traced directly to the Aryan northerners. They left a body of sacred scriptures learned by heart by their priests and referred to as law, **the Vedas**. The word *Veda* means "knowledge" in Sanskrit, the Indo-European language of the Aryan people. The Vedas are long poems composed of many individual couplets, each giving some proverb or principle of their religion. They originated in the heroic tribal days of the invaders. These scriptures describe the duties of men and the divine social order given to the Aryans by their gods. Most of what we know about the Vedic society comes from the longest of them, the *Rig Veda*. This poem mentions many aspects of Aryan life.

The Hindu priests were charged with preserving the Vedas in their exact wording. The poems are strictly metered and easy to memorize. In the priestly schools masters taught their students to sing the verses; a master sang each line, and then it was repeated by the students. Each line would be sung and repeated several times so as to memorize it. Hindu priests today sing the Vedas by repeating each line at least once.

The Aryan society was tribal. The tribesmen enjoyed making warfare and rode horse-drawn chariots into battle. Cattle stealing and fighting were the chief occupations of Aryan warriors. Each tribe was ruled by a hereditary king or prince, called a **raja**. The prince had absolute power over his tribe, and the tribe had absolute power over the conquered people. The rajas fought among themselves. Then, as their families grew and there were more sons to divide the inheritance between, they grabbed more lands from Dravidians to the south.

Between 1000 and 600 B.C. the Aryans outgrew the Indus valley and spread into the Ganges plains. And by the 600s there were 16 large Aryan states in north India. A major war, probably fought around 900 B.C., became the subject of India's national epic, the *Mahabharata*. This poem, with 100,000 couplets, is the longest poem known. Its moral subject is

The Vedas: Indian poetic scriptures.

Raja: A hereditary prince, or king, of India.

Hindu priests studying.

The *Mahabharata*

In the kingdom of Bhaarata, the next king of the Kurus is blind. But the law says that no blind man can be made king. He passes the kingdom to his brother, Pandu. When Pandu dies, the kingdom should have gone to Yudhisthira, son of Pandu. The sons of the blind king, the Kauravas, want the throne. They cheat at dice and win the kingdom from the Pandavas. The Pandavas must hide in the forest for 12 years, and then be unrecognized for the next year, or spend another 12 years in the forest. A long and destructive war follows between the cousins. The leader of the Pandavas is Arjuna, a noble young prince. The god Krishna takes a part in the action in a human disguise as Arjuna's charioteer.

After a terrible battle that lasts 18 days, the Pandavas are victorious and the Kauranas are all slain on the battlefield. Arjuna and his brothers rule the kingdom wisely and well for many years.

Above: Arjun Nrittam is a ritual folk dance based on stories from the *Mahabharata* epic. Below: A battle scene from the *Mahabharata* epic.

The *Bhagavad Gita*

The *Mahabharata* contains a long central section called the *Bhagavad Gita*, or "Lord's Song." It is a sermon given to Arjuna on the battlefield by Krishna, his charioteer. The *Bhagavad Gita* is the most popular scripture of Hinduism. It is read by many for its answer to the question of human suffering. It offers the idea of reincarnation to assuage our doubt and fear.

Arjuna sees his cousins, who were his childhood playmates and friends, their brahmins, gurus, servants, soldiers, wives, and children, before him on the battlefield and is struck with sympathy for them. "How can I take the lives of my kindred?" he says. "Would it not be better to give up the kingdom rather than cause suffering to those I care for?" Krishna exclaims, "Let them perish, prince, and fight!" His sermon gives three reasons for this cold-blooded counsel: First, the soul is immortal, only the body dies; thus Arjuna is not killing his cousins but doing them a favor. Second, his duty as a prince is to fight, since that is what a prince is, a killer. Third, if he does not fight, he will be called a coward, not a prince. He must detach his inner "self" from the act he must do. His duty as a prince is all that matters.

Arjuna's older brother Yudhisthira is even more unhappy at what they must do, and cries, "There is nothing more evil than a warrior's duty!" He begs Krishna to stop the carnage. He then curses dharma, the law of the universe that assigns and defines duties. Tragically, Yudhisthira comes at last to the city of the gods. He sees his enemies, the Kauranas, eating and drinking and feasting with the gods. His brothers, the Pandavas, are in torment in a burning pit. The gods tell him that his cousins earned their reward by going to war as their duty demanded, but he and his brothers have earned torment for refusing to live out their appointed destiny. After torment and further rebirths, he may learn to live out his dharma better.

Dharma: The overarching law of the universe.

ambition and duty, and its spiritual subject is **dharma**, the law of the universe.

The war is the occasion for finding out the demands of duty and what dharma entails. It is a tragic story of defeat in victory.

The Indian Caste System

The Aryans were very race conscious and brought with them a rigid class structure. While almost all ancient societies (right up to the 1800s) had class distinctions and roles (the son of a farmer would be a farmer, the son of a cabinetmaker would be a cabinetmaker and that of a nobleman a nobleman), India's class structure was exceptionally strict and was the basis for all social life. The Aryans themselves were fair-skinned, large-framed, and light-haired, their conquered subjects were dark and small. The word for caste—*varna*—means "color."

Brahmins: The highest class in Indian society, the priest class.
Kshatriyas: The warrior class.
Vaishyas: The merchant class.
Sudras: The servant class.

Indian society was divided by the Vedas into three *varnas*, or classes: **brahmins, kshatriyas, vaishyas**. At the top were the priests, or brahmins, who performed the sacred rituals to the gods. Next was the warrior class, or kshatriyas, the kings and nobles who ruled and fought for the tribe. Third was the merchant and artisan class, or vaishyas, who carried on trade and made items to sell. These three classes made up Aryan society on the long migration across the Middle East. Added to these traditional Vedic groups was a fourth, called the **sudras**, who were descendants of the original Indian people conquered by the Aryans. They were the servants and farm workers of the other three classes.

Pariahs: The outcasts of society.
Caste Structure: A strict hereditary societal structure.

Outside and below all the other four castes are the untouchables, **pariahs** or *harijans*. These pariahs were perhaps the original inhabitants of the subcontinent, already enslaved to the Dravidian peoples the Aryans conquered. This rigid hereditary social system is called the **caste structure**. Marriage was permitted only within the same caste. Occupations and personal contact with members of other castes are limited by rigid rules to this day. The belief is that if one obeys the rules of caste, reincarnation into a higher caste is possible. The universal ministry of Mother Teresa to the poorest of the poor in Calcutta was an unprecedented work of mercy in India's society. She ministered to all the outcasts and not only touched the "untouchables," but tended them with love. Her Missionaries of Charity continue her work.

Origins of Indian Religions

The Vedic people also brought with them their own religion, which was based on the worship of nature gods. Their **pantheon** of gods and heroic stories about the gods were similar to those of the Greeks and Romans: supermen whose actions set the world in place. The Indo-European trifold deity was made up of three brothers: Brahman, Indra, and Varuna. These brothers correspond in many ways to Hades, Poseidon, and Zeus. The chief god of the Vedic people was Indra, the war god, though their priests worshiped Brahman, the god of enlightenment. The Vedic pantheon had some 33 gods, but local deities and the gods of the conquered peoples were added to the original group until hundreds of gods were part of the worship of the Indian civilization.

Pantheon: a group of gods.

A major religious change occurred in Aryan society around the 600s. While the rajas and their warriors continued to steal cattle and make petty wars to consolidate their growing kingdoms, the priestly caste came to be more influential than the warriors and their kings. In the eyes of the people the priests were more important than kings. They knew the complex rituals for controlling the gods. Kings had to defer to them and buy their favor. To escape the restrictions of the priests, men wandered off into the wilderness to live as hermits in search of spiritual knowledge. They undertook heroic fasts and self-denials. They sang and danced unaware of anyone near them. They went into long trances. These hermits lived on charity as they wandered from village to village, teaching their wisdom and blessing their benefactors without ritual spells or formulas.

A new religious attitude, the pursuit of religious wisdom, grew out of these hermits' wanderings. It transformed Indian life. The new teaching was set forth in a series of teaching poems called the Upanishads, the "Meditations." The Upanishads counsel intuition over learning and self-denial over earthly pleasures. The goal is to liberate the soul from earthly desires and pains. The Upanishads incorporated earlier gods into the Aryan pantheon. Brahman creates the universe, and is accompanied by two other gods, Shiva, who destroys creation, and Vishnu, who preserves the universe that Brahman creates. These gods were married; the wife of Shiva was the most

Vishnu

A Gupta cave painting in Ajanta, India, depicts Prince Gautama.

important to Hindu religion. She was called Parvati, Kali, or Durga. The Upanishads also introduced the idea of reincarnation and the transmigration of souls, a belief that must have originated with the first peoples of India and been accepted only gradually by the ruling Aryans.

Reincarnation is the belief that the immortal soul does not die once to live forever in eternal reward or punishment, but that the soul is reborn in another creature after death. The station of life that one is reborn to is based on how good the life was that has been lived. The soul is "reincarnated" many times. This belief directly supports the caste system which teaches that each caste has earned the privileged life or the difficult life that he or she is born into.

The Upanishads developed the idea of "the universal spirit." The many and various gods of the Vedic religion were seen as various aspects of the universal spirit. Hinduism, the religion that developed out of Vedic origins, allowed for many types of worship and many types of gods. Its gods were all nature spirits and aspects of the universal spirit, sometimes identified with Brahman, sometimes thought to be beyond even Brahman.

Buddhism

In the 6th century B.C., an Indian prince, Siddhartha Gautama, made his own spiritual journey and taught a new way of spiritual enlightenment. This method of spiritual growth came to be named "Buddhism" from its founder, Siddhartha, who was later called Buddha, or "enlightened one."

According to Siddhartha, sorrow and suffering came from desire. The answer to sorrow was, for him, to purify the spirit through right thinking and conduct. Siddhartha did not abandon all the gods of the Vedic religion, but he taught that the rituals were of no use. Men of all classes flocked to his message. The new religion spread quickly throughout northern India. Persons were attracted to its simplicity and to its lack of class distinction—so different from Hinduism. Even though it did not entirely break off from Hinduism until later years, Buddhism became the major rival to Hinduism in India for several centuries.

Indian Buddhist missionaries carried Buddhism to Tibet and China and to Burma, Thailand, and Southeast Asia. Buddhism became the

The Legend of the Buddha

The golden Buddha of Tikse Gompa in Ladakh, India.

At his birth, a soothsayer prophesied that Siddhartha would see four signs that would convince him of the misery of the world. He would then choose to be either a universal teacher or a universal tyrant. To prevent that prophecy from coming true, his father tried to shelter him from all sickness and decay and surround him with youth and beauty and pleasure. One day, Siddhartha was riding in his hunting preserve when he came on a gnarled and feeble old man who had somehow wandered into the park. He had never seen an old person. He asked his charioteer what this creature could be and was told it was "Old Age." On the ride home, he passed a beggar covered with sores and shivering with fever. "What is the matter with this man?" he asked. "Sickness," was the reply. Just then a funeral procession rounded the corner, and seeing the corpse he asked, "What is this?" "Death," he was told. He left the palace and walked off to find the answer to the three riddles: Old Age, Sickness, and Death. Finally, in his 36th year, he sat down under a great fig tree. It would come to be known to Buddhists as the *bodhi*, the tree of wisdom. He vowed to sit there until he had solved the three riddles of suffering. For seven weeks he sat, fasting and thinking. At last he entered a state of mind that seemed neither being nor nonbeing, a timeless realm of meditation. Buddhism would later call that state Nirvana, "detachment." In that moment he became the Buddha, the "Enlightened One."

majority religion in the island of Sri Lanka, south of the Indian mainland. It is the majority religion in Burma, Thailand, Cambodia, and Vietnam.

Jainism

Another group of holy men began to roam through the villages at about the same time as the Buddha's followers. The called themselves Jains, "conquerors." Their leader was another tribal prince, Vardhamana, who like Siddhartha had renounced his privileged status because the pitiful state of human society had horrified him. He was called the Mahavira, or "Great Hero." The way of life he founded became another major religion of India.

The Mahavira taught that the soul, in tiny portions, was present in all living things. Men, women, animals, flies and insects, plants and worms in

Followers of the Jain sect, known as "White-Clad," wear white robes and mouth coverings to keep from inhaling and killing insects.

the ground—all—were caught in the cycle of reincarnation because of past crimes and offenses. The only way to achieve release from continual rebirth and suffering was to renounce destruction of any kind. Even a seemingly peaceful action such as tilling the soil or walking on the road involved harm if a worm was disturbed or an ant crushed.

The Mahavira's first followers thought of themselves as living symbols of respect for life. They walked about only in daylight to avoid injuring any life by not seeing it. They carried brooms to sweep insects from their path and wore veils to avoid inhaling even a gnat. Eating meat was strictly forbidden and they walked around naked, for clothing was made either from animal skins or from plants.

After his death, the Mahavira's followers took his message to all of India. Although such severe renunciation was rare (usually only by monks), many laymen and families joined the ranks, supporting the monks and taking periodic retreats to liberate their souls. Jain missionaries went as far west as the Middle East, where the Greek historian Herodotus remarked on them. He thought all Indians were Jains. Later Jains were unwilling to be warriors or to take up the plow, so they turned to trade and commerce, forming an important part of India's merchant class.

Indian Roman Catholics leave the Sacred Heart Cathedral, New Delhi, India.

Christianity

The basic Christian message was and is the forgiveness of sins and the redemption of suffering through Christ's death and passion. This is a message of great hope and breaks the hopeless cycle of belief in reincarnation. Christianity was first brought to India in the time of the apostles. The apostle Thomas is credited with carrying the Gospel to the west coast of

India. The Mar Thoma Church is the descendant of Thomas's evangelization. Hundreds of years later, in the 1600s, Portuguese explorers and traders brought missionaries and began the Catholic Church in their colonies. St. Francis Xavier began his missionary work among the poor in the Portuguese colonies and had his greatest success there. Ringing bells, he would walk among the people of the streets and sing hymns and play games with the children until someone would talk to him; then he would tell them about the Savior. In the 1800s the English brought Protestant Christianity to India with their rule. There are now Catholics, Protestants, and Mar Thoma Christians (Thomas's original church) in the subcontinent.

The Great Empires of India 330 B.C.–A.D. 1948

The Mauryan Empire

The first Indian Empire was the Mauryan Empire (330–180 B.C.), whose founder was Chandragupta Maurya. Maurya was the son of a common herdsman, not of the kashtriya caste at all. Although he was born to a humble family, he secured the throne of a local prince in northeast India along the Ganges River. After this he turned west and evicted the Greeks, conquering the local cities and tribal rajas until he ruled over the entire north of India.

The Macedonian Greek conqueror, Alexander the Great, had brought his army down out of Persia into the Indus valley because he had heard of the great wealth of its cities. He found small states, all at war with each other, that he easily defeated and added to his realm. When he left to return to Babylon and home, he left behind garrisons and commanders who made western India a Greek state. Greek influences would continue to come to India from the northwest out of Persia and Bactria for hundreds of years.

It is told that when Chandragupta Maurya was a boy, he met Alexander face to face, and spoke with him. He was struck by the conqueror's personality. What Alexander said to him is not known, but the lad reported that some days later, while he kept watch over his flocks, he fell asleep, and the spirit of Alexander, in the form of a lion, came to him. He woke with

A profile portrait of Seleucus I Nicator (358 or 354–281 B.C.) who was the emperor of the area comprising Syria and Iran.

a real lion licking his body. The brahmins said that was an omen that he would become royalty, saluted by Alexander.

Maurya was adopted by a wise brahmin, Kautilya, who became his teacher and adviser. Kautilya set him on the throne of the kingdom and became his first minister. At Kautilya's urging, Maurya forged a union of several kingdoms and tribal republics in eastern India into one large kingdom, then sent his new army into the Indus valley to bring the states of the west under his control. Kautilya understood that India would always be open to invasion from the northwest, where the republics and kingdoms had been weakened through war with Alexander and his Greek governors. Alexander had proved that a determined conqueror could overwhelm the region. The best defense against recurring invasions from the west would be an Indian Empire.

The Greek king of Persia, Seleucus I, tried to retake the lands Maurya had seized, but in 305 B.C. was forced to turn around and leave India forever. Maurya's chariots and elephants then moved north to the foot of the Himalayas and added Kashmir and the rest of northern India to the kingdom's Ganges and Indus River valleys.

The Mauryan capital was Pataliputra, a city in the Ganges plain with timber walls and large stone houses for the nobles. Maurya ordered all the rajas of his realm to move to his capital, where he could keep an eye on them. The gardens and parks and wide streets made it a city of beauty.

A Greek ambassador, sent by Seleucus to Pataliputra, wrote home to his king that there was no theft or other crime to be seen in all the great city of Pataliputra. Rather, the people of the city seemed to be skilled in all the arts, to live luxuriously, and to leave their property unguarded and doors unlocked. But the crime rates were probably kept so low because Maurya visited such terrible punishments on those guilty of thieving, raping, assault, and public drunkenness. The king believed that crime should be dealt with quickly and harshly so that those who might *even think* of doing harm would quake with fear.

Women were able to read and were accomplished in the arts. However, upperclass women were forced to marry at a shockingly young age. A man of 24 or older might marry a girl of eight, and most marriages were for girls between 12 and 14.

The agricultural lands around the capital and in the conquered cities were all the property of the king. The peasants sometimes had to give up a third or even a half of their produce to the royal collectors, but they were exempt from military service or any other obligations to the state. The Mauryan Empire reduced the free hermit caste, farmers and servants, to a state of near serfdom, and recruited its military manpower among the many younger sons and dependents of the kashtriya caste who had been deprived of their estates and kingdoms. Brahmins were not required to do military service or to pay taxes, but brahmins had to be educated for government administration. Maurya himself was drawn to the Jain sect more than to the Hindu and ignored his brahmins.

As he grew older, Maurya began to fear assassins. He was afraid to eat meals that had not been tasted by a slave. And he never slept in the same room twice in a row. Guards surrounded his sleeping rooms, where lights burned all through the night.

A Hindu man walks along the sacred Ganges river where many bathe to wash away sin; others cast the ashes of the dead into the river, believing their loved ones will go straight to heaven.

A secret service of government spies was formed to report on the activities of local governors and rajas and to keep him informed of any plots to rebel, or corrupt his appointed magistrates. Maurya asked them to watch the most trivial activities of his courtiers, and to report everything that his possible rivals might say or do. The slightest hint of disloyalty or a word spoken innocently but with some double meaning could get a noble torn apart by lions or crushed by the feet of royal elephants. People whom the aging king thought dangerous might disappear without a trace. Ten years of such fear and watchfulness ate up his peace while he ruled the largest empire India had ever seen.

After 20 years of rule, Maurya began to surround himself with frivolous entertainment—dancing girls and courtesans. He no longer trusted his wives, not even the woman he had loved since his youth. He seldom left his palace except for the necessary public festivals and rituals. When India was hit by a 12-year drought and the Ganges itself dried up to a trickle, a Jain sage told him he alone could save the land by leaving his throne and withdrawing into a hermitage. To end the drought, Maurya abdicated in favor of his eldest son, Bindusara, and went to the southwest with a group of naked Jains. There, free at last of the fears that had tormented him for

10 years, the shepherd boy who became an emperor died of starvation. He fasted to death, praying for his people he thought wanted to kill him.

Ashoka the "Saint"

For 25 years, Maurya's son Bindusara ruled the empire his father had so wonderfully organized. His people called him "Slayer of Enemies," because he spent his energies in warfare on the borders of the empire. He kept the policies of his father and brought the empire to a state of high prosperity and contentment, despite the harsh laws and strict controls.

When he died he named a younger son, Ashoka, to the throne; Bindusara thought Ashoka was the most ruthless of all his sons, and capable of keeping the empire together. Ashoka followed the example of his father and set out to be a ferocious and feared master of the land. His first act was to order the death of his 95 brothers. He wanted no rivals to the throne left alive. Then he made total war on the southeastern coastlands of India, the region called Kalinga. His armies left the region burned and devastated. Whole villages and cities had been put to the sword, and thousands of people of all castes were forced to leave their homes and move to underpopulated regions of the empire the young king wanted filled up.

View of the Great Stupa, built by Ashoka, through the East Gate, at Sanchi, India.

Ashoka visited his new territory and there had a conversion of heart. He was horrified by the suffering he saw. He recoiled from his father's and grandfather's tyrannical ways and determined to change both his life and his empire. He studied Buddhism and took himself off for a 265-day retreat. When he returned, he issued edicts that would bring his people happiness and his kingdom closer to a Buddhist paradise. He organized a council of theologians to codify the Buddhist scriptures, the sutras, and to make a formal religion of the Buddha's ideas.

Buddhism did not become the official religion of his empire, but it gained royal support and Ashoka himself was converted to its tenets. The great king sent Buddhist missionaries to Tibet, where it became the dominant religion, and to China, where it grew more slowly. Missionaries from Ashoka's court carried Buddhism to Sri Lanka, where it became the official religion for many years.

In his own kingdom, Ashoka put the benevolent and humane ideals of Buddhism into practical forms. He appointed "Officers of Righteousness" to oversee local officials and promote welfare and happiness among all classes. They were to be the ultimate judges, responsible for preventing wrongful imprisonment and punishment. In all his provinces he encouraged advances in medicine, ordering herbs and healthful foods to be planted where they had not been known. He gave up the ancient Aryan amusement of the hunt, which must have been a great sacrifice for a prince of his class, and forbade the killing of animals that were not to be used or eaten.

The old Brahmin separation of the castes had no place in his ideas of administration, and men of all castes were advanced in his service according to their achievements. Brahmin anger smoldered but was kept in check by the authority of Ashoka's personality and by his ruthless spy network.

The Mauryan Empire placed representatives of the central government in every village. Records were kept of births, deaths, taxes, and all manner of commerce. Also, there were rules and laws for every profession and line of work. For example, washers of clothes would be punished if the stones they used in their work were too sharp and ruined the clothes. And woe to the doctor whose patient died because of negligence!

He renounced war for political reasons and himself taught his soldiers that a man should behave toward others as he would wish them to behave towards himself. The neglected army grew weak. Less than 50 years after Ashoka's death in 232 B.C., the Mauryan Empire fell apart, as his descendants quarreled over the succession. The Brahmins came back to power in

Map of the Gupta Empire.

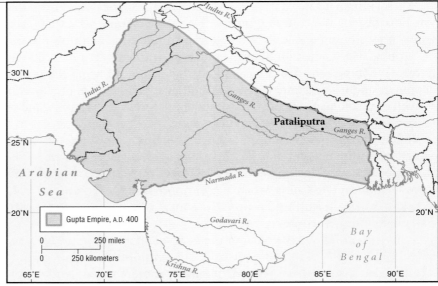

Gupta painting fragment, with heads from Ajanta, India, about A.D. 500.

the warring states. Buddhism fell out of favor, and Hinduism became again the dominant religion.

The Indian Classical Period (A.D. 320–650)

After the death of Ashoka, the Mauryan Empire began to splinter. Various families vied for leadership, until a new Maurya emerged to unite India by force: Chandragupta Gupta, whose family was to rule northern India for the next 150 years. This time brought prosperity and relative peace to northern India, and set the stage for a flowering of architecture and the arts.

Because of the prosperity of India during this "golden age, " a life of leisure, learning, and courtly life became available to many people, not just a small elite. The educated were expected to become good musicians, artists, and poets. Refined painting from this period has been preserved and is admired today. Stone replaced wood to build temples. The distinctive artistic styles of Indian sculpture and painting were first formed in this period.

Mathematics and science also flourished in India during the Gupta "golden age." The Indians were expert in mathematics and introduced the decimal system and the concept of zero, which was carried by Middle Eastern traders to Europe. Indian mathematicians calculated a value for *pi* more accurately than the Greeks. And a prince named Brahmagupta taught a theory of physics that included gravity.

The Mughal Empire (A.D. 1526–1707)

After the "golden age" of rule by the Guptas, there was a period of relative peace in northern India. This period ended around 1000, when a new power, the Turks, brutally conquered and despoiled the cities of northern India.

The Turks were devastatingly effective in their multiple raids against northwest India, demolishing Hindu temples, which they considered unholy, and killing tens of thousands of people. Although they totally dominated northwest India, the Turks had little impact on the rest of India at this time. Turkish power in northwest India ebbed and flowed for the next several hundred years.

The Islamic conquerors, who left the greatest lasting impact on India, were called the Mughals. The English word "mogul," meaning someone with great power and influence, came from the name of these rulers. They came from central Asia and fought with fury, eventually taking over northern India. They were also Turkish, but their king claimed descent from Timur and Genghis Khan, the famous Mongol Khans. Thus their name, Mughal, is a corrupted form of mongol. Their reign was not as short as the Muslim dynasties because of the wisdom of a new Turkish leader, Akbar. Akbar realized that not only to conquer but to *rule* India, he would need the help of the Indian nobility. By respecting the Hindu religion he won the support of the Indian ruling classes.

The time of the Mughals was like a second golden age for Indian culture. This time the culture was a combination of Indian Hindu culture and Turkish Mughal culture. The language of the nobles became Persian, the language of the conquering Turks. There was a great flowering of the Persian language in India. There was also a period of creative achievement in art

Akbar's expedition by boat to the eastern provinces. A.D. **1602–1604.**

and music that sprang from the Persian/Indian culture.

The architectural legacy of the Mughals includes the Taj Mahal. With its dome and arches, its graceful marble tracery and its harmonious gardens, the Taj Mahal has been called the most beautiful building in the world. It was built by the Mughal king Shah Jehan as a memorial to his beloved wife, Mumtaz Mahal. She was the most beautiful woman he had ever seen; they loved each other deeply and had 14 children. When she died from a fever at age 39, the distraught king decided to erect in her memory the most beautiful building human ingenuity could design. He sought out and hired the greatest artists and architects of all India and set them to creating designs for his memorial. They presented design after design. At last, the perfect image was set before him, one that would honor his beloved. It took over 20,000 workers and 22 years to construct. Inside, the body of Shah Jehan lies in a marble sarcophagus; in another sarcophagus, exactly like his, rests his beloved Mumtaz.

The British Raj

After the Mughals, India fell into political chaos. Princes and kings made
themselves independent of any central
authority. The maharajahs of larger
states and the rajas of smaller ones
made war on their neighbors. Into this
conflict came the Europeans in the
1600s. The Portuguese had already
established trading colonies at Goa and
Bombay. The French and the English
hastened to get a toehold in the enor-
mously profitable trade with India—
precious jewels, gold, and rare spices.

The Prince of Wales in
India; an elephant
salute. About 1878.

English interests were placed by the
government in the hands of the East India Company, a trading company
that was allowed to hire its own armies, make treaties with the rajas, and
impose its own laws on the territories it gained. By the end of the 1700s,
all India was in English hands, and the English East India Company was
running a subcontinent. But in time, mismanagement forced the English
government to take over the company's rule of India, and for the next 150
years India was part of the British Empire. The Indian princes were put on
government payroll, and the British ran the huge subcontinent as their
primary colony. English railroads, schools, roads, and physical improvements were as much a part of the government of India as were English law
courts and administrators. The British raj continued until 1948 when
independence was achieved through the efforts of Mohandas Gandhi and
his supporters.

Chapter 12 Review

Let's Remember   Write your answer in a single complete sentence.
1. What is the common language of modern India?
2. What are the Vedas?
3. To what does the Varnas refer?
4. What was the first Indian Empire?
5. What is the Taj Mahal?

Let's Consider   For silent thinking and a short essay or for thinking in a group with classroom discussion:
1. The divisiveness of the many languages of India.
2. The structure of Harappa as a city.
3. The power of memory, especially keeping the Vedas in mind.
4. Life in a rigid caste system.
5. How India was changed by the British Empire.

Let's Eat!

The distinctively Indian spice, curry, is used to season food and also to help digest food. Recipe for chicken curry: Heat 3 T. oil in a skillet. Add cut-up chicken tenders (about 2 C.) and 1 sliced onion to skillet. Add ½ C. chicken broth, 1 C. raisins, 1 sliced apple, 1 sliced green pepper and 2 T. curry powder. Heat for ½ hour; serve over rice. (Serves 4)

Chapter 13

Africa: The Enduring Continent

Africa was the first home to all members of the human race, spread now throughout the whole world. The earliest human-like creatures yet discovered have been found in the Olduvai Gorge region in Uganda, in Kenya, and in Somalia. Not enough is known about them or their migration to other continents to say anything about their history. Only the record of their bones and simple stone tools survives. The oldest stone tools found anywhere come from the highlands of Uganda.

The hot climate of Africa provides a severe challenge to the people still there, but there are other challenges as well. The vast majority of Africa's soils are poor and not suitable for farming; most of the continent is open grassland. It has many tropical diseases and **voracious** insects that torment the inhabitants of most areas of the continent. The Sahara, a huge desert, lies just south of the north African coast, making land transportation extremely difficult from north to south. Also, water is scarce in many parts of Africa, not just the vast deserts, making any kind of settled life very difficult. With these challenges, the African peoples—both present and past—require fortitude, toughness, and teamwork just to survive.

Voracious: having a great, destructive appetite.

The Geography of Africa

Africa is the second largest continent, so huge that the United States, Europe, India, and Japan could easily fit into Africa with space left over. Africa is surrounded by oceans on all sides, except for a small land bridge that connects it to Asia. The equator roughly bisects the middle of the

Nations and boundaries of Africa today.

African continent, and all the areas of the continent are hot. In the center of the continent and along the western coast are the famous jungles of Africa.

Africa may be divided into six broad areas: North Africa, the Sahara Desert, West Africa, East Africa, Central Africa, and southern Africa. All six areas are marked by extremes of nature.

North Africa is the part of Africa that touches the Mediterranean Sea. Its civilization has always been part of the greater Mediterranean world. Because the northern coast of Africa was on the trade route of the lower Mediterranean, this part of Africa was well known to Phoenicia, Greece, and Rome. These ancient states also colonized North Africa and made it part of the ancient civilized world. Later, in the 7th century, Muslim Arabs conquered the entire area. Because of its rich history of original Egyptian, Phoenician, Roman, and Arab conquerors, North Africa's fascinating history is different from that of the rest of Africa. The modern-day countries that comprise this area are Morocco, Algeria, Tunisia, Libya, and Egypt.

The Sahara: Below the fertile and inhabited northern coast lies the vast Sahara Desert. The Sahara is by far the largest desert in the world and stretches from the Atlantic Ocean on the west to the Red Sea on the east. It covers three and one-half million square miles. The Sahara was once a grassland, or savanna, before the end of the last ice age. Traces of a herding life and tribes of nomads living on the grasses and oases have been found. With the retreat of the ice, the Earth's climate shifted, and hot, dry winds turned much of the Sahara into sand wastes. Today, the southern portions of Morocco, Algeria, Libya, and Egypt, as well as most of Mauritania, Mali, Niger, and Chad, lie within the Sahara Desert, as well as the northern half of Sudan.

West Africa consists of the countries along the west coast of Africa. This fertile and rich area contains grasslands, rain forests, and farmlands. Many small states lie on the western coast of Africa; Senegal, Gambia, Guinea Bissau, Guinea, Sierra Leone, Liberia, Ghana, Burkina Faso, Togo, and Nigeria.

East Africa has high mountains, making it a separate geographical region from the Sahara to the north and west, and the rain forests of western and Central Africa. The Great Rift valley runs down East Africa north to south, marking the meeting place of the African and Indian continental plates.

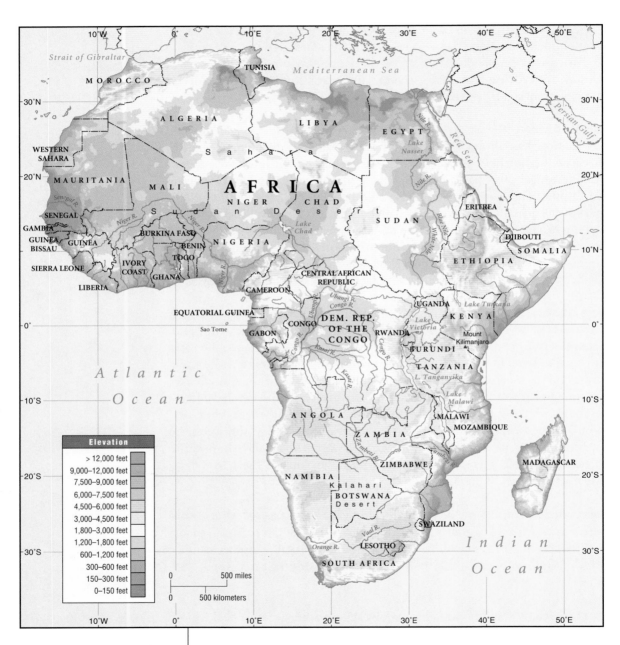

Topographical map of Africa, with color-keyed elevation table.

Volcanoes are still active there. Mount Kilimanjaro is an active and grow-ing volcano in Kenya, and the highest mountain on the continent. The fer-tile volcanic soil of these mountains is agriculturally rich, aided by the warm but wet climate. The countries of East Africa are Sudan, Ethiopia, Eritrea, Somalia, Kenya, Uganda, and Tanzania. East Africa is the home of two of the earliest African civilizations, Kush and Ethiopia.

Central Africa is the very large region drained by the Congo River basin flowing west to the Atlantic, and the Zambezi River basin flowing east to the Indian Ocean. The equator runs through Central Africa, and it con-tains the thick forests of the famous African jungle. Beyond the forested areas are bands of grassland, called savannas.

Southern Africa is drier than Central Africa and less mountainous than East Africa. The Kalahari Desert divides it from its neighbors to the north. It contains the nations of Namibia, the Republic of South Africa, Botswana, Zimbabwe, Lesotho, and Swaziland. South Africa is rich in min-erals and developed farmland. The Republic of South Africa is an indus-trialized country with modern cities and transportation. Southern Africa is home to the Bushmen, a people that roamed the whole continent and parts of Europe in prehistoric times but now are confined to the fringes of the Kalahari Desert.

The Lakes and Major Rivers of Africa

In the center of the continent are three large lakes, formed in the deep chasms of the African Rift: Victoria, Tanganyika, and Malawi. The largest is Lake Victoria, almost an inland sea, between Kenya and Uganda. Lake Victoria is only slightly smaller than Lake Superior in North America. The waters of Lake Victoria are the source of the southern branch of the Nile. Lake Tanganyika drains west into tributaries of the Congo, and Lake Malawi drains south and east into the Zambezi. These three lakes are high in the mountains, and hold their waters for the lowlands below.

Four major rivers are an important part of the geography of Africa: the Nile, the Congo, the Niger, and the Zambezi. Although it isn't a major river, there is a very strange river in Africa, the Okovango in Botswana; it never reaches the sea. Instead, it is a river that ends in swamps and the desert of the Kalahari in South Africa.

The Nile is the longest river in Africa. It starts in two places. The headwaters of the southern branch (the White Nile) are at Lake Victoria, in the mountains of Uganda. The eastern branch (the Blue Nile) begins at Lake Tana, in Ethiopia. The two branches flow northward until they meet at Khartoum, capital of Sudan. The Nile provides water for living and farming for those on its banks, and abundant silt to Egyptian farmers who till the fertile soil that the Nile leaves behind.

The Congo is the second longest river in Africa. It begins in the Katanga plateau and flows north to the central part of the Democratic Republic of the Congo (formerly Zaire) and then turns south and flows to the Atlantic Ocean. It does not form a delta, but runs through a deep canyon to the ocean. The Congo River is the highway of the Democratic Republic of the Congo. From dugouts piloted by village people to modern riverboats and huge commercial transports, the Congo makes movement possible in the dense rain forests of Central Africa.

The Niger is the third longest river; it begins in Guinea in West Africa. It first flows northeast to Mali before turning south, flowing through Nigeria and Benin, then ending its journey to the sea at a large delta in Nigeria. This river is very important to the people of West Africa who live on its banks. Water from the river allows farming and commercial fishing.

The Zambezi is the fourth of the great rivers of Africa. It flows east from the same high country where the Nile and the Congo begin. It passes through thick forests in Zambia and Mozambique and enters the Indian Ocean.

Early Africans

Roughly 30,000 years ago Africans were making sophisticated stone tools. These Africans were ancestors of the peoples who are found on the continent today: Afro-Asian, Bantu, Pygmies, and Bushmen.

The Afro-Asians were ancestors of the people living in northern Africa today. They had light brown skin and were of medium height. Some older books refer to this physical type as Caucasoid, or Hamitic, but the newer term is Afro-Asian.

The Bantu peoples lived in the sub-Saharan plateau and along the fringe of the forest region. They were tall, large framed, dark ebony in color and had wiry, tightly curled black hair. They are now called the Blacks, or Bantu, and inhabit most of the continent today.

The Pygmies were similar to the Bantu except for their small stature—only four and one-half feet tall. They inhabited forest regions around the Congo basin, and now are greatly reduced in number. They have always lived by hunting and planting small plots of vegetables and maize.

The Bushmen lived in the eastern and southern savannas. They were slight of build, of medium height, and had light copper-colored skin. They had almond-shaped eyes (the epicanthic fold) common to Oriental peoples, and tightly curled dark hair. They were a nomadic people, living by hunting and gathering only. Farming is still not their ordinary practice. Their paintings on the rock faces of cliffs and outcroppings of stone are very like the prehistoric paintings in the caves of Europe. Whether they once lived so far north is not known.

A pygmy chief sits on a wooden stool.

Bushmen hunt with bows and arrows.

The Earliest Civilizations in Africa

Around 5500 B.C. the climate of the Sahara was wet and cool. Previously, the whole continent's climate had been dry; after a period of wet, it returned to dry again. In 5500 B.C., however, the grasslands of the Sahara were lush and rivers ran across them to the south into the Niger and east toward the Nile. The dry riverbeds can still be seen in the desert. Fish and game were plentiful, and generations of hunters and herdsmen lived comfortable lives. Then around 3000 to 2500 B.C. the climate changed again. The rains stopped, the rivers dried up, the forests and grasses died. The long disaster of the drying up of the Sahara helps explain why the history of Africa after 2000 B.C. goes in two directions.

The Saharan peoples who lived in this once-bountiful hunting land dispersed in three directions. Some went north to the coasts of the Mediterranean; some went east to the treacherous but fertile valley of the Nile; some went south into the heart of the continent.

Tissili Desert, a portion of the Sahara Desert that extends into Algeria.

To the north of the vast and soon-to-be desert, the high civilization of Egypt emerged. South of the desert the peoples had to work out their lives alone, cut off from the ideas of the peoples of the Mediterranean. They had to cope with a vast but inhospitable land: heat, poor soil, dense jungles, barren mountain slopes, deep and broad rivers full of predators and parasites, and everywhere the ravenous insects with their disease-laden stings and bites.

The Kingdoms of the Nile—Kush and Axum

The first civilization in Africa was the civilization of the Nile valley, and its influence may have given birth to the first kingdoms to blossom outside Egypt's borders, the Nile kingdoms of Kush and Axum.

Around 750 B.C., the princes of Kush made their capital at Napata, near the upper reaches of the Nile, and built a city influenced by Egyptian building styles. Greek writers refer to Kush as Aethiopia (Land of the Fire-Eyes), and to Kushites as Ethiopes, but Kush is unrelated to the Ethiopia of modern Africa.

Constant war with Egypt for a thousand years had left a deep impression on the Kushites. They developed a civilization that was Egyptian in appearance, but it was their own in its forms and character. The worship of the Egyptian god Amun was made part of the royal ritual in imitation of the court life of the pharaoh, but their king was not worshiped as a living god—as the pharaoh was in Egypt. Later, as the Sahara grew ever more dry and the pastures around Napata dried up, the capital was shifted to Meroe, farther south, and Egyptian ideas and influences were thoroughly **assimilated** into distinctly Kushite forms. Palaces and stone cities rose along the Nile. In Meroe the kings built pyramids, not as grand as those of Egypt, but with a

To Assimilate: To absorb one culture into another.

remarkable style and dignity. Iron was abundant around Meroe, and the kings of Kush made great use of the technology of ironworking. The capital grew into a great metalworking center. Heaps of iron waste may still be seen in the ruins.

The kings of Kush conquered their old foes the pharaohs in the 8th century and made themselves for a brief time pharaohs of Upper and Lower Egypt. Kushites managed to tame the African elephant and use elephants in war. The lion and the elephant appear in their art, replacing their earlier depiction of Egyptian gods. The kingdom of Kush loved new things and sent emissaries to all the lands of the Mediterranean. Their ships, from ports on the Red Sea, traveled to India. The apostle St. Philip met an official of the queen of Meroe, whom the Bible refers to as an Ethiopian, on the road from Jerusalem, and St. Philip expounded to him the Gospel of the Lord Jesus.

Around A.D. 300 the kingdom of Kush and the Kushite civilization seem to have faded after invasions by wild Nubian tribes and the kings of Axum in what is now called Ethiopia. Why or by what hand the end came, no one knows. The last king of the Kushites was buried in a tiny pyramid, a sad imitation of the tombs of his ancestors. His name was Malequerabar. That is all that is known of him. No other kings are recorded on the stones of Meroe.

The largest site of Kush civilization burial pyramids lies north of Khartoum, along the Nile River in ancient Meroe, Sudan.

Two hundred years later, in the 500s, the Nubian invaders in the Kushite towns produced their own culture, Christian Nubia. Monks from Constantinople were sent by the Emperor Justinian to convert Ethiopia, and they stopped in the towns of Nubia.

The Church in Nubia was only a hundred years old when it was cut off from the rest of the Christian world by the Muslim conquest of Egypt. Its kings and bishops knew nothing of the developments of the Christian world of Europe or Constantinople, and had only themselves and their faith to rely on. Believing the rest of the world had fallen to the Muslims, they thought that they alone were left to keep Christianity alive. They made constant war on the Muslim governors of Upper Egypt and declared

Preaching from the Cave

The missionary to the Nubians was named St. Julian, and he brought the Nubians to Christianity in A.D. 543. Julian, a European, was so stricken by the heat that he confined his preaching and priestly work to the evenings and nights. During the days, Julian floated in a pool of water in a cave, unable to breathe in the outside air. Did Julian have a bad heart? Was he so fat that he could not stand the heat? What did the pagan Kushites make of the spectacle of a pink-skinned evangelist who spent all day floating in the water inside a cave? Whatever they thought, they came in crowds to listen to him and to be baptized.

themselves the protectors of Egypt's Coptic Christian minority. The Muslims of Egypt under the sultan, Saladin, sent troops south to stamp out this nuisance. In A.D. 1276 the first of the three Nubian kingdoms was overcome, the middle kingdom fell a century later, and the last of the

The Christian kingdoms of Nubia, which is on the Nile River, and Ethiopia.

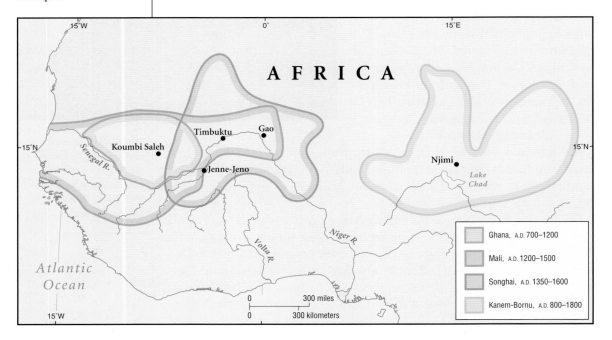

AFRICA

Atlantic Ocean

Koumbi Saleh
Timbuktu
Gao
Jenne-Jeno
Njimi
Lake Chad

Senegal R.
Volta R.
Niger R.

15°W   0°   15°E
15°N

0   300 miles
0   300 kilometers

	Ghana, A.D. 700–1200
	Mali, A.D. 1200–1500
	Songhai, A.D. 1350–1600
	Kanem-Bornu, A.D. 800–1800

Nubian Christians fell to Muslim **scimitars** in the early 1400s. For nine hundred years, the Nubians of old Kush had held out against the Muslim armies. These Nubians worshiped Jesus Christ as Lord and Savior. In their monasteries and domed churches, they honored the Madonna and all the apostolic Saints, just as St. Julian had instructed them.

Scimitar: A curved sword.

The kingdom of Axum arose to the south and east of Kush in the mountains of Ethiopia. There is an Ethiopian legend that relates a strange and mythical origin of these people. The legend relates that the queen of Sheba went up to Jerusalem to judge the reputation of Israel's king Solomon for wisdom. There, Solomon fell in love with her and she bore him a son whose name was Menelik; he became the mythical founder of the Ethiopian royal line. (The Ethiopian royal line traced its descent from Menelik and in fact, not legend, this royal line became a dynasty that would last into the 20th century; its last emperor was Haile Selassie.) In the legend, it was said that Menelik was harassed by his relatives as he grew up, and he was forced to flee Sheba with the treasures of his mother and father. He led his band of warriors into the mountains of Ethiopia, where he founded his kingdom, worshiped God in the Israelite manner, and preserved the ways of his father into the future. Among the treasures he was reputed to have left to his heirs was the Ark of the Covenant. Legendary tradition held that Solomon's Israelite son sent the ark to his half-brother, Menelik, to keep it safe.

The legend of the queen of Sheba and her son, Menelik, is based on a more complicated and factual history. The Sabaeans, a people of the southern tip of Arabia, established trading posts on the African coast near their homeland. Some 500 years before Christ, a number of settlements on the African coast near the mouth of the Red Sea merged with the local peoples to develop a culture all their own. They moved inland into the sparsely settled mountains and built a city there safe from Red Sea pirates and wandering nomadic tribes. By A.D. 200, the city was called Axum, and the people of the mountains that it commanded were called Amharic. Christian missionaries reached Axum in the 400s from Antioch in Syria. A hundred years later, the same missionary, St. Julian, who suffered so from the heat and converted the Nubians, went to Axum. In his extraordinary report to Constantinople,

The Queen of Sheba visits King Solomon of Israel.

In an early 12th century painting, the Virgin and Child stand with an unnamed martyr and Queen Martha of Nubia, holding a crucifix.

he said that the Christian king there was dressed in white linen, adorned with gold and pearls, that his throne was a gilded chariot drawn by elephants, and that Greek was the language of the court!

Truly, the kingdom of Ethiopia did have a highly developed literary tradition, a literary language spoken by the nobles and upper classes of Axum called Geez. Further, Ethiopia had its own translation of the Scriptures into Geez, done by Syrian monks when the country was converted. The ancient Ethiopians developed their own version of Christianity when their country, like Nubia, was cut off by the Muslims from the rest of Christianity. By the 1200s, Muslims and primitive pagan tribes surrounded the mountain kingdom, and its ports on the Red Sea coast were forbidden to Christian travelers from the mountains. King Lalibela in the 12th century built some of the most unusual structures in the world, 10 churches cut into the rock of the hills around his capital, but cut *down*, down in vast shafts below ground level. Within the churches huge halls with pillars and arches, false windows and hidden rooms are carved out, just as if these had been erected *above* ground.

The Legend of Prester John

During the late Middle Ages in Europe, a legend grew up of a great Christian kingdom on the other side of Muslim-controlled lands. A semimagical king named Prester John, who had virtual immortality, ruled this mythical kingdom. He said he would wage war against the Muslims until the Christian crusaders of the West joined forces with him and then eliminate the Muslims. In fact, Portuguese explorers, venturing into the mountains of East Africa in search of the fabled Prester John, found an Ethiopia in structure very like the kingdoms of medieval Europe! They found proud and independent nobles bound by oaths of loyalty to their king, a hierarchy of lesser nobles and lords below them, and landless peasants laboring for all. There were monks, abbots, and bishops with their parish clergy worshipping as professed Christians, but in strange and mysterious liturgies and in an ancient sacred language. To the surprise of the Europeans, the Ethiopians would not make alliance with these Christians from the West. They thought the Portuguese immoral because they showed no solidarity with each other. A French traveler to Ethiopia in the 1830s recorded: "They [the Ethiopians] live together in reciprocal dependence and solidarity, which they value and consider a matter of pride. A man with no fixed obligation to his society was, in their eyes, outside of society."

All African societies valued family and community. Similarly, Ethiopians determined morality by social service. A man's moral duty was to serve the group. Not only complex and ancient cultures like Christian Ethiopia, but primitive tribal society with no apparent structure at all understood that morality was duty for the common good of the group over self-interest. The harsh climate and life of ancient Africa left its mark on all African cultures. Group solidarity was needed in order to survive.

The Sudanic Civilization

Everywhere, African culture grew out of conditions peculiar to the continent. Fighting to survive in the hostile climate and terrain, African societies devised a diversity of methods for staying alive and living joyfully. One scholar of Africa has said that Africa's history is a story with two major themes: (1) the restless movement of peoples over enormous distances and obstacles, and (2) the isolation and self-containment of individual communities.

After a period of development as hunter-gatherers and farmers, Africans south of the Sahara Desert—the area the Arabs named the Sudan—developed a unique culture we call the Sudanic civilization. Four Sudanic kingdoms grew into almost imperial size between A.D. 700 and 1800. These kingdoms of the Sudan were: Ghana (not the modern country called by that name), 700–1200; Mali (again, not the modern country) 1200–1500; Songhai, 1350–1600; and Kanem-Bornu, 800–1800.

The Sudanic societies were headed by a king of a tribe, which might be quite small or large. The king was thought to be divine, and was kept from contact with the rest of the tribe. It was thought that the health of the king was needed for good weather and crops. The king could not die a natural death. If his own death seemed imminent from illness or age, he would be ritually killed. This was not a feudal society; royalty was not passed down in families. Rather, the king was the head priest, and the priestly class determined the king by election or magical divination.

In these societies the king, as a divine being, ruled absolutely. Wives, drink, food, crafts, and items for trade were collected for him from his subjects. He also controlled all trade. This order of society influenced all

Map of West African
Kingdoms—Ghana,
Mali, Songhay,
Kanem-Borno.

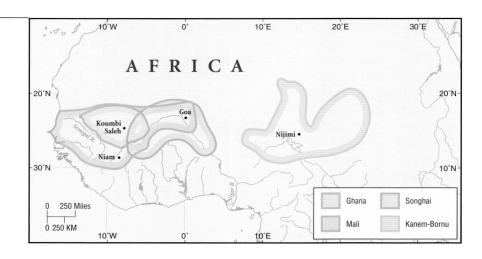

**A traditionally dressed
member of the Bantu
tribe Ndebele.**

the peoples of West and Central Africa, and became the model for all the Bantu kingdoms of Central and southern Africa.

The wealth and power of the kingdoms of the Sudan were built on gold. The trade in gold went back to the days of the Phoenicians and the Carthaginians, but with the Arab conquest of North Africa in the 7th century, it expanded to include new items of export from the West African coastlands. Gold was exchanged for salt, priceless in the hot and saltless lands of inner Africa. Salt was the prince of commodities, and Arab merchants were quick to perceive the value of their cheaply produced salt to the gold-rich petty kings of the south. On trains of camels, the Arabs carried tons of salt to the south and brought home gold beyond their dreams. Salt was not only useful to make foods savory, but it was essential for health among peoples who lost so much water through heavy perspiration in the intense heat.

Another "product," but in no way savory, soon found its way into trade—trafficking in slaves. The great kingdoms of the Sudan grew as the kings conquered their neighbors to accumulate the gold and slaves that the traders demanded for their salt. Empires rose and fell on the market price of salt and slaves.

Along with the merchants came Muslim zealots and teachers who converted the pagan tribes of the Sudan to Islam. The cities that grew up as trading centers and royal capitals became centers of Islamic learning; one of these, the Islamic center of Timbuktu, grew world-famous.

Burial of a Sudanic King

Kings in Sudanic cultures were not allowed to die a natural death. Poisoning or ritual asphyxiation were used to hasten death when a king's time to die was near. Somehow it was thought that if a king died a natural death, the fertility of the land would die also. The king would be buried with his favorite furniture, food, and the bodies of his servants and aides, their throats slit, to follow him in death.

The empires of the Sudan also inspired the kingdoms of the coastal forests to expand their borders and conquer their neighbors. The kings of Benin and Ashanti resisted Islam but learned from their northern neighbors the art of slaving and of war. By the 1600s, the coastal kingdoms of West Africa were ready to trade with Europeans for gold and slaves, just as they had learned from their Muslim neighbors.

The Djinguereber Mosque dates from the early 14th century. Timbuktu, Mali.

The Arab Empire in Africa

In A.D. 639, Arab Muslims conquered Egypt. It took them less than a century to dominate northern Africa and attack Europe through Spain. During this time, however, Muslim Arabs did not so much conquer northern Africa as convert it. Rapidly, Christianity was replaced with the Muslim religion. In fact, the Berber peoples of North Africa seemed to welcome the Arabs as liberators from the oppression they felt from the Christian Byzantine Romans who ruled them. While this is readily understandable in rural areas where sympathies could be with the rough invaders, it is harder to understand in the cities. While the culture of the new rulers was not Christian, the ease with which the city folk adopted the new religion suggests that, at least for many, the roots of their Christian faith had not run deep.

As a consequence of the Arab ascendancy in the late 600s and early 700s, all of northern Africa became part of the larger Muslim civilization. Also, in time, the Berber tribesmen carried the Muslim faith across the Sahara to the Sudan, where the countries of the savanna below the desert also became Muslim. But the Muslim faith carried to central Africa was

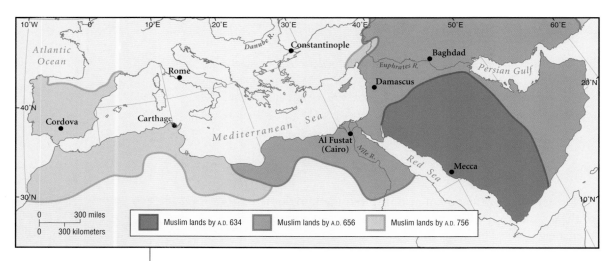

Map of Arab kingdoms and Arab influence in Africa.

not a strictly Arab faith. The Muslims had assimilated the learning of the West, and by this time it was the faith of Mediterranean Africans, carrying with it the influences of Romans, Greeks, and Christians.

The Slave Trade

In the 17th century the demand for slaves to work the crops of European colonies in the Americas grew. European traders turned to western Africa for slaves. In exchange for guns and other goods, many African chiefs collected slaves from their neighbors inland, and traded them to slavers on the coast. If you were convicted of a crime, had debts, or your family had debts, or even if the chief didn't like you, you could be sold as a slave.

As the value of a slave grew greater than the value of gold, the kings of the coast made war on weaker neighbors to capture whole villages or peoples for the slavers. The slaving wars disrupted Sudanic life and tribal allegiances for centuries.

Arab slavers on the east coasts set up slave-trading towns from Somalia to Mozambique. The slave trade affected Africa both east and west. But the coming of the Europeans in the 1400s had the most destructive effect, since the new plantations of Brazil and the Caribbean Islands seemed to have an insatiable appetite for new slave labor. The

Portuguese, who had first explored the African coasts, stepped in to corner the new trade.

It is impossible to describe the horror of African slavery. Usually betrayed by a rival tribe, people were broken up from their families and cultures, never to see them again. Then they were loaded aboard ships with too little air and space. If they survived this, and many did not, most became agricultural workers with no rights, no pay, and no chance for improvement. Access to slaving areas was restricted, for it was feared that if Europeans not involved in the slave trade were to see it, it would be stopped.

A slaver walks among his African slaves in the hold of the slave ship *Gloria*.

The economic and political effects of slavery varied in Africa. Western Africa, with a large population, did not suffer terribly from the loss of people but rather from the weakening of family ties and communal obligations, the essence of African morality. In Central and East Africa, however, the loss of population was devastating. Slaving took its toll on those left behind. Villages starved because their young men and women were no longer there to work the fields.

The Kingdom of Kongo

The Portuguese adventurer Diego Cao sailed down the west coast of Africa in 1482. He was the first European to make contact with the kingdom of Kongo, the largest kingdom in Central Africa. Portuguese interest in Kongo grew rapidly. And the kings and nobles of Kongo found everything European fascinating. They entered into trade with the Portuguese for European cloth, tools, furniture, and wine. They offered high wages to Portuguese carpenters and masons to come and build new palaces and cities for the African kingdom. The Manikongo, supreme king, Nzinga a Nkuwu, converted to Christianity and was baptized as Joao (Hongo) II, in honor of the king of Portugal, King Joao I.

Kongo became a Christian kingdom, and the grandson of the Manikongo Joao II, Henrique, became the first black African bishop in the Catholic Church in the early 16th century. The nobles followed their king's lead and accepted the Faith. Many of the Bakongo people also were baptized and a

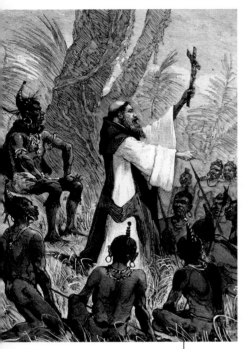

A Franciscan missionary brings the Gospel of Christ to the people of the Congo.

flourishing church seemed to be growing in the Congo River basin. Portuguese missionaries and Congolese converts set out into the interior with the Gospel.

But the Portuguese greed for gold and slaves worked steadily against the efforts of the Portuguese government and the Catholic bishops to make Kongo into a Christian kingdom. Through the 1500s the slave trade grew, and local African warlords and magistrates sold their people or made war on their neighbors to collect enough slaves. Then control of his provinces and local governors broke down when the Manikongo tried to limit the effects of the slave trade on his population. Relations between these two powers, Portugal and Kongo, were overshadowed by the transatlantic slave trade and drained Kongo of its manpower. Letters from the Manikongo to the kings of Portugal complained of the Portuguese betrayal of their word. Committed as they were to the common good, Africans could not understand this disregard of honor.

After two centuries of Portuguese influence, Kongo was a Europeanized African kingdom, but its control of its provinces was nominal only, its traditional morality had evaporated, and its new Christian faith had been distorted.

The desperate Manikongo at last decided to expel the greedy and treacherous Portuguese slave traders and mercenaries from his land. The

Map of the Kingdom of the Congo.

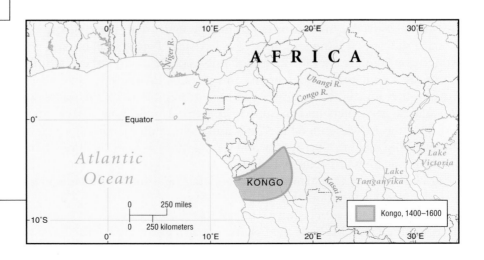

Kongo army was called up from all the provinces. But fewer than half responded. Kongo was defeated by the Portuguese at the battle of Mbwila. The head of the Manikongo was cut off, and displayed in the chapel on the bay of Luanda, where the explorer Diego Cao had first landed in Kongo.

A Warrior Queen

In the 1620s, Dona Anna de Souza Nzinga became a brilliant, warrior queen in the Kongo. She was the daughter of the king of Ndongo, a subordinate kingdom to Kongo. Her brother murdered her son, the logical heir, and seized the throne. Dona Anna fled to the bush and hid. When her brother found that he could not deal with the Portuguese, he called her back and made her his deputy to negotiate with the Europeans. She was baptized at this time.

When the Portuguese betrayed their treaty, she found allies among the Jaga, a fierce and less civilized people, and killed her brother to avenge her son. She raised a huge army of followers—her Jaga allies, her own countrymen, and hundreds of escaped slaves and displaced people. She kept a traditional-style royal court that moved with her and her army from camp to camp. She dressed like a man, in defiance of African custom. Through all these years, she kept a priest at her side and heard Mass daily. Her religion and her actions were in conflict. For nine years she fought the Portuguese until she was finally defeated in 1656. She remained queen of Ndongo until her death in 1663. Her sister, Dona Barbara, was made queen after her death, and made peace with the Europeans.

The Africanization of the New World

The large numbers of slave workers imported from Africa could not fail to affect the life of the regions where they were enslaved. Portuguese Brazil, along with French, Spanish, and British islands became, in effect, extensions of African culture. Mexico and the United States were influenced by their African immigrants as much as by their Native Americans and Europeans. The contributions of Africans to the countries of the Americas make African sub-Saharan culture a world culture as well as a

Early African artifact

A woman wears traditional African clothing to an African American festival in New Jersey.

continent-wide African civilization. African social mores and African religion have continued in Afro-American communities throughout the New World. European society both in the Americas and Europe has assimilated many aspects of African art, its musical forms and its dance, and its visual patterns and images.

The effect of West African sculpture and representation of the human form on the painting of early 20th-century European modern art is one of the most obvious influences. Popular music in the United States and Europe is now a blend of European melodies and African rhythms and harmonies. Bright colors in geometric patterns are so familiar in the decorative arts that their African origin is almost forgotten.

African Resources and Food

Africa's most valuable resources are fossil fuel, precious jewels, and metals, including abundant copper and gold. But these blessings carried difficulties. It was gold that attracted mercenary foreigners.

Cuisine: A style of cooking.

Staple African foods—peanuts, sweet potatoes, okra—are so much a part of the **cuisine** of all lands today that their origin is unknown to most. A world without the humble peanut and peanut butter is unthinkable. The sweet potato is used in many recipes. Okra and filé are the essential ingredients in gumbo, and blackened meat and fish are now popular in all parts of North America.

The Religious Influence

Most black African peoples believed in a supreme being, a creator god who held the welfare of human beings, his special creation, close to his heart.

The monotheism of Islam and Christianity was easily translated through this deity. Other gods were also worshipped—spirits of nature and the elements—and these became identified with Christian saints and Islamic angels and prayed to by people who considered themselves good Christians or Muslims.

African religion today still includes all the acts of daily life, every action having a religious significance. Great events are particularly marked with ceremony and ritual: birth, marriage, children, successes and failures, and death. Sacrifice, the offering of things precious to the worshipper or traditionally connected to the spirit invoked, are offered in recognition of the important event or the on-going life of the family. Special gifts are traditionally given to each god, including animal sacrifice and, formerly, human sacrifice. Whiskey and corn meal are the traditional gifts to the ancestors of the family.

A child seen carrying peanut plants.

Slavery and Colonialism

The chief marks of African religion are social—group cooperation and duties to family and guests. The need for cooperation and mutual aid in order to survive has made African religion focus on a sense of obligation to other people. This was undermined by the slave trade, which weakened family ties. The disruption left the continent open to conquest by the European powers in the 19th century. European **colonialism** was the result.

By the end of the 19th century, all of the African continent was claimed by one or other of the European powers, who had divided up the continent into colonies. European governments and companies extracted profits but also brought stability, peace, and a degree of civilization with them. Independence did not come to the European African colonies until after the Second World War. African-run governments or minityrants now rule all the former European territories. Traditional African social structures and royal lines no longer exist.

In the New World, African family ties remained strong, even withstanding the breakup of families by the slave system. Although Africa produced no major technology, its influence on art and music has been just as meaningful to human development.

Colonialism: The control of a region by a more powerful foreign nation.

Chapter 13 Review

Let's Remember   Write your answer in a single complete sentence.
1. Where does the Nile River originate?
2. What was the first civilization in Africa?
3. Who was St. Julian?
4. What is Timbuktu?
5. Why did the Portugese think they had found Prester John?

Let's Consider   For silent thinking and a short essay, or for thinking in a group with classroom discussion:
1. Why the Sahara might have become a desert.
2. The fate of Kush and its disappearance.
3. The effect of slave trade upon African life.

Let's Eat!

Peanuts are an African vegetable.
Recipe for African Peanut Soup: In large pot, place the following: 2 T. oil, 1 onion and 1 green pepper (chopped), 2 cloves garlic (pressed). Saute until brown. Add 1 can of crushed tomatoes and 4 cans chicken broth. Bring to a boil and add ½ C. uncooked rice and ¼ teas. Pepper. Simmer for ½ hour. Add ½ C. peanut butter. Stir until smooth and serve. Sprinkle with crushed peanuts on top.

Chapter 14

Russia:
The Third Rome

For seventy-four years, from 1917 to 1991, the deeply Christian nation of the Russians was ruled by an **atheist** regime determined to overthrow all other governments in the world. Thus, in the 20th century, the religious and largely isolated Russia became "the Evil Empire" and took its place among world powers with its new political religion, **Communism**. It devoted its vast resources to spreading Communism to all other lands.

While Catholics all over the world, following the Marian apparitions at Fatima in 1917, began praying for Russia's conversion, Russia—renamed the Union of Soviet Socialist Republics—tried to eliminate all religions, especially its own Orthodox Christianity, and promote violent revolution everywhere. At last, in 1991, the atheist Soviet regime collapsed, setting its tributary satellite countries free and restoring the basic rights of its citizens. Today's Russian republic struggles to overcome the economic and cultural damages of the Communist years. All religions, especially the Orthodox Christian faith, are free to worship once again and are reviving in an amazing way. How did so deeply religious a nation as Russia abandon its Christian past and submit to an atheist tyranny? The answer lies in Russia's history and tradition.

Atheist: One who denies the existence of God.
Communism: A social theory that advocates common ownership of property and equal distribution of wealth.

St. Basil's Cathedral in Moscow.

The Geography of Russia

The history of Russia has been shaped by her geography. Russia is the largest country on Earth, extending from central Europe across the eastern end of the continent and the cold wastes of Siberia to the Pacific coasts

Russia today.

of Asia. It has vast stores of natural resources and a diverse population comprised of more than 200 nationalities and many languages.

However, nature and geography have been harsh on Russia. More than 80 percent of the country is north of the latitude marking the U.S.-Canadian border. There are no protective mountain ranges to stop the freezing arctic winds from coming down over the plains, or hostile invading peoples over the vast flat land. The country falls into two regions: European Russia (the original Russian homeland in eastern Europe) and Asian Russia (the lands added by the empire in the 16th and 17th centuries—the vast expanse of northern Asia called Siberia).

European Russia has no mountain ranges to act as natural boundaries, only a huge rolling plain stretching from the Baltic Sea in the north to the shores of the Black Sea thousands of miles to the south. On the far eastern boundaries of Russia are the Ural Mountains (the dividing line of Europe and Asia) and on the southeast are the Caucasus Mountains.

Asian Russia (Siberia on the north and the Turkish steppes to the south) is sparsely populated and has harsh weather conditions. It is a frozen waste for most of the year, its northern running rivers are frozen except for a brief

Topographical map of European Russia, with color-keyed elevation scale.

summer thaw, and its plains and low mountains are inaccessible except by air. The southern steppe contains two landlocked seas, the large Caspian Sea, fed by the Volga River, and the Aral Sea, damaged in the 20th century by failed Soviet land-reclamation projects, so that it is now only a third of its original size. Siberia contains the world's largest and deepest freshwater lake, Lake Baykal.

In the first centuries of the Russian nation, a huge forest covered all the northern half of the Russian plain. The Slavs, a people living in southern Europe near the Carpathian Mountains, entered this forest, cut trees, and planted fields in the rich soil. The snowy winters were long and harsh, but the summers gave bountiful crops. The southern half of the land, the Russian **steppe**, was open grassland, warm and inviting. Nevertheless, the Slavs feared the steppe, because wave after wave of barbarian enemies came across it out of Asia and there was no way to defend against them on the open plain.

Steppe: vast, treeless plains in Europe and Asia.

Over the centuries, the Russian people were attacked so often that they came to fear strangers and to close themselves off from the rest of the world. They had tried to defend themselves against first the Huns, then the Khazars, then the Mongols, who killed and enslaved the hardy settlers. The Slavs were raided and taken into captivity so often that their name, Slav (which meant in the Slavic language "the glorious people"), became the word in western Europe for a captive laborer: slave.

Despite the easily invaded land, Russia has one great geographical advantage: a network of easily traveled rivers. The Dniester (NYEHSTER) and Dnieper (NYEPPER), the Don and the Volga, flow south into the Black Sea and the landlocked Caspian Sea. The Vistula, the Neva, and the Dvina all flow north into the North Sea and the Baltic Sea. All these rivers rise near each other in the central watershed of the continent that is the Russian heartland. A simple **portage** across land could put a transcontinental trader or traveler back on the water quickly. The route up and down the Dvina and Dnieper Rivers gave the Vikings a trade route to Byzantium, while the Volga to the Caspian Sea brought the northerners down to Baghdad.

Portage: A route for carrying boats overland between bodies of water.

The rivers of European Russia with the traditional cities of Kiev, Novgorod, Smolensk, and Moscow.

A Viking, Rurik, and his Germanic warriors, carved out a kingdom for themselves among the Slavs along the Dnieper River, and built a fortress that would become the city of Kiev. Rurik's warriors were called the *Rus*—meaning "red-haired"—and gave their name to the people they ruled.

The "Constantine" of Russia

The Christian message came to Russia in the 800s, when two Greek siblings, St. Cyril and St. Methodius, were sent as missionaries to the Slavic regions of Bulgaria, Russia, and Yugoslavia. The brothers developed a written alphabet based on Greek, and using this, they translated the Scriptures and liturgical books into the Slavic language. This written language developed by St. Cyril and St. Methodius became the Russian alphabet, similar to the Greek. Though the region remained largely pagan, Christianity began to spread steadily.

The Vikings were absorbed into the Slavic people they ruled, and the heirs of Rurik took Slavic names. Then in the late 10th century, Vladimir of Kiev, the pagan ruler of a newly unified Russia, decided that a national religion was needed. So he went shopping for a religion for his people. He invited envoys from neighboring countries to come to Kiev to tell him all about the benefits of their religions. Vladimir considered, but then rejected, Islam and Judaism. As for Christianity, he was unimpressed by the envoys of the Latin Church and thought the Byzantine one would better suit the Russian people. Vladimir decided to send some of his own men to Constantinople to investigate. So enchanted were his emissaries by the splendor of the city, the cathedral (Hagia Sophia), and the richness of the liturgy, that they ran out of words to describe it: "We knew not whether we were in heaven or on Earth." That settled the matter for Vladimir, and the Russian Church developed out of Byzantine Christianity.

In 988 Vladimir invaded Kherson, a city in the northern region of the eastern empire. From there he sent a marriage proposal—under threat of attack—to Anna, the sister of the Byzantine emperor, Basil II. Basil said his sister could not marry a non-Christian, but Vladimir replied that he had decided to convert. Vladimir was baptized in Kherson, and then withdrew his troops from the city. He married Anna, and upon his return home he released his pagan wives. He then ordered all his Russian subjects to be baptized. After so dramatic a beginning, his remaining years were spent rather uneventfully, establishing Christianity throughout his kingdom.

Christ with Saints: icons in the Cathedral of St. Sophia, Kiev, Ukraine.

The influence of Byzantine culture on Russia was evident in both politics and culture. Politically, the Byzantine imperial ritual and bureaucracy were the models for Russian royal ceremonies and civil services for centuries. Culturally, the style of icon painting, liturgical music, church mosaics, and church architecture that developed in Russia was imitated from Byzantine models.

Russian Christianity was always drawn to the ceremony and ritual of the Byzantine liturgy, and to the monastic ideal of renunciation and devotion to prayer. Humility and poverty, imitating the life of Christ and Jesus' mercy and forgiveness, were the ideals of Russian Christianity as they were of Latin Christianity. The Russian monks sought out remote places for their hermitages and communities. Like many peasants and pioneers, the monks went deeper into the forests searching out uninhabited land farther and farther from the cities. In the 1200s St. Sergius founded the Holy Trinity monastery north of Moscow. Holy Trinity-St. Sergius became the central community of Russian monasticism.

Mongol Invasion

Towers of Trinity Monastery of St. Sergius, founded in 1345 by St. Sergius Radonezh; the Trinity Monastery has been a center of Russian Orthodoxy for hundreds of years.

In 1206, an event in Asia changed Russia's history forever. The Mongol prince Genghis Khan united all the tribes of the Mongol people and invaded China. He conquered that old empire in a matter of years, and then turned to the west to make himself master of the known world. The Russians tried to stop the Mongols in 1223 at the Battle of the Don, but lost and were decimated. The Mongols crushed their captured Russian princes to death under a heavy wooden platform. The Mongol victors held a victory feast while nearby their victims bled and suffocated.

In 1237, the Mongols returned under Batu Khan, a grandson of Genghis, and all Russia was forced to pay tribute to the Khan and his forces. Batu reduced the Russian people to abject poverty and slavery. He then swept toward western Europe, defeated the Poles and Hungarians, and reached the Adriatic Sea. But Batu withdrew suddenly at the news of his brother's death, and the West was spared. But Mongol generals, under

Moscow mural depicting St. George blessing Grand Duke Dimitri Donskoi and his army on their way to do battle with the Mongols at Kouliobo.

Kublai Khan and his successors, continued to ravage Russia and to exact crushing tribute from its cities for the next two centuries. Russian slaves were regularly shipped down the rivers to the markets of Persia or marched into the interior of Asia and China. Slavers tried to hide the nationality of Russian slaves, claiming that they were "Lithuanians," or "Swedes," because the Russians had the reputation of making trouble.

In 1378 a descendant of the line of Rurik, the Grand Prince Dimitry of Moscow, refused to pay the tribute and defeated a small Mongol army. The Mongols rode north to put down this upstart Russian. Unexpectedly, at the juncture of the Don and Nepryavda Rivers, a much smaller Russian force routed the Mongols. The princes of Moscow became the leaders of the resistance to Mongol oppression. Mongol control was broken by a series of battles and internal civil wars over the next hundred years. Muscovy, the region around Moscow, became the center of Russian life so that the bishop-patriarch of Russia moved his see to Moscow.

The effect of Mongol control on Russia was disastrous. Russia was cut off from Byzantium and from the West as well. It was forced to devote all its resources to defense and tribute money to the Mongols. Despotism and serfdom began under the Mongol rule.

The freedom and democratic laws that characterized the Kievan kings, and energized the people to set out as pioneers into the undeveloped forests and grasslands, was wiped out. Instead, Russian rulers began to imitate the Mongol khans in their harshness and cruelty.

To escape the oppression of their own despotic local lords, their *boyars*, peasants fled their homes with their families and claimed lands farther north in the forest away from Mongol raids or **boyar** taxation. The Russian Empire grew by accident as its people sought the liberty of the wilderness. These frontiersmen, refusing the rule or authority of the landed

Boyar: The land-owning aristocrats of Russia.

Ivan III Vasilyevich, Grand Prince of Moscow.

aristocrats, were called Cossacks. Soon large communities of Cossacks were found along the Dnieper River in the heart of Ukraine, and on the eastern and southern borders of the kingdom, spreading into the steppe with their horse herds, or turning the empty forest into farmland.

Ivan the Great

The Muscovite prince most responsible for the success of Moscow was Prince Ivan III, called Ivan the Great. Ivan was a contemporary of Italy's Michelangelo and Leonardo de Vinci. He added the independent republic of Novgorod to Moscow's realm, and conquered Tver to the northwest of Moscow, then the Kievan princedoms of Chernigov and Smolensk. When Ivan died he had all of the lands of Russia under his control. His nation was one people with a common language, united in religion and in resisting Mongol oppression. With all of the Russians united under the Moscow prince, internal fighting ceased, and Russia began to see itself as a nation united against the world.

The consolidation of Muscovy under Ivan the Great was the most important development in Russian history. It gave a sense of national identity to the Russians, and a power capable of protecting the people from their traditional enemies. Enemies surrounded Muscovy. The Mongols were in the east and south; Poland and Lithuania—Roman Catholic , with a Western culture—on the north and west; the Teutonic Knights of Prussia, and the large kingdom of Sweden in the north.

Ivan set out to make Muscovy a recognized nation, legitimate in the eyes of other nations. He was unaware of developments in the West, but knew how to impress the East. In 1475 he married Sophia Paleologos, niece of Constantine XI, last emperor of Byzantium. He declared that his marriage made him the rightful heir of the Eastern Empire. He added the Byzantine double-headed eagle to his family crest and took for himself the two titles of the Byzantine emperors: czar (caesar) and **autocrat**.

Ivan instituted a court ceremony imitating the pomp of Byzantine rituals; he succeeded in stupefying visiting ambassadors and princes. Imitating Byzantium, Ivan ordered three huge cathedrals built to adorn the Kremlin, his Moscow fortress-palace. *Kremlin* is the Russian word for fortress. Every major city had its own kremlin, but Moscow's became the most famous. Ivan's churches were impressive examples of medieval Russian architecture. The churches of the Assumption, the Archangel, and the

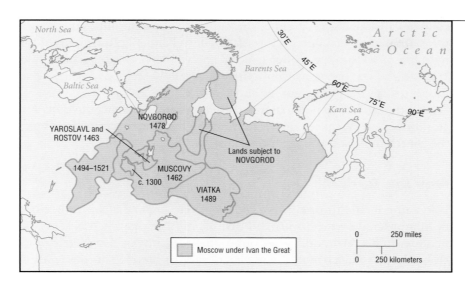

North Sea

Arctic Ocean

Baltic Sea

Barents Sea

Kara Sea

30°E
45°E
60°E
75°E
90°E

NOVGOROD
1478

YAROSLAVL and
ROSTOV 1463

Lands subject to
NOVGOROD

1494–1521

MUSCOVY
1462
c. 1300

VIATKA
1489

Moscow under Ivan the Great

0   250 miles
0   250 kilometers

Moscow's expansion under Czar Ivan the Great.

Annunciation still stand in the modern Kremlin, a memorial to Ivan and the creation of the Russian nation.

The Russian church, to advance Muscovite authority, developed the doctrine of Moscow being the Third Rome, heir to the world authority of Rome, and its successor, Constantinople. The church was divided, however. The Christian ideals of poverty and humility contrasted with the power of rulers and the wealth of bishops. Some churchmen argued that the church must be wealthy in order to fulfill its obligations of charity and to attract men of quality to the priesthood. Others advocated a return to the

The Kremlin in Moscow.

contemplative and ascetic life of the old monks and hermits, and a complete separation of church and state. The religious argument over the morality of wealth and power affected the whole of the Russian people. What Russia was becoming (powerful and worldly) seemed to betray what Russia had always been (humble and ascetic).

Ivan the Great was not able to resolve the issue in his own lifetime. But grandson, Ivan IV, called "the Terrible," brought the aristocratic boyars and the church under his truly autocratic fist.

Ivan the Terrible

Ivan came to the throne in his late teens. He knew that his father had been murdered by the boyars and that his mother's family had kept him prisoner in his boyhood. He set out to make the boyars completely powerless. To do so he created a new class of service gentry. This new class of

Ivan the Terrible (1530–84), Czar of Russia.

men had distinguished themselves in battle. Ivan gave them great estates and peasants, but with a catch to keep them loyal. The service gentry understood that they were to furnish the czar with soldiers and officers as needed, and that their lands could be taken away at the czar's whim. Additionally, a dreaded army of landless fanatics, the *oprichniks* (the set-apart men), was created to serve the czar alone, and sent to terrorize the boyars and destroy those who spoke out against the czar. After eight years of *oprichnik* terror, the boyars as a class were politically broken. The Russian landed aristocracy became the servants of the throne.

Czar Ivan became fascinated with the English, and sent a marriage proposal to Queen Elizabeth I. She refused, and he then negotiated for the hand of an English noblewoman. He imported English workmen and engineers to start factories and workshops in Moscow, and brought Germans from the Protestant states of Prussia and Brandenburg to settle along the Volga in lands taken from the Mongols. The Russian word for foreigner was *German.*

Tragically, Ivan went violently insane in his later years. He maintained a 20-year war with Sweden and

Poland that nearly bankrupted the treasury and cost thousands of Russian and Polish lives. He tortured his supposed enemies cruelly. His armies were sent on suicide missions or to build impossible bridges and roads. He feared everyone was trying to kill him and that his sons were plotting to assassinate him. In a fit of madness he killed his eldest son with the spear-tip of his scepter-staff. He wandered howling through the halls of his palace, screaming so loudly that his cries were heard outside the Kremlin. He abandoned Christianity, imprisoned and killed the Moscow patriarch, and sought out witches and magicians from the pagan peoples of the far north. Carried on a chair into his treasury, he would hold precious jewels next to his skin and watch for them to change color. His witches had told him that poison and disease could be detected by its effect on the color of precious stones. Finally, one day he had a convulsion, fell from his throne, and died within the hour.

Alexis I (1629–1676), second Russian Czar from the Romanov family.

The Dynasty of the Romanovs

After Ivan the Terrible's death, his idiot son Feodor ruled for fourteen years. Feodor died childless and the line of Rurik the Viking ended. Russia was racked by civil wars until Michael Romanov, a distantly related boyar, was crowned czar in 1613. Romanov founded a line that would rule Russia until the Revolution of 1917. Under the Romanovs, Russia became more autocratic and despotic, although as much by accident as by intent. The factions of the aristocracy and the military could not agree on anything, and the country faced ruinous debts from Ivan's wars and disruptive policies. Placing all power in one man's hands seemed the only solution.

Czar Alexis Romanov, Michael's son, arranged a **codification** of the laws in order that "law and justice shall be equal in all things." Despite its intention, "The Code of 1649" created a caste system for Russia and kept peasants, taxpayers, army recruits, and officials tightly under the control of the Moscow government. Serfdom, the denial of the right of peasants to leave their landlords, came about naturally. The peasantry was hereditary; sons could not leave the household of their father. Townsmen, moreover, were bound to their towns, and all occupations were made part of the civil service, and kept track of by a growing bureaucracy. Everyone was required to carry identification and produce it on demand. The civil service was organized in military ranks and titles, and officers of the government were required to wear uniforms like army officers. Government

Codification: the arrangement of laws or writings into a systematic form.

employees handed their offices to their sons, so that the civil service became hereditary as well.

Yet some runaway peasants and townsmen made their way to the south and east along the Don River and the Volga and became cossacks—lawless frontiersmen, defying czar or landlord. The 1600s saw several cossack rebellions that became legendary in Russian folklore.

One reform of the Romanov czars caused untold misery and social disruption: the reform of Russian religion in 1652. Russian Christians were deeply attached to the ritual forms of the faith, and tried to observe every detail of the ritual that came from St. Cyril and St. Methodius and the first missionaries. In particular, the liturgy was still said in Church Slavonic, the language of the medieval past. But the brilliant and scholarly patriarch of Moscow, Nikon, persuaded Czar Alexis to reform Russian religion. Nikon had decided that the Russian ritual deviated from the original forms of Byzantium. He decreed that every detail of contemporary Greek practice should be adopted. The most controversial of his changes was the making of the sign of the cross with three fingers, not two. To many Russians this was not just a change in symbolism, but also a change in theology. The liturgies were rewritten to conform to the current Greek texts, not Slavonic. Much that was loved of the tradition was sacrificed. Everywhere the Russians were to obey these reforms on pain of death or exile. The czar's police backed up the patriarch's demands, and punishments were swift and fearful.

A large segment of the Russian clergy and people refused to go along with Nikon's "reforms." They rebelled against both patriarch and czar. Calling themselves Old Believers, they asked: "Why, if Holy Russia was third Rome, should she change her ways? Were not the reformers the true

Seagoing cossacks.

heretics? Did not Byzantium, Second Rome, fall to the Turks because it was weak in faith, while Moscow defeated the Mongols because it held fast to the true faith?"

The Old Believers were not only opposed to the new reforms, but to the whole idea of czarist autocracy—serfdom, despotism, and Westernization. Many clergy and aristocrats suffered for this rebellion, and a long-lasting schism split the Russian Church, a schism that went to the heart of national unity. Old Believers continued to worship and communicate in secret societies over the next two centuries. They thought of themselves as being like the Christians in the days of the Roman persecutions, meeting in the catacombs. The cooperation of the church with the state gave the state rule over the church and the church dependent on the czar for its existence. So under Peter the Great, the Russian Church became another bureau in the state apparatus. By Peter's ordinance, priests who heard seditious remarks during confession were required by law to report them to the police.

Peter the Great

Michael Romanov's great-grandson, Peter, brought Western technology and thought to Russia. When Peter was crowned in 1696, at the young age of 24, he determined to bring Western engineers and thinkers to Moscow. To accomplish his goal, he set about learning everything about the West that he could. In disguise and accompanied by his closest friends, Peter undertook a trip to Germany and England. In his disguise, he worked as a stonemason, a carpenter, a blacksmith, and a dentist. He even kept a bag of human teeth to prove his skill and talent!

In his youth he showed great curiosity about mechanical structures, and spent hours with the practical German and Danish technicians of Moscow's "German" quarter. There he learned a principle that he used in his later reign: advancement should be based on merit, not rank or origin. Later, he would choose his assistants from the lowest levels of society, and maintain a regiment of 300 young nobles, all serving as enlisted men, until one by one they distinguished themselves or mastered their jobs; then he would promote them to officer rank. If they consistently failed, he would leave them in the enlisted rank.

Czar Peter the Great in European armor, 1717.

Isolationism: The policy of a nation which cuts itself off from contact with other nations.

In domestic affairs, Peter had only one goal: to bring Russia out of its **isolationism** and force it to accept Westernization. He ordered Russian men to shave their beards and to wear Western clothes. Those who refused could be stopped on the streets and forcibly shaved by the police. They were made to pay a "beard tax" if they persisted in being unshaven. Internal civil wars broke out all over Russia, and were put down, one by one, over the years of his reign. The Old Believers were persecuted, crushed, and driven underground; they become a dangerous secret society.

In foreign affairs, Peter had two goals: warm water ports for Russian trade and acceptance of Russia as a world power. He conquered the last Tartar forces of the Crimea and built a fleet on the Black Sea, which had been the private lake of the Ottoman Turks. In the north, he made war on Sweden, which at that time controlled the coast of the Baltic Sea. In 1703 he seized the mouth of the Neva River and began to build a city to be named for him, Petrograd, or St. Petersburg. St. Petersburg was built on swampy ground that had to be drained and filled. It had to be both a seaport and a fortress. To build his city he dragged thousands of Russian peasants into the cold and unhealthy swamps and there starved, beat, and drove them to their deaths for the sake of the great project. The great city is today a memorial to the heroic and nameless men who suffered and died to create it. Later, he forced the Russian nobility, on pain of death or exile, to move to St. Petersburg and to build stone mansions there for themselves and their families; he could keep a better eye on them if they lived nearby. The example of Louis XIV of France and his palace of Versailles was Peter's model. It would be not only the "Window on the West," it was to be his new capital, an enlightened European metropolis, far from the superstition and rebellion of medieval Moscow.

Peter defeated the Swedes, the Turks, the Poles, and his own rebellious cossacks in a series of wars. His military adventures added modern Lithuania and

St. Petersburg. View of the Troizkoi Bridge by J. Schroeder.

Latvia to his territory and pushed the Russian border south to its present place. By creating of a modern army and navy, he placed his country militarily among the great powers of Europe. After Peter, all European alliances had to take account of Russia in the balance of power.

Peter's legacy was the Westernization he had so fiercely championed. Russia did become a world empire and a world culture, but it was at the heavy cost of widespread suffering and deep division in the national soul. Westernized aristocrats, deriving their wealth from the agricultural labor of their serfs, learned to speak French and to dress in French and English fashions, to travel to foreign capitals and to engage in Enlightenment debates. Their peasants, on the other hand, spoke an archaic Russian, and they lived in hopeless poverty and ignorance. The growing middle-class of Russian townsfolk remained bound by the caste system to a life of little comfort or near-poverty. The great cities were mired in slums and decaying industrial neighborhoods. Russian religious faith was as strong as ever, but trust in the institutional church was forever broken. Ritual and faith grew farther apart. Enlightenment ideas drew the privileged rulers in one direction, while Russian realities drew the uneducated poor in another. Into this crisis a third movement came, Slavophilism, an attempt among many educated Russians to restore the traditions and faith of the Russian past to full power.

Armies of Napoleon

In 1811, the French armies of Napoleon invaded the Motherland of Holy Russia. Opposition to this "atheist revolutionary" became a crusade. Russians of all classes eagerly joined the war effort. The armies of Czar Alexander I fell back, luring the French deeper into the Russian plain as winter came. Finally, at Borodino, outside of Moscow, the Russians attempted a stand and were defeated. Moscow fell to Napoleon. But, the Russian winter of 1812 did what the armies of Russia had failed to do. Napoleon's frozen and starving troops straggled back across the thousand miles of Russia leaving the Russians in possession of their land. The Russian composer Tchaikovsky celebrated this event in the famous *1812 Overture*. The war provided material for *War and Peace*, the greatest Russian novel, by Leo Tolstoy.

The war against Napoleon angered the upper classes because of the inefficiency of the czarist government, and brought more Russians into contact with the West and with Western ideas of government. The new

Napoleon and his soldiers return from Moscow.

Anarchist: One who believes that any government is bad and works for its destruction.

ideas of "democracy" and "republicanism" swept through the educated classes. Secret societies of military officers tried to overthrow the government and establish a republic. The Decembrist Revolution, an attempted military coup, was stopped only at the last moment. Other secret societies worked for reform and change in all aspects of Russian life. The universities became hotbeds of revolutionary fervor. Nicholas I feared this growing mass movement. He empowered the secret police to arrest anyone suspected of revolutionary ideas or speech. Thousands were sent to the new prison camps in Siberia.

In 1861, before Abraham Lincoln's Emancipation Proclamation freed the slaves in America, Czar Alexander II freed the serfs of Russia by imperial decree. The peasants were now free to leave and seek employment in the cities; industry grew and took in this new source of labor. But freed serfs who stayed on the land were not given free land as they had expected, and were forced to pay for their tiny plots over the years, keeping them in debt to the government. Resentment grew.

In 1883, Alexander II was assassinated when someone from a revolutionary secret society of **anarchists** threw a bomb into his carriage. The secret police sent even more people to Siberia. His son, Alexander III, feared revolution and change as much as he feared assassination. He began a campaign to force all the various nationalities under Russian rule to speak Russian and to accept the Russian Orthodox faith. Many Catholics, Protestants, Jews, and Muslims were fined and arrested as disturbers of the peace. Persecution of Jews became so intense that millions of Russian Jews left their homes and emigrated to America and England.

Alexander III's son, Nicholas II, inherited a raging country, divided and resentful at every level of society. He believed that the old Russian ways ought to be brought back again and the Russian faith revived. Nicholas II wanted to be a true Christian monarch. He was a loving family man and devoted to his German-princess wife, the granddaughter of England's Queen Victoria. He spent most of his time with his family away from Moscow and St. Petersburg and left the running of the country to trusted minis-

Alexander II of Russia, Czar of Russia (1818–1881); an active promoter of reform who was responsible for the abolition of serfdom in 1861.

ters. The situation was fast getting away from him and his government.

Industrialized Russia

Russia had become one of the industrial powers of the world, fourth largest producer of iron and coal. Russian industry employed over 2 million factory workers. Like workers the world over, Russian workers were underpaid and overworked. They wanted the right to organize into labor unions, like workers in the

Nicholas II (1868–1918), Czar (1894–1917), pictured with his family: Duchess Olga, Duchess Marie, the Grand Duchess Anastasia, the Czarevitch (young Czar) Alexis, the Grand Duchess Tatiana, and his wife the Czarina.

Western countries. But the secret police arrested labor organizers and broke up strikes with violence.

Into this boiling pot came the ideas of a 19th-century German intellectual, Karl Marx, who described an ideal world where the working **proletariat** made the decisions about their own future, and property was held in common for the common good. His description of history as a continuous class warfare convinced many European intellectuals that only violent revolution would bring about significant change. Secret Marxist societies, called *soviets*, sprang up all over Russia. In 1905, when there was an uprising of industrial workers in the cities, Russia barely escaped revolution. The czar and his ministers tried to loosen control by establishing a parliament on the English model, but too much of the old machinery remained in place.

Proletariat: Member of the working class.

Suddenly and violently, the military alliances of the preceding century drew all of Europe into the war that we now call World War I. Russia entered it on the side of the French and English, facing the armies of a highly prepared and trained Germany. The war with Germany caught Russia by surprise. Russia did not have the transportation or supply systems necessary to feed and clothe her massive armies. Its soldiers fought in the mud of the trenches through three winters without proper clothing or shoes, and with little ammunition. The death toll was staggering.

After three years of fighting, Russia was ready to sue for peace. The czar refused. In March of 1917, riots broke out in every major Russian city. The parliament declared a provisional government and on March 15, 1917, Nicholas II abdicated the throne. All over Russia, the *soviets* took power

Lenin speaking in Red Square to Russian soldiers. Moscow, May 1919.

from the local government and refused to acknowledge the authority of the new provisional government. The troops at the front began to desert in droves.

The Germans, to weaken Russia further, urged the *soviet* revolutionaries to take up arms against the czar. They sent to Russia a revolutionary by the name of Vladimir Ilich Ulyanov, better known by his revolutionary alias—Lenin—under whom more people were killed than under Hitler. Lenin had been living in Switzerland with a price on his head from the Russian secret police.

Lenin was a former law student who joined the revolutionaries when his brother was arrested and executed by the secret police. He then studied revolution and Marxism. A spellbinding speaker and ruthless leader, he had become well-known in revolutionary circles in Russia. His return provoked the *soviets* of St. Petersburg to rise up against the provisional government in November of 1917 and seize control of the country. The November revolution marked the end of traditional Russia.

After the uprising, the provisional government fled the city and tried to reorganize loyal supporters in the countryside. Civil war followed from 1917 to 1921. Lenin's band of revolutionaries, the Bolsheviks, took charge of the revolution and made peace with Germany.

The Bolsheviks sent Czar Nicholas and his entire family into exile in the east, and executed every one of them the next year. The Russian church considers the czar and his family to be martyrs for the faith.

The Bolsheviks, shortly after taking power, renamed themselves Communists. They promised land for the peasants and an end to all class distinctions. Women were given the vote, and titles of aristocracy were abolished. A grim equality supposedly was all over Russia.

Then Lenin grew afraid of his own people. His right-hand man, Leon Trotsky, disagreed with him on some issues. Trotsky fled Russia in fear of his life and was later assassinated in Mexico. The old one-man rule, autocracy, appealed to the Russian mind as the solution to inner strife. Lenin's Communist secret police were in fact more ruthless and demanding than their czarist predecessors. Millions were starved to death in the Ukraine during the enforcement of collective ownership of the land. Then the leaders of the November revolution themselves met death in Communist prisons. Russia became a vast and cruel prison for its own people. It is estimated that as many as 10 million people died in the Ukraine alone.

Lenin spent the last years of his life trying to turn Russia into a Marxist workers' utopia with himself the all-powerful leader. To accomplish this end, he murdered his opponents remorselessly, both royalists and fellow Bolsheviks, and he made his Russia, now called the Union of Soviet Socialist Republics, into the engine of world revolution. He died in 1924 and was succeeded by Joseph Stalin, a man even more cruel and ruthless in the pursuit of power than Lenin.

Joseph Stalin, during the final illness of Vladimir Lenin in the early 1920s, was plotting to take all power for himself upon Lenin's death.

The Direction of Modern Russia?

The history of Russia is a story of heroes and heroines, of saints and monstrous evil. The Russian contribution to world civilization has been mixed, both good and bad like most countries. Although Russian Soviet agents have subverted democracies and waged wars of revolution, though millions have died for czarist and communist ideologies, Russian authors and artists have created masterpieces of human imagination. Russian painters, such as Kandinsky and Chagall in the 20th century, changed our concept of art. Russian music continues to influence the world. The glories of Tchaikovsky, Mussorgsky, and Rachmaninoff in the 19th century, and Stravinsky and Prokofiev in the 20th will never be forgotten. Russian novelists have left a treasure house of stories for the world's edification and entertainment; Pushkin, Gogol, Tolstoy, and Dostoyevsky are the greatest names of a long list of great Russian writers and poets.

Improvisation (Little Painting With Yellow). Abstract painting by Wassily Kandinsky, an originator of modern theories of art.

Larger than life, the great men and women of Russia move across the stage of the past. Despite their accomplishments, the rise of an "Evil Empire" spread Communism to many other nations in the 20th century and made the USSR a world power to be feared and its people pitied and prayed for. Indeed, the whole Christian world has prayed for the conversion of Our Lady's "darling country" ever since the apparition at Fatima in 1917. The fall of the Communist state in 1991 opened Russia to a new relationship with the West and to a renewal of Christian religious fervor. The future destiny of so great a people remains to be seen.

Chapter 14 Review

Let's Remember   Write your answer in a single complete sentence.
1. Where does Russia get its name?
2. What alphabet does the Russian alphabet come from?
3. Why did Vladimir of Kiev send emissaries to Constantinople?
4. Who were the cossacks?
5. What is the Kremlin?

Let's Consider   For silent thinking and a short essay, or for thinking in a group with classroom discussion:
1. The influence of Byzantium on Russia.
2. The effects of the Romanovs' reforms of the Russian church.
3. Peter the Great's methods for Westernizing Russia.
4. Germany sending Lenin back to Russia.
5. The effects of the apparition of Our Lady of Fatima on the conversion of Russia.

Let's Eat!

Beet soup has been a staple of Russian cuisine for centuries. Here's a recipe for an easy-to-make borscht, cold beet soup: Chop up fine the beets from two cans of sliced beets (save the liquid). Put chopped beets in a 2-quart covered glass dish. Add the liquid and one can of chicken broth. Stir in the juice of 1 lemon, 2 T. sugar, 1 teaspoon salt. Cover and put in the microwave for 10 minutes. Remove and chill until ready to serve. Serve with a dollop of sour cream over the top of each bowl. 4 small servings.

Chapter 15 North America: Land of Opportunity

Though it began as a small and rough country, a mere youngster to its old-world ancestors, the United States quickly rose in stature to become the foremost defender of human rights, an industrial and military superpower, and the world's leader in democratic government and humanitarian aid.

In the 20th century three regions, previously regarded as mere backwaters or additions of Europe, became important world cultures in themselves: the Russian Empire in Europe and Asia, the United States in North America, and the many states of Latin America. Russia as the Soviet Union became one of the two superpowers of the last half of the 20th century. The United States became the other. The United States of America emerged as the defender of the anti-Communist Free World and the major industrial power of the globe. The countries of the Americas, English-speaking and Spanish-speaking, brought new ideas and new possibilities to the older cultures that had previously defined human civilization. In the competing cultures of the modern

A pioneer family makes a rugged new home.

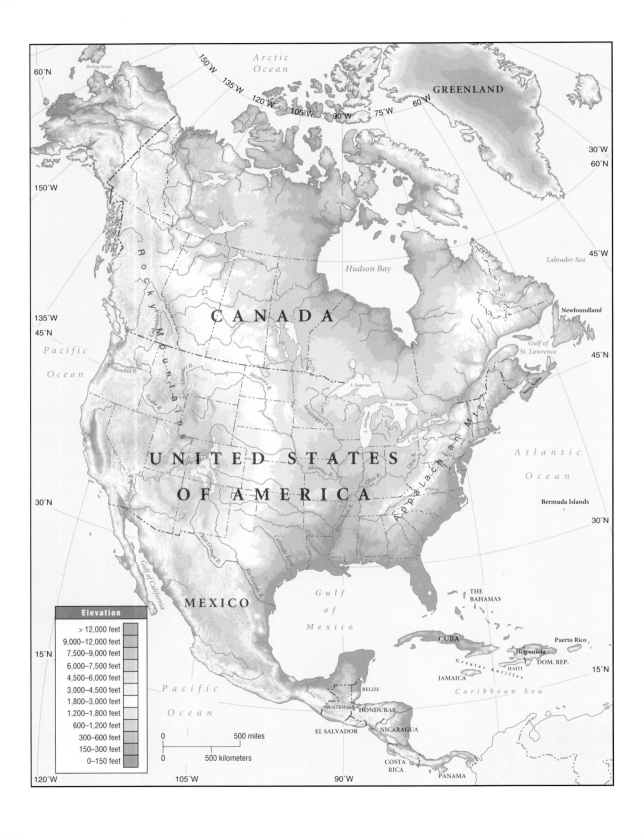

60°N

*Arctic
Ocean*

150°W

135°W

120°W

105°W

90°W

75°W

60°W

GREENLAND

30°W
60°N

Bering Strait

150°W

45°W

Labrador Sea

Hudson Bay

C A N A D A

Newfoundland

135°W
45°N

Pacific

Ocean

R   o   c   k   y   M   o   u   n   t   a   i   n   s

Columbia R.

Snake R.

Columbia R.

Missouri R.

Missouri R.

L. Superior

L. Huron

L. Michigan

L. Ontario

L. Erie

*Gulf of
St. Lawrence*

45°N

Nova Scotia

A   p   p   a   l   a   c   h   i   a   n   M   t   s   .

Atlantic

Ocean

U N I T E D   S T A T E S

O F   A M E R I C A

Mississippi R.

Missouri R.

Ohio R.

Ohio R.

30°N

30°N

Bermuda Islands

Colorado R.

Rio Grande R.

Rio Grande R.

Colorado River

Mississippi R.

Gulf of California

MEXICO

Gulf

of

Mexico

THE
BAHAMAS

CUBA

Puerto Rico

Hispaniola

DOM. REP.

HAITI

Greater Antilles

JAMAICA

15°N

15°N

Pacific

Ocean

BELIZE

Caribbean Sea

GUATEMALA

HONDURAS

EL SALVADOR

NICARAGUA

COSTA
RICA

PANAMA

Elevation	
> 12,000 feet	
9,000–12,000 feet	
7,500–9,000 feet	
6,000–7,500 feet	
4,500–6,000 feet	
3,000–4,500 feet	
1,800–3,000 feet	
1,200–1,800 feet	
600–1,200 feet	
300–600 feet	
150–300 feet	
0–150 feet	

0   500 miles

0   500 kilometers

120°W

105°W

90°W

world, the United States of America, as the inheritor of European Christian tradition, made itself a world culture, influencing the ideas and styles of all the world. The rapid growth of population and wealth has been helped by the land and weather of the North American continent; few countries have had such a favorable geography and climate for their growth and success.

A full account of the founding and development of the United States is given in the next text book, *One Nation Under God*, but in order to place the United States correctly within the world cultures, a brief analysis of the country is given in this chapter.

How Settlement of the United States Moved from East to West

When Europeans first came to the Atlantic seaboard, old forests covered the land as far as the Appalachian Mountains to the west and far beyond. The Native American tribes who lived there were unable to resist the European settlement; and land was there for anyone with enterprise, determination, and courage. European colonists spread into the interior rapidly, and this "can do" spirit of the early settlers became part of the American people. Because land was available, the old European ways of aristocratic authority and feudal organization never developed in the English-speaking colonies. The experience of the Spanish settlers in Mexico was different.

Colonial life: "Sunday morning at St. Thomas's church in Garrison Forest."

Thirteen English colonies with independent governments were established along the eastern seaboard. In the north, the colony of Massachusetts was followed by the colonies of Rhode Island, Connecticut, and New Hampshire. The city of Boston was the major port and metropolis. The territories that are now the states of Maine and Vermont were part of Massachusetts and New York. In the middle of the seaboard, the Dutch settlers surrendered their land along the Hudson River to England,

Opposite: A map of North America, with color-keyed elevation scale.

Map of the first European colonies—English, French, and Dutch—in America.

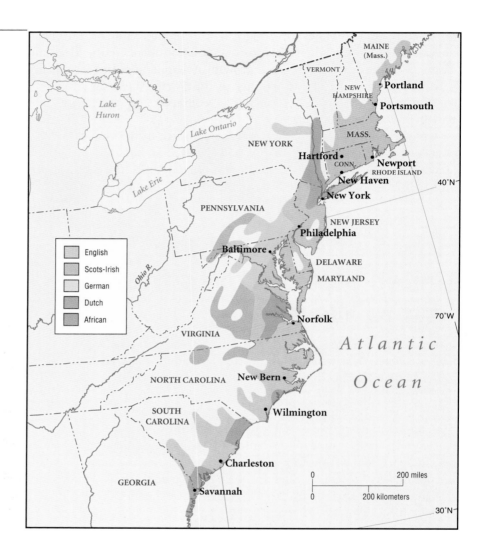

and it became the colony of New York. The port city of New York changed its name from New Amsterdam to New York. Pennsylvania's major city, Philadelphia, was the third largest city of colonial days. The colonies of Delaware and Maryland were founded on the peninsula that sheltered the great Chesapeake Bay. Maryland was originally a colony for English Catholics, but it soon became Protestant, like all the other colonies. Everywhere harsh colonial laws discriminated against

Catholics. The leader of the southern colonies was Virginia, the first to be settled by Englishmen. To its south were the colonies of North and South Carolina, and last, the colony of Georgia, sharing an uneasy border with Spanish Florida.

The French territory of Canada lay to the north of the St. Lawrence River, and to the west of the Appalachian Mountains. Later it would become a British possession, but it was not one of the original thirteen colonies. British arms would prevent its being added to the new United States after Independence.

Pioneers traveling down the Ohio River in a flatboat.

England and France had fought for hundreds of years in Europe, and they continued in their American colonies. France claimed the region now known as Canada at the same time as England claimed the coastland that is now the United States. After his ordination as a Jesuit priest in 1636, Saint Isaac Jogues was sent to America as a missionary. He evangelized the areas around the great lakes, in what is now Canada and New York State. He and other brave missionaries were martyred in Auriesville, New York during the period of 1642–1649. The first of these North American Martyrs was Rene Goupil, a layman and doctor, who was tomahawked for making the sign of the cross on the brow of a child. Isaac Jogues was also martyred in the same way in 1646. A little later, Jogues' murderer was captured by the French and handed over to the Algonquins, with orders not to torture him. Before his execution, one year later, the young brave was baptized, taking the name Isaac Jogues! Other French explorers and missionaries journeyed deep into the continent and discovered the Mississippi waterway, and went down the river to the Gulf of Mexico. French settlers followed and built towns along the Mississippi and Ohio Rivers at Vincennes on the Ohio and St. Louis and New Orleans on the Mississippi. The European Seven Years' War, 1756–1763 (called here the French and Indian War), ended with the French surrender in the New World in 1760. England gained French Canada and all the lands east of the Mississippi. The French gave the lands west of the Mississippi to the Spanish, for a time.

Daniel Boone (1734–1820) during his last years, in the wilderness he loved and spent his entire life exploring.

Access to land continued to shape the American character throughout the 19th century. No titled aristocracy came over from the feudal traditions of Europe—no dukes, counts, marquises, etc. Gentlemen there were, but they were never as rich or as independent as in Great Britain, and a colonial aristocracy was never established. This was because poorer settlers and new immigrants could leave their employers and landlords and move on into the west and the free land of the wilderness.

In England, for instance, a gentleman could have a steady income from his estates. This was because relatively few people below the level of gentlemen owned any land, but had to rent it from gentleman landlords. In America, gentlemen did not have such a steady source of income, for there were not as many tenant farmers to rent land. Too often, colonial gentlemen worked as traders or farmers, to keep up the appearances of being gentlemen. Benjamin Franklin made his fortune as a printer in Philadelphia. Later, he sold his business, and lived the life of leisure. He was, then, considered a gentleman by English society.

Daniel Boone

In the 1760s, with French opposition ended, frontiersmen pushed southwest over the Appalachians. The most famous of these wandering frontier hunters was Daniel Boone. Born in 1734, Boone had served in the British general Braddock's regular and militia army during the French and Indian War. Boone lived through the massacre of Braddock's troops at the disaster of Fort Duquesne caused because General Braddock refused to abandon the European fighting style of lines of riflemen firing in ranks. The Indians quickly learned to shoot into the ranks and disrupt the English formation. Boone and the other survivors of Braddock's disastrous defeat survived because they knew how to fight Indian style, as individuals, and so were able to support themselves in the long retreat back to English territory. In 1769, Boone began to explore the Kentucky country, and opened up the Wilderness Road through the Cumberland Gap for pioneer emigrants. As he traveled across the Appalachians into the west, Boone looked for the best route for wagons to get through. Boone's trail followed the old trails created by buffalo herds that once roamed along the east coast as well as the western plains. These huge herds cut out paths across the mountains in their annual migrations from east to west. The east coast buffalo were driven across the Mississippi by the encroaching settlements, but the huge herds survived on the Great Plains into the late 19th century. The buffalo, the major food source for nomadic Indian tribes, also fed and clothed the new European settlers.

Boone was typical of the rugged pioneers of the western lands. He could barely read or write, but he knew wood-lore and survival skills that saved his life many times. Men like him had been exploring and hunting in the forests for over a century. They came to be called "Long-Rifles," after the firearms they carried and used so accurately. The Long-Riflemen made annual hunting trips into the forests in small parties of three or four men, or, like Boone, traveled alone. For months they would be cut off from civilization and their families, collecting furs for sale in the eastern cities, and living off the hunt and the work of their own hands. They developed a scorn of the rules and conventions of city life, and a sense of independence and freedom that spread to those back in the colonies. These frontier heroes were praised in legends and popular ballads.

Boone brought his family, his wife and sons, with him to make a new life in the Kentucky wilderness. The settlers had moved into lands that were claimed by several Indian nations and used by them as sacred hunting and fighting grounds, where war parties could meet and settle quarrels without taking the fight into the permanent towns. *Kan-tu-kee*, the Shawnee name for the territory, means: "Dark and Bloody Ground."

Boone was honored as one of the first settlers of Kentucky, but his illiteracy and lack of business skill left him in the mercy of the tax men and con men who followed the settlers into the wilderness. He lost his lands through debt and was forced to move farther west when he was an old man. He died penniless in the western wilderness.

Beginnings of Civilization in the Western Territories

While the settlements along the east coast were being established, the west coast was also beginning to be settled. Spain, Russia, and England all had hopes of settling and claiming the west coast, but it was Spain's missionary efforts and the effort of one missionary that stood out above all others. In what is now California, a remarkable Franciscan priest began establishing missions, despite his frailty. From 1769 until his death in 1784, Father Junipero (whoo-nee'-pay-roe) Serra established 21 missions spanning a distance of 700 miles on foot (The *Camino Real* (ca mee'-no ray-al)). Established each approximately on day's journey apart, from San Diego to San Francisco, the missions provided centers of trade, education, and worship, all central to the formation of civilization. Father Serra not only greatly influenced the people of his day—baptizing and confirming thousands of new converts—he also left a great legacy that still stands today in the California Mission Trail and the Faith which is found all throughout California.

The Colonies Go to War

When the English Parliament, in the name of the king, increased the taxes on trade in the American colonies, the colonists resisted. Finally, a congress of representatives of all the colonial assemblies was called to meet in Philadelphia. They called themselves the Continental Congress. A British army landed in Boston to enforce the rule of the mother country, and the colonial militias of Massachusetts rose to defend their homes. The other colonies sent volunteers to help Massachusetts where the British troops had landed. They also landed in New York. The conflict spread. Congress appointed George Washington of Virginia to command the congressional army of militias and volunteers. The Colonies were now at war.

Washington was a remarkable man. Large of frame, already middle-aged, Washington was a Virginia landowner and planter. He had served as

American colonists and British soldiers fight at the top of Breed's Hill (Bunker Hill). The battle was a costly victory for the British.

a commander of troops in the French and Indian War. He had also been part of the Braddock expedition, and had been largely responsible for keeping the remnants of Braddock's army alive and together until they got safely back to English territory. He was a man of natural authority and common sense who commanded respect and devotion from his men. A more perfect choice for commander of the undermanned and poorly supplied Continental army could not have been found. He was faced with impossible odds fighting an experienced British Army with an untrained Militia. His men from Massachusetts refused to get along with the men from Pennsylvania; New Yorkers quarreled with Virginians. Washington's task was to keep his junior officers from shooting each other as well as to keep his troops from losing too many battles in the war. His policy of retreat and caution in the first years almost lost him his command, as Congress pushed for more energetic engagement with the British. But Washington's persistence and caution kept his army alive through the terrible winter encamped outside Philadelphia at Valley Forge. With the aid of Lafayette and French troops, Washington defeated the British at Yorktown in the last year of the war, 1781.

As the war progressed, it became obvious to Congress that the colonies had to declare themselves an independent country from England and the king. The task of writing the official notice of independence was assigned to a committee headed by the Virginian Thomas Jefferson. On July 4, 1776, the Continental Congress ratified The Declaration of Independence.

The Declaration of Independence stated why Congress thought it necessary to gain independence of the colonies from Great Britain. The first section invokes the "self-evident" truth that all men are created equal: "that they are endowed by their Creator with certain **inalienable** Rights, that among these are Life, Liberty and the pursuit of Happiness." Jefferson's claim that "all men are created equal" stated a cherished ideal of the frontier spirit that made up the American character. It would remain an assumption of American thought through all the formative years and beyond.

Inalienable: incapable of being lost, taken away, or surrendered.

Independence

England finally surrendered to Washington's army, and the independence of the colonies was recognized in the Treaty of Ghent, 1783. The colonies now had to figure how best to govern themselves according to the ideals and principles of their own spirit of independence and self-reliance, as well as their tradition as law-abiding Englishmen. The first attempt, called the Articles of Confederation, failed because of the rivalries of the regions

The Constitution, an original edition from September 1787, shown as it was first issued: written entirely on one side of one large sheet of paper, in the finest manuscript handwriting.

Constitution: The document that contains the written laws of a society.
To Ratify: To approve formally.

and colonies and international relations and trade. In 1787, a Constitutional Congress, presided over by the national hero, George Washington, met in Philadelphia and began to work out the principles of a national **constitution**—the agreement between the colonies as to how they would cooperate in a new country.

The Constitution of the United States of America was presented to the delegates on September 7, 1787, and sent to the separate state assemblies for **ratification**. The questions the Constitutional Convention dealt with were those raised by the American spirit of independence and equality under the law. No one wanted too much power in one man's hands, or in one faction. No one wanted one region to dominate the others, or the large states to dominate the small. Moreover, each free man deserved the right to vote for his laws and government.

After months of debate, the convention came up with a Constitution that called for a three-part government: a legislature, an executive, and a judiciary. The legislative body, like the English Parliament, a Congress, would represent all the voting citizens—a lower house, the House of Representatives, like England's House of Commons, would have proportional representation; and an upper house, the Senate, like England's House of Lords, would admit two representatives from each state. The executive officer, in the place of a king, was to be called the president. Indirectly, the people, through the Electoral College, would elect him. Finally, the proposed Constitution established a Supreme Court whose members, appointed by the president with the consent of the Senate, would serve for life. This, the delegates hoped, would free the court from political pressures.

The Electoral College was to be made up of electors who would vote for the president; each state would elect a number of electors proportional to their population. The people would, in effect, vote for the elector who would vote for the president. This put a buffer between the people and the president, since most of the Constitutional Convention delegates mistrusted full democracy. The president would be commander-in-chief of the armed forces and would have veto power over congressional legislation, which could be overridden by a two-thirds majority in both houses.

Thomas Jefferson

The system of checks and balances, of election of representatives by the people, and of appointment of senators by state governors—all—assured general representation as well as checks on democratic majorities. The system of choosing a chief executive, the president, through elected electors kept large states or majority factions from dominating the presidential office. The Supreme Court judges would be chosen on merit and be free of political pressures. The three branches of the government would balance each other's power and keep all officers honest and responsive to their people.

The last question to be taken up was directly tied to the principle of equality—slavery. The colonies, like all the New World, had accepted the ancient, but dreadful, custom of slavery. All the thirteen colonies had legal slavery, though the southern colonies had many more slaves than the northern New England colonies. Slavery had made the fortunes of large landowners in Virginia and the Carolinas, where tobacco and other labor-intensive agriculture supported the economy. Indian slaves had proved unreliable and dangerous, so the colonists had turned to the African slave trade, importing thousands of captives from the West African coasts. Washington and Jefferson were both slave owners, though both men freed their slaves after the Revolutionary War. Even in

Two cabins once occupied by slaves on Boon Hall Plantation, built from bricks made on the plantation, around 1743, near Charleston, South Carolina.

the southern states, there was a general distaste for the institution of slavery and a desire to bring it to an end soon.

The convention was faced with a double question: how to end slavery without bankrupting the southern states, and how to treat slaves in any population count that would determine representation in Congress. If all men are equal, and have a right to representation, how should slave-men be regarded in apportioning that representation? Free population in the southern states was smaller than free population in the northern states, yet the southern states covered more land and had larger populations of free men plus slaves. The Constitution attempted a double solution for the twin problems: (1) by ordering the end to importation of any more slaves, 20 years after ratification (1808), and (2) to count only ⅗ of all slaves in the population into the state's official congressional size. It was a lame compromise, and would only bring trouble later.

There was also dissatisfaction among the delegates over the failure of the American Constitution to protect their citizens against certain abuses that Englishmen had fought to end. The basic Constitution spoke about the rights of the states against the federal government, but did not touch on individual concerns. At the last minute, 10 amendments were added to the Constitution, covering the rights of citizens and protecting individuals' lives against government infringement. The Bill of Rights, as these first 10 amendments were called, stated the rights of free men that the federal government could not abuse. Included among those rights are the right to freedom of religion, and the right to freedom of speech, the right to own and bear arms, the right to free assembly, free press, and other protections of life and property.

At last, the Constitution was accepted by all 13 states and became the law of the land in June 1788. Shortly thereafter, the states chose George Washington to be their first president. Washington served two terms (he refused a third term), and was followed by John Adams of Massachusetts, then Thomas Jefferson of Virginia, and then James Madison, also a Virginian.

The United States Expands

The United States expanded rapidly over the next two decades. In 1793 and 1794, the 14th and 15th states, Kentucky and Tennessee, were admitted to the Union. Then came Ohio, Indiana, and Michigan. In 1804, the year of the French naval defeat by Lord Nelson at Trafalgar, the French ambassador suggested to President Jefferson that the United States might

Map of the Oregon territory, secured by treaty from England in the 1820s.

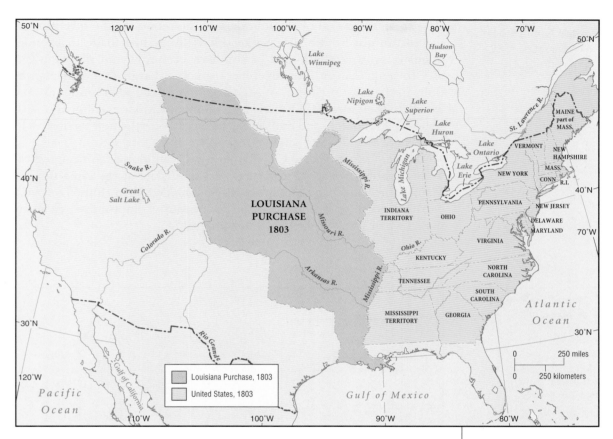

Map of the Louisiana Purchase. This addition to the national territory was negotiated by President Thomas Jefferson to keep France, Spain, and England at a safe distance.

want to purchase the lands claimed by France on the United States' western border. When asked what kind of land was included in the territory called Louisiana, Napoleon's French foreign minister shrugged: *"Je ne sais quois."*—"I do not know."

President Jefferson added these huge French territories west of the Mississippi River to the national territory. The "Louisiana Purchase" cost $15 million. It doubled the size of the country, and gave the United States access to the Pacific Ocean. A treaty with England later secured another large portion of land, the Oregon Territory, in the 1820s.

As the new territories were settled, the question of statehood brought up the unresolved problem of slavery. The northern states had abolished slavery within their borders, but the southern states had kept it, despite

Cotton Gin: A machine that separates seeds from cotton.

the urging of several of the founders of the republic. The invention of the **cotton gin** by the New Yorker Eli Whitney had made that labor-intensive crop the backbone of southern economy, and slavery was a way to make cotton-growing very profitable. Large slave-run plantations in the new territories of Mississippi and Louisiana brought quick wealth to their owners. The new lands along the Missouri offered wealth to both slaveholders and antislavery farmers. Were the new territories to be slave or free?

The Kentuckian Henry Clay fought for a compromise in Congress, in 1820: Missouri would be admitted as a slave state at the same time as Maine, a free state, and slavery would be excluded from all the Louisiana Territory north of latitude 36°30'. The Missouri Compromise was abandoned when Texas applied for statehood in 1845.

Map of the Republic of Texas.

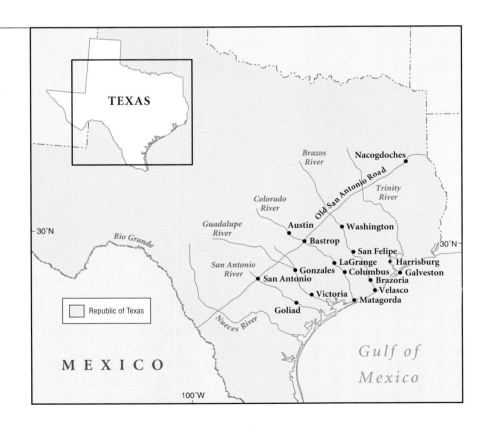

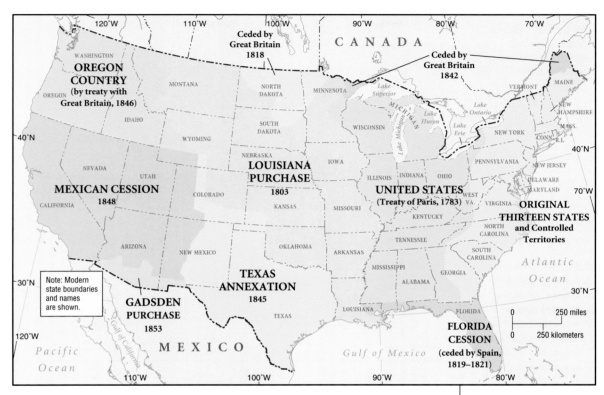

Map showing all the new territories added to the United States, including the ones ceded from Mexico.

Trouble in Texas

Trouble in Texas began when Mexico achieved independence from Spain. The Mexican Constitution was ratified in 1824, taking account of the large number of American settlers already within its province of Texas. But in 1830, General Santa Anna had seized control of the Mexican Republic and abolished the Mexican Constitution. In 1835, an assembly of Texans, both English-speaking and Spanish-speaking, declared independence, and called themselves the Republic of Texas. A war with Santa Anna confirmed Texan independence. The new Texas Republic elected its first president: Sam Houston, a former Tennessean, who commanded the Texan troops in defeating Santa Anna at the Battle of San Jacinto. Ten years later, in 1845, the young Texan Republic offered its lands and armed forces to the United States and asked to be **annexed** as a slave state. A slave-holding Texas unbalanced the slave and free states in Congress and unraveled the Missouri Compromise.

Annexation: The incorporation of a territory into a larger political body.

Map of the United States divided between the Union and the Confederacy.

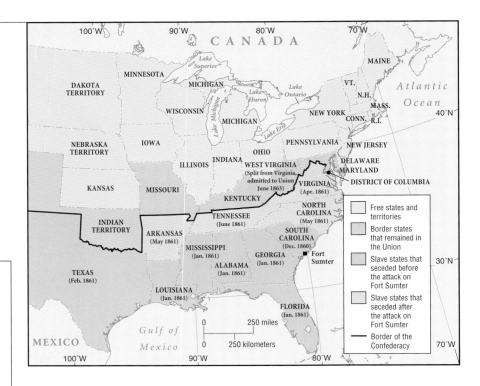

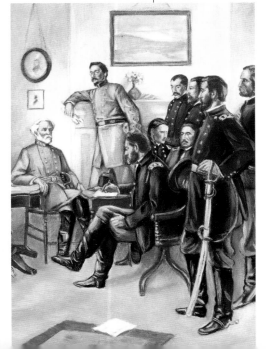

Robert E. Lee surrenders the army of Northern Virginia to Ulysses Grant at Appomattox Courthouse. General Lee is surrounded by Union officers.

Mexico and the United States were inevitably drawn into war, as the demand for more open lands fueled American politics. In 1846, President James K. Polk declared war on Mexico. In 1847, an American army fought its way to a bloody victory on the slopes of Chapultepec Hill, the fortress overlooking Mexico City. The rich territories of California and New Mexico were forfeited by Mexico to the United States.

The Civil War

Territorial expansion made the issue of slavery more obviously a moral issue, one that could not be avoided. Christianity sorely challenged Christians to recognize human dignity. Conflict over slavery continued to be the chief political issue until the election of Abraham Lincoln, an antislavery candidate of the new Republican

Party, as president, in 1860. The slave states prepared to resist or secede if abolition was made mandatory; South Carolina chose secession. Eleven of the 13 states followed suit. Lincoln then declared war on the secessionists. The most costly war in the new republic's history began with the South Carolinians' attack on Fort Sumter, a fortress in Charleston Harbor, which Lincoln refused to turn over to the state government and had reinforced with fresh troops. The first shot of the war was fired at 4:30 A.M., April 12, 1861. Four years and many many thousands of dead later, the southern states, the called the Confederate States of America, surrendered on April 9, 1865, Palm Sunday.

Ruins of the arsenal and surrounding neighborhood in Richmond, Virginia, as Union forces found them on entering the Confederate capital, April 13, 1865.

The Civil War left the southern states ruined and their manpower decimated; the southern railroads were destroyed, and the economy was annihilated. Subsequent acts of the Union Congress to punish the confederate states—the 10-year period called Reconstruction—left the South far behind the other states economically. The slaves were free, but there was no employment for them. They were "freed" into desperate poverty. Their former masters were outnumbered and feared the restless and uneducated former slaves in their midst. After Reconstruction was lifted, there were laws passed which prevented blacks from sharing in the privileges of whites. The former slave states mostly passed these laws, called **segregation**, but the northern states also legislated against their black citizens. (These laws were not struck down until the Supreme Court ruled against segregated schools in 1954. Following that ruling, segregation laws were struck down or voted out one by one.)

Segregation: the division or separation of the races.

The ideal of equality was not forgotten during the decades of segregation, however. The issue of racial justice continued to confront Americans through the whole of the 20th century. Civil rights led to human rights, and the United States became the leading advocate for justice and human rights in the 20th century. The experience of the two world wars, the second being clearly a fight for justice and human rights against tyranny and racial oppression, linked the traditional American themes to the fight against

Communism which followed the Second World War, as a fight for human freedom and civilization.

As the States sought racial justice, so they sought human justice against the lie of German Naziism and Soviet atheist Communism. America's military forces and thousands of American lives were sacrificed in the wars against Naziism and Communism in order to allow the rest of the world to hope for freedom and prosperity without despotism and tyranny.

Chapter 15 Review

Let's Remember   Write your answer in a single complete sentence.
1. England fought a war with what other European power for control of North America?
2. Why was Congress dissatisfied with George Washington's leadership?
3. What state has been an independent republic?
4. "Segregation" means what?
5. How does "balance of powers" describe the U.S. Constitution?

Let's Consider   For silent thinking and a short essay, or for thinking in a group with classroom discussion:
1. Are Christian principles behind the "republicanism" of our founding?
2. Why do we consider Washington a great man?
4. Could Civil War have been avoided?
5. What could be called the principles of American culture?

Let's Eat!

A Colonial Recipe for Deep-Dish Apple Pie.
Pare and thinly slice 5 pounds of apples. Place one-third of the apples in a baking pan. Sprinkle with ⅓ C. sugar and dot with 3 T. butter; sprinkle lightly with cinnamon. Continue with 2 more layers of apples, sugar and butter, and cinnamon. Sprinkle with dusting of nutmeg before covering with a piecrust. Bake 40 minutes, or until brown and apples are thoroughly soft.

Chapter 16 Latin America: a Sleeping Giant

L atin America is the world's greatest melting pot of cultures. Nowhere else have all the major cultures met in such a profusion of immigrants and natives. American Indians, Europeans, Africans, Japanese, Hindus and Muslims from India, all cooperate in the huge urban areas of all the Latin American countries. The population of Latin America is growing very fast. In some countries, the majority of the population is under 15 years of age. These young men and women will either infuse the world with a revival of faith and enterprise, or else they will burden the world by continuing their history of bloodshed. What becomes of Latin America in the century to come will affect the whole world.

South America is part of a world culture called Latin America. Latin America is a large cultural region that includes all territories in the Western Hemisphere south of the United States: the Islands of the West Indies as well as Mexico, Central America, and South America. In the 15th and 16th centuries, southern Europeans—especially Spaniards and Portuguese—began to settle in Latin America. These early settlers brought their Catholic religion and customs as well as their languages along with them. The languages of southern Europe developed from Latin, and for this reason the cultural region is still called Latin America. Today, the majority of Latin Americans speak Spanish. The Brazilians speak Portuguese.

Mexico, Central America, and the South American continent have abundant natural resources: vast rainforests and timberlands, rich grazing and farmlands, and large deposits of valuable minerals. But, because of the continuing clash of cultures and forms of government, most South

American countries have been too politically unstable to take full advantage of their natural riches.

The Geography of Latin America

Latin America has nearly every type of landscape: mountains, jungles, plains, deserts, and coastland. From tropical forests in the equatorial belt to temperate grasslands in the southern half of the continent, its climate is as varied as its land: heavy rains, steamy heat, dry desert, and icy cold. The equator runs through northern Brazil, Ecuador, and southern Colombia, so, in general, most of the continent has warm weather all year. Only in the high Andes Mountains is it always cold. The Atacama Desert, in northern Chili, is one of the driest places on Earth. Incredibly high, cold, snow-covered peaks and active volcanoes (many over 20,000 feet) make up the Andes Mountains. The range stretches 4,500 miles along western South America from Venezuela in the north to Tierra del Fuego on the southern tip of the continent.

The largest tropical rain forest in the world is found in the Amazon River Basin. The Amazon River flows 4,000 miles eastward from the Peruvian Andes Mountains to the Atlantic; only the Nile River in Africa is longer than the Amazon. This hot and moist area, the Amazon Basin, covers two-fifths of the South American Continent and contains more kinds of plants than any other place in the world.

Extending eastward from the Andes, the Central Plains cover about three-fifths of South America. These plains are drained by huge river systems, the Amazon and Plate, which empty into the Atlantic. There are very fertile plains and grasslands, especially in Argentina and Venezuela; many prosperous ranches and extensive farmlands are supported by the rich soil of these plains. There are also spectacular waterfalls, huge lakes, and rocky, windswept islands.

People of the Amazon rain forest paddling a canoe on the Amazon River.

Opposite: A map of Latin America, including Mexico and the Caribbean Islands.

Mexico is geographically part of North America, but its history and traditions make it part of Latin America. Its geography is rugged, but hospitable to human life. The coastal plain along the Gulf of Mexico is semitropical forest.

MEXICO

Gulf of Mexico

THE BAHAMAS

CUBA

Atlantic Ocean

20°N

HAITI

DOM. REP.   PUERTO RICO

JAMAICA

BELIZE

GUATEMALA   HONDURAS

Greater Antilles

EL SALVADOR   NICARAGUA

CENTRAL
AMERICA

COSTA
RICA

Caribbean Sea

10°N

PANAMA

VENEZUELA

GUYANA

COLOMBIA

SURINAME   FRENCH
GUIANA

Marajo Island

0°

ECUADOR

Amazon R.   Amazon R.

*Pacific
Ocean*

PERU

BRAZIL

10°S

SOUTH
AMERICA

A
N
D
E
S

BOLIVIA

PARAGUAY

20°S

Cabo Frio

30°S

ARGENTINA

CHILE

URUGUAY

*Atlantic
Ocean*

40°S

Elevation	
> 12,000 feet	
9,000–12,000 feet	
7,500–9,000 feet	
6,000–7,500 feet	
4,500–6,000 feet	
3,000–4,500 feet	
1,800–3,000 feet	
1,200–1,800 feet	
600–1,200 feet	
300–600 feet	
150–300 feet	
0–150 feet	

0   500 miles

0   500 kilometers

FALKLAND ISLANDS

SOUTH GEORGIA ISLAND

Strait of Magellan

50°S

The central plateau rises rapidly to a mile above sea level. Volcanic activity has left a layer of rich soil over the plateau that had one of the three high civilizations of pre-Columbian America, the Toltec-Aztec. The coastal peninsula of Yucatán was home to the Maya, and the high Andes Mountains of Peru on the South American continent were the home of the Inca Empire. Mexico's northern region is mountainous and arid, with two large deserts, the Chihuahuan and the Sonoran. A long peninsula on the west, Baja (BA•hah) California, shelters the Gulf of California, one of the richest marine-life regions of the world.

The Story of Latin America

Latin America's story begins with the three high Stone Age civilizations that flourished in Meso-America and the west coastal range of the Andes: the Toltec/Aztecs, the Maya, and the Inca. Indian culture contributed to the modern Americas its vibrant and colorful arts. The modern history of the culture begins with the European discovery of the American continents by Columbus in A.D. 1492.

Columbus did not know where he had landed when he sailed to the west in order to reach the East Indies. His conviction that he could reach the Indies by sailing west was a miscalculation—Columbus underestimated the circumference of the Earth. According to his reckoning, the Earth's circumference was 25 percent smaller than it actually is.

Portrait of Columbus and Queen Isabella on one of his many visits to ask her help to reach the Indies.

Columbus

Columbus had a mission; he was to carry the Catholic Faith to the heathens overseas. In 1486, Columbus obtained an audience with Isabella, Queen of Castile and León. Perhaps it was the mystic in Columbus that appealed to the devout and mystical queen. Whatever the reason, on April 17, 1492, the Catholic sovereigns agreed to finance Columbus's expedition to the Indies. Columbus was given a fleet of three very small ships, or caravels, which set sail from Palos harbor on August 3, 1492. The largest of these ships was the Santa María, which was Columbus's flagship. The other two caravels were called the Pinta and the Niña.

Opposite: A topographical map of South America, including Mexico and the Caribbean, with a color-keyed elevation scale.

After 35 days at sea, Columbus lands on an island, which he calls San Salvador, off the tip of Florida, taking possession "in the name of Our Lord Jesus Christ, for the crown of Castile."

Demarcation: The marking off of a territory.

In those days, most sailing ships hugged the coasts, rarely venturing out onto the open sea. The sailors did not fear sailing off the end of the world, for they knew the world was a sphere. They feared that they would run out of water and food on shipboard and they worried that there would be no wind to blow them back to Spain. By October 10, the crews had had enough. Open mutiny broke out. Hiding his own uneasiness that there was no land in sight, Columbus tried to encourage his men. He agreed that, if after two or three days no land was sighted, the fleet would return home. Finally at 2 A.M. on October 12, the crew heard the cry of "Tierra! Tierra!"— "Land! Land!"

Columbus landed on a small island, which Columbus named San Salvador (Holy Savior). The same day, October 12, Columbus and his men went ashore. Taking the flag of Castile and León in his left hand and his sword in his right, and placing one knee on the sand, Columbus ordered the planting of the cross in the name of the Catholic kings and the Catholic Church. Thus Columbus reached land—but was it the Indies?

On Christmas day, tragedy struck. Columbus's ship, the Santa María, struck a reef in a bay off the north coast of Hispaniola. Befriended by the native inhabitants, Columbus and his men built a fortress from Santa María's salvaged planking. Since it was the Christmas season, the fortress was christened Navidad (Nativity)—the first Spanish settlement in the New World. In January 1493, the Niña and the Pinta returned to Spain, after a stormy crossing, arriving on March 15.

The new pope, Alexander VI, took an interest in Columbus's discoveries. Pope Alexander, a Spaniard, issued a papal decree in 1493, the year of Columbus's return, titled *Inter Caetera,* in which he set a **demarcation** line in the Atlantic to forestall disputes between Spain and Portugal over the new lands. All lands, decreed the pope, west of the demarcation line would fall to Spain; those east of the line would fall to Portugal. Spain and Portugal renegotiated the line farther west through the Treaty of Tordesillas. This new line secured Brazil for Portugal, because it jutted out east of the line.

Other explorers did not have Columbus's religious motive. In 1513, a Spanish captain, Vasco Nuñez de Balboa, plunged into the interior of Darien (Panama) with 170 men. On September 24, from a mountaintop, Balboa sighted a new ocean. He called it the South Sea; later, men would call it the Pacific. Balboa took possession of this sea for Spain, and for a long time it would remain a Spanish-controlled ocean.

The greatest discovery and conquest, however, was reserved to a young adventurer, a native of that barren region of Spain, Estremadura: Hernán Cortés.

Hernán Cortés (1485–1547)

Few observers of his early life would have thought that Hernán Cortés could carry out the conquest of so great a kingdom as Mexico. Sent to college to study law, Cortés dropped out of school after only two years. The willful young man wasted years in foolish living, then went to the Indies to seek his fortune. In 1518, Cortés obtained the position of captain general of an expedition to exploit the riches of the mainland. Cortés's fleet landed off the coast of Yucatán in February 1519. His force consisted of 11 ships, 100 sailors, 553 soldiers, 2 heavy guns, 4 falconets (smaller guns), and 16 cavalry. Two missionaries also accompanied the expedition; one, the Dominican Father Bartolomé de Olmedo, softened Cortés's martial zeal, recommending patience and persuasion rather than force.

An important addition to the expedition was an Aztec Indian woman. After a battle fought in Tabasco in which the Spaniards defeated a force of 40,000 Indians, the **caciques** offered Cortés and his men 20 female slaves as a peace offering. Among these was the daughter of a Mexican cacique, who had been sold by her stepmother into slavery. Baptized, she took the name Marina, and became indispensable to Cortés as his interpreter.

After skirting the coast from Yucatán northward, Cortés landed on the coast of Mexico at the site of the modern city of Vera Cruz (means cross). It was Good Friday, April 21. Choosing a site a little farther up the coast, Cortés established a settlement there, naming it Villa Rica de Vera Cruz. When some of his men tried to return to Cuba, Cortés destroyed all but

Cacique: Chief or leader of an Indian tribe in areas dominated by Spanish culture.

Engraved portrait of Hernán Cortés (1485–1547), conqueror of Mexico.

one of his ships. His shocked troops cried out that their general had led them to Mexico to be butchered like cattle. Cortés replied that he had chosen his part: "I will remain here," he said, "while there is one to bear me company. If there be any so cowardly as to shrink from sharing the dangers of our glorious enterprise, let them go home, in God's name. There is still one vessel left. Let them take that and return to Cuba. They can tell there how they deserted their commander and their comrades, and patiently wait until we return loaded with the spoils of the Aztecs."

The men, their courage rekindled by these words, cried out: "To Mexico! To Mexico!"

Jade figure of the Aztec god Quetzalcoatl, rising from the jaws of the Feathered Serpent, just as the Morning Star rises from the Earth to herald the sunrise. He is wearing the collar symbolic of the sun.

The Aztecs

The natives of Mexico were unlike the gentle inhabitants of the Caribbean islands. As Cortés and his men had already noted in landing in this region, called Anahuac by its inhabitants, these Indians raised buildings and temple pyramids of stone instead of the dwellings of stick and thatch. They were very numerous, too, and dwelt in ordered towns surrounded by well-cultivated fields of maize, or Indian corn.

In the center of this land, in a city built in the middle of a lake, dwelt a powerful, warlike people—the Aztecs. Their king, since 1502, had been Montezuma II. In his 17-year reign, Montezuma had conquered the tribes of Anahuac, extending the Aztec Empire to its greatest.

According to their own history, the Aztecs had come from a region called Aztlan in the northwest. In the 14th century, they arrived on the shores of a lake in the high mountain valley of Mexico. There, they beheld an eagle, perched on the stem of a prickly pear cactus, its wings spread to the rising sun and a serpent in its talons. They took it for a sign from their gods to settle and raise their city, Tenochtitlán.

The Aztecs, once a relatively primitive tribe, learned the arts of civilization from their neighbor city, Tezcuco. By the 16th century, the Aztecs had advanced in agriculture and architecture, planting beautiful gardens and building a city that would earn the praise of their European conquerors. They also excelled in gold-work, displaying their craftsmanship in gold ornaments. With their hieroglyphic, or picture writing they recorded history and often wrote beautiful poetry. Oddly, though, no Indian nations, including the Aztecs, ever invented the wheel.

The Aztecs worshipped many gods. Among the most important was Huitzilopochtli (witsy•lo•POCT•lee), the god of war, born from his mother fully armed. Another important deity was Quetzalcoatl ("feathered serpent"), the god of the air. He had instructed men in agriculture, say the legends, in the use of metals, and in government. Their legends said that under him a golden age had flowered. Because he incurred the wrath of another god, he left Anahuac, going east over the sea. Quetzalcoatl, who was said to have white skin, dark hair, and a flowing beard, promised his followers that, one day, he would return, from the east over the sea.

It was said that when Quetzalcoatl returned, he would abolish a major act of Aztec worship—human sacrifice. One of the principal purposes of war for the Aztecs was to capture victims for sacrifice. Every festival, and there were many, was solemnized with human sacrifice. On the summits of the great pyramid temple, or teocalli, in the center of Tenochtitlán stood a large, rounded alabaster stone. A victim was led to the stone, his back forced against it, exposing his chest. A priest, his long hair matted with human gore, would then raise an obsidian knife, and after plunging it into the victim's chest, pull out the still beating heart. The heart alone was offered to the god; worshippers ate the discarded body—it was butchered and sold in the marketplace. The Aztecs are recorded as sacrificing about 20,000 victims each year.

The Spaniards Arrive

At the news of Cortés's landing, Montezuma was filled with apprehension—might this be the prophesied return of Quetzalcoatl? Reports seemed to confirm his fear: these strangers were white-skinned and bearded. Whatever Indian cities they entered, they freed victims intended for sacrifice. Montezuma was uncertain what to do. He invited Cortés to come to Tenochtitlán.

The Spaniards climbed to higher elevations. Below them stretched the great lake, with Tenochtitlán in its midst, and far away on the northeast bank, the city of Tezcuco.

Portrait of Montezuma II, emperor of the Aztecs.

Montezuma's city, Tenochtitlán, with its great buildings and temples, was so beautiful that the Spaniards were in great awe. Montezuma treated Cortés and his troops with hospitality.

Though Montezuma was gracious and kind, Cortés doubted his sincerity. The Spanish general also worried that his own men and their Tlascalan allies might do something to anger the Aztecs. To secure his position, Cortés decided on a daring plan. He would seize Montezuma. The captive monarch remained in confinement in the Spanish quarters, though he continued to hold court and act as the king of Mexico.

A new problem soon faced Cortés. The governor of the Indies, Diego Velásquez, sent against him an armada of 18 ships with 900 men and 1,000 Indians under the command of Pánfilo de Narvaez. Cortés again acted boldly. Leaving two-thirds of his force, 140 men, in Mexico, Cortés, with only 70 men, marched to the coast to meet Narvaez. Cortés was outnumbered, but he surprised Narvaez's troops and defeated them.

While Cortés was fighting Narvaez, the Aztecs rose against the Spanish troops in Tenochtitlán. Cortés marched back to Mexico. He entered the city unmolested, but soon found that the streets and rooftops were filled with armed Aztecs. Bloody fighting erupted. Montezuma, in an attempt to stop the violence of his people, dressed in his royal robes and bearing the wand of authority, climbed to the central turret of the Spanish quarters. He pleaded with his people to let the Spaniards depart, but his speech was cut short by a volley of stones from the street. Struck several times and seriously wounded, Montezuma died shortly thereafter on June 30, 1520.

The Spaniards did not remain idle. Leading a contingent of soldiers, Cortés drove the Aztecs from the great teocalli, destroying the image and temple of Huitzilopochtli. That same night, the Spaniards burned 300 houses close to their quarters.

The Spaniards' position, however, soon proved so desperate that Cortés planned a retreat from the city for the night of June 1. The attempt was dangerous, since the Spaniards, with their artillery and horses, along with their Indian allies, had to cross a long causeway where they would be exposed

The death of Montezuma, attacked by his subjects as he was held prisoner by Cortés.

to Indian assaults from the lake. Because the causeway was broken at intervals, and the bridges that normally closed the gaps removed, the Christians could be surrounded and slaughtered.

The Spaniards later aptly named that night of crossing "*La Noche Triste*", the sorrowful night. Some Aztecs, noticing the Spaniards' retreat, alerted the city. The beating of drums and the blasts of shell-trumpets sounded from the great teocalli as the Spaniards moved onto the causeway. Soon, thousands of Aztecs in canoes on the lake and from the city swarmed on the causeway. After passing the first gap over a makeshift bridge, the army was stopped at the second gap. Unable to extricate their makeshift bridge from the mud, the army was soon surrounded. As the Aztecs poured onto the causeway, the Spaniards lost all order; men and women (for some wives had accompanied their husbands) were slaughtered, or taken alive to be sacrificed. One woman, María de Estrada, defended herself with shield and broadsword as ably as any man.

The Spanish losses that night were serious. Many of the men (mostly from Narvaez's command) were drowned by the weight of the gold they had hidden under their clothing. All told, 450 Spaniards and 4,000 natives were killed. Most of Montezuma's treasure was lost, along with all the artillery and guns. A few days later, a broken and discouraged army marched into Tlascala.

But Cortés was not discouraged by his defeat and the condition of his army. He planned to take Mexico again. Fortune seemed to aid him. Another ally, smallpox, struck the Aztecs, who, having no immunity against the disease, died in great numbers. Among those who died was Cuitlahua, Montezuma's successor.

At Tlascala, Cortés ordered the construction of 15 small ships, called **brigantines**, so that he could assault Tenochtitlán by water as well as by the causeways. His total force consisted of 818 Spaniards, together with 87 cavalry and 25,000 Indian auxiliaries.

After crossing the mountains, Cortés's army took Tezcuco on December 31. From Tezcuco, he sent contingents of his armies to subdue the cities surrounding the lake of Mexico. The brigantines, which had been built at Tlascala and carried piece by piece over the mountains, were reassembled at Tezcuco. The causeways were blockaded and the great city cut off to starve. Finally, on April 28, 1521, after his soldiers had confessed their sins and heard Mass, the assault on the city began. As the brigantines were

The Great Tenochtitlán, by Diego Rivera. Detail: a vision of life in the Aztec city of Tenochtitlán.

Brigantine: A two-masted ship.

Origin of all human lands, from an Indian painted book of history showing Tezcatlipoca tempting the Earth Monster to the surface of the great waters by using his foot as bait. In swallowing his foot, the Earth Monster lost her lower jaw; hideously crippled, she was unable to sink and the Earth was created from her body. The symbols at the base of the drawing represent dates and, with the twelve dots also in the picture, signify the periods in the calendar when Tezcatlipoca was dominant over other forces.

launched, the Spaniards broke forth in a joyous "Te Deum" a hymn of praise to God.

The assault on the city would prove hard and bloody. A desperate people fought the Spaniards every block and street of the way. Pushing into the city, the army saw the streets strewn with the bodies of those dead from famine. In the houses slated for destruction, they discovered starving men, women, and children. When, in their slow progress, Cortés's army reached the marketplace, seven-eighths of the city had been laid waste. On August 13, 1521, the Spaniards overwhelmed what remained of the Aztec force. Though Father Olmedo charged the conquerors to treat the Indians with kindness, he was ignored by many of the Spaniards who in their lust for gold forgot Christian charity.

In 1522, Charles I made Cortés captain general and chief justice of Nueva España (New Spain), as Mexico was now to be called. From 1522 to 1524, Cortés labored to rebuild the city of Mexico. Using forced Indian labor, Cortés raised a city said to be more beautiful and rich than any in Europe. Encouraged by Cortés, many Spaniards settled in Mexico, where they mingled with the Indian population. Cortés zealously spread the Catholic Faith among the Indians. He requested the government to send over missionaries. Under Cortés, these missionaries established schools and colleges for the education of the Indians. They destroyed the native religion, but some of the missionaries translated the Aztec hieroglyphics and so preserved the knowledge of Aztec institutions and history. On every site of human sacrifice, the church performed exorcisms and erected churches to sanctify these terrible places.

Cortés then fell out of favor in the court of Spain. In 1540, he returned to Spain to plead his case before the king. Frustrated with the rebuffs he received from Charles, Cortés journeyed to Seville, planning to embark for Mexico. Instead, falling sick, Hernán Cortés, the conqueror of Mexico, died on December 2, 1547.

The Land-Grant System

When Columbus was made governor of Hispaniola, he rewarded his men by giving them land grants. Columbus called these land grants *repartimientos*—"partitions." Later, the Spanish crown called them *encomiendas*—"complimentary land grants"—and the beneficiaries of these grants, *encomenderos*. While strictly speaking the Indians on an *encomienda* were not slaves, their *encomendero* could force them to labor for him. Thus, on Hispaniola and other islands, colonists forced Indians to work in the fields and labor in the mines. Being unused to such labor, and having no immunities from European sicknesses, thousands of Indians died.

As governor of New Spain, Cortés also established *repartimientos*. Allowing the Indians to live in their villages under their native chiefs, Cortés passed laws regulating the number of hours an Indian was allowed to work and how much he must be paid. Cortés also required that *encomenderos* provide suitable religious instruction to their charges. Nevertheless, in Mexico, as well as elsewhere where the government was less benign, the Indians often were abused. The system turned the natives of the continent into serfs, bound to their lands and enslaved to their landlords. Mexico was perhaps the best ruled of the Spanish territories, and so kept the abuses of the system at a minimum. But the *encomienda* system invited abuses. It is considered the principal cause of the general poverty of the region today.

The Spanish crown justified the conquest of the Indians by appealing to the *Inter Caetera*—Pope Alexander VI's donation of the Indies to Spain. But some questioned the character of that donation—did it give Spain the right of conquest? Some argued that it didn't; the pope, they said, gave Spain the right to convert, not conquer, the natives. Among these latter was a Spanish lawyer turned priest who would become known as the "Defender of the Indians"—Bartolomé de Las Casas.

Bartolomé de Las Casas

Bartolomé de Las Casas probably heard a sermon preached in a straw-thatched church on the island of Hispaniola in 1511. Commenting on the text, "I am a voice crying in the wilderness," the Dominican friar, Antonio de Montesinos, asked, "Are these Indians not men? Do they not have rational souls? Are you not obliged to love them as you love yourselves?"

That the Indians as rational creatures were owed Christian charity and justice became the leading theme of Las Casas's life. Las Casas would spend the next 40 years arguing that, as human beings, Indians had equal rights to Spaniards. The Spanish crown, he argued, had no right to conquer the Indians by force. Though they could exercise overlordship over the

Bartolomé de Las Casas (1474–1566), Spanish missionary and historian.

Indians, Las Casas argued, Spaniards could not abolish Indian governments, nor enslave natives. The *encomienda* system, he said, was little better than slavery, and should be abolished. Force should never be used in preaching the Gospel, he maintained, and strenuously fought with those missionaries (most notably, the Franciscans) who baptized converts without first giving them sufficient instruction in the Faith.

The Spanish king appointed Las Casas bishop of Chiapas in southern Mexico in 1544. There, Las Casas enraged colonists by setting rigid standards *encomenderos* must meet before he would absolve them from their sins. He basically forbade the Eucharist to anyone who held an *encomienda*.

Las Casas was a stout defender of the Indians. Sometimes, though, in defending them, he exaggerated both Indian virtues and Spanish cruelty. His most famous work, *Brevíssima Relacion de la Destrucion de Las Indias (A Short Account of the Destruction of the Indies)* is filled with many gross exaggerations of Spanish cruelty, recounting events Las Casas could only know by hearsay. This work was translated into several languages and became the source of the "Black Legend" used to this day by Spain's enemies to discredit her.

Our Lady of Guadalupe.

Juan Diego and Our Lady of Guadalupe

On December 12, 1531, the Virgin Mary appeared to the Indian Juan Diego on Tepeyac hill—the site where an Aztec temple to the goddess Tonantzin had once stood. Appearing as an Aztec princess, the Virgin told Juan Diego to ask Bishop Zumárraga to build a church dedicated to her under the title of Nuestra Señora de Guadalupe. Zumárraga was, at first, unwilling to believe Juan Diego; however, when the Indian opened his tilma, or cloak, from which a flood of roses poured forth, the bishop changed his mind. Not only was it wondrous that the Indian should find roses in December, but upon the tilma appeared the image of the lady. Zumárraga commanded that the church be built on Tepeyac hill.

This apparition of the Virgin led to an amazing increase in native baptisms—thousands upon thousands converted. The Spanish government had not been remiss in trying to convert the Indians of Mexico, but because of the brutality of some of the Spaniards, many Indians had shunned the Church.

The Conquest of Peru

In 1532, Francisco Pizarro, with his brothers, began an expedition to Peru—an empire that rivaled the glory of the Aztecs. Climbing high into the Andes, the Spaniards found the fabled capital of the Inca Empire, Cuzco. It was indeed a city roofed with gold, or so it seemed to them. The walls and roof of the Temple of the Sun, the largest building in Cuzco, and the walls of the Incas' palace were hung with plates of gold to reflect the

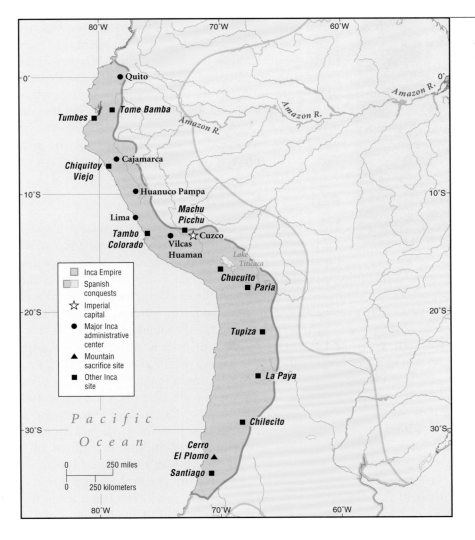

Map of the route of the conquerors of the Inca Empire.

Execution of the Incas of Peru **by Pizarro.**

life-giving rays of the chief god of the Inca. Pizarro captured the Incas, Atahualpa ("Inca" was the title of the king. The people are properly called the Quechua.) The Spaniards' horses sent fear into the massed ranks of the Incas' troops. The natives of Peru had never seen a horse, and thought the horse and rider were one beast. Ordered to bring the Spaniards a roomful of gold, the Inca and his nobles filled the throne room of the palace with the shining metal. Pizarro demanded more. While the gold was being collected, Pizzaro returned to the coast to send a message to Mexico, leaving his brothers in charge of the Incas and Cuzco. The Pizzaro brothers ordered the Incas killed—after Atahualpa fulfilled his promise to fill a second room with gold. Atahualpa's successor, Inca Manco, fled Cuzco with his nobles and fought a long struggle against the Spaniards until he was finally taken and killed. The whole of the rich Peruvian Empire was in Spanish hands.

Peru as a Spanish Colony

The division of spoils in Peru left the natives struggling for life itself. The native Indians were treated as serfs, bound to the land of their villages, and forced to work in mines and building projects. Thousands died in the first ten years of the colony. Pizarro built a new capital near the coast, the city of Lima, Peru. The lands were parceled out to Spanish landlords with the enslaved inhabitants of the region as part of the property, and a feudal kingdom was created, rich, cruel, and far from the control of Spanish law and Spanish justice. The Church alone tried to help the Indians and improve their lot.

Peru produced many holy men and women in colonial days, St. Rose of Lima and St. Martin de Porres are but the best known. Healer and wonder-worker, St. Martin was son of an African slave-woman and a Spanish owner. He brought comfort to the poor of Lima and inspired the rulers of the city to help their Indian serfs. St. Rose is credited with healings and a series of preternatural occurrences that saved Lima from a pirate attack. St. Turibius, bishop of Lima, fought for Indian rights and justice at the risk of his life. His efforts were finally rewarded when the king of Spain, Philip III, outlawed Indian servitude in 1601. St. Francis

Solano carried the Gospel deep into the Chaco jungle over the mountains, to the hostile and primitive savages who lived there. In old age he returned to Lima to preach to the wealthy of the city. His message brought about a revival of Christian faith and morality among the ruling classes of Peru.

Mexico in the 18th Century: A Typical Society of Spanish America

Like any society of the 18th century, Spanish America was compromised by injustice and social problems; but, in New Spain, Mexico, these had become entrenched, and a remedy was not available. The social structure provided opportunities for injustice. By 1800, the largest social group was the **mestizos**, those of mixed Indian and Spanish blood, who accounted for about 6 million of the population. Next there were the **creoles**, American-born persons of Spanish blood, who numbered about 3 million. Besides these groups, and, of course, the Indians, there were the *peninsulares* or *gauchupines*, those born in Spain, who were few in number, only about 300,000 in Mexico, but who controlled the majority of all political offices in the Spanish colonies.

Though the Church had sponsored schools and universities in New Spain from the beginning, illiteracy remained high. But republican philosophies began to influence the ruling classes and the creole intellectuals.

Saint Rose of Lima **by Carlo Dolci.**

Mestizos: A person of mixed Indian and Spanish heritage.
Creoles: American-born Spaniards.

Prelude to Revolution, 1808

The internal problems of South America and New Spain were not bad enough to bring on revolution. More serious events were happening across the Atlantic; Spain, at the opening of the 19th century, was rocked with civil war.

Charles IV had occupied the Spanish throne since 1788. But he angered Napoleon Bonaparte, the emperor of France, who had brought nearly all of Europe under his control. On May 6, 1808, Napoleon forced Charles IV and his son Ferdinand to relinquish all claim to the Spanish throne, and put his own brother, Joseph Bonaparte, in their place. A junta, or governing council, was formed to oppose Bonaparte. This council was taken over by an antiroyalist faction, which deposed Charles's son, Ferdinand VII. In 1812 they wrote a "liberal" constitution

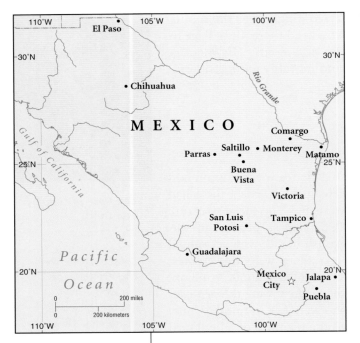

Map of Mexico showing the major cities in 1810.

that changed many traditional Spanish laws.

The Spanish constitution caused both royalists and republicans in the Americas to consider independence from Spain.

Priest Revolutionaries— Hidalgo and Morelos

Mexico's revolution began with two priests. The lower clergy had always protected the poor. Padre Hidalgo took great interest in the material welfare of the Indians. Leaving the spiritual concerns of the parish to one of his assistants, Hidalgo worked to promote the cultivation of grape vines and olive trees among the Indians, and introduced the silk worm. He also taught the Indians to make pottery and to tan leather. All these industries violated Spanish law.

Ordered to desist, he determined to fight. Five to six hundred men gathered around the priest, and as they marched from village to village, hundreds and thousands more joined them. By September 21, 50,000 Indians had joined Hidalgo, and all marched under a picture of Our Lady of Guadalupe. The peasant army brutally slaughtered any Europeans they found in the villages through which they passed. Hidalgo (now called "Captain General of America"), led this ill-disciplined and rag-tag mob toward the city of Guanajuato.

On September 28, Hidalgo's army invaded Guanajuato. Hidalgo pledged that he would spare all Europeans if the city surrendered. But, despite his pledge, a bloodbath followed. Following the massacre at Guanajuato, the bishop of Michoacán excommunicated Hidalgo and all his followers. Other bishops followed suit, and soon the Church was made to appear the enemy of the people and the friend of "oppressive" government.

During October, Hidalgo gained control of much of central Mexico west of Mexico City. Everywhere, the same mob violence was repeated. Hidalgo's tolerance of violence took its toll—he had hoped the creoles would rise with the Indians, but frightened by the violence, they joined forces with the royalists.

Hidalgo finally marched on Mexico City. At Monte de Las Cruces in the foothills overlooking the capital, Hidalgo's 80,000 met 6,000 Spaniards. The overwhelming rebel numbers forced the Spaniards to retreat to Mexico City. That night the rebels' camp fires lit the hills surrounding the city with a lurid glow. Some encouraged Hidalgo to strike the city, but Hidalgo hesitated, and finally decided to retreat northwest toward Guadalajara. Demoralized by the loss of a victory that seemed so clearly within their reach, thousands abandoned the rebel army. On November 7, Spanish troops defeated Hidalgo's remnant of 40,000 men at Aculco and drove them, reeling, toward Guadalajara.

Despite the defeat, Guadalajara greeted Hidalgo and his army with fiestas, and proclaimed the priest the liberator of his country. Gradually new recruits began to swell the numbers of Hidalgo's diminished force, until it once again boasted over 80,000 men. At Guadalajara, Hidalgo established a government and issued a proclamation granting freedom to slaves and delivering the lands they cultivated to the Indians. Hidalgo did not declare independence but proclaimed fidelity to King Ferdinand VII.

Meanwhile, the royal forces had retaken Guanajuato and were moving on Guadalajara. Against advice, Hidalgo concentrated his entire force of 80,000 at Calderón Bridge on the eastern outskirts of Guadalajara. A cannon ball, flying over the heads of the rebels, struck their munitions. The explosion created a grass fire that threw the rebels into confusion. Hidalgo and a small remnant of his force retreated northeast, toward Zacatecas.

At Zacatecas, a disgusted lieutenant removed Hidalgo from command of the army. The Spaniards seized Hidalgo and on the spot executed many of the lesser officers. Because he was a priest, Hidalgo was delivered over to the bishop of Durango for trial.

After trying him, the bishop of Durango removed Hidalgo's priestly dignity and delivered him to the state for

Mural painting by Juan O'Gorman depicts scenes from the Hidalgo Rebellion featuring the independence leaders Hidalgo and Morelos. From the National Palace, Mexico City, Mexico.

execution. Standing before a firing squad on July 30, 1811, Hidalgo calmly instructed them to shoot him through his right hand, which he placed over his heart. His head was displayed on the walls of Guanajuato, where for the next 10 years it remained, a grim warning to would-be revolutionaries.

Guerrilla Warfare in the Jungles

Severed heads couldn't, however, stop the revolution. Another priest, José María Teclo Morelos, had been operating in the south of Mexico since 1810. Hidalgo had sent him to the south to lead the revolution there.

Unlike Hidalgo, who had come from a middle-class creole family, Morelos was a poor mestizo from Valladolid. He had worked as a mule driver until, in his 25th year, he began to study for the priesthood. There he came under Hidalgo's influence. After he was ordained a priest, Morelos took a parish in Michoacán.

He had been a priest for over 10 years when he was sent to Zacatula on the Pacific coast by Hidalgo; Morelos organized a small force there. A skilled commander, Morelos favored the hit-and-run methods of guerrilla warfare (a strategy well-suited to the dense, jungle-like forests where he fought) rather than the pitched battle strategy of Hidalgo. The rebels were anonymous. Many of Morelos's soldiers were merely farmers who worked their fields until they were called—then they became rebel insurgents. When a battle ended, they returned to their fields. To punish and kill off these unknown insurgents, the Spaniards began to destroy entire villages.

Unlike Hidalgo, Morelos assembled a revolutionary congress and along with other revolutionary leaders issued a decree stating that "dependence upon the Spanish Throne ha[s] ceased forever and been dissolved." The declaration was made December 12, the feast of Our Lady of Guadalupe, "the Queen of our liberty," a day of national celebration.

The congress declared that the sovereignty of the state proceeds "immediately from the people." The congress abolished torture and said that slavery should be "prohibited forever and also distinction between classes,

Portrait of José María Morelos y Pavon (1765–1815), a Catholic priest and a revolutionary, who received the title of Generalissimo of the Mexican Army. He was executed by the Spanish.

leaving everyone equal, and Americans distinguished from one another only by their vice or virtue."

The new representative congress declared Morelos executive of the republic they had formed. Soon, however, the tide of war turned against the rebels. In December, Morelos tried to take Valladolid, but was defeated. When the congress reassembled at Tlacotepec, Morelos resigned as executive.

After Valladolid, many lost confidence in Morelos and the rebel forces began to break into factions. In the fall of 1815, Morelos himself was captured. Loading Morelos with chains, the royalists marched him triumphantly into Mexico City. He was executed after trial by both Church authorities and the state.

For a while it seemed as if the revolution had run its course. In 1814 Napoleon was defeated and Ferdinand VII returned to the Spanish throne. Though he swore to uphold the liberal constitution of 1812 that Cortés had written, he cancelled the constitution as soon as he had attained enough power.

Rebellion in Spain in 1820, however, forced Ferdinand VII to restore the constitution of 1812. Once again liberal reforms calling for, among other things, the seizure of property from the Church were imposed on Mexico. The "clericalists"—conservative creoles and members of the clergy— began to fear that the older order they so loved would be entirely destroyed. Union with Spain, they determined, was dangerous to that older order. So the royalists joined the independence movement. In 1821 Mexico was declared independent of the Spanish crown. At that time, Mexico's territory included not only the modern country, but California, Nevada, Arizona, New Mexico, and Texas, to the north, and Guatemala, Honduras, Costa Rica, and El Salvador to the south, in all a country larger than the United States.

Mexico's Agony

The revolutions of Hidalgo and Morelos failed, but Mexico feared further revolutions. In 1821, General Agustín de Iturbide offered a three-part program: a constitutional monarchy, protection for the Church, and equality for all citizens. His flag was a tricolor—red for the Indians, white for the

Portrait of Agustín de Iturbide.

Church, and green for independence. On September 27, 1821, Iturbide led his army into Mexico City. His victory ended three centuries of Spanish rule. Iturbide, however, set up a military dictatorship. He declared Mexico an empire, and himself the first emperor of Mexico, Agustin I. Two years later Iturbide left the Mexican treasury empty and fled into exile. (Returning with a price on his head, he was arrested and executed by his former followers.) A new government was then formed under the guns of General Lopez de Santa Anna and General José Antonio Echavarri. A new constitution was written.

The constitution of 1824 established a liberal republic on the model of the United States. It met the fate of all the other Latin American republics. The economy collapsed, corrupt officials stole public funds, powerful families grabbed communal Indian lands, and the suppression of the religious orders disrupted productively run Church lands. General Lopez de Santa Anna seized control of the government in 1830 and abolished the constitution. And he declared himself dictator for life.

Mexico's history for most of the rest of the century was a long, dismal failure. Santa Anna lost the northern province of Texas to the United States. The southern provinces of Guatemala, Honduras, Salvador, Nicaragua, and Costa Rica declared independence, and finally, Santa Anna was forced into exile. Mexico then fought the war with the United States that lost New Mexico, Arizona, Colorado, Nevada, and California.

In a brief interlude, the French conquered Mexico and made Maximilian I and his wife Carlotta the emperor and empress of Mexico. But their "empire" was ended with the return of the liberal president Benito Juarez, backed by United States arms. Juarez died of a heart attack in 1873, and was succeeded by another dictator general, Don Porfirio Díaz. He ruled Mexico for all but four of the next 35 years. There was peace and prosperity (at least for some) in Mexico, but at the price of some injustice. By his policy of *pan o palo*—"bread or the club"—Don Porfirio rewarded his "friends" and destroyed his enemies. In time a groundswell of discontent grew and toppled him—and plunged Mexico once again into a bloodbath of ideological hatreds.

Archduke Ferdinand Maximilian of Austria and his wife Carlotta.

The 20th century repeated the pattern of civil war and tyranny that kept Mexico, like so many Latin countries, a land of great wealth and grinding poverty. Díaz won an election over his opponent Francisco Madera, candidate of the National Catholic Party. Madera fled to the United States and proclaimed himself the legitimate president. In 1911 two brilliant guerrilla generals began the revolt that is known in Mexico as the Revolution. Pancho Villa led a band of bandit-revolutionaries in the northern provinces. Emiliano Zapata organized poor Indians into an army and drove off landlords, distributing the land to the Indians. When his troops came within sight of the capital, Díaz fled to France, where he lived until 1915. Madera returned, but he was afraid to take control. He held another election, but General Huerta seized power, murdered Madera, and attacked both Villa and Zapata.

Porfirio Díaz, President of Mexico.

U.S. President Woodrow Wilson wanted to help Villa, whom he misread as an advocate of democracy, and sent an American fleet to Vera Cruz. Admiral Mayo, the commander of the U. S. fleet, was provoked and occupied Vera Cruz. Both the Mexican government and the rebels were furious at American interference. General Obregón took Mexico City and Huerta fled. Another bloodbath between all the rebel forces now followed. An estimated 2 million people were killed as bandit bands raided and burned churches, destroyed ranches and estates, and looted small towns. Wilson withdrew support for Villa, who then raided Texas and New Mexico. Wilson then sent an expeditionary force under General John Pershing into Mexico. Pershing failed to arrest Villa and military intervention only increased Mexican anger at the "gringo giant" to the north.

The next president of Mexico, General Obregón, turned officially against the Church. His successor Calles was even more virulently anti-Catholic. "I have a personal hatred for Christ," he said. From 1924 to 1936, the government of Mexico waged constant persecution against Catholics. Many martyrs died for the Faith, among them Blessed Miguel Pro. But the persecution failed to enlist the sympathy of the Mexican people, whose faith remained firm, and a rebellion broke out all over Mexico. The movement was called the Cristero Rebellion. Its leader, Gonzalez Flores, was captured and executed. His cry as he was shot was, "¡Viva Cristo Rey!" It would become the battle cry of rebel armies in a war that lasted from 1927 into 1930.

It was not until 1979 that the ruling PRI, the single-party governing coalition first put together by Obregón and Calles and dedicated to an atheist state, relaxed the restrictions on Catholics that troubled the life of Mexico for 72 years.

Revolution in South America

Republican ideas were no less astir in South America. In Venezuela, General Simón Bolívar organized a coalition of Creole leaders across the north of the continent whose armies fought Spain for some 10 years until their independence was recognized. Bolívar won a final great victory at Ayacucho in Peru in 1824. He envisioned a nation like the United States, combining the governments of the several Spanish colonies into one union. But the several territories could not agree. Bolívar's united colonies quickly divided into Venezuela, Colombia, Ecuador, and Peru.

Argentina, led by José de San Martín, and Chile, led by Bernardo O'Higgins, had earlier achieved independence with the support of British agents and funding. Argentina broke apart with the secession of Uruguay and Bolivia. Landlocked Paraguay followed its neighbors. Paraguay immediately fell under the despotic control of General José Gaspar Rodríguez de Francia, who turned on his republican supporters and declared himself "El Supremo," and dictator for life.

General Simón Bolívar leads the fight for Colombian independence.

The Caudillo Undermines Republicanism

By 1826 Bolívar had accomplished the independence of all Spanish America.

The new governments, however, proved unable to maintain order or govern wisely. Wild ideas and experiments in political organization disrupted agriculture and left the Andes regions starving. The fanatics among the "republicans" turned on the Church and angered the poor, who were supported by the Church. The Indians were not interested in the ideas of independence and

Map of the campaigns of Simón Bolívar.

80°W   70°W   60°W

10°N   10°N

Maracaibo   Caracas
● Liberation of Venezuela 1817–18
Carabobo   *La Puerta*
Cúcuta   *Calabozo*
Angostura

Boyacá
Liberation of
Bogotá   Columbia 1819

Liberation of Quito   CAPTAINCY–
1822   VICEROYALTY OF   GENERAL OF
NEW GRANADA   VENEZUELA

Pasto   *Bombóná*
Pichincha   Quito

0°   0°

Gulf of   Guayaquil
Guayaquil

VICEROYALTY   B R A Z I L
OF PERU

Liberation
of Peru
1823–24   Trujillo

10°S   *Junín*   10°S
Callao
Lima   *Ayacucho*   UPPER
PERU

Bolivian independence   *Lake Titicaca*
established 1825   Arequipa   La Paz

Tacna   Potosí

20°S   *P a c i f i c*   20°S

O c e a n

VICEROYALTY OF
RÍO DE LA PLATA

CAPTAINCY–GENERAL
OF CHILE

✦	Battle
→	Bolívar's
⇢	campaign routes

30°S   Mendoza   30°S

Valparaíso   Santiago

Cancha Rayada   Liberation of
Chile 1819–21

Talca

Talcahuano

Concepción

40°S   40°S

80°W   70°W   60°W

Coups: a military seizure of the government.

republics. The Spanish crown, moreover, had protected them from the ruling classes of their countries. Revolts and **coups** became the pattern in South America. The rule of *caudillos*, strongmen with the support of the army, substituted despotism for the rule of law and tradition. The vast potential wealth of South America was siphoned off into a few hands and the bulk of the population was left in poverty.

The Empire of Brazil

Brazil won its freedom from Portugal without a revolution. During the Napolionic era, Portugal's king, Prince João, fled to Brazil with his family. After Napoleon's defeat, Joao returned to the Portuguese throne, but he left his son Pedro to govern Brazil. In 1822 Prince Pedro declared Brazil an independent empire and took his throne as Emperor Pedro I. A poor ruler, Pedro I was forced to abdicate in favor of his infant son Pedro II, only five years old, and a regent ruled for the child-king. Brazil fell into violence until Pedro II was 15, when he took control of the government from his regent.

Pedro was a prodigy. He had the wisdom and capacity of a much older man. Pedro II's amazing memory and brilliant mind directed 49 years of clearheaded rule. Pedro shared power with the landed and professional classes, and he gave Brazil a peace and prosperity unknown in the rest of the continent. Pedro said, "If I were not emperor, I should like to be a schoolteacher."

Under the empire, Brazil encouraged immigration from Europe, and thousands of Germans, Italians, and Spanish flocked to its shores. In the 20th century, large numbers of Japanese, Syrian, and Lebanese immigrants enriched the cities of Brazil.

Brazil's Indians were few, and unfit for much of the work. But African slaves, many brought over in whole villages, cleared the land and cultivated fields for the European landowners. By the time of the empire, the bulk of the population was of African descent. The Church's long opposition to slavery in Brazil gave moral force to an abolitionist movement. Antislavery societies secured a gradual abolition of slavery. First, children born to slaves were declared automatically free. Then, in the 1870s, all slaves over 60 years of age were freed. Finally, in 1888, the throne freed all slaves in Brazil.

Dissatisfaction with Emperor Pedro's children, who did not show their father's talents, and reluctance to have them inherit the throne brought the powerful families of Brazil to demand an end

1855 portrait of Emperor Pedro II of Brazil, by Menezes.

Historical map of Brazil in the 1890s.

to the monarchy. In 1889 Pedro II and his family abdicated and returned to Portugal. The political pressure created by the fact that both France and the United States had become republics led to the fall of the empire and the establishment of a democratic government. Except from 1964 until 1984, Brazil had presidents elected democratically.

Latin America Today

Political order and economic stability remain the primary problems in Latin countries. Social justice and general prosperity are now concerns for every level of society. The great natural resources of Latin America and the energy and hard work of Latin peoples have made prosperity possible. Latin artists and musicians are world famous, and Latin culture has entered the north as well as Europe. The next century may well prove to be the century of Latin America.

Chapter 16 Review

Let's Remember   Write your answer in a single complete sentence.
1. What were the three major American Indian civilizations when the Europeans arrived?
2. Cortés overcame what American Indian Empire?
3. Pizarro conquered what American Indian Empire?
4. The Cristero Rebellion troubled what country in the 1920s?
5. Simón Bolívar tried to establish what sort of government in South America?
6. What two countries in Latin America were for a time "empires"?

Let's Consider   For silent thinking and a short essay, or for thinking in a group with classroom discussion:
1. How did the *encomienda* system cause trouble for the future in Latin America?
2. Why did the Indians of Mexico and South America look on the Church and the Spanish crown as their protectors?

Rio de Janeiro

Let's Eat!

The tortilla has been eaten by the people of Central America for ages and is the basis of a burrito. Spread onto a tortilla (corn or flour) 2 T. of heated refried beans seasoned with chili powder to taste. Add slices of grilled beef or chicken and pico de gallo. Top with 2 T. of grated cheese. Spread sour cream over all. Roll into a burrito and enjoy.

Credits continued from page iv

p. 113 Charles Lenars; **p.** 114 Dallas & John Heaton; **p.** 116 above, Gian Berto Vanni, below, Archivo Iconografico, S.A.; **p.** 119 above, Bill Ross, below, Hoc Signo; **p.** 121 Robert Landau; **p.** 122 Ali Meyer; **p.** 123 Ali Meyer; **p.** 126, Yann Arthus-Bertrand; **p.** 127 above, unknown, below, Fulvio Roiter; **p.** 128, left, Adam Woolfitt, right, David Reed; **p.** 129 Archivo Iconografico, S.A.; **p.** 131 Jonathan Blair; **p.** 133 Araldo de Luca; **p.** 134 above, Christel Gerstenberg, below, Francesco Venturi; **p.** 135 Archivo Iconografico, S.A.; **p.** 136 North Carolina Museum of Art; **p.** 137 above, Archivo Iconografico, S.A., below, AFP; **p.** 138, Reuters NewMedia Inc.; **p.** 140, Bettmann; **p.** 141 unknown; **p.** 143, Robert Holmes; **p.** 145 Archivo Iconografico, S.A.; **p.** 147, Bettmann; **p.** 149, above, Christine Osborne, below, Paul Almasy; **p.** 152 Gianni Dagli Orti; **p.** 154 Bettmann; **p.** 155 Archivo Iconografico, S.A.; **p.** 156 Bettmann; **p.** 157 Stapleton Collection; **p.** 159 Archivo Iconografico, S.A.; **p.** 160 Bettmann; **p.** 161 Bettmann; **p.** 162 Bettmann; **p.** 163 Dean Conger; **p.** 164 Archivo Iconografico, S.A.; **p.** 166 Nik Wheeler; **p.** 167 Adam Woolfitt; **p.** 168 Gianni Dagli Orti; **p.** 169 Bettmann; **p.** 171 Bettmann; **p.** 173 Archivo Iconografico, S.A.; **p.** 174 Elio Ciol; **p.** 175 Elio Ciol; **p.** 176 Leonard de Selva; **p.** 177 Sandro Vannini; **p.** 179 Bettmann; **p.** 181 Bettmann; **p.** 183 left, John Heseltine, right, Bettmann; **p.** 184 Reuters NewMedia Inc.; **p.** 185 above, Bettmann, below, Archivo Iconografico, S.A.; **p.** 186 Bettmann; **p.** 187 left, Bettmann, right, Archivo Iconografico, S.A.; **p.** 188 David Lees; **p.** 189 Bettmann; **p.** 191 Vittoriano Rastelli; **p.** 192 Archivo Iconografico, S.A.; **p.** 193 Macduff Everton; **p.** 194 Angelo Hornak; **p.** 195 Hulton-Deutsch Collection; **p.** 196 Gianni Dagli Orti; **p.** 197 Bettmann; **p.** 199 left, Nevada Wier, right, John Slater; **p.** 202 Ann Purcell; **p.** 204 Richard Swiecki; **p.** 205 above, Archivo Iconografico, S.A., below, John Slater; **p.** 206 above, Chi Keung Ko, below, Asian Art & Archaeology, Inc.; **p.** 208 Christie's Images; **p.** 209 Warner Forman; **p.** 210 Stapleton Collection; **p.** 212 left, Richard Swiecki; right, Asian Art & Archaeology, Inc.; **p.** 213 Bettmann; **p.** 215 Hulton-Deutsch Collection; **p.** 216 J. Thomson; **p.** 217 Hulton-Deutsch Collection; **p.** 221 Craig Lovell; **p.** 220 Michael S. Yamashita; p. 222 Chris Lisle; **p.** 223 Barney Burstein; **p.** 224 Jed

Share; **p.** 225 Archivo Iconografico, S.A.; **p.** 226 Asian Art & Archaeology, Inc.; **p.** 227 Warner Forman; **p.** 228 Sakamoto Photo Research Laboratory; **p.** 229 above, Michael S. Yamashita, below, Asian Art & Archaeology, Inc.; **p.** 230 Peter M. Wilson; **p.** 231 Asian Art & Archaeology, Inc.; **p.** 232 Bettmann; **p.** 233 Richard T. Nowitz; **p.** 235 Alison Wright; **p.** 238 Roger Wood; **p.** 239 Charles Lenars; **p.** 240 David H. Wells; **p.** 241 both, Lindsay Hebberd; **p.** 243 Philip de Bay; **p.** 244 Charles Lenars; **p.** 245 Earl Kowall; **p.** 246 above, Robert Holmes, below, John MacDougall; **p.** 248 Bettmann; **p.** 249 Roman Soumar; **p.** 250 Richard A. Cooke; **p.** 252 Barney Burstein; **p.** 253 Philadelphia Museum of Art; **p.** 254 right, Pallaval Bagla, left, Seattle Art Museum; **p.** 255 Bettmann; **p.** 263 above, Tony Wilson-Bligh, below, Roger de la Harpe; **p.** 264 Tiziana Baldizzone; **p.** 265 Jonathan Blair; **p.** 267 Bettmann; **p.** 268 Roger Wood; **p.** 270 Charles Lenars; **p.** 271 Nik Wheeler; **p.** 273 unknown; **p.** 274 Chris Hellier; **p.** 275 Werner Forman; **p.** 276 Kelly-Mooney Photography; **p.** 277 Catherine Desjeux; **p.** 279 Roger Ressmeyer; **p.** 283 Dean Conger; **p.** 284 Sergievo Posad; **p.** 285 Franciose de Mulder, **p.** 286 Archivo Iconografico, S.A.; **p.** 287 Archivo Iconografico, S.A.; **p.** 288 Bettmann; **p.** 289 Bettmann; **p.** 290 Archivo Iconografico, S.A.; **p.** 291 Archivo Iconografico, S.A.; **p.** 292 Gianni Dagli Orti; **p.** 294 above, Bettmann, below, Hulton-Deutsch Collection; **p.** 295 Bettmann; **p.** 296 Novosti; **p.** 297 above, Hulton-Deutsch Collection, below, Philadelphia Museum of Art; **p.** 299 Museum of the City of New York; **p.** 301 Bettmann; **p.** 303 Bettmann; **p.** 304 unknown; **p.** 306 Bettmann; **p.** 308 Joseph Sohm; **p.** 309 above, Burstein Collection, below, Kevin Fleming; **p.** 314 Bettmann; **p.** 315 Medford Historical Society Collection; **p.** 319 Owen Franken; **p.** 321 Bettmann; **p.** 322 Bettmann; **p.** 323 Bettmann; **p.** 324 Werner Forman; **p.** 325 Archivo Iconografico, S.A.; **p.** 326 Bettmann; **p.** 327 Charles Lenars; **p.** 328 Werner Forman; **p.** 329 Bettmann; **p.** 332 Bettmann; **p.** 333 Arte & Immagini srl; **p.** 335 Charles Lenars; **p.** 336 Bettmann; **p.** 337 Bettmann; **p.** 338 left, Austrian Archives, right, Bettmann; **p.** 339 Bettmann; **p.** 340 Bettmann; **p.** 342 Archivo Iconografico, S.A; **p.** 344 Richard T. Nowitz.

Index